Strategy and Supply

Strategy and Supply

The Anglo-Russian Alliance, 1914–17

KEITH NEILSON
Royal Military College of Canada

London
GEORGE ALLEN & UNWIN

Boston   Sydney

George Allen & Unwin (Publishers) Ltd,
40 Museum Street, London WC1A 1LU, UK

George Allen & Unwin (Publishers) Ltd,
Park Lane, Hemel Hempstead, Herts HP2 4TE, UK

Allen & Unwin Inc.,
9 Winchester Terrace, Winchester, Mass. 01890, USA

George Allen & Unwin Australia Pty Ltd,
8 Napier Street, North Sydney, NSW 2060, Australia

First published in 1984

British Library Cataloguing in Publication Data

Neilson, Keith
    Strategy and supply.
1. World War, 1914–1918 – Diplomatic History   2. Great Britain –
Foreign relations – Soviet Union   3. Soviet Union – Foreign relations –
Great Britain
I. Title
940.3'22'41   D621
ISBN 0–04–940072–X

Library of Congress Cataloging in Publication Data

Neilson, Keith.
    Strategy and supply.
Bibliography: p.
Includes index.
1. World War, 1914–1918 – Diplomatic history. 2. Great Britain –
Foreign relations – Soviet Union.   3. Soviet Union – Foreign relations –
Great Britain.   4. Great Britain – Foreign economic relations – Soviet
Union.   5. Soviet Union – Foreign economic relations – Great Britain.
6. Great Britain – Military relations – Soviet Union.   7. Soviet Union –
Military relations – Great Britain.   I. Title.   II. Title: Anglo-Russian
alliance, 1914–17.
D621.G7N44 1984   940.3'22   83–24361
ISBN 0–04–940072–X

Set in 10 on 12 point Plantin by Phoenix Photosetting, Chatham,
and printed in Great Britain by Biddles Ltd, Guildford, Surrey

Contents

Preface

'The War lasted three years or the duration. . . . At the beginning the Russians rendered great assistance . . . by lending their memorable steamroller and by passing silently through England one Sunday morning before breakfast with snow on their boots.'[1] This comedic view of Anglo-Russian relations in the First World War has lasted long after the publication of Sellar and Yeatman's classic spoof of English history. While the Eastern front is no longer what Churchill called 'The Unknown War', Russia's relations with Britain during the First World War have been reduced to the status of a gigantic footnote to the opening of Anglo-Soviet discourse following the close of hostilities.[2] This relegation of Anglo-Russian relations to the dustbin of history is unfortunate, for it has led to an incomplete understanding both of the complexities of the war and of the events which came after it.

The principal aim of this work, then, is to remedy this deficiency by providing an account of the workings of the Anglo-Russian alliance in the period from the beginning of the war to the end of 1917. To do this has proved more difficult and complicated than it first appeared. While doing the research for this study, it became evident that the relations between Britain and Russia during the war were determined by the events of the war itself. From a British perspective, and that is the perspective of this study, the course of the alliance was determined by the amount which it was felt that Russia contributed to winning the war: Russia was judged primarily by whether or not she could provide a military presence on the Eastern front such that Allied victory would occur. Therefore, any discussion of the workings of the alliance had to take place within the context of British military strategy in the First World War. Here was the problem.

British histories of the First World War tend to see strategy in terms of two patterns.[3] The first is as civil–military relations or, to use Major-General Sir Henry Wilson's felicitous terms, a clash between 'brass hats' and 'frocks'. The second is as a struggle between two strategic schools of thought, the 'westerners' versus 'easterners' controversy. Both of these patterns are useful for the study of war, in particular as they put the British military experience in the general context of political life in Britain. Despite this undoubted value, neither of these patterns is satisfactory for an understanding of the workings of the Anglo-Russian alliance during the war. To this end, a new view of strategy is required.

In creating this new pattern, the most obvious point which needs to be understood is that Britain did not fight alone. Instead, Britain was part of an alliance, a fact which meant that strategic decisions were made within the context of group endeavour. Here lies the weakness of the two conventional views of British strategy; both tend to view British decision-making as if the government and its advisers had the latitude of action during the war which they supposedly enjoyed in peacetime. On the contrary, considerations of France and Russia (and, later, the United States) affected nearly all aspects of Britain's endeavours during the war. The decisions – military, diplomatic and economic – which were taken must be seen in the light of the alliance.[4] For this reason, much of this study is taken up with creating a new, 'alliance' view of British strategy, one which takes into consideration the impact of Russia and the Eastern front in particular on British planning.

A discussion of the impact of Russia on the creation of British policy has involved another problem. Just how and by whom were the decisions taken which shaped Anglo-Russian relations? With the outbreak of hostilities, the prewar bodies which served as the focus of foreign policy were gradually augmented by a number of other organisations which came to have a great impact on the determination of British policy with respect to Russia. Just as the organisational framework for dealings with Russia changed, so too did the individuals who made the decisions within the framework. Military men gained a prominence in decision-making unthinkable prior to the war. The Liberal government of Asquith was replaced by a coalition and then by Lloyd George's amalgam. The creation of new departments of state and the exigencies of war brought new men into the corridors of power. Since the attitudes and beliefs of these men had an impact on their decisions, it has been necessary to identify those who played a major role in shaping Anglo-Russian relations and to determine what were their attitudes towards Russia.

Military strategy involves far more than moving coloured pins on a map.[5] With the failure of the prewar plans of all the belligerents, the

First World War became a 'total war', one which taxed the abilities of all combatants to mobilise their economic, financial and demographic resources. Here an intimate co-operation (or, often, a lack of co-operation) grew up between Britain and Russia. In order to maintain Russia's military effectiveness, Britain became Russia's financier and armourer to an extent both unimagined and unimaginable before 1914. This posed many problems for the alliance, not the least of which were administrative. As a consequence, a substantial portion of this work deals with the complex negotiations between Britain and Russia over such seemingly non-military matters as the shipment of gold, the arrangement of credit and the creation of the administrative bodies to deal with such negotiations. Similarly, much time is spent discussing the more obviously military parts of the economic co-operation between the two countries, things such as the purchase of shells and guns.

While the war brought an end to much of prewar diplomacy, foreign relations of a sort not easily distinguishable from the traditional 'old diplomacy' continued on throughout the period of hostilities. These relations dealt with a number of interrelated matters: war aims, separate peace and the means to bring further members into the alliance against the Central Powers. To some extent, then, part of this work is an endeavour to place these elements of the 'old diplomacy' between Britain and Russia in their proper context of the totality of relations between the two countries. For the most part, military strength and victories determined diplomacy.

A note of explanation is required about the scope of this study. It is not intended to be a balanced account of the working of the Anglo-Russian alliance. The method employed here, of looking closely at the decisions taken by a number of individuals who formed the British élite dealing with Russia, cannot be extended to the Russian side of matters due to the limitations of sources. Until Soviet archives are open to Western scholars on a basis equivalent to that of the Public Record Office, such a study is impossible. However, I have attempted to provide a degree of balance by utilising Soviet monographs and specialised studies dealing with the war. While this naturally leaves this study with a leaning towards the British view of events, it is hoped that an understanding of the Russian point of view emerges as well. That at least is the intention.

In dealing with topics Russian there are several standard matters which need to be delineated. The first concerns transliteration. I have followed in general the Library of Congress system, but have omitted the apostrophes signifying hard and soft signs. In addition, when a proper name has a well-known English form, I have used that form at the expense of consistency. Finally, I have made no effort to change the contemporary transliterations used in direct quotations. Thus, for example, the name of General M. V. Alekseev will appear often as 'Alexeieff' or other variant. In all cases, the context and suitable imagination make the reference clear. The second matter which needs explanation is the system of dating used. While it is mildly anachronistic, I have used Western-style dates for all events whether they occurred in the West or in Russia. Since this is essentially a study of the British side of the Anglo-Russian alliance, it has been more convenient to use the Gregorian calendar throughout rather than the Julian calender employed in Russia until 1918.

Notes

1 W. C. Sellar and R. J. Yeatman, *1066 and All That. And Now All This* (New York, 1932), 114.
2 Two recent works have brought the Eastern front and the Russian army into clear focus: N. Stone, *The Eastern Front 1914–1917* (London, 1975) and A. K. Wildman, *The End of the Russian Imperial Army The Old Army and the Soldiers' Revolt (March–April 1917)* (Princeton, NJ, 1980). The best recent Soviet account is I. I. Rostunov, *Russkii front pervoi mirovoi voiny* (Moscow, 1976). There is no study of Anglo-Russian relations covering the entire period of the war. The interest of scholars has been focused on the origins of Anglo-Soviet relations and Anglo-Russian relations have consequently been treated cursorily, serving only as background material; see the classic study by R. H. Ullman, *Anglo-Soviet Relations 1917–1921* (3 vols, Princeton, NJ, 1961–72), I, 3–57. The most recent work, M. Kettle, *Russia and the Allies 1917–1920* (London, 1981), I, devotes more space to 1917, but is not particularly valuable.
3 A good summary of and introduction to the usual ways of viewing the First World War is D. R. Woodward, 'Britain in a continental war: the civil–military debate over the strategical direction of the Great War of 1914–1918', *Albion*, 12 (1980), 37–65. Two interesting exceptions to the usual ways of looking at wartime strategy are J. Gooch, 'Soldiers, strategy and war aims in Britain 1914–18', in Hunt and Preston (eds), *War Aims and Strategic Policy in the Great War* (London, 1977), 21–40, and D. M. Schurman, 'Historians and Britain's imperial strategic stance in 1914', in Flint and Williams (eds), *Perspectives of Empire* (London, 1973), 172–88. On the need to ask new questions about the war, see J. P. Campbell, 'Refighting Britain's great patriotic war', *International Journal*, 26, 4 (1971), 686–705.
4 There have been some excellent studies of particular aspects of the Anglo-French and Anglo-American alliances; see, in particular, G. H. Cassar, *The French and the Dardanelles: a Study of Failure in the Conduct of War* (London, 1971); J. K. Tanenbaum, *General Maurice Sarrail 1856–1929: the French Army and Left-Wing Politics* (Chapel Hill, NC, 1974); D. F. Trask, *The United States in the Supreme*

War Council (Middleton, Conn., 1961); the same author's *Captains and Cabinets Anglo-American Naval Relations, 1917–1918* (Columbia, 1972) and W. B. Fowler, *British–American Relations, 1917–1918: the Role of Sir William Wiseman* (Princeton, NJ, 1969).

5   This point has been made clearly by M. Van Creveld, *Supplying War Logistics from Wallenstein to Patton* (Cambridge, 1977). See also the essays in F. Dreisziger (ed.), *Mobilization for Total War: the Canadian, American and British Experience 1914–1918, 1939–1945* (Waterloo, Ontario, 1981).

Acknowledgements

Many people have been kind enough to lend me their support and encouragement while I wrote this book, and it is my pleasure to be able to thank them publicly. The late Professor C. J. Lowe suggested this topic: I hope that I have fulfilled some of his expectations. Norman Stone supervised the doctoral thesis of which this is an outgrowth. His constructive suggestions and tolerance of my ideas I greatly appreciate. Dr Kathleen Burk made available to me her unrivalled knowledge of Anglo-American finances during the First World War, a fact which allowed me to treat a complicated subject more thoroughly than would otherwise have been the case. Dr David French has given me the benefit of his familiarity with the files of the Public Record Office, which led to the discovery of many valuable documents. My colleague at the Royal Military College of Canada, Dr Hamish Ion, took time off from his own writing to read my entire manuscript and to offer valuable suggestions for its improvement. That this was done in such a tactful and agreeable fashion is something beyond the call of duty and for which I am thankful. Special thanks are due to Dr B. J. C. McKercher, friend and fellow historian. We have spent many enjoyable hours discussing various aspects of British diplomatic history from which I have gained many insights into the decision-making process in British government. The debt which I owe him with respect to chapter 1 of this book will be obvious to all those who read his forthcoming study of Anglo-American relations (*The Second Baldwin Government and the United States, 1924–1929: Attitudes and Diplomacy*, Cambridge University Press). Finally, I should like to thank my colleagues at RMC for allowing me to bore them with my enthusiasm about the First World War: it has not gone unappreciated. None of the above bears any responsibility for what follows, and all the mistakes in both fact and interpretation are my own.

The following have graciously given me permission to quote from the material to which they own the copyright: Viscount Addison (the Addison mss); the British Library (the Balfour mss); the Earl Haig

and Trustees of the National Library of Scotland (the Haig mss); Mr
Julian Hardinge (the Hardinge mss); the Trustees of the Liddell
Hart Centre for Military Archives, King's College London (the
Kiggell and Robertson mss); Mr A. J. P. Taylor and the Trustees of
the Beaverbrook Foundation and the Clerk of the Records of the
House of Lords Record Office (Lloyd George mss); Mr David
McKenna (the McKenna mss), and the Warden and Fellows of New
College, Oxford (the Milner mss). Crown copyright material is
reproduced by kind permission of the Controller of Her Majesty's
Stationery Office. My sincere apologies are due to anyone whose
copyright I may have infringed unwittingly.

There are two particular debts of gratitude which I wish to
acknowledge. My mother, Agnes Neilson, brought a fine gram-
marian's eye to this work. The mistakes which remain do so as a
result of my stubborn refusal to see the error of my ways. My wife
Joan has contributed so much to my work that no listing of her help
would do it justice. Without her love and encouragement this book
would not have been completed and it is dedicated to her.

1
Men and Ideas

'In moments of crisis,' James Joll has observed, 'political leaders fall back on unspoken assumptions.'[1] The determination of these 'unspoken assumptions' is essential in dealing with Anglo-Russian relations during the First World War, for much of what transpired between the two allies is not readily intelligible without some knowledge of what the British thought and expected of Russia. Such determination is complex and difficult. Not only does it require discerning attitudes and values normally not committed to paper, but also it requires the identification of the individuals who were instrumental in the creation of policy.

Even prior to identifying these individuals, some preliminary remarks are helpful. An important consideration when dealing with British policy towards Russia is what the average educated Englishman knew of Russia. For most Britons, Russia was an exotic and mysterious land.[2] Russian xenophobia and the difficulties posed by the language meant that from the earliest contacts with Russia in Elizabethan times, 'Englishmen could never be well-informed about the country or its people'.[3] Although by the nineteenth century Russia had ceased to be a land populated by fabulous creatures, as A. G. Cross notes, 'perhaps on a psychological level, however, the transition from the strange to the familiar was never completed'.[4] Even the great sensation caused in European circles prior to the war by Russian ballet and opera – the latter with its 'brilliant quasi-oriental exoticism' in colour and costume – must only have reinforced the impression that Russia was somehow barbarous and extra-European.[5]

More important for a study of Anglo-Russian relations was the existence of several firmly held beliefs about Russia. The first was that Russian government was arbitrary and oriental in nature.[6] As a result of this misgovernment, the average Russian was felt to be drunken and boorish, and kept so deliberately as a consequence of repressive governmental policy. The advantages which Britons felt they enjoyed in terms of government had changed little since the eighteenth century.[7] The second important belief was that Russia was 'invulnerable' militarily and that her soldiers were capable of inhuman feats of bravery and endurance. A British evaluation of Russian soldiers in the Seven Years' War – 'they cannot be defeated; they must be killed' – was not appreciably different from remarks made of their performance in the Russo-Japanese war 140 years later or, indeed, in the First World War itself.[8]

A final word should be said about British public opinion and Russia, since Anglo-Russian relations depended in the last resort on some sort of public acceptance of Russia as an ally.[9] In many ways Russia was both an unlikely and an embarrassing ally in 1914. Many of the reasons which had led to a virulent Russophobia in the nineteenth century still existed upon the outbreak of war.[10] To a British public weaned on the beliefs of liberalism, autocratic Russia seemed a socially and politically reactionary backwater. As well, Russia was a long-time rival of the British Empire, a rival which over the last half-century had swallowed Central Asia and now threatened India from the borders of Persia. Indeed the *rapprochement* between the two powers signalled by the signing of the Anglo-Russian convention in 1907 was unique in that it united the more extreme elements of both political parties in opposition: the Liberal Radical faction, because of their revulsion for reactionary Russia, and the Unionist circle, because of their dislike for expansionist Russia.[11]

On the other hand, many of those qualities which made Russia an unattractive partner before 1914 made her a desirable ally upon the outbreak of war. By September of that year, one of the more enduring myths of the war, the 'Russian soldiers with snow on their boots', had already come into existence, as the once-dreaded Russians had become the handmaidens of righteousness against the fiendish Hun. Special precautions taken by the Foreign Office to prevent any unwarranted reports of 'Cossack outrages' of the sort that had inflamed prewar opinion against Russia proved unnecessary after hostilities commenced, as British public opinion readily accepted the value of Russia as an ally.[12] With Parliament mostly dormant during the war, public opinion generally set no limits to British policy with respect to Russia.[13] That policy was the province of a small group of men.

The widened range of contacts – military, financial, economic and diplomatic – between Britain and Russia during the war caused a major problem in the creation of British policy towards her eastern ally. Prior to the war British foreign policy was determined, nearly exclusively, by the Secretary of State for Foreign Affairs and his advisers within the Foreign Office.[14] Operating in what A. J. P. Taylor has called a 'government of departments', Sir Edward Grey, as Foreign Secretary, established foreign policy in the personal fashion which Canning, Palmerston and Salisbury had enjoyed before him.[15] With Russia as an ally, the nature of relations between the two countries changed and became less a matter of traditional foreign policy and more a matter of total governmental policy directed towards winning the war. Thus the Foreign Office was compelled to seek advice from other departments of state to a degree unthinkable prior to 1914.[16] As these departments, particularly the Treasury, the War Office and the Ministry of Munitions, had little if any experience in dealing with Russia, the Foreign Office continued to administer British policy; but that policy was no longer the exclusive creation of the Foreign Office.

Keeping this in mind, the problem arises of pinpointing the individuals who established British policy towards Russia. This is difficult, as the responsibility for creating this policy was spread widely. Still, this is not a reason (or at least not a satisfactory reason) for not attempting to do so. While there was no single body within the government which had exclusive control over Britain's relations with Russia, there was a group of individuals who by dint of position, knowledge and influence tended to determine the policy. In the sense suggested by D. C. Watt, these individuals constituted an élite group concerned with the formulation of Britain's policy towards Russia.[17] It was their 'unspoken assumptions' which were significant for British policy.

As Watt argues, this élite group centred on the Cabinet and found the rest of its members among the diplomatists, civil servants and military men who dealt with Russia. The aim of this élite was to manage relations with Russia in such a fashion that she might be the strong ally necessary to help win the war. This much was agreed on by all members of the élite. Little else was. Differences in political affiliation, in departmental responsibility, in strategical opinion and in temperament all combined to ensure a wide divergence of conviction when the means to make, and the possibility of making, Russia an effective ally were discussed. Nor was this élite group static throughout the war. The political portion had a large turnover as the Liberal government turned into a coalition in 1915 and later, in 1916, into a second coalition with more drastic changes in personnel. Such shuffling of position was not confined to the politicians, for the bureaucracy of government was also affected by the war.[18] The decline of the Foreign Office has been mentioned, but other changes, like the creation of the Ministry of Munitions and the rise of the Treasury's influence in the functioning of the alliance, also had a major impact on the composition of the policy-making élite.

Despite such caveats, it is not impossible to discern the élite which established British policy towards Russia. Certain individuals played, and continued to play for long periods, prominent roles in shaping and implementing this policy. For convenience they can be divided into three main categories, roughly by the function which they performed in creating policy. The first category includes those politicians who either took a major interest in forming policy with respect to Russia – generally due to the portfolio which they held – or whose influence in the government was such that they affected what policy was adopted. These men made the final decisions with respect to British policy and, on occasion, even were responsible for its inception. Generally, however, the creation of policy initiatives was the responsibility of the second category of the élite, the civil servants who dealt with Russia and Russian matters. With some important additions, this meant the staff at the Foreign Office, the filter through which information from and communications with Russia passed. Although the role of the Foreign Office with respect to policy concerning Russia declined sharply in 1917, its influence remained substantial throughout the period under consideration. This was particularly true with respect to the interpretation of the information about Russia provided by the third category of the élite. This was comprised of the individuals who represented Britain in Russia and who were the source of the fact (and occasionally the fiction) upon which the other members of the élite based their decisions.

Before going on to discuss the individuals who made up this élite, it is necessary to explain why certain other people have been excluded from it. Among the political élite, one would expect to find the Secretary of State for War, the Chancellor of the Exchequer and the Minister of Munitions, given the importance which these departments had for Anglo-Russian relations. However, not all those who occupied these posts have been included here. Lord Derby, Secretary of State for War under Lloyd George, has been omitted because of his lack of initiative with respect to Russian policy. General Haig, the Commander-in-Chief of the British forces in France, once contemptuously dismissed Derby as 'the feather pillow [who] bears the mark of the last person who sat on him'; when it came to Russia, the 'last person' was normally General Robertson, the Chief of the Imperial General Staff (CIGS).[19] In a similar fashion neither Reginald McKenna nor Andrew Bonar Law, successively Chancellors of the Exchequer, have been included since neither put forward much in the way of policy with respect to Russian finances. McKenna also lacked the political clout to make his suggestions heard.[20] Christopher Addison, who succeeded Lloyd George as Minister of Munitions, never became more than a caretaker, the man who kept running the Ministry that Lloyd George had created.[21]

The exclusion of Lord Milner from the political élite requires special explanation. Milner virtually became Lloyd George's 'Minister for Russia' in 1917, travelling to Petrograd for the inter-Allied conference and then heading the interdepartmental committee set up to deal with Russian matters which bore his name. There are two reasons for his omission. First, the Petrograd conference was of such significance that it will be dealt with in a separate chapter making treatment here unnecessary. Second, the Milner committee was largely an administrative body which carried out decisions made elsewhere and was rarely involved in policy creation.

Among the bureaucrats omitted, perhaps the most surprising is Maurice Hankey, the secretary to the Committee of Imperial Defence (CID) and, successively, to the War Council, Dardanelles Committee, War Committee and War Cabinet. While Hankey has generally been acknowledged to have had great influence on British policy formulation during the war, his influence on British Russian policy appears to have been minimal.[22] Thus, while Hankey undoubtedly played an important role in the war, he finds no place in the policy-making élite for Russia. Similarly with Sir Eyre Crowe. While Crowe would have been impossible to omit prior to the autumn of 1914, the Assistant Under-Secretary at the Foreign Office lost much of his influence at that time.[23] As a consequence, Crowe was shifted to the Contraband Department at the Foreign Office where, although he dealt with Russia, his overall influence on

Anglo-Russian relations diminished sharply. Another important omission is General Charles Callwell. As Director of Military Operations (DMO) at the War Office from 1914 to the end of 1915, Callwell was at the centre of military deliberations concerning Russia.[24] As well, he was intimately connected with providing munitions for Russia, serving on the War Office's Russian Purchasing Committee and later with the Ministry of Munitions and Milner Committee. There is no doubt that Callwell should be a member of the élite, but the absence of any private papers for him and the fact that the official War Office files that dealt with his Russian activities no longer exist has made his inclusion impossible.

The Politicians

On the outbreak of war, Sir Edward Grey was the unchallenged leader of the Asquithian government with respect to foreign policy.[25] Long a friend of the Prime Minister and allied to him politically, the Foreign Secretary's position within the Liberal Party was near-impregnable. More than this, he had won a wide general following due to his 'transparent sincerity and honesty' and 'courage, skill and steadfastness'.[26] Still, Grey did not lack for critics. As mentioned, the Anglo-Russian convention of 1907 had unleashed a barrage of bipartisan complaint upon him. However, his continued offering of the olive branch to the Germans and his adroit handling of the Balkan wars in 1912–13 had convinced his Radical critics of his dedication to peace, while his firmness with Germany over the Moroccan crises had silenced his Unionist detractors.[27] As a Cabinet colleague wrote of Grey in April 1913, 'I do not believe that Canning or Palmerston ever stood higher.'[28] In 1914 Grey was clearly master in his own house.

Russia had been at the centre of Grey's policies since he had come to office in 1905.[29] Grey realised that Britain, as a sated power, had little to gain from any changes in the status quo. His policies, as a consequence, were designed to prevent or at least to put into acceptable and pacific channels any attempts at change. German attempts to challenge Britain's predominance led to the development of a feeling of Germanophobia at the Foreign Office, but Grey never totally succumbed to it.[30] Instead, he turned to two policies, the maintenance of the *Entente Cordiale* with France and the reduction of the outstanding colonial issues with Russia, as a means of reducing European tensions. These policies were not anti-German nor, in the case of the latter, pro-Russian; they were instead what might be termed policies of self-interest, despite their appearance in German eyes. While both policies involved Britain closely with Russia, there never existed any military alliance between them.

Grey's primacy in determining British foreign policy did not last the war.[31] Many of the reasons for this were personal in nature. First, he was shattered by his failure to avoid the war that his policies had been designed to prevent. Second, his health deteriorated during this time, the failure of his vision necessitating long periods of rest and inactivity. This accelerated the rate at which the Foreign Office lost control over the creation of foreign policy. The third and most important reason for Grey's loss of control over policy was his own belief that 'in war words count only so far as they are backed by force and victories'.[32] With Russia as a militarily important ally, Grey felt that the primary role of his department was 'to preserve solidarity among the Great Allies' by ensuring Russia's unflagging support of the Allied cause.[33] He believed that the Foreign Office should not attempt to direct British policy.

None the less, while the decline of the Foreign Office and of Grey was complete by 1917, with the latter out of office and the former reduced to what Lord Bertie, the British ambassador to France, termed a 'pass-on department', during the first two years of the war Grey was at the centre of the élite which determined British policy with respect to Russia.[34] Nearly all information to and from Russia passed through his hands, and his voice was heard in all policy-making debates. While he deferred much of the initiative that was formerly his to the new military voices in the government, he did not cease to add his expertise to the ways in which these initiatives were carried out.

Much of the reason that Grey accorded such a high priority to Russia stemmed from the views of Lord Kitchener of Khartoum, the Secretary of State for War.[35] No man was identified as closely in the public eye with British prestige and military prowess as was 'K of K', and during the war he basked in a public adulation which made him nearly beyond reproach. Whether or not this high regard was justified remains a contentious point, but such contention in no way obviates the fact that it did exist and that it gave special weight to Kitchener's pronouncements.[36] Not that such popularity was necessary for the Secretary of State's view to be accepted within the government. His colleagues, as well as the public, initially felt him to be the man of the hour and accorded him and his military ideas the deference which his outstanding career suggested was his due. They, of course, lost both their awe of Kitchener and their belief in his infallibility more quickly than did the multitude for whom he remained the ultimate hero until his death in June 1916.

From the outset, Kitchener viewed the war as one to be fought in partnership with Britain's allies and felt that it would not be a short one. As a consequence, the Secretary of State paid careful attention to his French and particularly to his Russian allies. While he was ignorant of some of the changes which had been effected in the British army because of his long service away from England, Kitchener had a keen awareness of the relative strengths of the Allies and the Central Powers.[37] His service in India, in particular, had made Kitchener quite appreciative of Russian strength, both actual and potential.

As Russia's failure to carry the war through to victory in 1917 is often read retroactively to mean that she achieved little and was a negligible quantity prior to it, it is instructive to determine the prewar British evaluation of the Russian army. Generally speaking, British estimates of Russia's military capability were favourable. Even during the defeats of the. Russo-Japanese war, a British observer could write that 'the uninterrupted series of Russian defeats tends to make the Russian Army appear greatly inferior to what it really is' and conclude that 'the [Russian] Army, taken as a whole, is distinctly a good one'.[38] Kitchener shared this view and defended it tenaciously against those, like the CID's initial secretary, Sir George Clarke, who felt that Russia's defeat by Japan meant that 'for ten years at least the Russians will not be in a position to undertake another campaign closely resembling Manchuria in size'.[39]

By 1914 the majority of British military opinion had stopped considering Russia as a military threat, not because she was no longer considered capable militarily, but simply because it was clear that Britain had no defence against her. This, coupled with the growing German menace in Europe, had focused the attention of the General Staff on the continent where it was felt the British Expeditionary Force (BEF) could play a significant role.[40] Further, the signing of the Anglo-Russian convention had satisfied many that a political solution had been found to the defence of India, a defence which was impossible militarily.[41] By 1914 confidence was high that the Franco-Russian combination was at least a match for the Central Powers. The continuing Russian military build-up, the so-called 'Great Programme' which aimed at making her the predominant military power in Europe by 1917, only fed this belief.[42] For example Major-General Sir Henry Wilson, the DMO, wrote optimistically in March 1914 on a report about the burgeoning Russian army: 'It is easy to understand now why Germany is anxious about the future & why she may think that it is a case of "now or never".'[43] Given his acceptance of Russia's strength and his disregard of the British territorial system, Kitchener quite naturally felt that British policy must necessarily be tailored to keep Russia firmly in the alliance, at least until Britain had raised massive armies of her own.

Kitchener was not in any sense pro-Russian. For example, he was not enthusiastic about the need to cede Constantinople and the Straits to Russia in order to ensure her firm adherence to the alliance.[44] But, as it became clear that the war would be a long one, there seemed no alternative to providing Russia with all the support she required to maintain an effective fighting force in the field. Contemptuous of the French army – he had told the CID in 1911 that the Germans would scatter it 'like partridges' – and concerned about the minuscule BEF, Kitchener felt that the Russian presence in the East was essential to the security of the British and French lines in the west.[45] When it became clear in the spring of 1915 that Russia would require substantial external aid – primarily munitions – to remain an effective ally, Kitchener immediately turned British resources to this end. That his efforts were generally unsuccessful was due to Russian intransigence about accepting his help and to the general British inability to provide the desired supplies rather than to any lack of appreciation of Russia.

Despite the essential soundness of his views concerning Russia, Kitchener was gradually removed from the élite which determined Britain's Russian policy during the autumn of 1915. His place as chief military adviser was taken by General Sir William Robertson, who became Chief of the Imperial General Staff (CIGS) in December of that year. The inclusion of Robertson among the politicians requires at least some justification, not least because 'Wully' himself would have resented it. Still, as V. H. Rothwell has noted, as CIGS Robertson 'was in effect a senior member of the War Cabinet', equivalent in the hierarchy to other members of the élite.[46]

Robertson attended all meetings of the various bodies set up to direct the war, presented papers outlining his position and defended them tenaciously, serving as far more than a technical adviser. His comments ranged over the entire compass of the war effort, including matters like war aims, a negotiated peace and conscription, underlining just how artificial the distinction between military and non-military matters was in time of war.

Robertson has become identified as one of the archetypal 'westerners' in British military thinking and it is not surprising that this should be so. The CIGS had been one of the leaders in the prewar movement within the army to establish a continental commitment and it was his refusal during the war to countenance Lloyd George's strategic alternatives which caused Robertson's dismissal in 1918. Throughout the war, the CIGS was a steady advocate of the need for a strong Western front and by the spring of 1917, with revolution in Russia, he was convinced that the war must be won in France alone if need be. However, this should not be taken as suggesting that Robertson never placed any value on, nor paid any attention to, Russia.

Early in 1915, when Russian arms still appeared capable of winning the decisive victory which prewar strategy had predicted, Robertson showed his keen awareness of his Eastern ally. For instance, in mid-February he wrote to Callwell that Russia's setback in the Carpathians was certain to have a 'big effect', especially in the Balkans. He believed that final victory, however, required an offensive on both fronts – in his own words it would be 'absolutely necessary'.[47] When Robertson joined the élite as CIGS, his immediate concern was twofold; first to concentrate Britain's efforts in France and to end sideshows elsewhere, and second to establish closer co-operation among the Allies. He moved immediately to improve his liaison with Russia by sending Callwell there to find out 'what the real state of affairs . . . is and when they will be ready'.[48] The date of any offensive, Robertson realised, 'must depend on the various allies'. While the CIGS often found Russian generals 'troublesome', he never ignored them. As long as Russia was capable of mounting a significant military effort, Robertson never ceased to try to co-ordinate British policy with Russian wishes.

Kitchener placed more importance on Russia than did Robertson, largely because in 1914 Russian arms seemed the only hope for a rapid decisive victory (or the prevention of a similarly rapid defeat).

In 1915 Russia's collapse and the possibility of a complete German victory in the east meant that Kitchener had to extend as much support as possible to bolster Russia. With the British army still in its developmental stage and the French ineffectual in attack, Kitchener necessarily shaped his policy around Russia. During Robertson's ascendancy, all this changed. The British army became a major force in the war and, the longer the conflict continued, seemed the key to eventual victory. Any hope that Russia would win the war by her own exertions had ended during the long retreat of 1915, and Robertson viewed her only as an adjunct to victory, and an unreliable one at that. The style of the two men was certainly different – the contrast between Robertson's efficient War Office and that of 'K of Chaos' must have been immense – but the two men varied little in stragetic approach. In the end, both were 'westerners'; the variance in their policy towards Russia was a function of their time in office. While Robertson was more blunt with and impatient of his Russian allies than was Kitchener, it was not because the former was anti-Russian and the latter pro-Russian; changed circumstances required changed policies.

While Robertson and Kitchener were primarily responsible for military policy towards Russia, a third member of the élite must be considered in this respect. In 1914 Winston Churchill, the First Lord of the Admiralty, was the *enfant terrible* of British politics.[49] Just 40 years old, he was the youngest man by far in a key position to determine British policy. Despite his personal and familial ties to the military and regardless of his obvious intellectual gifts and capacity for hard work, Churchill was not accepted unreservedly by his colleagues. The inconsistencies of his political career, his tendency to self-aggrandisement and what Asquith, the Prime Minister, termed his lack of a 'better sense of proportion' often made his associates sceptical of his ideas and suspicious of his motives.[50] Even so, there can be no doubt that prior to the fiasco of the Dardanelles, and later in 1917 when he had restored his reputation somewhat, Churchill was at the centre of war policy.

In military terms Churchill undoubtedly was an 'easterner'. If one accepts Captain Roskill's contention that the policy of the 'easterners' was in reality a 'maritime policy', then the adherence of Churchill – always a man to identify closely with the interests of his own portfolio – is easy to explain.[51] But what of Russia? Churchill was initially a firm believer in Russia's military strength. At the end

of August 1914 he wrote that 'Russia is unconquerable', and put
forward a variety of plans for joint Anglo-Russian operations.[52] He
always preferred, as he wrote to Asquith at the end of 1914, 'to
concert our action with our allies, and particularly with Russia'.[53]
This was never more in evidence than during the Dardanelles
campaign, which he always justified with references to the aid that it
would provide for Russia. Churchill was not, however, an uncritical
supporter of Russia. In the autumn of 1917 when her military
capacity seemed almost nil, he opposed sending further supplies to
that country. Thus, while Churchill's strategical views place him in
the 'easterners' camp, his view of Russia varied according to her
military strength.

Chancellor of the Exchequer, Minister of Munitions, Secretary of
State for War, Prime Minister: the list of high wartime offices alone
would justify the inclusion of Lloyd George as a member of the
policy-making élite. Still, his inclusion needs explanation. He had
made his national reputation prior to 1914, beginning with the
conflict in South Africa, as a man opposed to war.[54] He had
continued, along with Churchill, to be the leading Radical member
of the Liberal government until 1914, but, unlike Churchill, had
neither familial nor personal military experience or connection.

By 1914, though, Lloyd George had had some experience in
foreign affairs despite his commitment to Radical causes which
involved him primarily in domestic politics.[55] Since 1911 he had
served on the Cabinet committee created to review foreign policy.
His interest in the budget automatically had involved him in such
military matters as the naval estimates. Nor should it be assumed
that his entire nature was towards pacifism; it was his celebrated
Mansion House speech in 1911 that underlined the British
determination to stand firm against Germany. Despite this at the
beginning of the war Lloyd George was an unlikely candidate to be a
fashioner of war policy. This came about due to two factors: his
importance within the Liberal Party and his desire to 'get on with'
the war.

It was this latter desire, connected with Lloyd George's celebrated
call for men of 'push and go' to run the war effort, that ensured his
entrance to the circle that determined war policy. Lloyd George
never was convinced of the soundness of the arguments of the
'westerners'. He believed that the war could best be won by
providing arms for the large number of Russian troops which he

believed were available and by concentrating British diplomatic and military efforts in the Balkans in conjunction with Russia. Those who opposed these views, like Robertson, or who seemed not to be capable of carrying them out, like Grey and Kitchener, earned Lloyd George's dislike and opposition.

The strengths of Lloyd George were clear to his contemporaries.[56] The 'Little Man' had a nimble mind, great charm and presence and a dynamism second to none. He was at his best in conversation, detested written argument and was contemptuous of expert opinion which opposed his own convictions.[57] In his dealings with Russia, which often involved complicated technical matters relating to finance and supply, these latter qualities were weaknesses. His ignorance of technical matters and his refusal to read reports which might have overcome this shortcoming often produced ideas which any careful examination would have shown to be doubtful at best. To take just one example, Lloyd George's desire to bring Japanese troops to the Russian front showed momumental ignorance of both geography and logistics.[58] His clash with Robertson over the shaping of British policy towards Russia was not just one of opinion; it was a clash of personality and method.

Arthur Balfour's political career seemed behind him at the outbreak of war. A former Prime Minister, he had resigned the leadership of the Unionist Party in 1911 and, well into his 60s, seemed unlikely to hold major office again.[59] However, the man who was considered paradoxically the 'finest brain that has been applied to politics in our time' and a 'philosophic idler', was destined to be at the centre of British policy-making.[60] The inclusion of a member of the opposition party in the inner circle of those who dealt with Russia was unusual. It was possible only because Balfour's age and reputation were beginning to make him a non-party figure (later he was regarded by some Unionists as Asquith's 'tame elephant').[61] Balfour's long experience in defence matters made him a natural conduit through which information could be channelled to the opposition without resort to formal coalition. This made Balfour's position, in his own words, a 'delicate and difficult' one, but once coalition occurred his situation was regularised and, as First Lord of the Admiralty and later Foreign Secretary, he remained influential throughout the war.[62]

While Balfour had little prior knowledge of Russia, unlike most of his colleagues he did not always have a high regard for Russia's

military capability. Writing to Hankey early in 1915, Balfour made
his doubts about Russia plain: 'if the Russians are as strong as they
profess to be, (of which so far I have seen no signs) they ought not to
have the same difficulty in an offensive on the Eastern frontier as we
are experiencing on the Western.'[63] But Balfour's position on
strategy was rarely straightforward. In the same letter to Hankey,
Balfour went on to deny the validity of any of Hankey's proposed
'easterner' alternatives to the Western front. As no one yet
contemplated a Western front without one in the east, Balfour's
argument implicitly recognised the importance of Russia while at the
same time questioning her strength. Such fine argument was typical
of the man, and of his ability to look at both sides and put them in
perspective. On the other hand (to use a phrase Balfour himself often
employed), Balfour lacked initiative; as Selborne noted of him, 'he
had the vision the P.M. lacked, but it led to nothing'.[64] Still, Balfour
had the prestige, the knowledge and the position to ensure that his
opinions were sought and heard, and for this he must be included in
the élite.

The Prime Minister, Herbert Asquith, was the final member of
that group. This is ironic since at the outbreak of war he clearly
stood first among them and was in complete command of his
government. However, Asquith's talents – impartiality, the ability to
find a compromise among differing opinions, a tendency to delay
decisions when no compromise seemed likely – were ill-suited to
wartime.[65] He 'lacked drive', as Lloyd George put it, and seemed
not to have the ruthlessness necessary (except when his political
position seemed threatened) to take the hard decisions which the war
required.[66] An ideal Prime Minister for the peacetime Liberal
Cabinet with its diversity of opinion and outstanding talents,
Asquith was unwilling to impose a policy upon it during the war.

Such unwillingness was unfortunate, for while he was Prime
Minister only Asquith had the requisite authority, moral and legal,
to influence the other political members of the élite. In particular,
Asquith had Kitchener's confidence, which was unusual given the
Field Marshal's generally low opinion of politicians.[67] Further, only
Asquith could overcome Grey's 'certain awkward inflexibility' on
matters where the Foreign Secretary was sure of his ground.[68] But,
as the editor of the *Manchester Guardian*, C. P. Scott, noted
exasperatedly in 1911, even before the war Asquith 'never attempted
to influence him [Grey] at all'.[69]

As a result Asquith failed to implement a comprehensive policy with respect to Russia and her place in the war. In general he supported the consensus, which meant, during the first year of the war, that he gave weight to the views of Kitchener and Grey. In Asquith's government, which 'practised individual enterprise in politics as rigidly as in economic affairs,' departmental autonomy was sacrosanct and expert knowledge was the key to influence.[70] The Prime Minister largely ignored the policies proposed by Churchill and Lloyd George because of the former's bumptiousness and impetuous nature and the latter's lack of expertise. Only when their policy proposals (like Churchill's for the Dardanelles) were supported by more knowledgeable or cooler heads did Churchill and Lloyd George find Asquith in support. As long as Asquith was in office, he was the final arbiter in all debate. When his mode of operation was found inadequate, the call for 'hard-headed war by ruthless methods' proved irresistible.[71]

Several things stand out about the political élite. First, it was drawn from a wider social and educational background than was normal.[72] Men like Robertson and Lloyd George in particular lacked either the aristocratic birth or the schooling normally considered a prerequisite for high office. Second, only three of its members – Grey, Kitchener and Robertson – could claim specialised knowledge of Russia. Third, only an overlapping trio – Churchill, Kitchener and Robertson – had any previous military experience or knowledge of military affairs. As Anglo-Russian relations during the war were dominated by military considerations and required some awareness of Russia, this meant that considerable deference was given to the opinions of others. In this war the non-political, specialist members of the élite, both in Britain and Russia, attained greater influence over Anglo-Russian affairs than would have been otherwise the case.

The Civil Servants

At the centre of the group of civil servants who helped to determine policy with respect to Russia was a small group of men at the Foreign Office. This, the so-called War Department, was created shortly after the outbreak of war by amalgamating the existing Western and Eastern Departments and dealt, as one of its members later put it, 'with the political (as contrasted with contraband) affairs of practically all the countries of the world'.[73]

The men at the Foreign Office were a much more homogeneous group than were the political members of the élite. While this 'close-knit family' underwent substantial expansion during the war, it retained its social and educational homogeneity throughout and emerged from it with 'some of its pre-war personnel and character' intact.[74] Despite the decline in the importance of the Foreign Office mentioned above, several members of the War Department, along with the Permanent Undersecretary (PUS), continued to influence Anglo-Russian relations throughout the war. Their prewar experience, the fact that they dealt with Russia and Russian affairs on a day-to-day basis and the lack of such knowledge among the political élite made the Foreign Office advisers irreplaceable. When other departments, such as the Treasury, began to deal with aspects of British policy towards Russia, the Foreign Office offered advice and opinion about what course of action should be followed. Exclusivity in the creation of policy ended during the war for the Foreign Office, but influence over it did not.

It is impossible to speak of a Foreign Office opinion about Russia. While Russia was acknowleged by all to be important, the élite members varied in their views of her. Nevertheless, the two men who served as PUS during the war, Arthur Nicolson and Charles Hardinge, were united by the fact that they had been prominent in advocating and creating the Anglo-Russian convention.

Sir Arthur Nicolson became PUS in November 1910 after a career full of dealings with Russia.[75] While serving with the British legation at Tehran in the late 1880s, Nicolson had become convinced that only a British understanding with Russia could ensure the British position in Central Asia.[76] As ambassador to Russia from 1906 to 1909, Nicolson managed the complicated and difficult negotiations which led to the signing of the Anglo-Russian convention. There can be no doubt that Nicolson was the most ardent Russophile at the Foreign Office. Harold Nicolson wrote of his father's liking for Russians and 'le charme Slav', while Nicolson himself could write of his 'beloved Russians'.[77] His liking for Russia was not only evident in his private capacity: Nicolson believed, as he wrote to Grey in 1911, that 'our understandings with Russia form the basis of our present foreign policy'.[78] On such matters as the Baghdad railway policy debate in 1911 and 1912, Nicolson sought to impose his pro-Russian views on British policy.[79] Such manoeuverings led eventually to a clash with Grey in 1914 when the Foreign Secretary began to take a firmer line with Russia over Persia.[80]

Prior to 1914 Nicolson wished to make the informal *Entente* between Britain and Russia into a formal alliance. The PUS certainly had no doubt that should war occur, Britain would, as 'a matter of course', enter on the side of the French and the Russians.[81] While this belief, and Nicolson's championing of Russia, could plausibly be interpreted as resulting from a fear of Russia, it is not likely that this was the case.[82] Rather, it was the general growth of Germanophobia at the Foreign Office that gave support to Nicolson's pro-Russian policies. Although Nicolson's interest in and influence over policy at the Foreign Office waned for the most part after 1914, this was not true with respect to policy towards Russia. True to his longstanding preoccupation with Russia, Nicolson continued to pay close attention to Anglo-Russian relations until he resigned in June 1916.

Nicolson was succeeded as PUS by his 'intimate and trusted friend', Charles, Lord Hardinge.[83] Hardinge and Nicolson had known each other for thirty years, having met as junior members of the British delegation at Constantinople in the 1880s. Despite his being nearly ten years younger than Nicolson, Hardinge's progress in the diplomatic ranks had been swifter due to his social connections. In 1904 he had been made ambassador to St Petersburg, and in 1906 had become PUS. In these two positions Hardinge had been instrumental in the improvement of Anglo-Russian relations. Hardinge had, however, formed his opinions about Russia long before. While serving as first secretary in Tehran from 1896 to 1898 and subsequently in St Petersburg until 1903, Hardinge had been humiliated by Britain's powerlessness in Central Asia in the face of a hostile Russia.[84] In 1903 Hardinge was offered a position back at the Foreign Office and accepted it because, as he later put it, 'I felt the absolute necessity of coming to some sort of agreement with Russia . . . [and felt] that, in accepting the UnderSecretaryship at the Foreign Office, I would be able to impress my views in this respect upon the higher authorities.'[85]

Thus, when Hardinge returned to the Foreign Office as PUS in 1916, he entered as a man with full knowledge and awareness of Russia. The change from Nicolson to Hardinge was not a change in expertise, but in attitude. Nicolson had become increasingly pessimistic about the possibility of winning the war; Hardinge was optimistic. Nicolson was incurably Russophile; Hardinge was less so, although before the war Haig had accused Hardinge of having a 'blind belief' in Russia.[86]

Hardinge returned to a Foreign Office transformed by the war.[87] A vastly increased work-load and Grey's diminished influence had reduced the paramountcy of the Foreign Office. This, combined with Hardinge's personal problems, undoubtedly made the PUS less influential than before.[88] However, like Nicolson before him, Hardinge did not let his impact on Russian policy end. His familiar 'H' and minutes continued to appear on key telegrams. In addition Hardinge maintained an extensive private correspondence with the British ambassador in Russia, Sir George Buchanan. While Hardinge could complain about the decline of the Foreign Office's influence, writing to Buchanan in 1917 that 'we have two diplomacies – one the Foreign Office and the other "amateur", running side by side', the former Viceroy still kept his own hand in the creation of these two diplomacies.[89]

George R. Clerk was the head of the War Department for the duration of the war and was, as a consequence, the right-hand man to both Nicolson and Hardinge. At the outbreak of hostilities, Clerk was head of the Eastern Department and the Foreign Office's leading expert on Near Eastern affairs. Nicolson's debility meant that extra work fell on Clerk and in Zara Steiner's words, 'Crowe and Clerk seem to have been omnipresent.'[90] Of course, given the minuscule size of the War Department, even Nicolson at the height of his powers could not have prevented its members from working until 'all hours of the night'.[91] The 'Third Room', as the War Department was termed, never exceeded six clerks in number. Clerk became the man at the Foreign Office most intimately connected with Russia. When British diplomats returned from Russia, it was to Clerk or the PUS that they generally reported. One of these diplomats, the British Acting Consul at Moscow, R. H. B. Lockhart, remembered the personable Clerk warmly: 'He had something more than a kind heart. He had a first-class brain and a judgement of men and affairs that was rarely at fault.'[92]

Clerk was no stranger to Russian affairs. As head of the Eastern Department and having spent time at Constantinople prior to the war, he was intimately aware of Russia. That country's importance to the Balkan wars – wars which had made the Eastern Department 'the hub of the diplomatic universe' prior to 1914 – gave Clerk experience of Russia.[93] His connections with Russia increased during the war. In 1917 he was selected to go to Russia as the Foreign Office's representative to the Petrograd conference. In the

gloomy Russia of early 1917, Clerk adopted the hopeful attitude that
Russia would remain in the war whatever might be her postwar
political situation.[94] Even by the end of the year, Clerk had not
abandoned Russia. He was unwilling either to support the various
White groups springing up in Russia or to forsake the Bolsheviks:
British policy, he felt, should *'festina lente'*.[95] Such optimism was not
universally shared at the Foreign Office.

Lancelot Oliphant ably seconded Clerk in the War Department.
From a distinguished Scottish family and only in his early 30s when
the war began, Oliphant already had served eleven years in the
Foreign Office, was the Persian affairs expert there and
second-in-command of the Eastern Department.[96] Oliphant's earlier
postings at Constantinople and Tehran had brought him into contact
with Russian affairs. It was not surprising that he should play a
major role in determining British policy towards Russia during the
war.

The tone of Oliphant's minutes reveal the caution which he used
in dealing with Russian affairs. Generally he took the worst possible
view of events in that country. By doing so, Oliphant was a useful
foil to Clerk, who usually tended to see only silver linings where
Russia was concerned. An example illustrates this difference.
Writing in mid-June 1915 Buchanan reported the news of the public
unrest in Moscow. Oliphant's minute was typical of his attitude:
'This cannot', he wrote, 'fail to have a disquieting result so far as the
Balkans are concerned.' So, too, was Clerk's rejoinder: 'Yes, but it is
a healthy symptom, if only the Russian Govt. respond in a spirit of
recognition.'[97] Oliphant's caution often verged on pessimism; it did
not prevent his being an astute observer of Russian politics. For
example, early in April 1917 he was quick to realise the 'impotence'
of the Provisional government, and wrote a week later that they
would not 'increase their strength by procrastination'.[98] His attitude
towards the Bolsheviks was even less charitable. He opposed any
recognition of them at all, was certain that they would 'capitulate
entirely' to German demands and regarded them as 'part and parcel
of the enemy camp'.[99]

Clearly there was no unanimity of opinion about British policy
towards Russia at the Foreign Office: Hardinge was more optimistic
than Nicolson, Nicolson more Russophile than Hardinge, and
Oliphant more pessimistic than Clerk. However, there were certain
assumptions about Russia which most of the Foreign Office held in

common with educated opinion outside it. First, Russian public life
was generally held to be corrupt and Russian officials were 'apt . . .
to put commissions into their own pocket.'[100] (Nicolson, of course,
rejected this point of view. He minuted on the same telegram that
there 'were no grounds whatever' for such an opinion.) Nicolson's
disbelief aside, it was commonly assumed throughout the Foreign
Office that Russian bureaucrats and even politicians were able to be
bought. Just before the November revolution, for example, it was
felt that 'some Bolsheviks' could be bribed away from following
what was seen as a German-inspired policy, and Buchanan was
forced to defend the head of the Provisional government, Alexander
Kerensky, against charges of being in German employ.[101]

The second common assumption was that the Russian
government, being an autocracy, was necessarily 'reactionary'. As a
consequence the Foreign Office tended to identify their interests and
those of Britain with the liberal members of the Duma. For example,
when the conservative N. A. Maklakov resigned as Minister of the
Interior in June 1915, Nicolson noted that this was a 'fortunate'
event.[102] In September when the Emperor Nicholas II unilaterally
prorogued the Duma, thwarting any attempt to have responsible
government forced on him, Clerk viewed the situation 'as most
serious' and Nicolson felt the action 'most regrettable'.[103] Men like
I. I. Goremykin, until February 1916 the Russian Prime Minister,
were held to be typical of 'reactionary' Russia and were believed
responsible for the dismissal of more liberal ministers. When
Goremykin's own dismissal was adumbrated in a telegram from
Buchanan, Oliphant's minute nicely summed up opinion at the
Foreign Office: 'we can only hope that this forecast may prove
correct.'[104]

Interestingly, it was not so much that those in the Foreign Office
believed that the policies of liberal ministers would be reversed by
more 'reactionary' ones; rather they feared that such appointments
would hamper Russia's long-term ability to carry on the war. When
the archetypal Russian liberal, Sergei Sazonov, in Lockhart's words
'the most reliable of the Tsarist ministers'[105] was dismissed as
Foreign Minister, Oliphant again spoke for the Foreign Office when
he wrote that

> this incident can scarcely be regarded without grave concern for
> the future. Even though Russia's foreign policy may not be

modified, the internal situation may become very restless with a weakening in foreign affairs as a consequence. I fear that the reactionaries are miserably shortsighted.[106]

Hardinge was more dramatic: 'when we first heard the news [of Sazonov's dismissal]', he wrote to Buchanan, 'we had a feeling of despair.'[107]

This belief in liberal Russia, shared also by the British representatives in Russia as will be shown later, was somewhat naïve. Liberal strength in that country was never much more than a chimera.[108] The Foreign Office's belief in it reflected more their own aspirations for Russia's future than any concrete reality. In some ways this assumption did not seem to affect decisions taken about Russia adversely. Men who had spent their careers working with the less-than-liberal governments of places like Persia obviously had learned to set aside their prejudices and deal with governments as they found them. This belief meant, however, that political events in Russia were always seen as a struggle between good and evil, with the liberals taking on the guise of the former and 'official Russia', the Emperor's circle of conservative advisers, being seen as the latter.

Such a view of political events made the Foreign Office morbidly sensitive about the long-term stability of the Tsarist regime. As mentioned, any dismissal of a liberal minister tended to trigger such fears, but there was a general concern about the inefficiency of the Russian administration as well, an inefficiency which was felt might lead to revolution. The anxiety about Russia's internal situation was intimately linked to worries about her ability to prosecute the war and to a fear that this might lead to the signing of a separate peace by Russia. The latter was a particular concern and surfaced periodically throughout the war. With the precedent of the Russo-Japanese war in mind, where internal problems had forced the Emperor to sign a humiliating peace, such fright was understandable.

For the most part, it was assumed at the Foreign Office that internal change in Russia was inevitable but that it would not take place until after the war.[109] Even so, as early as October 1915 Buchanan was given permission to speak to the Emperor about the need for reform of his government in order that the war effort might be maintained. Such an initiative, it was realised, was a breach of protocol but, as Nicolson noted realistically, 'as we are allies in war we can speak more freely on internal affairs than would be possible or proper in peace time.'[110] Such efforts were repeated right up to the time of the first revolution, but to no avail. The Emperor, contrary to the hopes and expectations of the Foreign Office, put his faith in his own loyal band of intimates and not in liberal Russia. Whether or not this helped to cause the revolution is a debatable point, but it was not doubted in the Third Room.[111]

Although the Foreign Office provided the majority of the civil servants who made up this portion of the élite, the widened range of contacts between the two countries during the war meant that other departments and other men came to share this responsibility. This was particularly true with respect to finance and supply, and these specialties produced two more men, George Macauley Booth and John Maynard Keynes, who must be included among the élite. Their inclusion also illustrates a more general feature of the British experience in the First World War: the way in which those normally outside the government were brought in to deal with the problems caused by the war.[112]

Booth's involvement with Russia came about largely by accident. The son of Charles Booth, the social scientist, and related to the Macauleys on his mother's side, George Booth had no previous connection with Russia.[113] He had gone into the family shipping business as a young man and had pursued an unremarkable career as a prominent businessman. His involvement with Russia grew out of the fact that in the autumn of 1914 Lord Kitchener began to investigate purchasing military supplies for Britain in the United States. Through mutual friendships (and aided by the fact that Kitchener's sister was married to one of Booth's relatives), Booth joined Kitchener in this process, utilising his family's extensive network of business contacts in the United States. Gradually, Booth became part of all Kitchener's efforts to organise Allied supply, particularly that for Russia. Although Booth joined the Ministry of Munitions when that body was formed in June 1915, he did not cease to deal with matters of Russian supply for the War Office. This bureaucratic awkwardness was eliminated in July 1916 when the War Office handed over responsibility for supplying Russia to the Ministry of Munitions. In 1917 he was made a member of the Milner committee, where he acted as the liaison between it and the Ministry of Munitions.

In addition, Booth had other ways of influencing British policy towards Russia. First, he was a friend of Keynes (through the latter's sister-in-law) and thus could make personal appeals whenever Russian finances were involved in discussions about munitions. Second, he was also a friend of H. Llewellyn Smith, the man who had set up the co-ordinating body (called the *Commission Internationale de Ravitaillement* – CIR) at the Board of Trade to deal with inter-Allied purchasing and who later became the general secretary at the Ministry of Munitions. This friendship ensured that the CIR, the War Office and the Ministry always were aware of what the others were doing for Russia. Finally, Booth had the social connections to ensure that his opinions would be heard, regardless of his official position. His younger brother Tom, for example, had gone to Harrow with Churchill, no small advantage when the latter was Minister of Munitions. In short, Booth acted as the lubricant which oiled the awkward machinery set up to deal with the supply of Russia. As Lloyd George summed him up, 'though known . . . as a man of "push and go", he [Booth] was neither, but had other invaluable qualities. He was rather a conciliator than a compeller. I found his tact and geniality invaluable in a Ministry of energetic talents.'[114]

Keynes's involvement with Russia sprang from the same sort of circumstances as did Booth's. On 1 August 1914 Basil Blackett, senior clerk in the Treasury's 1D (or Finance) Department, asked Keynes if he could 'pick [his] brains for [his] country's benefit'.[115] This was the beginning of Keynes's work with the Treasury, work which became full-time by the beginning of 1915. Like Booth, Keynes had no prewar connection with Russia. After Cambridge he had worked at the India Office for two years and then had returned to academe at King's College Cambridge. However, given his association with the ultra-progressive Bloomsbury set, it is unlikely that Keynes had any positive views of Russia and her reactionary government.[116]

If Keynes was ignorant of Russia when he joined the Treasury in 1915, he had full opportunity to remedy that state of affairs during the next three years. As a member of 1D, Keynes became the man responsible for the financing of Allied purchases overseas. Russia was a major troublespot.[117] By 1916 Keynes had developed at least some opinion of Russia as a financial partner. He told the Board of the Admiralty that Britain had only one real ally in the financial sense and that was France; the rest, including Russia, were 'mercenaries'.[118] Russia was, as the Treasury euphemistically put it,

one of 'our less wealthy' allies, and Keynes was continually
frustrated by Russian attempts to avoid the controls established for
inter-Allied purchase abroad and by her seemingly endless demands
for credit.[119] In 1917 Keynes was given even more responsibility for
Russia. First a new department, the 'A' division with Keynes as its
head, was set up at the Treasury to deal exclusively with Allied
purchasing. Second, he became a member of the Milner Committee
and for a time its secretary, doubly ensuring that he would be
involved with all Russian problems. Given the importance of finance
in Anglo-Russian relations during the war and the lack of financial
expertise among the political élite, Keynes is an obvious addition to
the civil service élite.

This élite provided the politicians with the specialised knowledge
which was pertinent to Anglo-Russian affairs. As a consequence, it
was these specialists who generated the policy alternatives from
which the political élite had to choose. Whether or not their
suggestions were made official policy of course depended on those
in the policital élite, but there is little doubt that the influence of
the civil servants was substantial. Even these experts, though, as
well as the political decision-makers, had to rely on another group
of men for information about current events in Russia. While
men like Hardinge and Nicolson, with their first-hand knowledge
of Russia, required less guidance than did men like Asquith and
Lloyd George, all were dependent upon the third element of the
decision-making élite, the network of British representatives in
Russia.

The Representatives

The head of the British representatives in Russia was the
ambassador, Sir George Buchanan.[120] His appointment to St
Petersburg in 1910 at the age of 56 'must have meant', as his
daughter later put it, 'the fulfilment of his dreams'.[121] Even more,
the fact that he was given the sensitive and important Russian post
over the heads of those senior to him was a sign of the special favour
which Buchanan enjoyed both with Sir Edward Grey and within the
Foreign Office.

As a diplomat, Buchanan was to the manner born. The son of Sir
Andrew Buchanan, he was born in the legation in Copenhagen
where his father was the minister. He joined the diplomatic service

in 1876 and made steady, though unspectacular, progress through the ranks, serving largely though not exclusively in the German-speaking areas of Europe. It was as chargé at Darmstadt that Buchanan came to the attention of Queen Victoria due to the old Queen's lively interest in the marital problems of her immense family. This royal connection led to a warm relationship between the Queen and the young diplomat.

In 1903 Buchanan was made Consul-General at Sofia. At the time he regarded this as a dismal prospect; he wrote to the incumbent PUS, Sir Thomas Sanderson, 'I had asked for bread and you have given me a stone.' However, as it turned out, Sanderson's reply that Sofia was the 'school for Ambassadors' turned out to be more prescient than Buchanan's lament.[122] Sir George's tactful handling of the Balkan crisis in 1908 led to his receiving an official commendation from Grey and showed him to be perfectly qualified for the ambassadorship in Russia.[123] As Grey told Buchanan when offering the latter the appointment to St Petersburg, the post there required 'constant tact and skill', qualities which Buchanan had demonstrated so well in the Balkans.[124]

Within the Foreign Office Buchanan was highly regarded. All were aware of his skill in handling the most delicate matters with, as Nicolson put it in 1915, 'tact & circumspection' and were confident of his ability to make the British point of view clear to Russia.[125] Equally, the Foreign Office had confidence in Buchanan's evaluation of events in Russia. Clerk's minute on one of Buchanan's telegrams in August 1917 was typical of the respect accorded to the ambassador's views: 'Sir G. Buchanan's forecasts are always most carefully weighed and never given except on grounds of which he is very sure.'[126] The abortive attempt to replace Buchanan as ambassador in 1917 came about as a result of a political decision and did not reflect views at the Foreign Office. As Hardinge wrote to Buchanan there was 'absolutely no' desire there to remove the ambassador from his post.[127] The inspiration for this attempt came from a belief among the political élite that Buchanan was tied too closely to the old regime to be acceptable to the Provisional government and also may have reflected Lloyd George's impatience with 'old diplomacy' of which Buchanan was the epitome.[128]

After the war there was widespread criticism of Buchanan.[129] Some Russian *émigrés* accused him of having fomented the revolution, while in England many felt that he should have been able to work the diplomatic miracle of keeping Russia actively in the war. An examination of Sir George's activities from 1914 to the end of 1917 makes clear the inanity of these charges. Throughout the war, Buchanan's major concern was the fighting capacity of Russia. To him, such a capacity was linked to internal reform in Russia. As early as 13 September 1914 he wrote to Nicolson to wonder whether or not the Emperor would take the 'golden opportunity' which the political truce caused by the outbreak of war had presented to satisfy the 'legitimate demands of the people' for more participation in government.[130] In the autumn of 1915, after the disastrous military defeats of the summer and the political unrest, Buchanan felt obliged to speak to Nicholas about Russia's internal political situation. Buchanan made attempts of a similar nature both in 1916 and 1917, each time suggesting to Nicholas that governmental reform was necessary in order to hold the country together for the war effort.

These efforts, coupled with the fact that Buchanan was in frequent touch with Russian liberals and was 'moreover in sympathy with their aims', undoubtedly led to the rumours that the British ambassador had caused the revolution.[131] In reality, Buchanan was always quite certain, as he told Grey, that there would be no revolution 'so long as the war lasts'.[132] The counsellor at the St Petersburg embassy, F. O. Lindley, made clear the position of those in Russia and their surprise at the overthrow of the Emperor, shortly after the March revolution:

> I wonder if you all think the Embassy very blind not to foretell what has happened. I don't myself think we have been; we knew the Army was disaffected from top to bottom, though the Government here would not believe it, but I rather expected they would worry on without an actual explosion until peace came.[133]

These were scarcely the words of those who had incited a revolution, and such sentiments were shared at the Foreign Office. Clerk noted on Lindley's remarks that 'I don't think that anyone will accuse the Embassy of blindness. Everyone could see the powder lying about . . . but it was so easy to sweep the powder up, and it scarcely seemed possible for human folly and obstinacy to go so far.'[134]

The idea that Buchanan could have kept Russia in the war needs little refutation. From the time of the first revolution, Buchanan was aware of the danger which political unrest presented to the Allied cause. By 26 March 1917 he wrote that 'hopes which I at one time entertained of war being prosecuted with greater energy and efficiency are gradually dwindling'.[135] Buchanan continually chivvied the Provisional government to increase its military effort and warned it, just as he had the Emperor, of the political dangers which he perceived. He refused to support any attempt at counter-revolution against the Provisional government not because he supported the latter body, but because it 'could only lead to civil war and end in a disaster'.[136] In short, Buchanan attempted in 1917 to do what he had done before the revolution: to ensure the best possible military effort by Russia against Germany. The collapse of Russia was a result of the internal situation in that country, a situation which Buchanan was powerless to remedy.

R. H. B. Lockhart, the Acting British Vice-Consul in Moscow, was just 27 years old when the war broke out.[137] By the end of the war he was the official British representative to the Bolsheviks and the man at the centre of Anglo-Soviet relations. This spectacular rise was due to a number of things: the illness of the British Consul in Moscow led to Lockhart's assuming the duties of the Consul, the heightened significance of Moscow in British thinking during the war due to the importance of its industrial and political scene and, most of all, the initiative and hard work of Lockhart himself. The son of a well-to-do Scottish family, Lockhart had entered the Foreign Office after a less-than-successful attempt at a business career in south-east Asia, an attempt distinguished only by a demonstration of his ability to master foreign languages quickly. This exceptional linguistic skill came to Lockhart's aid when he was sent to Russia in 1911.

Upon arrival in Moscow, the young Scot lived at the home of Madame Ertel, the widow of the noted novelist. He rapidly learned Russian and was introduced into the whirl of prewar Moscovite social life.[138] 'A cheerful young man with a taste for gypsies, wine and dancing', Lockhart soon made himself popular among the liberal circle which frequented the Ertel establishment.[139] There his friends included M. V. Chelnokov, the former mayor of Moscow and future head of the All-Russian Union of Cities; Prince Lvov, organiser of the Union of Zemstvos and future leader of the Provisional government; A. I. Guchkov, the founder of the Octobrist party and another luminary in the Provisional government, as well as other prominent political and industrial figures.[140] Thus in June 1915 when Moscow was swept with riots and political unrest, Lockhart was in an ideal position to be aware of the political currents there and to provide informed commentary on them. As the summer of 1915 wore on, Lockhart's work began to command respect at the Foreign Office. As A. Nicolson wrote in August on one of Lockhart's efforts, 'this is a most useful despatch. Moscow opinion is of the highest value', and Clerk, a month later, noted on another dispatch that 'Mr. Lockhart's report is, as usual, well written, convincing'.[141] Lockhart's worth was apparent as well to Buchanan, and it was typical of the ambassador's relations with his subordinates that he made certain that full credit was given to Lockhart for the work that the latter had done. Buchanan made it clear to the Foreign Office just how much he relied on the Acting Consul's information: 'Thanks to the exceptional position which Mr. Lockhart has created for himself at Moscow, and to his intimate relations with many of the leading political men, his reports on the internal situation are always most valuable.'[142] Such backing made Lockhart, as Clerk was to inform him later, 'the man whose opinion of Russia and Russian affairs counted most [with the Cabinet]'.[143]

Lockhart's full value lay not only in the fact that he had established useful political connections in Moscow, but also in the wide range of activities in which he participated there for the British government. For example, Lockhart ran the Moscow branch of the British propaganda mission in Russia and managed to place items favourable to Britain in the Russian press by means of his wide range of acquaintances in newspaper circles.[144] As well, he helped organise and maintain the Anglo-Russian friendship group in Moscow. In February 1917 Lockhart arranged for the British contingent which had come to Russia for the Petrograd conference to meet with leading Russian liberal political figures. At this time Lockhart became friends with George Clerk, the Foreign Office's representative at the conference, a situation which undoubtedly gave even more weight to his reports subsequently.[145]

Of course, Lockhart had his weaknesses as well as his strengths. The very social qualities which allowed him to make such close friendships among Russian liberals tended to make him see things exclusively from the viewpoint of his friends. While Buchanan, too, had a bias in favour of the liberals, the ambassador had the detachment afforded by maturity and professional training which his younger colleague lacked. This lack of detachment, coupled with Lockhart's romantic entanglements, ultimately resulted in his advice becoming discounted in England, but this did not occur until 1918, during the Bolshevik ascendancy.[146] Until that time, Lockhart was an essential part of the information-gathering network in Russia.

Information about Russia did not arise solely from diplomatic sources. The British government also had a number of representatives in that country who were responsible for providing the essential opinions on military matters upon which so much of British policy was based. The principal British military representative in Russia, in title if not in fact, was Lieutenant-General Sir John Hanbury Williams, the head of the British Military Mission. As Lloyd George later put it, Hanbury Williams 'was a soldier perfectly adapted to represent the country at a Headquarters where the Commander-in-Chief was a Grand Duke, followed by an Emperor'.[147] Descended from a prominent family – a direct ancestor had been British ambassador to the court of Catherine the Great – Hanbury Williams was sent to Russia on the outbreak of war in order to provide a man of suitable rank and social standing to act as a direct link between Kitchener and the Russian Commander-in-Chief, the Grand Duke Nicholas Nikolaevich. Upon arrival Hanbury Williams found himself in a difficult position. With 'a very sketchy idea' of Russia and speaking no Russian, he was entirely dependent on such information as the Grand Duke and the French-speaking members of his staff were willing to provide.[148] This was not much. Convinced that the British were merely an annexe of the French, and intensely suspicious of the discretion of diplomats (through whom Hanbury Williams reported), the Grand Duke refused to give Hanbury Williams any but the most general and vague account of the Eastern campaign.[149] To make matters more difficult, Hanbury Williams was resented deeply by the British military attaché in Russia, Lieutenant-Colonel Alfred Knox, as the latter felt that he should have been given Hanbury Williams's appointment.[150] As a consequence, cut off both from Russian information and from support by Knox, Hanbury Williams initially found himself at loose ends at *Stavka* (the Russian General Headquarters).

However, by the end of 1915 the man whom Lockhart described as a 'charmer, who was popular with everyone' had established himself firmly at *Stavka*.[151] His combination of tact and good manners, plus the growing importance of the British contribution to the war, gradually made Hanbury Williams '*persona gratissima*' to the Russian authorities. He even managed to establish warm relations with the Emperor himself, an important consideration when Nicholas assumed personal command of the Russian army in September 1915.[152] Despite this improvement in his position, Hanbury Williams never was able to provide military information about Russia commensurate with his high station. As a result in 1916 Robertson made an effort to replace Hanbury Williams with someone who spoke Russian and thus could forage for information independent of the Russian authorities.[153] This replacement did not occur. Supported by Buchanan, who noted that Hanbury Williams 'has rendered me valuable assistance by his tactful treatment of the many difficult questions which he had to discuss at Headquarters', and by George V, who told Lord Derby that 'the Emperor treats him [Hanbury Williams] with absolute confidence and talks to him about everything', Hanbury Williams was kept on in Russia until after the March revolution.[154] His social and personal qualifications became less valuable with the fall of the Emperor, and he was replaced soon thereafter.

Hanbury Williams was unable to provide accurate and comprehensive information about Russian military affairs. This problem was mitigated somewhat by the fact that, in Knox, the British government had a representative who 'was better informed than the Russian General Staff themselves' according to the Russian chargé d'affaires in London.[155] Knox came to Russia in 1911. Prior to this he had been aide-de-camp to Lord Curzon while the latter was Viceroy and had spent the period from 1908 to 1911 on the General Staff at the War Office. A physically imposing Ulsterman who spoke Russian fluently, Knox soon established himself as an expert on the Russian army. On the outbreak of war, he was sent to the front with the Russian army, as much to keep him apart from Hanbury Williams as to provide first-hand commentary on the battles.[156] As it became clear that the war would be a long one, Knox's ability to obtain information independent of the Russians became invaluable.

This ability was recognised by all. Even Hanbury Williams, who found Knox 'not even civil', was warm in his praise for Knox's talents.[157] 'He is a very able officer', wrote Hanbury Williams to Kitchener in July 1915, '& knows much more of the Russian Army & its details than any other foreigner.'[158] Knox's letters and dispatches provided a detailed critique of Russian military capacity, often in blunt and colourful language, which went beyond a mere catalogue of events. Due to his many friendships in the socially élite Guards regiments – Knox was attached to them in Poland in 1915 and 1916 – he was well-informed about the political situation in Russia and was able to place his military evaluations in the overall context of Russian governmental affairs.[159] As a consequence of his ability Knox became, in the words of one of his subordinates in Russia, 'the real link with the country, the most authentic channel of information for the Ambassador'.[160] Buchanan was well aware of Knox's value; as he wrote to Nicolson at the beginning of 1916, Knox 'has . . . an exceptional knowledge of the Russian military authorities'.[161] Knox's talents were recognised in the political circles of England.[162] In May 1916 Lloyd George complained, unfairly as it turned out, that Knox's exceptional abilities were being ignored by the War Office, and by 1917 his reports were being circulated freely to the War Cabinet. The minutes of one meeting of that body noted that 'although General Knox had never erred on the side of optimism, his information in the long run generally proved to be accurate.'[163]

During the war there was a move to bring Knox back to England. Primarily this was due to his inability to get along both with Hanbury Williams and with the members of the British intelligence and propaganda mission in Russia.[164] In each instance it was chiefly Knox's pride which was at the root of the trouble. Knox felt that his own abilities were being called into question when others were sent to Russia, particularly when so many of them spoke no Russian and had little knowledge of the country. At the beginning of 1916 General Callwell went to Russia in an attempt to ease the quarrels between Knox and his opponents, essentially with the intention of bringing Knox back to England. Thanks to a determined effort by Buchanan on Knox's behalf Callwell changed his mind. Instead, he arranged compromises about jurisdictions of duties which satisfied Knox's bruised feelings. Even so Knox's attitude was soured by clashes of personality and a general unhappiness over a lack of rapid promotion. Clerk wrote early in 1917 that 'we've got too many capable soldiers here [in Russia], all treading on one another's heels and out for spiking one another's guns.'[165] Only a common desire to win the war and an effort by Buchanan to foster harmony between Knox and the others enabled a working truce to be maintained.

When Knox accompanied the Russian army in the autumn of 1914 it became evident that an assistant military attaché would be required in Petrograd to act as a liaison between the Russian War Ministry and the British embassy. Fortunately, a man of outstanding merit, Captain James Blair, Gordon Highlanders, was available. Blair had been educated at Winchester for a career in the diplomatic service but had enlisted in the Boer War as a private instead.[166] He decided to make a career of the army and won distinction in India both for his athletic and linguistic prowess. Having attended and passed Staff College in 1912–13, Blair was assigned on language leave to Russia. At the outbreak of war, in an unusual burst of common sense, the War Office made Blair assistant military attaché, a position he retained until the end of 1917.

In temperament, Blair was the antithesis of Knox. Hanbury Williams noted that 'Blair is much better to deal with' than Knox, while another of his colleagues remembered Blair for his readiness to help with unpleasant tasks and his 'nice, considerate' manner.[167] Even Knox found no fault with him, describing him as 'the best of fellows and the most loyal of helps'.[168] Different as their personalities were Knox and Blair found common ground in their similarly high abilities. While Knox roved with the Russian army, Blair spent his time mostly in Petrograd; while Knox dealt mostly with the fighting capacity of the army at the front, Blair worked primarily with matters concerning munitions at the rear.

Blair had the difficult and often unpleasant task of explaining to the Russians the reasons why some contracts placed abroad by the Imperial government were not fulfilled and why an unlimited amount of munitions was not available for the Eastern front. Blair managed it well. Buchanan was fully satisfied with Blair's performance, writing on one occasion that 'Major Blair speaks Russian and is on the best of terms with Russian military authorities. He has been of greatest assistance to me and is thoroughly conversant with details of negotiations regarding ammunition.'[169] In addition to his duties regarding munitions, Blair also spent part of his time aiding the intelligence mission and generally lending assistance wherever it was needed. Either resplendent in his kilt (of which a dumbfounded Russian general remarked 'Le costume est pittoresque mais il me semble plus propre à l'amour qu'à la guerre.') or out walking with his wife and infant son, Blair served as a stabilising force for the British representatives in Russia.[170] His reports, based on information culled from the Russian War Ministry and from his own investigations, were a model of informed comment. While lacking Knox's gift for the colourful phrase, Blair provided information of the highest calibre for the British political leadership in Whitehall.

Buchanan, Lockhart, Hanbury Williams, Knox and Blair were the essential sources of information about Russia during the war. Interestingly, however, their information was not passed on to the government as a whole. After passing through the War and Foreign Offices, the bulk of it normally reached only an élite group of politicians, roughly corresponding to those discussed above.[171] Many of those excluded were aware that they did not possess full information about military affairs. As Austen Chamberlain, the Secretary of State for India, wrote to Hardinge in October 1915 about a military matter: 'I understood that it [an earlier opinion of Chamberlain's] was shared by those members of the Cabinet who are most immediately concerned with the conduct of the war and have the most detailed information both of our resources and of the call which may be made upon them.'[172]

Initially, this inner group included Asquith, Kitchener, Grey, Churchill and the King.[173] Balfour soon came to be included in this group, but Lloyd George did not, although after he became Minister of Munitions, information about Russian supplies was passed along to him. Lloyd George was not a man to take such exclusion lightly and, in May 1916, raised the issue of access to information at a meeting of the War Committee.[174] Robertson, who as CIGS received copies of all information from Russia as a matter of course, promised that full knowledge would be made available to the entire War Committee. In practice substantial amounts were excised from, for example, Blair's reports prior to their wider distribution.[175]

Such restrictions had several effects. First they made those, like Lloyd George, who were excluded from inside information susceptible to other, often less informed, sources of knowledge. Much of Lloyd George's attack on Grey for the failure of Britain's Balkan diplomacy was based on the credence which the Welshman gave to the views of the Buxton brothers, Noel and Charles, who undertook a private mission to that region in 1914 and 1915.[176] Similarly Lloyd George seems to have formed many of his views about Russia and particularly Russian munitions from the accounts given to him by Bernard Pares, the historian of Russia who served briefly for the Foreign Office in that country in 1914 and 1915.[177]

While Pares possessed expert knowledge of Russia (although somewhat flawed by an extreme bias in favour of liberal movements there), he was not aware of Kitchener's efforts to help Russia with regard to munitions. Lloyd George, cut off from official sources of information, took much of Pares's information as gospel. Second, such informal contacts no doubt led to Lloyd George's later preference for special missions and the 'new diplomacy', as he likely felt that men like Pares and the Buxtons had provided better value than had traditional sources and channels of information.

More generally, the restrictions placed upon information about Russia meant that public opinion, and even government opinion outside the élite, was shaped largely by newspaper reports from Russia. In some ways this was not altogether bad. Harold Williams, sometime correspondent for both *The Times* and the *Guardian*, probably knew more of Russia than any other foreigner and often advised Buchanan on political matters.[178] Williams was particularly close to the Russian Cadet Party as his wife, Ariadna Tyrkova-Williams, was one of its mainstays.[179] Other men of high ability, like Pares and Arthur Ransome of the *Daily News*, also provided expert commentary based on their close connections with the Russian intelligentsia.[180] The problem was that the correspondents generally had little contact with official Russia and even less sympathy with it. As Ransome later wrote, 'we were all firmly on the side of the Russian parliament, the Duma, as against the Autocracy . . . and were alike in coming to suspect that the Duma was much more pro-English than the Autocracy.'[181]

While similar views existed in the Foreign Office and among some of the official British representatives in Russia, at these levels a corrective existed. British officials at least had regular contacts with the 'Autocracy' and could maintain a more balanced picture of events. Hanbury Williams, Knox and Blair, in particular, dealt directly with the Russian government on a day-to-day basis and, while they often complained of its inefficiency, their reports were useful to balance the overwhelmingly pro-Duma views of the newspaper correspondents and of men like Lockhart. The impact of newspaper articles on the government was lessened only in 1917 when the Department of Information was set up which provided the War Cabinet with a comprehensive survey of the information which was received about Russia.[182] While members of the élite never had to rely on newspaper sources for their information about Russia, they had to work with those who did. For this reason, the general attitude of the correspondents in Russia is important for an understanding of the underlying factors which helped to create British policy.

Between 1914 and the end of 1917, British policy towards Russia was created by an élite group of men. These men had to deal with a wide variety of problems centred on the prosecution of the war. The possible solutions to these problems were limited sharply by the fact that Russian participation in the war was felt to be essential to an Allied victory. The strength of this feeling largely determined the substance of Anglo-Russian relations.

Notes

1   J. Joll, *1914 The Unspoken Assumptions* (London, 1968), 7.

2   On the British attitudes towards Russia, see M. S. Anderson, *Britain's Discovery of Russia 1533–1815* (London, 1958) and the editor's introduction to A. Cross (ed.), *Russia Under Western Eyes 1517–1825* (London, 1971), 13–47.

3   Anderson, *Britain's Discovery*, 15.

4   Cross, *Russia Under Western Eyes*, 14.

5   On the Russian ballet in England, see W. Bridges-Adams, 'Theatre', in S. Nowell-Smith (ed.), *Edwardian England 1901–1914* (London, 1964), 393–94; for opera, F. House, 'Music', in ibid., 440, 443–5.

6   Cross, *Russia Under Western Eyes*, 42–3; Anderson, *Britain's Discovery*, 19–26, 99.

7   Cross, *Russia Under Western Eyes*, 43, 211.

8   As cited in Anderson, *Britain's Discovery*, 112. Compare with General Staff, *The Russo-Japanese War* (3 vols, London, 1908), III, 160, 169–70, and B. Pares, *A Wandering Student* (Syracuse, NY, 1948), 190–228.

9   On public opinion and the making of foreign policy, see two works by K. G. Robbins, 'The Foreign Secretary, the Cabinet, Parliament and the parties', and 'Public opinion, the press and pressure groups', both in F. H. Hinsley (ed.), *British Foreign Policy Under Sir Edward Grey* (Cambridge, 1977), 3–21, 70–88.

10 J. H. Gleason, *The Genesis of Russophobia in Great Britain* (Cambridge, Mass., 1950), 272–90. The best introductions to Anglo-Russian relations in the period from 1907 to the outbreak of war are D. W. Sweet and R. T. B. Langhorne, 'Great Britain and Russia, 1907–1914', in Hinsley (ed.), *British Foreign Policy*, 236–55 and Z. Steiner, *Britain and the Origins of the First World War* (London, 1977), 79–93, 110–27.

11 ibid., 83; A. J. A. Morris, *Radicalism Against War, 1906–1914* (Totowa, NJ, 1972), 52–70. J. A. Murray, 'Foreign policy debated: Sir Edward Grey and his critics, 1911–1912', in L. P. Wallace and W. C. Askew (eds), *Power, Public Opinion and Diplomacy* (New York, 1959), 143–6.

12 On Cossack outrages, see K. Neilson, '"Joy Rides"? British intelligence and propaganda in Russia, 1914–1917', *Historical Journal*, 24, 4 (1981), 890. The Foreign Office was not convinced that Russia would be an acceptable ally to the British public and began a concerted propaganda campaign on Russia's behalf, see H. W. Koch, 'Das Britische Russlandbild im Spiegel Der Britischen Propaganda 1914–1918', *Zeitschrift für Politik*, 27, 1 (1980), 71–96.

13 P. Fraser, 'The impact of the war of 1914–1918 on the British political system', in M. R. D. Foot (ed.), *War and Society* (New York, 1973), 124.
14 Steiner, *Britain and Origins*, 129–89.
15 A. J. P. Taylor, *English History 1914–1945* (Oxford, paper 1970), 14.
16 Naturally other departments had been consulted on particular issues prior to the war. During the war, such consultation was the rule.
17 D. C. Watt, 'The nature of the foreign-policy-making élite in Britain', in D. C. Watt, *Personalities and Policies* (London, 1965), 1–15. I use Watt's narrow definition, as outlined on pp. 3–9.
18 For studies on the effect of the war on various branches of government and creation of new departments, see K. Burk (ed.), *War and the State: the Transformation of British Government, 1914–1919* (London, 1982).
19 As cited in Taylor, *English History*, 53.
20 Despite his friendship with Asquith, McKenna did not influence major political decisions. At the Treasury policy initiatives with respect to Allied finance generally came from civil servants like Keynes.
21 On Addison, see K. and J. Morgan, *Portrait of a Progressive* (Oxford, 1980).
22 Hankey has been well-served by S. Roskill, *Hankey Man of Secrets* (3 vols, London, 1970–4). Typical of the praise given Hankey for his efforts in the war are found in I, 629-34.
23 See E. T. Corp, 'Sir Eyre Crowe and the administration of the Foreign Office, 1906–1914', *Historical Journal*, 22, 2 (1979), 452–3.
24 Callwell left his own entertaining account of his activities, *Experiences of a Dug-Out 1914–1918* (London, 1920).
25 See Z. Steiner, 'The Foreign Office under Sir Edward Grey', in Hinsley (ed.), *British Foreign Policy*, 22–69; K. Robbins, *Sir Edward Grey* (London, 1971), 372; S. Koss, *Asquith* (London, 1976), 144.
26 E. David (ed.), *Inside Asquith's Cabinet. From the Diaries of Charles Hobhouse* (London, 1977), 230.
27 H. S. Weinroth, 'The British Radicals and the balance of power, 1902–1914', *Historical Journal*, 13, 4 (1970), 679–80; M. L. Dockrill, 'British policy during the Agadir crisis of 1911', in Hinsley (ed.), *British Foreign Policy*, 271–87. The Unionists had reasons of their own, stemming from a desire to maintain the concept of bipartisan foreign policy, for not troubling Grey unduly after 1911; see K. M. Wilson, 'The opposition and the crisis in the Liberal Cabinet over foreign policy in November 1911', *International History Review*, 3, 3 (1981), 399–413.
28 Crewe to Hardinge, 16 April 1913, as cited in D. McLean, 'English Radicals, Russia, and the fate of Persia 1907–1913', *English Historical Review*, 93 (1978), 351.
29 This is, of course, debatable; I base it on the premise that only Russia was central both to British imperial interests and to her concern about the balance of power in Europe. See K. Robbins, 'Sir Edward Grey and the British Empire', *Journal of Imperial and Commonwealth History*, 1, 2 (1973), 213–21, for a discussion of how the two issues were linked in Grey's mind.
30 See, for example, his resistance to the Germanophobes in 1911; Dockrill, 'Agadir Crisis', 275–9.
31 R. M. Warman, 'The erosion of Foreign Office influence in the making of foreign policy, 1916–1918', *Historical Journal*, 15, 1 (1972), 133–59.
32 Grey of Fallodon, *Twenty-Five Years* (2 vols, New York, 1925), II, 165.
33 ibid., 166.
34 Bertie to Hardinge, 25 June 1916, Hardinge Papers, 22.
35 For Kitchener's views on Russia's importance in the war, see K. Neilson,

'Kitchener: a reputation refurbished?', *Canadian Journal of History*, 15, 2 (1980), 207–27.

36 For a discussion of Kitchener's great popularity, see G. H. Cassar, *Kitchener: Architect of Victory* (London, 1977), 177–82.

37 ibid., 184–5, 198–201; Neilson, 'Kitchener', 207–8.

38 General Staff, *The Russo-Japanese War*, III, 210.

39 As cited in P. Towle, 'The Russo-Japanese war and the defence of India', *Military Affairs*, 44, 3 (1980), 114.

40 J. McDermott, 'The revolution in British military thinking from the Boer war to the Moroccan crisis', *Canadian Journal of History*, 9, 2 (1974), 171–2; J. Gooch, *The Plans of War: the General Staff and British Military Strategy c. 1900–1916* (London, 1974), 278–95.

41 Towle, 'The Russo-Japanese War', 114.

42 Stone, *Eastern Front*, 18, 37–43; P. Towle, 'The European balance of power in 1914', *Army Quarterly and Defence Journal*, 104, 3 (1974), 333–9, 342. On the Russian naval buildup, see K. F. Shatsillo, 'O disproportsii v razvitii vooruzhennykh sil Rossii nakanune pervoi mirovoi voiny (1906–1914 gg.)', *Istoricheskie zapiski*, 83 (1969), 123–36.

43 Minute by H. Wilson, 27 March 1914, WO 106/1039.

44 See his comments in 'The Dardanelles. Note by the War Office', Kitchener, 28 May 1915, Kitchener Papers, WO 159/7.

45 As cited in Sir P. Magnus, *Kitchener: Portrait of an Imperialist* (London, 1958), 279. See also C. E. Callwell, *Field-Marshal Sir Henry Wilson: his Life and Diaries* (2 vols, London, 1927), I, 103, where Kitchener is said to have told Sir Arthur Nicolson that the French army was 'rotten'.

46 V. H. Rothwell, *British War Aims and Peace Diplomacy 1914–1918* (Oxford, 1971), 6.

47 Robertson to Callwell, 17 February 1915, Robertson Papers I/8/7.

48 Robertson to Haig, 5 January 1916, Robertson Papers I/22/8.

49 On Churchill in the war, see M. Gilbert, *Winston S. Churchill*, Vol. III *The Challenge of War 1914–1916* (Boston, 1971) and Vol. IV, *1917–1922* (London, 1975).

50 H. H. Asquith, *Memories and Reflections* (2 vols, Boston, 1928), II, 82.

51 Roskill, *Hankey*, I, 152–3.

52 Churchill to N. Buxton, 31 August 1914, as cited in T. P. Conwell-Evans, *Foreign Policy from a Back Bench 1904–1918: a Study Based on the Papers of Lord Noel-Buxton* (London, 1932), 89.

53 Churchill to Asquith, 29 December 1914, as cited in Gilbert, *Churchill*, III, 313.

54 See the account in M. G. Fry, *Lloyd George and Foreign Policy*, Vol. I *The Education of a Statesman: 1890–1916* (Montreal and London, 1977), 39–62.

55 M. L. Dockrill, 'David Lloyd George and foreign policy before 1914', in A. J. P. Taylor (ed.), *Lloyd George: Twelve Essays* (London, 1971), 3–31. Fry, *Lloyd George*, I, adds detail but does not change substantially the views outlined in Dockrill.

56 Studies on Lloyd George have become an industry. A good introduction both to them and to the wide range of contemporary opinion about the man himself is D. Brooks, 'Lloyd George, for and against', *Historical Journal*, 24, 1 (1981), 223–30. What is required for a deeper understanding of Lloyd George are some detailed studies of his ministerial career in order to discover how effective he was in transforming his political successes into tangible achievement. The one such study which examines the period of the war, R. J. Q. Adams, *Arms and the Wizard: Lloyd George and the Ministry of Munitions 1915–1916* (London, 1978) is useful, but tends to accept Lloyd George's own evaluation of his achievements too uncritically and discusses little about supply and the Allies.

57 David (ed.), *Hobhouse Diaries*, 72, 76; R. Rhodes James, *Memoirs of a Conservative: J. C. C. Davidson's Memoirs and Papers, 1910–1937* (London, 1969), 52–3; J. A. Salter, *Memoirs of a Public Servant* (London, 1961), 61–2.

58 See the scathing comments by Davidson in Rhodes James, *Memoirs of a Conservative*, 52–3.

59 On Balfour, see his most recent biography, M. Egremont, *Balfour: a Life of Arthur James Balfour* (London, 1980). His political decline prior to 1914 is in P. Fraser, 'The Unionist debacle of 1911 and Balfour's retirement', *Journal of Modern History*, 35, 4 (1963), 354-65.

60 The positive view is that of Austen Chamberlain as cited in B. Tuchman, *The Proud Tower, a Portrait of Europe Before the War: 1890–1914* (New York, 1967), 53; the negative view is from Lady A. G. Lennox (ed.), *The Diary of Lord Bertie of Thame 1914–1918* (2 vols, London, 1924), II, 99, diary entry, 30 December 1916.

61 The phrase is that of P. Fraser, 'The impact of war', 131; see also M. D. Pugh, 'Asquith, Bonar Law and the first coalition', *Historical Journal*, 17, 4 (1974), 833.

62 Balfour to Lansdowne, 9 January 1915, as cited in B. E. C. Dugdale, *Arthur James Balfour* (2 vols, New York, 1934), II, 97; and see Egremont, *Balfour*, 264–5.

63 Balfour to Hankey, 2 January 1915, Balfour Papers, Add MSS, 49703.

64 As cited in Egremont, *Balfour*, 274.

65 Koss, *Asquith*, 160–2; C. Hazlehurst, 'Asquith as Prime Minister', *English Historical Review*, 85, 336 (1970), 516–29.

66 D. Lloyd George, *War Memoirs of David Lloyd George* (6 vols, London, 1933–6), II, 1006–10.

67 Grey, *Twenty-Five Years*, II, 247.

68 R. Jenkins, *Asquith: Portrait of a Man and an Era* (New York, 1966), 152.

69 Diary entry, 1 December 1911, in T. Wilson (ed.), *The Political Diaries of C. P. Scott 1911–1928* (London, 1970), 57.

70 A. J. P. Taylor, 'Politics in the First World War', in A. J. P. Taylor, *Politics in Wartime and other Essays* (London, 1964), 15.

71 ibid., 13.

72 On nineteenth-century political élites see J. Alt, 'Continuity, turnover and experience in the British Cabinet 1868–1970', in J. Alt and V. Herman (eds), *Cabinet Studies* (London, 1974); W. L. Guttsman, 'Aristocracy and the middle class in the British political élite, 1886–1916', *British Journal of Sociology*, 5 (1954), 12–32; and R. Wilkinson, 'Political leadership and the late Victorian public school', *British Journal of Sociology*, 13 (1962), 320–30.

73 L. Oliphant, *An Ambassador in Bonds* (London, 1946), 35; the changes in the Foreign Office during the war are treated in Z. Steiner, 'The Foreign Office and the war', in Hinsley (ed.), *British Foreign Policy*, 516–31.

74 Z. Steiner and M. Dockrill, 'The Foreign Office reforms, 1919–21', *Historical Journal*, 17, 1 (1974), 151.

75 Nicolson's career is in H. G. Nicolson, *Sir Arthur Nicolson, Bart., First Lord Carnock: a Study in the Old Diplomacy* (London, 1930). His career with respect to Russia may be followed in detail in Z. Steiner, *The Foreign Office and Foreign Policy 1898–1914* (London, 1969), especially 121–52 and Steiner, 'The Foreign Office under Sir Edward Grey', 42–56.

76 Nicolson, *Lord Carnock*, 60.

77 ibid., 246–7; Nicolson to Buchanan, 15 March 1915, Nicolson Papers, FO 800/377.

78 Nicolson to Grey, 6 April 1911, as cited in S. A. Cohen, 'Sir Arthur Nicolson

and Russia: the case of the Baghdad railway', *Historical Journal*, 18, 4 (1975), 865.
79 ibid., 863–72.
80 Steiner, 'The Foreign Office under Sir Edward Grey', 56.
81 Dugdale, *Balfour*, II, 85.
82 This has been argued by K. Wilson, 'British power in the European balance, 1906–14', in D. Dilkes (ed.), *Retreat from Power: Studies in Britain's Foreign Policy of the Twentieth Century*, Vol. I *1906–1939* (2 vols, London, 1981), I, 34–41. This has led to some controversy; see the quotation-mongering correspondence in the *Times Literary Supplement*, various issues in April–June 1981. While Nicolson and Hardinge obviously feared Russian intentions in Central Asia, during the war their primary interest was in victory and all else was secondary.
83 Nicolson, *Lord Carnock*, 206; Hardinge's career may be followed in B. Busch, *Hardinge of Penshurst : a Study in the Old Diplomacy* (Hamden, Conn., 1980).
84 Hardinge of Penshurst, *Old Diplomacy: the Reminiscences of Lord Hardinge of Penshurst* (London, 1947), 70–80.
85 ibid., 84.
86 Haig to Kiggell, 5 April 1911, Kiggell Papers, I/8.
87 Steiner, 'The Foreign Office and the war', 516–31.
88 Hardinge had suffered an assassination attempt just prior to the war which had left him with some physical disability. In addition, both his wife and son had died in 1914.
89 Hardinge to Buchanan, 25 June 1917, Hardinge Papers, 33.
90 Steiner, 'The Foreign Office and the war', 516 and 519.
91 Sir L. Collier, 'The old Foreign Office', *Blackwood's Magazine*, (September, 1972), 260.
92 R. H. B. Lockhart, *Retreat From Glory* (London, 1934), 65.
93 Collier, 'The old Foreign Office', 257.
94 Clerk to T. Russell (Balfour's political secretary), 30 January 1917, Miscellaneous, FO 800/383.
95 Minute by Clerk, 21 December 1917, FO 371/3017/240433.
96 Oliphant, *Ambassador in Bonds*, 1–35.
97 Minutes by Oliphant and Clerk, both 14 June 1915, FO 371/2452/77065.
98 Minute by Oliphant, n.d., FO 371/2996/73018, telegram of 8 April 1917; minute by Oliphant, 14 April 1917, FO 371/2996/76703.
99 Minute by Oliphant, 29 November 1917, FO 371/3017/226991.
100 Minutes by C. G., 11 October 1914 and A. Nicolson, 12 October 1914, FO 368/1077/44234.
101 Buchanan to FO, 23 October 1917, FO 371/2999/201697A.
102 Minute by Nicolson, 21 June 1915, FO 371/2452/80972.
103 Minutes by Clerk and A. Nicolson, both 17 September 1915, FO 371/2454/133004.
104 Minute by Oliphant, 1 October 1915, FO 371/2454/141732.
105 R. H. B. Lockhart, *British Agent* (New York and London, 1932), 120.
106 Minute by Oliphant, 23 July 1916, FO 371/2750/144394.
107 Hardinge to Buchanan, 26 August 1916, Hardinge Papers 24.
108 R. Pearson, *The Russian Moderates and the Crisis of Tsarism 1914–1917* (London, 1977), 174–81. A good introduction to the complex subject of Russian liberalism is C. E. Timberlake (ed.), *Essays on Russian Liberalism* (Missouri, 1972) and especially, on the weakness of the liberal movement, the contribution by T. H. von Laue, 164–81. The outstanding Soviet work is V. S. Diakin, *Russkaia burzhuazia i tsarism v gody pervoi mirovoi voiny* (Leningrad, 1967).

109   See Buchanan to FO, 12 October 1915, Grey Papers, FO 800/75. 'I do not personally believe that so long as the war lasts there is a serious danger of revolution.'
110   A. Nicolson to Grey, 18 October 1915, ibid.
111   See minute by Clerk, 7 April 1917, FO 371/2996/72662.
112   The most evident instance of this was the Ministry of Munitions; see Adams, *Arms and the Wizard*, 38–55.
113   On Booth's career, see D. Crow, *A Man of Push and Go: the Life of George Macauley Booth* (London, 1965).
114   Lloyd George, *War Memoirs*, I, 251.
115   As cited in E. Johnson (ed.), *The Collected Writings of John Maynard Keynes*, XVI, *Activities 1914–1919, The Treasury and Versailles* (London, 1971), 3.
116   For Keynes's association with Bloomsbury, see P. Levy, 'The Bloomsbury Group', in M. Keynes (ed.), *Essays on John Maynard Keynes* (Cambridge, 1975), 60–72.
117   On the structure of the Treasury, see H. Roseveare, *The Treasury: the Evolution of a British Institution* (New York, 1969), 230–41.
118   Johnson (ed.), *Keynes*, XVI, 187.
119   Treasury minute, 14 September 1914, as cited by K. Burk, 'The Treasury: from impotence to power', in Burk (ed.), *War and the State*, 85.
120   There is no biography of Buchanan. His career may be followed in his *My Mission to Russia and Other Diplomatic Memories* (2 vols, London, 1923) and two volumes by his daughter, M. Buchanan, *Ambassador's Daughter* (London, 1958) and *The Dissolution of an Empire* (London, 1932). The latter two are also valuable for the character sketches of Sir George contained in the prefaces, by Lockhart and Sir George Arthur respectively.
121   Buchanan, *Ambassador's Daughter*, 88.
122   As cited in ibid., 53.
123   Buchanan, *Mission*, I, 86.
124   Grey to Buchanan, 16 July 1910, as cited in ibid., 89–90.
125   A. Nicolson to Grey, 18 October 1915, Grey Papers, FO 800/75.
126   Minute by Clerk, 30 August 1917, FO 371/2998/170957.
127   Hardinge to Buchanan, 25 June 1917, Hardinge Papers 33.
128   The official reasons are in 144th meeting of the War Cabinet, 23 May 1917, Cab 23/2. The suspicion of Lloyd George's motives is in Buchanan, *Ambassador's Daughter*, 173, 202–3; and Buchanan, *Dissolution*, 289.
129   See Buchanan, *Mission*, II, 92–106 for his discussion of them and his own defence. Lockhart also defended Buchanan against such charges in his preface to Buchanan, *Ambassador's Daughter*, xiv–xv.
130   Buchanan to A. Nicolson, 13 September 1914, Nicolson Papers, FO 800/375.
131   Buchanan, *Mission*, II, 96.
132   Buchanan to Grey, 12 October 1915, Grey Papers, FO 800/75.
133   Lindley to Clerk, 20 March 1917, FO 371/2996/72662.
134   Minute by Clerk, 7 April 1917, ibid.
135   Buchanan to FO, 26 March 1917, FO 371/2995/64191.
136   Buchanan to FO, 5 September 1917, FO 371/3015/174458.
137   Lockhart's early career can be followed in his own *British Agent*. The best survey of his career is the editor's introduction in K. Young (ed.), *The Diaries of Sir Robert Bruce Lockhart* (New York, 1973), 7–21.
138   See the description of prewar life in Buchanan, *Dissolution*, 12–25. There is an excellent account of the Ertel establishment at this time in T. Connell, *Wavell: Scholar and Soldier* (London, 1964), 66–74.
139   R. Hart-Davis (ed.), *The Autobiography of Arthur Ransome* (London, 1976), 231.

140 Lockhart, *British Agent*, 74–5, 77–8, 103.
141 Minute by A. Nicolson, 24 August 1915, FO 371/2454/117006; minute by Clerk, 23 September 1915, FO 371/2454/136408.
142 Buchanan to FO, 6 October 1916, FO 371/2745/212146.
143 Lockhart diary entry, 31 March 1932, Young (ed.), *Lockhart Diaries*, 212.
144 Discussed in Neilson, '"Joy Rides"?', 894, 905.
145 Clerk was so pleased with Lockhart's work that when Clerk became Minister at Prague after the war he asked for Lockhart as his Commercial Diplomatic Secretary; Lockhart, *Retreat*, 39 and 171.
146 For Lockhart's failure in Russia, see R. K. Debo, 'Lockhart Plot or Dzerzhinskii Plot?', *Journal of Modern History*, 43, 3 (1971), 413–39.
147 Lloyd George, *War Memoirs*, III, 1579–80.
148 J. Hanbury-Williams, *The Emperor Nicholas II As I Knew Him* (New York, 1923), 1.
149 Hanbury Williams to Creedy (Kitchener's private secretary at the War Office), 8 October 1914, Kitchener Papers, PRO 30/57/67. This was a constant theme of Hanbury Williams's letters throughout 1914. On Russian fears, see minutes on FO 371/2095/56275. Later, Hanbury Williams got his own cypher and reported directly to Kitchener; see Grey to Balfour, 27 December 1915, Balfour Papers, Add MSS 49731.
150 Hanbury Williams to Kitchener, 9 July 1915, Kitchener Papers, PRO 30/57/67.
151 Lockhart, *British Agent*, 137.
152 Buchanan to Grey, 15 October 1914, FO 371/2095/59973.
153 119th meeting of the War Cabinet, 16 April 1916, Cab 23/2.
154 Buchanan to Hardinge, 3 July 1916, Hardinge Papers 23; George V to Derby, 29 September 1916 as cited in R. S. Churchill, *Lord Derby 'King of Lancashire'* (London, 1959), 224.
155 C. Nabokoff, *The Ordeal of a Diplomat* (London, 1921), 121.
156 See Callwell to A. Nicolson, 6 July 1915, FO 371/2454/90634.
157 Hanbury Williams to Kitchener, 19 March 1916, Kitchener Papers, PRO 30/57/67.
158 Hanbury Williams to Kitchener, 9 July 1915, ibid.
159 See the memoirs of one such prominent Guardsman who discusses his time at the front with Knox, P. Rodzianko, *Tattered Banners: an Autobiography* (London, 1938), 169–73, 177–8, 183–6, 190–5.
160 W. Gerhardi, *Memoirs of a Polyglot* (New York, 1931), 103.
161 Buchanan to Nicolson, 20 January 1916, Nicolson Papers, FO 800/381.
162 There is ample testimony about Knox's high ability in memoirs; typical are Lloyd George, *War Memoirs*, I, 454 and W. S. Churchill, *The World Crisis* (6 vols, London, 1923–31), II, 27.
163 152nd meeting of the War Cabinet, 31 May 1917, Cab 23/2.
164 See Neilson, '"Joy Rides"?', 898–9.
165 Clerk to Russell, 30 January 1917, Miscellaneous, FO 800/383.
166 Biographical information on Blair is from his obituary notice written by Knox, 'James M. Blair', *Slavonic and East European Review*, 4 (1925/6), 482–4.
167 Gerhardi, *Polyglot*, 126–7.
168 A. F. W. Knox, *With the Russian Army 1914–1917: Being Chiefly Extracts From the Diary of a Military Attaché* (2 vols, London, 1921), I, 40.
169 Buchanan to FO, 25 June 1915, FO 371/2454/84484.
170 G. T. Marye, *Nearing the End in Imperial Russia* (Philadelphia, 1929; reprinted New York, 1970), 72.
171 This opinion is based on an examination of the circulation lists noted on the reports of the attachés, WO 106/987–1132.

172   A. Chamberlain to Hardinge, 8 October 1915 as cited in Sir C. Petrie, *The Life and Letters of the Right Hon. Sir Austen Chamberlain* (2 vols, London, 1939–40), II, 36–7.

173   See, for example, FO 371/2095/50911 and 59975 and Buchanan to Nicolson, 24 February 1915, Nicolson Papers, FO 800/377.

174   Meetings of the War Committee, 10 and 30 May 1916, Cab 42/13/6 and Cab 42/14/12.

175   For evidence of the editing done on reports from Russia, see the remarks by G. M. W. Macdonogh (the Director of Military Intelligence) on Knox's dispatch, 8 September 1916, WO 106/1026.

176   On the Buxtons's mission and its impact on Lloyd George, see Conwell-Evans, *Foreign Policy from a Back Bench*, 88–115; Fry, *Lloyd George*, I, 280–5. The Buxtons continued to be active in attempting to influence British policy in Eastern Europe after their mission; see H. Hanak, *Great Britain and Austria-Hungary during the First World War* (London, 1962), 135–50. Not everyone held a high opinion of N. Buxton; Asquith described him as 'an amiable nincompoop': as cited in K. Robbins, 'British diplomacy and Bulgaria 1914–1915', *Slavonic and East European Review*, 49, 117 (1971), 567.

177   On Pares and Lloyd George, see Pares, *Wandering Student*, 209–11; B. Pares, *My Russian Memoirs* (London, 1931), 338–40; Grey to Lloyd George, 20 July 1915, Grey Papers, FO 800/99 and 'Memorandum on Russian munitions', Pares, July 1915, Lloyd George Papers D/12/2/5.

178   Newspaper reportage in the First World War has been criticised sharply, see P. Knightley, *The First Casualty* (New York and London, 1975), 79–112, and, particularly in Russia during the revolution, 137–70. Knightley refers to Williams as 'the worst of the war correspondents' (169) for the latter's coverage of the Civil War. Such a view reflects the attempt to impose contemporary standards on the past and must be contrasted with the views of those who knew Williams; see S. Hoare's preface to A. Tyrkova-Williams, *Cheerful Giver: the Life of Harold Williams* (London, 1935), ix; Lockhart, *British Agent*, 141; Hart-Davis (ed.), *Ransome*, 167.

179   See the discussion of her role in W. G. Rosenberg, 'Kadets and the politics of ambivalence, 1905–1917', in Timberlake (ed.), *Russian Liberalism*, 151–3, 157–9.

180   Pares, *Russian Memoirs*, 343 following; Hart-Davis, *Ransome*, 171–271.

181   ibid., 195.

182   The Department of Information was created at the end of January 1917 under the control of John Buchan. It worked in close connection with the Foreign Office until 1918 when it was made into the Ministry of Information. The task of providing summaries about Russia for the War Cabinet, however, remained with the Foreign Office in the guise of a new body, the Political Intelligence Department (PID). This PID was established by transferring the intelligence branch from the Department of Information to the Foreign Office; see P. M. Taylor, 'The Foreign Office and British propaganda during the First World War', *Historical Journal*, 23, 4 (1980), 875–98.

2

Waiting for the Steamroller

'Fancy Russia the saviour of civilization!'[1] This incredulous, half-amused remark by Sir Francis Bertie, the British ambassador at Paris, encapsulated for a number of reasons the British attitude towards Russia in the early part of the war. While historians conventionally refer to the Triple Entente as if Britain, France and Russia were aligned formally with each other both in war and in peace, this was not the case. Although France and Russia were bound by military convention, Britain and France were not, despite the staff talks begun in 1905.[2] And if the military link between Britain and France was tenuous, any Anglo-Russian military convention was nonexistent.[3]

The British conception of their role in a continental war was not one which encompassed a major commitment of British troops to the continent.[4] Rather it was generally assumed that Britain's role would be her traditional one, consisting of blockading the coasts and offering financial support to her allies, with the British Expeditionary Force (BEF) serving more as a psychological symbol of commitment than as a major striking force. This was linked closely to the generally held opinion that such a war would necessarily be of brief duration.[5] The orthodox view held that a war would be over in six months, decided either by a rapid series of armed clashes or by the financial collapse of the belligerents. In all of these British projections about war, the amount of Anglo-Russian co-operation or even interaction would be slight. The Russian 'steamroller' and the French army would crush the Germans between them, while Britain mainly watched.

The first five months of the war shattered these illusions. The French débâcle in August made it clear that Russia was indeed needed as the saviour, if not of 'civilization', at least of the Allied cause. A quick Allied victory largely depended on Russia. By Christmas of 1914 the idea that Russia would win the war singlehandedly began to fade. The fact that the war showed signs of lasting well into 1915 meant that Russia's ability to carry on a long war had to be considered. In particular, this meant that Britain had to worry about Russia's shortages of munitions and her shaky credit abroad. The end product of this concern was the beginning of an Anglo-Russian financial and economic co-operation which lasted until the end of 1917. But, while a belief in Russia's omnipotence began to wane by December, Russia's continued successes in the Carpathians during the winter encouraged those who hoped that the munitions shortages could somehow be overcome and victory achieved. This fond hope lasted until the spring of 1915 when the breakthrough of the Central Powers on the Eastern front made it plain that the Russian 'steamroller' would at the very least be delayed.

Thus, during the first nine months of the war, considerations of Russia were necessarily central to all of British policy. Nowhere was this more evident than with respect to Grey's diplomacy. His first goal once war began was to ensure Allied solidarity against the Central Powers. In essence, this meant ensuring continued Russian participation, for neither Britain, committed to preventing a German domination of Europe, nor France, with substantial parts of her territory occupied by Germany, could afford a negotiated peace. Grey's second priority was to attract new adherents to the Allied cause or, at worst, to prevent neutrals from joining the camp of the Central Powers. This again hinged on Russia. As most of the uncommitted nations were situated in the Balkans where Russian interests and influence were paramount, Grey's diplomacy was inextricably linked with that of Petrograd.

During the first six weeks of the war, with the immediate fate of the West depending on the success or failure of the Schlieffen plan, British attention to the Eastern front and co-operation with the Russians was cursory.[6] On the other hand, this was a period of intense diplomatic activity. Immediately upon the outbreak of war, the Russian Foreign Minister, Sergei Sazonov, began to search for allies in the Balkans. His search was a difficult one, for the Balkans was a tangle of conflicting aims and deep-seated enmities. In addition, several countries involved in that region's politics seemed unable to decide whether or not to commit themselves definitely to one side or the other. Italy and Romania refused to honour their alliance commitments to the Central Powers; Turkey signed a convention binding her to the Central Powers but did not implement it. Italy and Romania became the keys to Sazonov's attempt to unlock the Balkans.[7]

Initially Grey was enthusiastic about Russian attempts to bring Italy into the war. The accession of Italy to the Allied cause, it was generally thought, would have the effect of bringing in Romania as well and the 'Balkan bloc' against the Central Powers would be well on the road to completion.[8] Italian intervention did not occur so easily. Italy was reluctant to commit herself to either camp as it was not clear that a victory by either side would be advantageous to her. Italy had long-term aims in the Balkans which would be threatened by an *Entente* victory, yet equally feared an expansion of Austro-Hungarian influence in that region. In such circumstances the Italian foreign minister, Antonio di San Giuliano, rejected the offers made by Sazonov and Grey in early August. He was content to wait until the military situation became clearer before making any Italian commitments.

The Romanian position was essentially similar.[9] Ion Bratianu, the Foreign Minister, kept a foot in each camp and consulted with San Giuliano about possible co-operation between Romania and Italy. An equivalent stance also was taken by Bulgaria.[10] The Bulgars feared an attack from either Greece or Russia and were willing to commit themselves to the Central Powers only if, as the Austrian ambassador wrote to his Foreign Minister, 'Turkey and Romania [were] absolutely secure.'[11] Although a Turkish–Bulgarian accord was signed on 19 August, it required an additional assurance by Romania before it came into effect. As Romania remained neutral, the accord was rendered nugatory. The Bulgarians decided to listen instead to the offers of the *Entente* and await the outcome of military events.

For the British, Turkey was the pivot in the Balkans. Turkish intervention on the side of the Central Powers would affect the British position in the Moslem world adversely, particularly in Egypt and India. During the third week of August, the issue of Turkey dominated discussions in the Cabinet.[12] When the Greeks offered an immediate unequivocal commitment to the Allies on 18 August, the issue came to a head. Grey feared that an acceptance of the Greek offer would offend Turkey: it was also unacceptable to Russia. Sazonov rejected any Greek aid without concessions by her to Bulgaria and was concerned that Greek aid would complicate the issue of Constantinople. As a result, the British rejected the Greek

offer. Grey preferred to work with Russia in order to bring about a
larger Balkan bloc. As Asquith later remarked, 'The three *Entente*
Powers . . . agreed that the separate entry into the war of Greece was
not desirable, at any rate, so long as Turkey remained neutral, as it
would prejudice any attempt to form a Balkan bloc.'[13] Over the next
two weeks, Sazonov and Grey tried to wring concessions from the
Balkan states in an attempt to establish the bloc, but by 4 September
it was clear to Grey that such a confederation could not be achieved.
Faced with a situation in which concessions made to any Balkan state
might force the others into the arms of the Central Powers, Grey
preferred to push for the creation of a neutral zone.[14] As long as
Turkey remained out of the war, having no allies in the Balkans was
preferable to an expanded conflict which would lessen the
opportunity to end the war quickly.

Grey's policy was not that much different from San Giuliano's,
and both policies depended on the military situation. By the middle
of September the Anglo-French victory on the Marne and the
Russian successes against Austria-Hungary made the diplomatic
situation in the Balkans more fluid. San Giuliano immediately began
a campaign to ensure that Italy did not miss her opportunity by
waiting too long.[15] On 16 September he began negotiations with
Grey, offering Italian intervention in exchange for Anglo-French
destruction of the Austro-Hungarian fleet, a move which would
permit Italian expansion into the irredenta on the Adriatic. In
addition, San Giuliano moved to make Italy a more attractive catch
for the *Entente*. He began negotiations with Romania for joint action,
negotiations which would allow him to imply that Italian intervention would naturally bring in Romania as well.

Despite his success in concluding the Romanian–Italian
agreement of 23 September, San Giuliano's hopes for favourable
terms from the British were not realised.[16] First, Grey refused to act
as Italy's advocate with Russia: the Foreign Secretary had no
intention of asking Russia for concessions in the Balkans in the hope
of obtaining an Italian military assistance of dubious value. As
Nicolson noted on 20 September, 'beyond, I hope, drying up the
channel through which supplies flowed to Germany, I doubt if
Italy's assistance will be of much advantage.'[17] Second, the Russian
advance in Galicia slowed down in the second half of September,
removing the impetus behind San Giuliano's search for favourable
terms. Realising the weakness of the Italian army, aware of the need

to prepare public opinion for war and believing that no decisive military campaign would occur the rest of the year, the Italian government decided to postpone any decision to intervene until the spring of 1915.

Bratianu managed a greater success.[18] While his bargaining position had been weakened by the Russian successes and a growing popular agitation for Romania to enter the war on the side of the *Entente*, Bratianu managed to convince Sazonov that Romanian neutrality by itself was worthy of reward. As a consequence, on 9 October Romania received a Russian guarantee of Transylvania and a promise of a division of Bukovina along ethnic lines between Russia and Romania in exchange for the latter's neutrality. The signing of this agreement, negotiated by Sazonov without Grey's knowledge, put an end to any hope the *Entente* had of creating a Balkan coalition against the Central Powers. Despite the best efforts of the Buxton brothers, Bulgaria remained unwilling to enter without a Romanian guarantee and extensive concessions from the Serbs and Greeks.[19] While Grey was willing on 24 November to join in a note from the *Entente* promising Bulgaria unspecified territorial gains should she enter the war, no doubt he preferred her neutral if Bulgaria's aspirations would offend all other Balkan states. Only Turkey's entry into the war would make the situation different.

Grey's involvement in the complex negotiations in the Balkans was subordinate to that of Sazonov. This subordination was an inescapable corollary to the relative military strengths of Britain and Russia. While Russia was putting a millions-strong army in the field and Britain was contributing a bare hundred thousand, Grey would have been irresponsible to have attempted to dictate to Sazonov. Only in dealings with Italy, where naval considerations played a role, was Grey's position paramount.[20] Italian intervention at an Italian price was not worth offending Sazonov. Grey's awareness of the divergence of the military strengths of the Allies was evident. In mid-September the Russians asked whether or not the Anglo-French forces in the west planned to advance into Germany itself. Grey's reply on 19 September was revealing. After stating that he assumed that the western Allies would 'press home every advantage', he went on to add that 'as the French army is so much more numerous than the force we can yet send abroad, the question . . . is at present primarily one to be answered by [the] French commander-in-chief.'[21] While Grey did not forego adding his voice to Allied diplomacy, he was unable to force any solution upon the recalcitrant Balkans without Russian concurrence. A Balkan remedy required military medicine.

Without a thorough prewar understanding, Britain and Russia were each unsure of the other's intentions. By the middle of September the Russian Commander-in-Chief, the Grand Duke Nicholas Nikolaevich, was concerned that the western Allies might not carry the war into Germany itself. For the British part, Kitchener was uncertain as to the Russian plans for further action. The Grand Duke treated Hanbury Williams 'as [a] Military Attache of a foreign army in peace time' with the result that there was little co-operation between British and Russian military authorities.[22]

For Kitchener, such a situation was not acceptable. The Secretary of State for War was not convinced of the strength of the Anglo-French position in the west and feared that in the case of a deadlock on the Eastern front Germany would be able to break the Allied lines in the west. As he informed Buchanan on 4 October,

It is most important that we should be kept accurately and continually informed as to [the] real progress of the fighting on the Eastern frontier of Germany in the next few weeks. Upon this will depend the critical decisions that we shall have to take as regards sending troops abroad or keeping them at home.[23]

Kitchener went on to outline his fear that a 'deadlock' in the east would lead to 'an attempt to land German troops in England' producing a situation 'that would not only be critical but fatal.' The Eastern front was essential to Kitchener's thoughts on strategy.

Kitchener's concern about discovering Russian aims was well founded. While Sir John French and his staff optimistically pondered whether or not the Russians would be in Breslau by 15 October, in reality the Russian army was involved in a futile series of manoeuvres in Poland caused by the divided councils within the Russian military hierarchy.[24] These manoeuvres resulted in the Russians' achieving little against the Germans in early October. The failure of the Russians to renew their offensive into Silesia made the situation 'perilous' for the Allies in the west, Kitchener informed the Russian ambassador in London, Count Benckendorff.[25] Even more irritating was the fact that no news about Russian intentions was forthcoming. In frustration, Kitchener had Grey inquire through

Bertie what information the French government had concerning the Russian front.[26] By 14 October the situation was so serious that one Cabinet member noted: 'As to Russia either our attache is a very incompetent person, or else the Russians don't let him send us what he knows, at all events we are in complete ignorance of the situation there, and so it appears are the French.'[27] To remedy this, Kitchener went so far as to suggest that General Sir Arthur Paget be sent to Russia to act as a high-level conduit for information between *Stavka* and Kitchener. While the information problem cleared up sufficiently so that Paget's mission became a temporary rather than a permanent one, Kitchener's concern with obtaining accurate information from Russia indicated clearly the significance which the Eastern front held for him.[28]

Much of this concern derived from his fears for home defence. Throughout October, in the face of Churchill's assurance that invasion was impossible, the Secretary of State maintained that 'if things went seriously wrong in France' as a result of events in the east, Britain herself would be threatened. As Kitchener stressed to the Cabinet, the two fronts were 'interdependent'.[29] By the end of October there was a growing disappointment with Russia's military effort. This was particularly true in France, where Bertie noted in his diary on 20 October, 'here they complain of the slowness of the Russian progress'.[30] Equally discouraging, it seemed likely that Russia would concentrate her offensive efforts against Austria-Hungary and would not make a 'big advance' against Germany until 'she was thoroughly prepared'. Such an eventuality was exactly what Kitchener dreaded. As early as 20 September, Kitchener had urged Grand Duke Nicholas to carry out his plan for an advance in the direction of Berlin, and by the beginning of November the continuation of Russian attacks on Germany seemed essential.[31] The desperate fighting around Ypres, the fear that Russia would go on the defensive against Germany and the fact that influential naval authorities were not convinced that a German invasion of England could be prevented, seemed to presage the gloomy scene which Kitchener had envisioned in his telegram to Buchanan at the beginning of October.

The major significance of Russia for Britain throws some light on the British promise of November that Russia should have Constantinople in any postwar settlement. There has been a wide variety of explanations put forward for the British decision. The two most recent and contradictory theories are that Grey gave Russia a promise of the Straits in order to keep her from obtaining gains in eastern Europe and hence upsetting the balance of power on the continent, and that it was a fear of Russian advances in Persia which triggered the concession of Constantinople.[32] Neither of these explanations seems adequate and neither reflects the situation as it existed.

When the Turks shelled the Russian Black Sea ports on 30 October, it was the final event which decided the British about the Straits. With Russia enjoying military success against Austria-Hungary and with Turkey's entry into the war, it seemed only natural that Russia should concentrate her forces on the south-western and Caucasian fronts at the expense of a drive against Germany. In addition, since the beginning of the war, influential Russians had suggested that a separate peace with Germany was the natural course for Russia to take.[33] The time seemed ripe for Russia to consider her options. Here was Kitchener's fear at its worst and Grey no longer was bound by concerns about the Moslem world. The issue now was what could Britain offer Russia to keep her fixed on the German front. Britain could offer no immediate assistance in the form of an increased military effort on the Western front. As Kitchener told the French President, Raymond Poincaré, and Generals Foch and Joffre at Dunkirk on 1 November, the British could put a million men in France by the beginning of July 1915, but 'before that date, do not count on anything.'[34] In these circumstances Grey attempted a two-pronged approach. First he informed Sazonov that the British were opposed to any major Russian attack against Turkey, arguing that 'everything in the war depends on the success of the Russian offensive against Germany and that nothing should be allowed to divert Russian forces from that object.'[35] Second Grey obtained the agreement of the Cabinet to cede Russia Constantinople. This latter move would, it was hoped, reassure Russia that her interests lay with the *Entente* and keep the Russians committed firmly to continuing the war against Germany. The promise of the Straits, as A. J. P. Taylor puts it, was 'the cheapest coin in which to pay' the Russians to carry on against the Germans.[36] While the 'Persian factor' was undoubtedly important to Grey and the Foreign Office, such a consideration did not override the concern that the Allies might suffer defeat in the west through a Russian defection.

By the middle of November the German attacks in the west tapered off as a new phase began in her policy. Troops were transferred from the west to the east in an attempt to inflict a decisive defeat on Russia in Poland, while offers of a separate peace were put forward through a variety of intermediaries.[37] These events caused a growing dissatisfaction with the western Allies in Russia, and on 4 December the Grand Duke Nicholas asked the British whether they intended to renew their offensive in Flanders in aid of the beleaguered Russians.[38] Such a course had the enthusiastic support of the British Commander-in-Chief in France, Sir John French. French wished to join General Joffre in an attack to clear the Belgian coast, a plan which had the endorsement of Churchill.[39]

By the middle of December French's plan had been abandoned, and his co-operation with Joffre's offensive had led to no great result. At this point, the news from Russia, which had been worsening in late November and early December with the collapse of the Russian offensive in Galicia, fulfilled Kitchener's fears. Reports of shortages of munitions on the Russian front, which had begun as early as 17 October and had continued throughout November, were confirmed fully.[40] Kitchener felt that this meant that the Germans would take Warsaw, and having consolidated their eastern position, would send large reinforcements to the west. Kitchener was not particularly optimistic that either the BEF or the French army could hold their lines in this event and felt that the French were living in a 'fool's paradise' if they believed so.[41]

The matter of the Russian munitions shortages introduces another aspect of Anglo-Russian relations during the war, an aspect which was to have major impact on the functioning of the alliance. The first instance of Anglo-Russian co-operation with regard to supply was seemingly insignificant. On 5 August the French ambassador to London, Paul Cambon, suggested that an Anglo-French body be set up in London for the efficacious purchase of supplies by the French government.[42] After two weeks of discussion, such a body was created, the so-called *Commission Internationale de Ravitaillement* (CIR), under the aegis of the Board of Trade. Initially the CIR was a purely Anglo-French arrangement, but when the Russian government inquired at the end of August about possible purchases to be made in Britain, the President of the Board of Trade, Walter Runciman, wrote to Grey:

If the Russian Gov't would make its purchases by the same method as the French Gov't in conjunction with our Admiralty & War Office, we should by that means avoid competing against each other to our mutual detriment. We could moreover give full detailed information and suggestions [to the Russians] as in the case of the French purchases.[43]

After consultation with the Admiralty, the War Office and the Treasury, the Foreign Office cabled Buchanan, suggesting that the Russian government nominate representatives to the CIR.[44]

This proposal was accepted by the Russians on 22 September, although final details of Russian membership, including methods of payment, were not completed until December. The Russian delegates to the CIR were M. V. Rutkovskii, the Russian commercial attaché in London; Lieutenant-General N. S. Ermolov, the military attaché, assisted by Colonel Nicolaev, and the naval attaché, Captain Volkov.[45]

The Russian adherence to the CIR, while it marked the beginning of Anglo-Russian co-operation in purchasing, by no means prevented the Russian government from ordering munitions independently from or in direct competition with the British. This proved to be a major point of contention between the two Allies. As early as October 1914 Cecil Spring-Rice, the British ambassador to Washington, wrote to the Foreign Office that 'from various sources I hear that British, French and Russians are competing in United States markets against each other' and later in the month added that there was 'great confusion and corruption' in the United States due to the Allied scramble for contracts there.[46]

In Britain itself there was not a central body strong enough to ensure that Russian government orders there were not harmful to the British war effort. For example, in mid-September Count Benckendorff wrote to the Foreign Office asking whether there was any objection to the Russian government's placing an order with Vickers for twenty anti-aircraft guns.[47] The British reply was revealing. H. Guthrie Smith, Director of Artillery at the War Office, noted that there were 'no objections if our orders are not interfered with. Vickers will probably say there will be no interference and we have no means of finding out whether this is correct or not.' Not surprisingly, four days later Vickers informed the Foreign Office that the Russian order in no way jeopardised the work which they were doing for the British government.[48]

Within the CIR things did not run smoothly. The Russian delegates were not advised by their government of purchases made in either the United States or Britain by various departments of the Russian government and this led to confusion and crosspurposes. Some of the British members of the CIR felt that the Russian members were simply not 'playing the game' and suggestions were made that the Russian delegates were demanding commissions as bribes. This sentiment was echoed by some departments of the Russian War Office. As Blair reported in January 1915, some Russian departments 'flatly refused' to place orders through the CIR as they felt that body was shot through with corruption.[49]

The difficulty of getting 'one neck to the bottle' for Russian purchasing overseas was to last until Russia left the war and proved to be a continual irritant to cordial Anglo-Russian relations.[50] Much of the problem stemmed from the prewar methods of purchasing foreign munitions used by the Russian government. Since about 1860, the Russian government had followed a programme of self-sufficiency with respect to munitions, but had utilised freely the expertise of foreign contractors.[51] Firms like Vickers, Schneider-Creusot, John Brown and others had contributed much to the creation of modern armaments industry in Russia. All of this had been carried on in a fashion quite similar to the general way in which foreign contracts were dealt with in Russia.

Contracts in Russia were normally awarded by bureaucratic fiat, with individual departments of state controlling their own purchasing. Serving as a liaison between these departments and the foreigners who wished to obtain contracts were a large number of middlemen and promoters who, for a fee, made certain that the two interested parties were brought together. The creation of the CIR threatened this existing system and with it the highly lucrative practice of 'finder's fees', fees not easily discernible from bribes. In such circumstances, it was no surprise that many Russian departments wished to circumvent the CIR and maintain the prewar practice. Equally important was the fact that the Russian War Ministry was highly compartmentalised. In particular the Main Artillery Department (*Glavnoe Artilleriiskoie Upravlieniie* or GAU) jealously guarded its prerogatives with respect to ordering abroad.

At the outbreak of war, such problems were exacerbated by the fact that Russia was split into two areas, a war zone controlled by *Stavka* and a rear area which remained under the control of the

Imperial government.[52] So tight was the division between these two areas that senior government officials had to get permission to travel to the front and communication between these two virtually independent governments was not frequent. Nowhere was this more evident than in dealings involving munitions. The strained personal relations between the War Minister, V. A. Sukhomlinov, and the Grand Duke Nicholas meant that only a tenuous link was maintained between front and rear. Had a short war ensued, problems with munitions would not have been as profound as they turned out; Russian stockpiles of war material were of the same order as other European armies. In a long war these problems were at times disastrous.

Of course, munitions had to be paid for as well as ordered. The unsatisfactory situation with regard to supply found its counterpart in the financial relations between Britain and Russia. In the latter case, the problems were caused less by shortages and matters of organisation than by differences of opinion between the financial experts of the two countries. The first attempt by the Russians to negotiate credit in Britain came in early September 1914. Benckendorff wrote to Arthur Nicolson outlining a scheme whereby the Russian government either would open a credit of £15 million secured by the gold reserves of the Russian State Bank, or would receive a credit of £15–20 million backed by an equal amount of Russian Treasury bonds to be held by the Bank of England.[53]

The British response was contained in a letter written by Sir John Bradbury, the joint permanent secretary to the Treasury.[54] The Treasury proposed that a loan of £20 million be made, secured by the shipment of £8 million worth of gold bullion from Russia to Britain, and the issuance of £12 million worth of Russian Treasury bonds in England. This loan was to be used to allow Russian firms to pay their English creditors, to permit the Russian government to pay the interest due on its external debt, and to finance Russian government purchases in Britain. The Treasury was not 'prepared to contemplate' any of the loan being used to purchase goods for Russia outside of Britain. This point of view was sent to the Russian government on 26 September.

When no Russian reply was made immediately, a further telegram was sent to Petrograd to underline the British position. The telegram was the work of Lloyd George's special Treasury Committee which the Chancellor had set up to deal with the problems caused by the war. The Committee stated in the telegram that the British proposals of 26 September 'were as favourable as they could possibly make' in the circumstances and that better terms seemed unlikely.[55]

Despite the take it or leave it nature of the British offer, the Russian government attempted to modify the terms of the proposal, although by mid-October they had accepted the bulk of the terms. Piotr Bark (later Sir Peter), the Russian Minister of Finance, spoke to Buchanan on 18 October and asked whether the gold could be held in Russia for the British government given the dangers of shipment. This was unacceptable, both to the Treasury and to the Bank of England. The maintenance of the exchange rate of the pound depended on the amount of gold deposited in London and the Russian gold was vital.[56]

The Treasury modified its position a few days later. The £20 million was not to be used solely to settle prewar commercial debts, nor was there to be a complete ban on the use of the loan for purchases abroad. Rather, the money would be available to finance current expenditures and to purchase goods abroad which could not be provided by the 'English market'.[57] With the failure of the Russian government to raise a loan in the United States, negotiations for which were being pursued simultaneously by the Russian government in that country, Bark agreed to the British proposals. On 26 October Benckendorff was authorised to sign for the £12 million in Russian Treasury bonds. The first British loan to Russia was a reality, a loan concluded solely on British terms.

The loan negotiations had pinpointed the problems which were to remain unsolved for the duration of the war. The Russians resented restrictions which the British Treasury wished to place on the money loaned, money which, after all, Russia was expected to repay with interest. At the same time, Bark felt that the British demands for bullion shipments were an unacceptable imposition on an ally, given the relative international strengths of sterling and the rouble.

British opinion about financing Russia's overseas purchasing was remarkably optimistic at this time. Two statements, by Basil Blackett and Sir George Paish (the latter the editor of *The Statist* and an adviser to Lloyd George), written at the end of October put the British view clearly.[58] Paish was convinced that there would be no difficulty in financing Russian purchases in the United States. 'If France can meet her own expenditures in the United States by sales of American securities,' Paish wrote, 'I apprehend no difficulty in

meeting the expenditures of England and of Russia.' Blackett was
less sanguine. Since the financial burden of Russian purchasing in
the United States would fall on British shoulders, Blackett felt that
a necessary concomitant should be the transfer of a 'substantial
amount' of gold from Russia to Britain. In addition, he desired the
creation of some financial equivalent to the CIR to ensure that the
Allies should not be 'bidding against each other in the American
money market as in the American horse fairs'.

By the beginning of December, the Russian government initiated
a new round of negotiations for a further British loan.[59] Bark asked
Buchanan to obtain the support of the British government for a
Russian attempt to raise further funds on the London market. Bark
needed this support as he did not wish to send more gold abroad and
Russian gold reserves just exceeded 50 per cent of the fiduciary
issue. The rest of the Russian bullion Bark needed to finance the
war.

At this point, a difference of opinion arose between the Foreign
Office and the Treasury about the Russian proposal. The Foreign
Office thought in strategic terms. Hugh O'Beirne, the counsellor at
the British embassy in Petrograd, had written trenchantly of the
problems of Russian war finance.[60] Russian expenses were £1
million per day for the war effort, and total resources were only
£245.7 million. At the end of 1914, by O'Beirne's reckoning, the
Russian government would have only about two months' supply of
funds left with which to carry on the war. As O'Beirne wrote to
Grey's private secretary, Sir William Tyrrell, on 8 December: 'over
here the financial question is becoming a rather burning one right
now', and added, with respect to the further export of Russian gold,
'I hope this won't have to be insisted on, because the idea causes the
greatest indignation here and besides it diminishes the Russn.
Treasury's ability to discount its bills with the State Bank, which is
the only visible means of financing the war just at present.'[61] In a
memorandum which was circulated to most of the political élite,
O'Beirne noted that Bark had stated that unless Russia received
more money from Britain, 'he [Bark] could not continue the war'.
Buchanan supported O'Beirne's views, and wrote to Nicolson
suggesting that Britain not insist on onerous terms for the new
Russian loan.[62]

Unlike the Foreign Office, the Treasury thought in financial
terms. The concern there was with the role that the Russians

expected the British government to play with respect to the loan. Did Russia merely want the Treasury to adopt a favourable attitude to the Russian loan or did Russia expect the British government to guarantee the loan? Further, the Treasury admonished the Russian government to bear in mind 'the dangers to the financial position' of Britain caused by the demands on her credit and on her 'comparatively slender stock of gold'. To prevent the erosion of British, and therefore *Entente*, credit, the British government had to 'take steps' to increase her gold reserves.[63]

On 15 December the Russian Treasury clarified its position on the proposed financial arrangement. Of the £100 million asked for by the Russians, about £30 million were required for war industry imports, a similar amount for the repayment of debts incurred previously by Russian industry, £15–20 million for orders placed in Britain, £5 million to service the Russian government debt in Britain and some small amounts for various Russian commitments in both Britain and the United States.[64] The following day Lloyd George raised the matter at a meeting of the War Council.[65] His presentation of the Russian position illustrated how narrowly the Treasury viewed the Russian war effort. Lloyd George loosely characterised the Russian demands as £30 million for 'internal industries', £30 million for 'municipal loans' and £40 million for 'the war'. The Treasury's attitude was that they would not have 'anything to do with' the £60 million not required for 'the war', and that the £40 million which the Treasury were prepared to offer as a loan would have to be repaid at 5–6 per cent. Any part of the loan spent outside of Britain would have to be 40 per cent backed by gold to be shipped to Britain. After deciding that the Treasury position should be phrased in 'more conciliatory terms', the War Council sent it as a basis for negotiation on 18 December.

This timing was ironic. On that same day Buchanan informed the Foreign Office that the Russian advance into Silesia would be indefinitely delayed due to munitions shortages.[66] This telegram confirmed the fears which Knox's information about Russian munitions production had raised earlier in the month. Combined with Kitchener's concern that the Russians would now begin a retreat to Warsaw and with the parlous state of Russian finances, the news of munitions shortages was disheartening. Gloom about the Eastern front was everywhere: Kitchener informed the War Council that his news about munitions was 'disastrous' and Bertie noted that 'the military opinion here [London] is that the Russians are done for, so far as offensive action is concerned, until July.'[67] Even in France where optimism about Russia normally exceeded that in England, 'they [the French] are losing confidence in the Russian "steamroller": there is not enough steam to make it act properly.'[68]

It was in this situation that Sir John French arrived in England on 20 December to plead for an offensive in the west. On that day, he and Kitchener had a long discussion of the military situation. Asquith, who had arranged the meeting of the two Field Marshals, noted the disparity of their opinions: 'I found K.[itchener], with his chart of Russian and German divisions, emphasizing the pessimistic point of view. French . . . would have none of it.'[69] The next day French had a long talk with Churchill. Again the talk centred around Russia. French conceded that 'the question is are the Russians so smashed that the whole weight is coming on our necks.' If that were true, Sir John was willing to 'simply hold on until we are all ready again'. In point of fact, the Commander-in-Chief of the BEF did not 'yet believe about the Russians, & [thought] that it may turn out to be less bad than we now think.'[70]

On 21 December Kitchener made an attempt to determine the true state of affairs in Russia. As he put it baldly to Buchanan, 'it is essential for us to know what the Russians intend to do.'[71] The key points, as far as Kitchener was concerned, were how far the Russians intended to retreat, how many German troops could be expected to be transferred to the west and whether or not the Russians had inflicted 'severe loss' on the Germans during the fighting in Poland. The answers to these questions, Kitchener made it plain, would determine British strategy in the west.

The Russian situation dominated the discussions at the War Council on 22 December.[72] French stated his case clearly at this meeting. He felt that the Germans would be unable to achieve a decisive victory against the Russians and would shift their troops westward for a spring offensive against the Allies in France. In the interim, Sir John wanted to launch an attack against the German lines. On the other hand, Kitchener 'presented the most gloomy view of the Russian position' and argued that forty German divisions would be transferred to the Western front should the Russians lose Warsaw.[73] Churchill was pleased to have 'an optimist at the front' in the person of French, but Asquith felt such optimism required the balance of 'a pessimist [Kitchener] in the rear'.[74] The pessimistic point of view carried the day, and the War Council instructed French to discuss with Joffre the effect of the Russian munitions problems on Allied plans.[75]

Despite the general despondency about the Russian situation, there were some who did not share it. Nicolson made his position clear in a letter to Balfour on 24 December.

> I am not perturbed as to Russia. And though her advance may be delayed, and though she may be suffering from anoemia in certain of her organs, a malady not peculiar to her, I am still confident that she will play her part to our satisfaction. We must be prepared for checks in this great war with so formidable an adversary. As to the *spirit* of the Russian people I have no doubt whatever.[76]

This reference to 'spirit' reflected the fact that there was a growing discontent in Russia with the Allies; 'gossipers' in Petrograd were 'grumbling ag[ain]st. the Armies in the West – ours & French – for not advancing more rapidly.'[77] In addition there were influential circles in Russia which were receptive to the increasing blandishments of the German government for a separate peace. As Balfour noted, among these Russians there was a belief that 'the whole weight of the war – both in blood and money – has fallen upon Russia . . . and that England has been very mean about her financial arrangements with Russia.'[78]

In Russia meanwhile, the British representatives made every effort to determine the true state of affairs with respect both to munitions and to the military situation. Buchanan dispatched Knox to *Stavka* on 24 December in order that he and Hanbury Williams might be able to obtain some information from the Grand Duke Nicholas. During the week Knox was at *Stavka*, he was flooded with bad news. The Russian Chief of Staff, General N. N. Ianushevich, told the British that no Russian offensive could be expected until July 'if Russia had to depend on her own resources.' In addition Hanbury Williams discussed matters with the Emperor and tried to point out the problems which Russia was bound to encounter in her munitions orders overseas.[79]

The question of munitions for Russia was a difficult one. By the end of December, the Russian government had made it clear that only immediate munitions support from the Allies would result in any Russian offensive in the near future. Beyond chivvying the Japanese to provide aid for Russia, no British help could be available for several months, much to the chagrin of some members of the government. As Lloyd George wrote angrily to Asquith at the end of December:

> No real effort has been made until this week to ascertain the Russian position. . . . Two months ago I pressed it on the War Office. Had it been done then we could have helped Russia whilst Archangel was still open, and saved her from the peril of exhausted caissons.[80]

While this attack had force, it ignored several facts.

As Buchanan noted, the Russians had kept the Allies unaware of their munitions problems, even though the French had inquired about them as early as September.[81] Also, the New Armies were more than absorbing all the output of the British war industries, and all the Allies alike were scrambling in the American market for munitions.[82] Once the Russians had chosen to reveal their deficiencies, Kitchener requested that they send an officer to Britain to outline their needs.

While the debate about munitions continued, Sir John French had returned to France determined to find support for his planned offensive. Before meeting with Joffre as ordered by the War Council, French had a paper drawn up outlining his point of view.[83] According to this, the Germans were unlikely to be able to force a quick decision in Russia and would be most likely to make a bold thrust against the Western front in April 1915. The pivotal issue would be whether the Allies could provide enough troops to counter this attack, a shrewd play by French to press for the transfer of the last remaining element of the regular army, the 29th division, from England to France.

On 27 December French and Joffre met at Chantilly to discuss the Russian impact on the Western front.[84] The French Commander-in-Chief professed optimism about the state of affairs in Russia. Joffre told French that victory could best be obtained by focusing all the efforts of the French and British armies on the Western front. In addition to carrying the possibility that a decisive victory could be won, such a move would prevent further forces from being sent eastward by the Germans to the Russian detriment. Joffre also noted that the French were moving to help the Russians with their munitions problems and doubted that the Russian shortages would be more than temporary. Such an account cannot be taken at face value. French as well as British representatives in Russia had been informed of the munitions crisis, and Joffre's optimism was no doubt a product of his desire to obtain as many British troops as possible for the Western front.

The pessimism which Knox's telegrams had engendered earlier in December must have been intensified by the arrival of his dispatches and those of Hanbury Williams at the end of the month.[85] They were filled with gloomy talk of shortages in ammunition, rifles and men. As Knox put it, 'the thick reserve columns that appear in the *Times* map in rear of the Russian front exist only in the imagination of the Military Correspondent.' Even so Knox was not pessimistic about the long-term situation, since he felt that 'the Russian army has done as well as anyone who knew anything about it expected. Its faults and difficulties were foreseen.' This was cold cheer to those British statesmen who had entered the war confident in the assumption of a six-months' conflict and of a Russian 'steamroller'.

By the end of 1914 it had become clear that the Russian army was not the decisive weapon that many had hoped it would be. Both Russian finance and production of munitions were suspect and Britain faced the prospect not only of financing the war but also of becoming the principal supplier of arms for Russia. The significance of Russia as an ally was not in doubt, despite these signs of weakness. Russia forced the Central Powers to maintain armies on two fronts, and she provided the source of the Allied superiority in manpower. Balfour spoke for British opinion when he wrote to Nicolson on 28 December: 'The war cannot possibly be conclusive in our favour unless the Western Allies have Russia wholeheartedly on their side till the end.'[86]

It was the Russian situation, as well as the stalemate on the Western front, that created the atmosphere which produced a series of papers designed to chart a strategic path for Britain in 1915. Churchill, Hankey and Lloyd George argued that attacks on German lines in France would yield no gains commensurate with the losses that they seemed certain to entail.[87] This sentiment, while not totally shared by Kitchener, must have seemed to him support for his own policy. His policy was based on delay. The Secretary of State for War wished to await the development of the New Armies and not to

use them piecemeal in France. On 2 January Kitchener wrote to Sir
John French to advise him that, as any penetration of the German
lines seemed unlikely, 'the feeling was gaining ground that although
it is essential to defend the line we hold, troops over and above what
is necessary for that service are better employed elsewhere.'[88]

Such an idea did not sit well with French, as it would mean the end of
his plans for an attack on Ostend and Zeebrugge. Against any diversion
of troops from France, French argued that while 'the Eastern theatre of
war is one in which a success on the part of the Allies would have the
most decisive results', a loss in France would be fatal. In no situation, not
'even in such a one as would arise if Russia were to be placed temporarily
hors de combat' could French accept a diversion of troops from France.[89]
French supported this letter by a memorandum on manpower. He
argued that the formation of new German armies would soon give them a
numerical superiority in the west, without major withdrawals from
Russia. He therefore advocated sending British reinforcements to the
continent in order to 'take the offensive at the earliest possible
moment.'[90] French's remarks were obviously designed to counteract the
Russian-based arguments which had frustrated his proposals at
Christmastime, but failed to consider the possibilities which the papers
of Churchill, Hankey and Lloyd George had raised.

All of the alternatives were discussed at the meeting of the War
Council on 8 January 1915.[91] Kitchener stated that a German
offensive in the west was likely and he read aloud French's letter of 2
January with its emphasis on the danger of a defeat in France. This,
Kitchener argued, destroyed any arguments for a major
commitment to any theatre other than France. But Kitchener was
not opposed to a limited involvement elsewhere. He stated that

> The Dardanelles appeared to be the most suitable objective as
> an attack here could be made in cooperation with the Fleet. If
> successful it would re-establish communications with Russia;
> settle the near Eastern question; draw in Greece and, perhaps,
> Bulgaria and Roumania, and release wheat and shipping now
> locked in the Black Sea.

Kitchener felt that this could be achieved with a force of 150,000
men. At this meeting no final decision as to where British efforts
should be concentrated was taken, although French's plan for an
attack on Zeebrugge was quashed.

What had prompted Kitchener's suggestion of an attack on the Dardanelles? The most likely explanation stems from the military situation. A War Office paper prepared at this time made clear the difficulties which Kitchener faced in formulating strategy. Passive defence in France would cause enormous problems, since

> Even at considerable military risk we must convince France, (still the predominant partner, on land, in the Western theatre) that we are ready and willing to do our utmost to cooperate with her; and even if France agrees to maintain a defensive attitude for the present, then she and ourselves must convince Russia that it is wise to do so in the interests of all.[92]

An even more dangerous result of passive defence in France was the possibility of suffering a major defeat there. In order to prevent either occurrence, the War Office suggested 'determined local offensive[s], aiming at the defeat of an appreciable section of the German line and not at a gain of ground'.

For Kitchener an attack at the Dardanelles was a more attractive alternative. If successful it would bring about the collapse of the Ottoman threat to the British empire, a threat which concerned Kitchener greatly. In addition it would help the Russians both by removing their Caucasian front and by opening up a year-round means of transport to the west via the Black Sea. It would also satisfy those for whom a passive military stance was unacceptable and would serve as a sop to those among the élite who preferred a commitment of British forces elsewhere than in France. Most of all, it would preserve Kitchener's options and allow him to avoid showing his hand until a later date when German intentions were clear and the New Armies were ready.

Kitchener's desire to play for time was evident at the War Council meeting held 13 January.[93] With Sir John French present to represent the view of the BEF, the discussion soon turned to the Russian front. When Grey demanded to know what the British intended to do in the interim until the Russians could renew their offensive in May, Kitchener made clear the Fabian nature of his Mediterranean proposal. Kitchener stated that the War Office (by which he meant himself) supported Sir John's plan but in the long run only. A decision on it, he felt, should be delayed until the end of February. This left the War Council with no policy at all, and this

unsettling vacuum accounts for the enthusiasm generated by
Churchill's suggestion that the Dardanelles could be forced by naval
efforts alone. In quick order the Dardanelles project was accepted as
British policy, although a Cabinet sub-committee was set up to
examine other potential British campaigns.

While the Dardanelles expedition had been accepted by the War
Council, the debate on strategy continued for the rest of January.
The key issue was the question of reserves and where they were to be
deployed. Arguments over forces like the 29th division dominated
strategical discussion. The final blow to French's plan for an attack
on Zeebrugge came not from the War Council but from Joffre and
intimately involved the issue of reserves. Joffre's decision to attack
the Germans in Champagne meant that the French Commander-in-
Chief expected John French to take over part of the French line in
order to free troops for the assault. On 21 January Alexandre
Millerand, the French War Minister, came to Britain to argue for the
immediate dispatch of available troops to France in support of
Joffre's offensive.[94]

He met with little success. Churchill, Grey and Lloyd George all
argued in favour of sending troops to the Mediterranean to help the
Serbs. Kitchener hedged. The Secretary of State for War advanced
the idea that the end of French's proposed offensive meant the end
of any commitment to send British troops to the continent. At this
suggestion 'Millerand stuck his toes in' and insisted that France have
priority over all other theatres.[95] Kitchener agreed that no Balkan
action could be taken at once, but did not promise to send any
reserves to France.

The whole matter of strategy was reviewed at the War Council
meeting on 28 January.[96] Much was made of the positive effects
which a victory at the Dardanelles would have. Grey was particularly
enthusiastic about the effect which a success in the Balkans would
have on the diplomatic situation there and Kitchener noted that if
the neutrals declared themselves on the Allied side the military effect
would be considerable. That afternoon Kitchener made his position
even clearer at a meeting of the sub-committee which had been
commissioned on 13 January to investigate Britain's military
options.

In a wide-ranging paper on strategy, Kitchener again emphasised
the importance which he placed on the Eastern front.[97] Since Russia
was essential to victory, Kitchener argued that all plans had to be

weighed to see how they would aid her. All schemes involving sending a major force to the Mediterranean Kitchener felt had the drawback that they would allow the Germans to transfer forces to the Russian front from France. Equally, such a move would offend the French, a point which Millerand's visit had underlined. Kitchener's 'final conclusion' was that Britain's best move was to send a token force to aid the Serbs, which could have the effect of bringing in the Romanians and Bulgarians. The main British forces should be kept (preferably in Britain) for the Western front. Both of these recommendations would aid the Russians: the first by providing new allies and the second by holding German forces in the west.

In the background of this debate about strategy was the ongoing concern over Russian finance and supply. While the British government had offered the Russians a loan of £40 million on 18 December, the terms of it had not yet been agreed to by the end of January 1915. The key issue was gold. On 23 December Bark asked the Treasury whether all funds spent in Britain required backing in gold, and wondered if Russia sent extra gold could the funds thus obtained be spent without restriction?[98] He also suggested that shipment of gold be delayed 'in view of the present unfavourable conditions of navigation'. The Treasury reply was succinct. Funds raised by the excess shipment of gold could be spent without restriction; however, all gold must be shipped 'without delay'.[99]

Bark was not yet willing to accept these terms. No doubt deliberately seeming to be obtuse, he assumed that the Treasury's reply meant that a £40 million loan could be obtained against the security of Russian Treasury bills only and that any gold shipped would create funds unbound by British fetters.[100] This interpretation did not find much favour at the Treasury. Concern there over the British gold reserve was becoming acute. Increased spending in the United States, it was argued, would inevitably cause the British gold reserves to be transferred across the Atlantic.[101] Short-term measures such as calling in loans would not suffice to maintain Britain's credit for long. Russia would have to contribute. In the Treasury's view, 'the [Russian] gold reserve lies idle' and would not be needed by that country until the postwar period. At present, Blackett argued for the Treasury, 'all impartial people would agree, [that the Russian gold can] be made most useful by sending it to London to form the basis of a large superstructure of credit for the benefit not of Britain alone but of the allies generally.'[102]

Broadly speaking he felt that all Allied loans had to be secured by gold, lest the credit of Britain be eroded abroad with disastrous consequences for the *Entente*. Since Russian and French gold was not wanted 'for our own use' but to defend the exchange, the *amour propre* of the Allies could be maintained by having all gold shipped to London kept earmarked as their property. In this way the Allies could legally declare this gold as part of their gold reserves. Bark's proposals thus were not acceptable to the Treasury. Further discussion of terms for a loan were deferred until a conference of the Allied finance ministers scheduled for the beginning of February in Paris could take place.

While the Treasury was negotiating Russian finance, efforts were being made to get to grips with the problem of Russian munitions. Kitchener arranged through Hanbury Williams for a representative of the Russian government to be sent to Britain to ensure closer co-operation concerning munitions. To this end, General Timchenko-Ruban was sent to England in late January as the Russian government's representative in charge of munitions procurement. As such, Timchenko-Ruban was the head of what was called the Russian Government Committee (RGC) in London, a body which included Rutkovskii and the other Russian delegates to the CIR.[103] Timchenko-Ruban's brief was to put an end to the free-lance purchasing by quasi-official Russian agents who were outside the jurisdiction of the RGC. The general was to be given 'all the information and instructions necessary to deal fully with all questions regarding orders', and Kitchener was asked to place orders in the United States on Russia's behalf in conjunction with him. On 25 January Kitchener agreed 'to do all in his power' to help the Russians, but requested a fuller disclosure of Russian requirements. At the same time, the Foreign Office attempted to help the Russian government sort out the horde of real and supposed arms dealers who had descended on Petrograd.[104]

Of these adventurers the most significant were the Canadians, 'Colonels' Mackie and Allison, who obtained a large contract for shells during January and February.[105] The Foreign Office had been warned about Allison as early as October 1914. His dealings in the United States were said to be 'deplorable'. The flurry of correspondence over this contract showed just how little co-ordination of effort as yet existed in Britain for the provision of Russian supplies.

Efforts to check on Allison and Mackie with Wyldbore Smith, the head of the CIR, revealed that the latter had no knowledge of the new Russian procedures for ordering munitions through Timchenko-Ruban.[106] As well, Wyldbore Smith professed ignorance of the War Office's attempts to find munitions supplies for Russia. While these organisational defects contributed to the problems experienced in providing supplies for Russia, a far greater obstacle to close co-operation was the fact, as the Foreign Office put it, that the British government was resented for 'not always letting the Russians have what they ask for'.[107] The Russian attitude, which persisted throughout the war, was that Britain was endlessly capable of producing unlimited amounts of armaments. British refusals to supply Russia, in this view, reflected her general niggardliness and lack of appreciation for her Ally.

This attitude was paralleled concerning finance and manifested itself at the Paris conference of Allied finance ministers held 4–5 February.[108] While Lloyd George had spent January mainly concerned with the strategical issues discussed above, he had not neglected preparing for the Paris meeting. Lloyd George was interested particularly in the question of gold and gold reserves. Two memoranda by Keynes encapsulated the Treasury's position.[109] Keynes argued that while the need for Russia to ship gold to Britain was irrefutable, it was politically inexpedient. Keynes therefore developed the policy outlined earlier by Blackett. Russian gold should be shipped to Britain where it would be stored, 'earmarked' as Russian property. In this fashion it would still be legally part of Russia's gold reserve, yet available to back Allied credit. While this was the main thrust of his argument, Keynes also felt that Russia should be encouraged to seek funds in money markets both in Britain and the United States independently. By this means, Keynes wrote, 'some sources of funds ought to be tapped which will never be reached by the issues of our own government.'

The conference was a highlight in financial relations with Russia. The Russian government obtained permission to raise £100 million, backed by the British and French governments, on the London and Paris markets. While the money was being raised the two western Allies would each lend Russia £25 million, these sums to be deducted from the issue when it was fully funded. On the other hand, Russia and France each agreed to lend the Bank of England

£12 million worth of gold if, during the next six months, the gold reserves of the Bank fell below £80 million. This gold was to be returned by the Bank of England to the Allies after the cessation of hostilities. Also, all the Allies agreed that it was in their best interest to form some sort of common purchasing commission for goods obtained from the United States.

The major disagreement at the conference was a proposal supported by both Bark and the French Finance Minister, Alexandre Ribot. This proposal called for the issue of a common loan, 'having the joint guarantee of all three powers.'[110] This idea was opposed strongly by the British. As Keynes argued, while France and Russia would thus be able to borrow a 'larger amount more cheaply . . . the joint guarantee is practically useless to us.' Such a guarantee would, Keynes thought, to some degree '*spoil our own credit*' and would result in Britain underwriting much of the French and Russian national debts without gaining any advantage. Keynes argued further that the effect of such a guarantee would be that France and Russia would have greater difficulty in mobilising their own internal financial resources, since they would rely on foreign sources instead. While Britain was willing to help her Allies, she was unwilling to give up control of the financial resources at her disposal. Despite such differences of opinion the Paris conference was a major success and the question of Anglo-Russian finance subsided until the summer of 1915.

At Paris Lloyd George had not confined himself to financial matters. Unwilling to allow his proposed Serbian offensive to die, the Chancellor had lobbied for a French commitment of troops to Salonika. Such a suggestion found a ready audience since many French politicians were seeking an alternative to the Western front and feared a British expansion in the Near East at France's expense.[111] Even Joffre's opposition failed to deny support to Lloyd George's idea, and the Chancellor returned to London determined to push for a British commitment in the Mediterranean.

At the War Council meeting of 9 February the entire issue was debated.[112] Kitchener found himself balanced between those – Lloyd George, Churchill and the ubiquitous Hankey – who preferred a British commitment in the Balkans and those – John French and Joffre – who favoured an enlarged commitment in France. The fact that the Russian army would be unable to renew the offensive until supplied with munitions, the interest of French politicians in Salonika and the possible diplomatic benefits of a Balkan success all combined to produce a decision to commit a British force to Salonika. Over the objections of the British military hierarchy in France, it was decided on 16 February to send the 29th division to Lemnos as a preparatory step for British action in the Mediterranean.[113]

The apparent success of the German offensive in Poland, which began 7 February, put an end to the Salonikan adventure. On 18 February Kitchener told the War Council that the Polish situation meant that it should 'consider very seriously' before sending the 29th abroad.[114] A major Russian reverse gave the Germans the opportunity to bring back 'great masses of troops' to the west, a movement which would require rapid reinforcement of the lines in France. While Kitchener danced to French and Joffre's tune, Lloyd George listened to a different drummer.[115] First the Chancellor argued that the Allied lines in the west were secure and did not require reinforcement. Second, he felt that Germany was bound to attack Serbia soon and that it was necessary to 'take risks in order to achieve a decisive operation, which might win the war.' Kitchener did not agree. The Secretary of State for War argued that the 'two divisions on the spot [that is, in Egypt]' were sufficient at first for any Mediterranean project. Should events necessitate, Kitchener added, he would dispatch the 29th to the Dardanelles, but before doing so '*he wished to wait until the Russian situation cleared up.*' Kitchener's views prevailed in the War Council and the Australian and New Zealand troops in Egypt were dispatched to Lemnos while the 29th was kept at home.

By 24 February it was clear that the Dardanelles would not fall to an exclusively naval assault. At the War Council that day, Churchill noted that a force of 100,000 men would be necessary to take the Straits.[116] Kitchener's concern with the Eastern front was evident. While he was 'less anxious' about the Russian situation and willing to 'risk a good deal' by sending the 29th to the Dardanelles as Churchill proposed, Kitchener warned of the 'rapidity' with which the situation in Poland could change. This certainly was not a blanket approval for the dispatch of the 29th. As Callwell wrote to Robertson concerning that pivotal force: 'Winston is bringing strong pressure to bear to get the 29th Division out, but K. is determined to keep it until he sees his way more clearly.' Kitchener realised that if

Joffre's contemplated offensive came into being, it would be 'imperative' that the BEF be supported with 'every man that can be got hold of', including the 29th.[117]

By 26 February Kitchener's fears about the Eastern front had materialised. At the War Council that day, Kitchener made it plain that he considered the interlocking nature of the Eastern and Western fronts far more important than the situation in the Mediterranean.[118] The German threat to the Warsaw–Petrograd railway made a German transfer of troops to the west possible, and Kitchener wanted the 29th division as a reserve 'to throw in at any threatened point.' Churchill and Lloyd George reacted angrily to this argument. Another naval fiasco similar to Antwerp would be dangerous to Churchill's career, and the First Lord was adamant in his demands for troops to send to the Dardanelles. Kitchener's answer was clear: the 'deterioration' of the Russian position necessitated the retention of a reserve. Lloyd George's argument took another tack. The Chancellor felt that Russia had suffered a 'collapse' which could be aided only by sending troops to the Balkans and bringing in the neutrals there on the Allied side. Kitchener vitiated this contention by arguing that Lloyd George had overstated his case; the Russians had done 'very well' and were in no danger of a total collapse. The 29th was retained in Britain.

At the same time as he was resisting pressure from his colleagues to send troops to the Dardanelles, Kitchener refused to bow to pressure from Millerand to send more troops, including the 29th, to France. When the French War Minister suggested that Kitchener was reneging on his earlier promise to send reinforcements, the Secretary of State for War's reply was glacial.[119] Millerand's complaints, Kitchener wrote, were 'not at all well founded'; the composition of forces to be sent to France a 'detail' not included in the agreement. And, Kitchener concluded, 'I think I might point out that, with regard to keeping engagements, our experience of our French allies on the subject in the Antwerp emergency hardly led me to think that they took such a rigid view.' This had its effect and Lord Esher, who often served as Kitchener's confidential go-between in dealings with the French, was able to report to the Field Marshal that Millerand 'understands now that Joffre will not *necessarily* get any more troops at all from you.'[120]

Despite Kitchener's uncompromising attitude, French pressure for more troops continued to mount. Paul Cambon, the French ambassador to London, called on Kitchener on 28 February, and reminded him that he had promised Joffre not to send the 29th division from England '*sans être d'accord avec le Général Joffre*'.[121] Joffre wanted Kitchener to send the 29th division to France in order that Sir John French would have sufficient troops to take over part of the line now held by Joffre. If this did not occur, it would 'render impossible' the projected French offensive.[122] Despite such lobbying, Kitchener maintained his position with respect to the 29th until 10 March.

Kitchener's fears were eased throughout March by the steady improvement in the Russian position. The success of her Carpathian offensive and the fall of Przemysl made things appear brighter in the east. With a decisive German victory less likely, Kitchener announced to the War Council on 10 March that the situation was 'sufficiently secure' to permit the 29th to go to the Mediterranean.[123] This transfer was a symbol of the British commitment to the Dardanelles and was soon matched by a similar French commitment, the latter engendered by Gallic fears that Britain would usurp French interests in the Near East.[124]

By the end of March, Anglo-French co-operation in the west also had been put on a better footing. At a meeting at Chantilly, Kitchener, French and Joffre agreed that the Russians would best be aided by a large Anglo-French attack at the end of April or the beginning of May.[125] Joffre was confident that a 'serious' German retirement could be achieved and noted that improved communications with the Grand Duke Nicholas meant that there would be closer co-ordination between the two fronts. While the conference served to improve Anglo-French relations, there was not a unanimous acceptance of Joffre's optimism on the British side. General Rawlinson, one of French's corps commanders and an old friend of Kitchener's from South Africa, wrote to the Secretary of State that he preferred small attacks which would kill Germans but not require much ammunition or risk many troops to Joffre's larger plan.[126] The direction of further military actions now awaited the opening of the spring offensives.

By the middle of February the preliminaries to the British attacks at the Dardanelles had changed the diplomatic situation in the Balkans. The most promising area for the British was Italy. Sidney Sonnino, who had taken over as Italian Foreign Minister upon the death of San Giuliano, presented Grey with a list of Italy's desiderata

for declaring war on 15 February.[127] When Grey sent this list to the
Allies, Sazonov made it plain that he found Italy's demands
excessive and that he placed little value on her military assistance.
Sazonov's diplomacy was based on his experience the previous
autumn in similar dealings in the Balkans and on his exaggerated
belief in Russia's military capacity. The Russian Foreign Minister
had decided that a Balkan bloc would be achieved only by Russian
victories, victories which would result in a bloc created on lines
favourable to Russian interests. As a result, Sazonov was cold to the
proposals which the Bulgarians and Romanians put forward in the
first months of 1915, preferring to delay negotiations in the
expectation of victory.

Some found Sazonov's attitude galling. 'Sazonov assumes the airs
of an all-round victor and dictator,' Bertie fumed on 7 March, 'the
part don't suit him, but who is going to bell the cat?'[128] Certainly not
Grey. On 3 March the War Council held a discussion concerning the
Italian demands, the Russian position and the issue of
Constantinople.[129] While Grey did not accept the Russian belief that
Italy's intervention would be of little use, he made it clear that 'it was
very important to avoid anything in the nature of a breach with
Russia, or any action which would incline Russia to a separate
peace.' Therefore he refused to support Italy's demands or to
countenance her fears of a too-great Russian success in the Balkans
and continued the negotiations with Russia. The complicating factor
was the Dardanelles. The need for troops to take the Straits was
manifest, but so too were the Russian objections to the participation
of other nations there.[130] With the push and pull over the 29th in full
swing, the only solution for Grey was a formal promise of the Straits
to Russia, a promise which it was hoped would end her objections to
Greek and Italian forces aiding in the attack there. When he made
this clear to the War Council on 10 March, his position was
accepted.[131] While Kitchener and Churchill felt that Britain should
take Alexandretta as her *quid pro quo*, it was decided that Russia
must be reassured first and that British compensation should be
discussed later. The Russian attitude towards Allied support
surprised many. As Balfour wrote to Lloyd George, the Russian
Foreign Office

> are not only indifferent to the augmentation of the Allied Forces
> by the adhesion of fresh states to the Entente: they appear

positively to *dislike* it. This would be perfectly intelligible if they themselves possessed an overwhelming strength in well-equipped armies: but if they are as ill-provided as in our moments of pessimism we suppose, their confidence is truly amazing![132]

All discussions now hinged on the military situation. Possible Greek support had ended on 6 March when the pro-Allied Prime Minister, Eleutherios Venizelos, had been forced to resign, and Bulgaria and Romania awaited the outcome of the attack at the Dardanelles. By the end of the month, agreement between Britain and Russia over Italian entry had not been achieved. The sticking point was Sazonov. The general improvement in Russia's military situation made him less likely to concede Italy's demands. As Bertie noted on 28 March of the Russian Foreign Minister, 'He thinks that the Russian victory at Przemysl makes him a dictator.'[133] While military events worked to Sazonov's advantage, quite the contrary was true for Grey. The failure of the Anglo-French bombardment of the Dardanelles made the British position there a matter of concern. Only the fact that Russia's Carpathian offensive came to a halt in early April, making Italian entry in the war militarily important for Russia, allowed Britain and Russia to agree on the terms to be offered to Italy. The Treaty of London, formally binding Italy to the *Entente*, was signed on 26 April; the period between the 9th and that date was required to finalise the details with Italy. This delay was fatal to the hope of creating a Balkan confederation. The Russian military collapse in May made it prudent for all concerned to await events.

This collapse was not a complete surprise to the British. For some time there had been a growing concern that Balfour's 'moments of pessimism' accurately reflected the munitions situation in Russia. Despite the Russian military successes in March, reports – 'jeremiads' as Callwell termed then – had continued to arrive at the War Office with news of serious munitions shortages on the Eastern front.[134] There was also concern about Russian purchasing abroad. British warnings concerning the bona fides of Mackie and Allison aside, in March the Russian government had signed two contracts with their firm for 5 million 3-inch shells. Other problems with overseas supply arose as well. Russian domestic production of shells was dependent upon fuses supplied by British firms and these were not forthcoming.[135] The shortage was due to the failure of Vickers to fulfil their contract and to an inordinate delay in Russian negotiations with another firm, Kings Norton, for further orders. In British eyes, the most important concomitant of this shortage was that, as Buchanan noted on 24 February, 'months will consequently elapse before the Russian Army will be in a position to take the offensive.'[136]

This news came at a critical juncture. The deliberations over the fate of the 29th division were in full progress and Buchanan's opinion warranted the fullest consideration. His report led to the first comprehensive statement which the British government had made concerning its ability to provide Russia with munitions. The War Office's outlook was bleak.[137] They could not think of 'any means' by which the Russian shortages could be overcome, either through ordering in Britain or the United States. The Foreign Office, the report went on, should inquire whether any help from France were possible. The War Office did have suggestions to improve things in the future. Eventual effectiveness depended on the implementation of a number of reforms by the Russian government. First, there must be a full disclosure of Russian needs. Second, it was 'indispensable' that all Russian purchasing in Britain and the United States be placed under a single man. This man, it was emphasised, must be capable of controlling 'the activities of the numerous Russian agents who appear to be competing with one another for the same articles in the same markets and none of whom appear to be cognizant of the instructions issued to their colleagues.' Kitchener had in fact gone some way towards solving this latter problem. At the end of February he instructed Hanbury Williams to ask the Grand Duke Nicholas to send an artillery specialist with wide-reaching powers to England.[138]

The inability of the War Office to find any aid for the Russians was an extreme irritant to Lloyd George. Early in March he demanded that a special body be formed to take over the area of munitions production. The Chancellor termed the War Office's statement 'almost a disastrous admission' and flayed that body for its inability to raise production.[139] Despite such criticism, at this same time Kitchener was making every effort on Russia's behalf to procure rifles in the United States. On 8 March Kitchener placed an order for 1 million rifles for Russia with the Westinghouse Electric Company. The following day Kitchener obtained an offer from the Bethlehem

Steel Company for 5 million complete rounds of 3-inch shell with delivery scheduled to begin in January 1916.[140]

Despite this, Russian discontent with the British grew. In particular this discontent centred around the British firm of Vickers. The failure of Vickers to fulfil its orders for Russia was especially galling to the Russians because of the position which that company had established in Russia before the war. In the years before 1914 Vickers had, in the words of its agent there, established 'a virtual monopoly for the manufacture of guns' and was 'absolutely in a paramount position in Russia'.[141] In 1911 that firm had been involved in creating the great naval base at Nicolaev on the Black Sea and two years later had won the contract to provide the expertise for the Tsaritsyn Gun Foundry. As another Vickers representative wrote to the firm in November 1912, the Russian government saw Vickers as 'the only firm capable of giving such advice and guidance as will enable the Russian [armaments] work to be carried on from beginning to end.'[142]

Vickers was particularly displeasing to the Grand Duke Sergei Mikhailovich. The former Inspector-General of Artillery had become head of a new committee, the Special Efficiency Commission for Artillery Matters (*Osobaia rasporiaditelnaia komissiia po artilleriiskoi chasti*) in January 1915 with a mandate to end the inefficiency and conflict between the Russian front and rear.[143] On 9 March Sergei told Blair that Vickers's protests that they had not been provided with Russian guns for test purposes were merely 'an excuse' for late deliveries.[144] Despite this, the Grand Duke pointed out that Sukhomlinov was prepared to enter into direct communication with Kitchener over munitions. In the interim required for future deliveries, he went on, Russia would be grateful for anything which could be done to ease the present shortages. The following day Kitchener replied that the War Office would do everything in its power to help the Russians and offered them a contract for 1 million Ross rifles with the first half million to be delivered by May 1916.[145]

Russian irritation with what they viewed as the British policy of promises today but supplies tomorrow was evident when Blair delivered Kitchener's offer of the Ross rifles to the Grand Duke. Sergei rejected the offer and 'repeatedly insisted' that the Russian need for supplies was now and not in the distant future.[146] Great emphasis was put on the need for Vickers to deliver the shells and fuses promised for March lest the Russian shortages prevent any offensives in the summer. The Grand Duke also argued that it would be 'very difficult' to place a man in London with the wide-ranging authority which Kitchener requested and noted that Timchenko-Ruban 'in fact was not fully qualified to have full powers.'

Kitchener made efforts to speed up the Vickers's orders.[147] The problem was that Vickers had contracted for more than they could deliver and not only Russian but also British orders were delayed. But Kitchener pointed out that he felt it 'most unwise' of the Russian government not to place orders on the assumption that a surplus would exist if the war ended in six months. The Russians did not agree. The irritation and disappointment which they had felt with the failure of foreign contractors to fulfil their orders, plus Grand Duke Sergei's confidence that all shortages would end by the autumn of 1915 due to increased domestic production, led to the creation of a new policy.[148] By the second half of March Sergei's interest turned away from orders for shells and rifles and towards the purchase of plants to produce these items in Russia. This policy was even more firmly followed in June, when General A. A. Manikovskii became the new head of GAU. This optimism was the equivalent of Sazonov's in the diplomatic field and no doubt resulted from the same cause, the illusion of Russian military success as exemplified by the fall of Przemysl.

Kitchener was not as confident about Russian capabilities. On 25 March he offered the Russians a contract for 5 million 3-inch shells from the American Locomotive Company with delivery to begin in the autumn. Sergei rejected this offer, pointing out that Russia already had 10 million shells on order abroad. Kitchener refused to let this offer drop so easily.[149] Knox had telegraphed of severe shell shortages within the Russian army and when Timchenko-Ruban informed Kitchener of the origin of the foreign order upon which the Grand Duke was depending, Kitchener noted, 'if these are the only outside orders for shell the Russia Government had got, the situation appears to be serious.'[150] Early in April, despite Sergei's earlier refusal of the American Locomotive contract, Kitchener went so far as to close the deal on his own, subject to price negotiation. Despite this initiative and a subsequent one, on 14 April a final rejection of the American offer was made by the Russian government.[151] By the end of that month it was clear that improved Anglo-Russian relations with respect to munitions would require some special negotiations with the Russian government. The Russian military disaster in May was to provide the impetus for them.

The first nine months of the war had brought about major changes in the nature of the Anglo-Russian alliance. At the beginning of the war, there was a sharp inequality between the forces of Britain and Russia. The Russian 'steamroller' was the weapon which would ensure an Allied victory; the British contribution was the diminutive BEF. While Kitchener accepted the fact of Russian strength, he believed that victory would result only when Britain had raised massive armies of her own. This he set out to do. In the meantime he feared a major German victory in the west and a subsequent invasion of England. As a result of this, he was inordinately sensitive to events on the Eastern front and based his policy on occurrences there.

The military importance of Russia placed severe restraints on British diplomacy. Grey needed first to ensure Allied solidarity at the outbreak of war and second to ensure that Russia did not leave the *Entente*. This first need meant that Grey could not take the initiative in negotiations with the Balkan states in August. Sazonov's determination to pursue his own policies meant that Grey could act only as a mediator and offer suggestions in keeping with the general thrust of Russian policy. Sazonov's unilateral agreement with Romania on 4 October hamstrung any further Allied attempts to create a Balkan bloc and made any progress in that direction dependent on military victory. Grey then centred his diplomacy on the one country where British influence exceeded that of the Russians: Italy. Even here, the need to maintain Allied solidarity and Sazonov's dogged opposition to Italian expansion in the Balkans meant that Russia had in effect a veto over Grey's negotiations.

The fear of a Russian withdrawal from the *Entente* also dictated that Grey pursue policies in line with Russian initiatives. Of the three major Allies, only Russia was in a position to sign an acceptable separate peace during the first nine months of the war. In addition, there were important circles in Petrograd who were in favour of such a move. The Germans were well aware of these facts and made a concerted effort to achieve a separate peace when the Schlieffen plan failed to win the rapid victory which it was designed to do. This situation, combined with the central place which Russia occupied in Kitchener's beliefs about Britain's own security, meant that Grey had to propitiate the Russians and soothe their fears about the firmness of the Allied commitment to the war. This circumscribed Grey's diplomacy in the Balkans. Nicolson's remarks about Balkan diplomacy in July 1915 applied just as aptly to the period during 1914 and 1915:

> Our diplomatic activity is largely concentrated on South-East Europe, and we have been in constant, and in some ways overlapping and contradictory, correspondence with our Allies. All our efforts have been directed towards securing the co-operation of some one of the Balkan States. . . . Each Foreign Minister has his own pet subject.

Nicolson felt that neither Bulgaria nor Romania would come in 'in view of the general military situation'.[152] This provides an explanation for the concession of Constantinople and the Straits. Asquith derided the Russian arguments during the negotiations leading to the Treaty of London as 'Sazonoff's piddling little points', but to Grey they were the essential items in maintaining the Anglo-Russian alliance.[153] Neither Kitchener with respect to military affairs nor Grey with respect to diplomatic ones could afford to ignore the interests of Russia.

The unexpected length of the war, its unparalleled use of munitions and the ineptitude of Russian bureaucratic arrangements led to a number of problems between the two Allies. These were exacerbated by what Knox termed the 'criminal secretiveness' of the Russians about the state of their supply situation.[154] By delaying informing the Allies of their difficulties until the middle of December, the Russians ensured that no relief could be provided until the end of 1915, too late for the campaigning season. Unfortunately, the Russians did not believe this. The prewar image of Britain as a world leader in munitions production which Vickers had done so much to promote, meant that the Russians could not accept the facts of the situation. Instead a new policy of reliance upon domestic production was adopted, a fact which did not reduce tensions over munitions in the future.

The purchase of munitions was intimately linked to the financial issues between the two countries. Finance was the only area where Anglo-Russian co-operation was not frustrated by bureaucratic difficulties to any great extent. This did not mean that there were no problems. While Russia had managed to obtain funds from Britain, this had been done at commercial rates. With Russian troop losses in the millions, such an attitude was repugnant to Russia. Similarly the British attempt to control Russian expenditure in America was viewed as undue interference in the affairs of an ally. As was the case with munitions, the Russians believed that British credit was limitless. This belief would remain for the rest of the war.

By the beginning of May 1915 a new shape was emerging to the Anglo-Russian alliance. The growth of the New Armies and a realisation that Russia was dependent upon Britain for finance and supply meant that Britain would no longer have to defer to Russian demands in the diplomatic sphere. The end of the 'steamroller' meant the end of Sazonov's period of dominance and the beginning of British independence. Russia was not a negligible factor at the beginning of May 1915, but British power and influence were increasing.

Notes

1 Bertie diary entry, 18 September 1914, Lennox (ed.), *Bertie Diary*, I, 34.
2 This notion has been dispelled in T. Wilson, 'Britain's "Moral Commitment" to France in August 1914', *Historian*, 64 (1979), 380–90; see Grey, *Twenty-Five Years*, I, 273–86.
3 The naval discussions between Britain and Russia in 1914 were not of a binding nature and Grey was reluctant that any military talks should ever be more than just discussion; see Steiner, *Britain and Origins*, 121–7 and note 6 below.
4 For the British plans of war, see M. Howard, *The Continental Commitment* (Harmondsworth, 1974), 31–52; Gooch, *Plans of War*, 165–97 and 278–98; S. R. Williamson, *The Politics of Grand Strategy* (Cambridge, Mass., 1969) and A. J. Marder, *From the Dreadnought to Scapa Flow*, Vol. I, *1904–1914 The Road to War* (London, 1961), 328–404. An excellent view of the overall aspects of prewar planning is D. French, *British Economic and Strategic Planning 1905–1915* (London, 1982). The Russians shared the British belief that the latter's contribution would be essentially naval; see D. V. Verzhkovskii and F. S. Krinitsyn, 'Plany voiny', in I. I. Rostunov (ed.), *Istoriia pervoi mirovoi voiny 1914–1918* (2 vols, Moscow, 1975), I, 202–6.
5 French, *British Planning*, 7–19 and 51–70; M. Ferro, *The Great War 1914–1918*, trans. N. Stone (London, 1973), 26–33, and L. L. Farrar, jun., *The Short War Illusion* (Santa Barbara, Calif., 1974), 4–7.
6 This reflected the lack of any prewar Anglo-Russian military planning; see N. D'Ombrain, *War Machinery and High Policy* (Oxford, 1973), 111–12. Gooch, *Plans of War*, 231–2, illustrates that plans to fight against Russia were more usual in Britain than were plans to fight with her in an alliance. During August 1914 Churchill did entertain some speculations about a joint Anglo-Russian amphibious assault in the Baltic; see Gilbert, *Churchill*, III, 52–3.
7 There is no comprehensive study of Russia's Balkan policy in the First World War. It can be pieced together from a number of sources: C. J. Smith, jun., *The Russian Struggle for Power, 1914–1917* (New York, 1956), 21–42 and 135–84;

W. W. Gottlieb, *Studies in Secret Diplomacy during the First World War* (London, 1957), 39–48 and 66–73; A. J. Rieber, 'Russian Diplomacy and Rumania', in A. Dallin (ed.), *Russian Diplomacy and Eastern Europe 1914–1917* (New York, 1963), 235–75; J. M. Potts, 'The loss of Bulgaria', in ibid., 194–234; W. A. Renzi, 'The Russian Foreign Office and Italy's entrance into the Great War, 1914–1915: a study in wartime diplomacy', *Historian*, 28, 4 (1966), 648–68, and R. H. Johnson, *Tradition Versus Revolution Russia and the Balkans in 1917* (Boulder, Col., 1977), 12–17 and *passim*.

8   C. J. Lowe and M. L. Dockrill, *The Mirage of Power* (3 vols, London, 1972), II, 170–2 and 186; C. J. Lowe and F. Marzari, *Italian Foreign Policy 1870–1945* (London, 1975), 133–7.

9   Rieber, 'Russian diplomacy', 235–46; G. E. Torrey, 'The Rumanian–Italian agreement of 23 September 1914', *Slavonic and East European Review*, 44, 103 (1966), 403–20.

10   Potts, 'The loss of Bulgaria', 194–208; Robbins, 'British diplomacy and Bulgaria', 564–8.

11   Von Hötzendorf to Berchtold, 2 August 1914, as cited in G. E. Silberstein, 'The Serbian campaign of 1915: its diplomatic background', *American Historical Review*, 73, 1 (1967), 53.

12   C. J. Smith, jun., 'Great Britain and the 1914–1915 Straits Agreement with Russia: the British promise of November 1914', *American Historical Review*, 70, 4 (1965), 1018–20.

13   Asquith's testimony to the Dardanelles Inquiry, as cited in ibid., 1020.

14   Rieber, 'Russian diplomacy', 245; Potts, 'The loss of Bulgaria', 208–9; M. G. Ekstein, 'Russia, Constantinople and the Straits 1914–1915', in Hinsley (ed.), *British Foreign Policy*, 425–6.

15   Lowe and Marzari, *Italian Foreign Policy*, 138–9; Torrey, 'The Rumanian–Italian Agreement', 414–15.

16   Lowe and Dockrill, *Mirage of Power*, II, 173–4.

17   Minute by Nicolson on Rodd (British ambassador to Italy) to Grey, as cited in ibid., 173.

18   Rieber, 'Russian diplomacy', 247–51.

19   On the Buxtons and their efforts, see Robbins, 'British diplomacy and Bulgaria', 567–8; Fry, *Lloyd George*, I, 280–5.

20   Lowe and Mazari, *Italian Foreign Policy*, 136.

21   Grey to Buchanan, 19 September, FO 371/2095/50911.

22   Buchanan to Grey, private and secret, 12 October 1914, FO 371/2095/58681.

23   Kitchener to Buchanan, 4 October 1914, FO 371/2095/55811.

24   Connell, *Wavell*, 96–7. Wavell had been summoned to French's headquarters to serve as a 'Russian "expert" '. On the true Russian military situation, see Stone, *Eastern Front*, 97–104.

25   As cited in V. A. Emets, 'O roli russkoi armii v pervyi period mirovoi voiny 1914–1918 gg.', *Istoricheskie zapiski*, 77 (1965), 80.

26   Kitchener to Grey, 13 October 1914, FO 371/2095/58929.

27   Hobhouse diary entry, 14 October 1914, David (ed.), *Hobhouse Diaries*, 197.

28   FO to Buchanan, private, 14 October 1914, Grey Papers, FO 800/74; Buchanan to Grey, private and secret, 15 October 1914, FO 371/2095/59971.

29   Lord Hankey, *The Supreme Command* (2 vols, London, 1961), I, 215–16; Asquith to George V, 22 October 1914, as cited in Smith, 'Great Britain and the 1914–1915 Straits Agreement', 1027. On the question and fear of invasion generally, see J. Gooch, *The Prospect of War: Studies in British Defence Policy 1847–1942* (London, 1981), 10–17.

30   Bertie diary entry, 20 October 1914, Lennox (ed.), *Bertie Diaries*, I, 55. See also

the call of 19 October by Raymond Poincaré, the French president, for the Russian 'steamroller' to begin, as discussed in Gottlieb, *Secret Diplomacy*, 47; Farrar, *Short-War Illusion*, 58.

31 See two notes by Kitchener, the substance of which was sent to Buchanan, 20 September 1914, FO 371/2095/50911.

32 Smith, 'Great Britain and the 1914–1915 Straits Agreement', 1033; Ekstein, 'Russia, Constantinople and the Straits', 423–35.

33 L. L. Farrar, jun., *Divide and Conquer: German Efforts to Conclude a Separate Peace, 1914–1918* (Boulder, Col., 1978), 9–13; R. Sh. Ganelin, 'Storonniki separatnogo mira s Germaniei v tsarskoi Rossii', in E. V. Tarle (ed.), *Problemy istorii mezhdunarodnykh otnoshenii* (Leningrad, 1972), 126–32.

34 Marshal Foch, *The Memoirs of Marshal Foch*, trans. T. Bentley Mott (New York, 1931), 162.

35 Bertie to Grey, private and confidential, 12 November 1914, Bertie Papers, FO 800/177, citing Grey's telegram to Sazonov. Sir John French held a similar view; on 15 November 1914 he wrote to Stamfordham (George V's private secretary) that 'the fact is that everything *depends on Russia* – we can hold on here without much difficulty but are not strong enough . . . to take a vigorous offensive', as cited in R. Holmes, *The Little Field Marshal John French* (London, 1981), 253, original emphasis.

36 A. J. P. Taylor, *The Struggle for Mastery in Europe 1848–1914* (Oxford paper, 1971), 543.

37 Farrar, *Divide and Conquer*, 7–16; Farrar, *Short-War Illusion*, 78–83.

38 Buchanan to Grey, private and secret, 4 December 1914, FO 371/2095/78627.

39 Magnus, *Kitchener*, 305–6; Field Marshal Viscount French of Ypres, *1914* (London, 1919), 304–7; Field Marshal Joffre, *The Memoirs of Marshal Joffre*, trans. T. Bentley Mott (London, 1932), II, 334–5; J. E. Edmonds (chief ed.), *History of the Great War based on Official Documents by Direction of the Historical Section Committee of Imperial Defence. Military Operations in France and Belgium* (14 vols, London, 1922–48), 1915, I, 16–18.

40 Buchanan to FO, private and secret, 11 December 1914, FO 371/2095/81443; Buchanan to A. Nicolson, private, 17 December 1914, FO 371/2095/83996.

41 Memorandum by Bertie, 18 December 1914, Bertie Papers, FO 800/177.

42 'C.I.R. establishment and function,' Duke, n.d., Wintour Papers, Mun 5/7/170/25. The first head of the CIR was U. F. Wintour of the Board of Trade and its first secretary was Sir Edmund Wyldbore Smith, also of the Board of Trade. Wintour moved to the War Office to become Director of Army Contracts (DAC) early in the autumn of 1914 and Wyldbore Smith became head of the CIR with Duke serving as secretary.

43 Runciman to Grey, 29 August 1914, FO 368/1077/44234.

44 FO to Buchanan, 11 September 1914, FO 368/1077/47816.

45 FO 368/1077/52115. The transliteration of the names has been standardised; see also A. L. Sidorov, *Ekonomicheskoe polozhenie Rossii v gody pervoi mirovoi voiny* (Moscow, 1973), 285–90 for a discussion of the Russian members and their duties.

46 Spring-Rice to FO, 9 October 1914, FO 371/2224/57870; Spring-Rice to Grey, private, 20 October 1914, FO 371/2224/61688.

47 Benckendorff to FO, 15 September 1914, FO 368/1085/49832.

48 H. Guthrie Smith to FO, 18 September 1914, ibid.

49 See the minutes on FO 368/1077/44234 and Blair's dispatch LXV, 23 January 1915, WO 106/989.

50 Spring-Rice to FO, 11 November 1914, FO 371/2224/70005.

51 The discussion of the relationship between Russia and foreign armaments

manufacturers is based on J. P. McKay, *Pioneers for Profit: Foreign Entrepreneurs and Russian Industrialization* (Chicago and London, 1970), 12–24, 56–62, 90, 211–15 and 268–94; C. Trebilcock, *The Vickers Brothers: Armaments and Enterprise 1854–1914* (London, 1977), 119–41; E. R. Goldstein, 'Vickers Limited and the Tsarist regime', *Slavonic and East European Review*, 58, 4 (1980), 561–9.

52 D. W. Graf, 'Military rule behind the Russian Front, 1914–1917: the political ramifications', *Jahrbücher für Geschichte Osteuropas*, 22, 3 (1974), 390–411.

53 Benckendorff to A. Nicolson, 11 September 1914, FO 371/2095/48674.

54 Bradbury to FO, 24 September 1914, FO 371/2095/52706.

55 Draft telegram given to Rutkovskii for Benckendorff, 5 October 1914, FO 371/2095/63685. The Treasury Committee was created by Lloyd George to deal with the financial problems the war was expected to create.

56 Buchanan to FO, private and secret, 19 October 1914, FO 371/2095/61096. A. Nicolson's minute on this telegram gives the Treasury's reaction to Bark's proposals.

57 Ramsay (Treasury) to FO, 21 October 1914, FO 371/2095/61886.

58 Both statements are contained in Spring-Rice's dispatch of 28 October 1914, FO 371/2224/69910.

59 Buchanan to FO, 8 December 1914, FO 371/2096/80352.

60 'Russian war finance', O'Beirne, 20 November 1914, FO 371/2096/78523; and similar comments in Buchanan's dispatch no. 278, 26 November 1914, FO 368/1088/81778.

61 O'Beirne to Tyrrell, 8 December 1914, Grey Papers, FO 800/74.

62 'Russian war finance', O'Beirne, 26 November 1914, FO 371/2096/81744 seen by Asquith, Grey, Kitchener and Lloyd George. Buchanan to A. Nicolson, 10 December 1914, Nicolson Papers, FO 800/376.

63 FO to Buchanan, 10 December 1914, FO 371/2096/1178.

64 Buchanan to FO, 14 December 1914, FO 371/2096/82652.

65 Meeting of the War Council, 16 December 1914, Cab 42/1/6.

66 Buchanan to FO, private and secret, 18 December 1914, FO 371/2095/83997; news of munitions shortages in Buchanan to FO, private and secret, 11 December 1914, FO 371/2095/81443 and repeated in Buchanan to A. Nicolson, private, 17 December 1914, FO 371/2095/83996.

67 Hobhouse diary entry, 22 December 1914, David (ed.), *Hobhouse Diaries*, 214; Bertie diary entry, 19 December 1914, Lennox (ed.), *Bertie Diary*, I, 79.

68 Bertie diary entry, 6 January 1915, ibid., I, 91.

69 Asquith, *Memories and Reflections*, II, 59.

70 Churchill (relating a conversation with French) to Kitchener, 21 December 1914, Kitchener Papers, PRO 30/57/72.

71 Grey to Buchanan, personal, 21 December 1914, Grey Papers, FO 800/74.

72 Asquith, *Memories and Reflections*, II, 60; Hobhouse diary entry, 22 December 1914, David (ed.), *Hobhouse Diaries*, 214–15. French, *1914*, 334–6.

73 Asquith, *Memories and Reflections*, II, 60.

74 ibid.

75 French, *1914*, 335–6.

76 A. Nicolson to Balfour, 24 December 1914, Balfour Papers, Add MSS 49748, vol. LXVI.

77 Hanbury Williams to Kitchener, 20 December 1914, Kitchener Papers, PRO 30/57/67.

78 Balfour to A. Nicolson, 21 December 1914, Balfour Papers, Add MSS 49748, vol. LXVI.

79 Buchanan to FO, private and secret, 26 December 1914, FO 371/2095/87147;

Knox, *With the Russian Army*, I, 218; Hanbury Williams, dispatch A1, 27–28 December 1914, WO 106/1103.

80 Lloyd George to Asquith, 31 December 1914, Lloyd George Papers, C/6/11/24.

81 Buchanan to A. Nicolson, 23 December 1914, Nicolson Papers, FO 800/376.

82 Generally, see G. Hardach, *The First World War 1914–1918* (London, 1977), 254–8; for a specific case study, K. Neilson, 'Russian foreign purchasing in the Great War: a test case', *Slavonic and East European Review*, 60, 4 (1982), 572–90.

83 'Appreciation of the situation, 24th December 1914', GHQ, France, Kitchener Papers, WO 159/2.

84 French, *1914*, 340–2; French to Kitchener, 28 December 1914, Kitchener Papers, PRO 30/57/49; Haig diary entry, 29 December 1914, Haig Papers, 100.

85 Knox's dispatches E, F and G (26 November, 29 November and 10 December 1914), WO 106/1048; Hanbury Williams's dispatches S through W (all of December), WO 106/1101. The quotation is from G.

86 Balfour to Nicolson, 28 December 1914, Nicolson Papers, FO 800/376.

87 Churchill's memorandum in his *World Crisis*, II, 18–21; Hankey's 'Boxing Day memorandum' in Hankey, *Supreme Command*, I, 244–50 and Lloyd George's 'Suggestions as to the military position', 1 January 1915, Cab 24/1/ G 2.

88 Kitchener to French, 2 January 1915, Kitchener Papers, PRO 30/57/50.

89 French to Kitchener, 2 January 1915, ibid.

90 Untitled memorandum, 3 January 1915, Cab 37/123/9.

91 Meeting of the War Council, 8 January 1915, Cab 42/1/12.

92 'An appreciation', n.s., n.d. (but January 1915), Kitchener Papers, WO 159/3.

93 Meeting of the War Council, 13 January 1915, Cab 42/1/16.

94 Untitled memorandum by Esher of a conversation with Kitchener, 22 January 1915, Kitchener Papers 30/57/57.

95 Callwell to Robertson, 30 January 1915, Robertson Papers I/8/1.

96 Meeting of the War Council, 28 January 1915 at 4 p.m., Cab 42/1/27.

97 Meeting of the War Council (sub-committee), 28 January 1915 at 6.30 p.m., Cab 42/1/27; 'The question of engaging forces elsewhere than in the Western theatre of war', Kitchener, n.d. (but prepared for this meeting), WO 106/1523.

98 Buchanan to FO, 23 December 1914, FO 371/2096/85819.

99 FO to Buchanan, 30 December 1914, FO 371/2096/86749.

100 Buchanan to FO, 1 and 4 January 1915, both FO 371/2446/549.

101 'The gold reserve and loans to foreign governments', Blackett, 5 January 1915, T 171/107.

102 'British loans to France and Russia', Blackett, 6 January 1915, ibid.

103 See Buchanan to FO, private and secret, 23 January 1915, FO 371/2447/9016 and attached correspondence.

104 Kitchener to Buchanan, 25 January 1915, ibid.

105 For the Canadians, see Neilson, 'Russian foreign purchasing', 578–85.

106 Wyldbore Smith to FO, 26 January 1915, FO 371/2447/9932.

107 FO to Wyldbore Smith, 27 January 1915, ibid.

108 The French account of the conference may be found sketchily in the memoirs of the French finance minister, A. Ribot, *Lettres à un ami: souvenirs de ma vie politique* (Paris, 1924), 79–89. Bark's views are in 'Finansovia sovershchaniia soiuznikov vo vremia voiny', *Krasny arkhiv*, V (1927), 50–63. The most complete account of the conference is that of A. L. Sidorov, *Finansovoe polozhenie Rossii v gody pervoi mirovoi voiny* (Moscow, 1960), 240–59.

109 'Russia' and 'Position of the Bank of Russia', both Keynes, 30 January 1915, T 171/107.

110 See 'Memorandum on proposals for a joint loan', Keynes, marked 'after Paris' in E. Johnson (ed.), *Keynes*, XVI, 73–4, original emphasis.
111 Cassar, *French and the Dardanelles*, 48–60; 71–5.
112 Meeting of the War Council, 9 February 1915, Cab 42/1/33; Callwell to Robertson, 4 February 1915, Robertson Papers I/8/2.
113 Meeting of the War Council, 16 February 1915, Cab 42/1/35.
114 Meeting of the War Council, 19 February 1915, Cab 42/1/36; Hobhouse diary entry, 18 February 1915, David (ed.), *Hobhouse Diaries*, 222. Sir John French, on the other hand, felt that the Russian withdrawals were 'only a strategic move', French diary entry, 13 February 1915, as cited in Holmes, *Little Field Marshal*, 268.
115 Meeting of the War Council, 19 February 1915, Cab 42/1/36, my emphasis.
116 Meeting of the War Council, 24 February 1915, Cab 42/1/42.
117 Callwell to Robertson, 25 February 1915, Robertson Papers I/8/10.
118 Meeting of the War Council, 26 February 1915, Cab 42/1/47.
119 Kitchener to Esher, 22 February 1915, Kitchener Papers, PRO 30/57/59.
120 Esher to Kitchener, 27 February 1915, ibid., original emphasis.
121 Memorandum of a conversation with Cambon, Kitchener, 28 February 1915, Kitchener Papers, PRO 30/57/57.
122 Copy of Joffre to Millerand, 1 March 1915 and Millerand to Kitchener, 2 March 1915, ibid.
123 Meeting of the War Council, 10 March 1915, Cab 42/2/5.
124 Cassar, *French and the Dardanelles*, 84–90.
125 The conference is noted and discussed in a memorandum by General Sir H. Wilson, 29 March 1915, Kitchener Papers, WO 159/7; Haig diary entry, 30 March 1915, Haig Papers, 101; Robertson to Callwell, 31 March 1915, Robertson Papers I/8/17 and Callwell to Robertson, 5 April 1915, Robertson Papers I/8/18.
126 Rawlinson to Kitchener, 1 April 1915, Kitchener Papers, PRO 30/57/51.
127 Lowe and Dockrill, *Mirage of Power*, II, 176–8; Renzi, 'Russian Foreign Office', 658–61.
128 Bertie diary entry, 7 March 1915, Lennox (ed.), *Bertie Diary*, I, 127.
129 Meeting of the War Council, 3 March 1915, Cab 42/2/3.
130 Gottlieb, *Studies in Secret Diplomacy*, 66–70; Hobhouse diary entry, 4 March 1915, David (ed.), *Hobhouse Diaries*, 226; Grey, *Twenty-Five Years*, II, 212–13.
131 Meeting of the War Council, 10 March 1915, Cab 42/2/5.
132 Balfour to Lloyd George, 5 March 1915, Balfour Papers, Add MSS 49692, vol. X.
133 Bertie diary entry, 28 March 1915, Lennox (ed.), *Bertie Diary*, I, 135.
134 Callwell to Robertson, 23 March 1915, Robertson Papers I/8/16.
135 Buchanan to FO, private and secret, 24 February 1915, FO 371/2447/22147; Blair's dispatch LXVIII, 23 February 1915, WO 106/992.
136 Buchanan to FO, private and secret, 24 February 1915, FO 371/2447/22147; Buchanan to A. Nicolson, 24 February 1915, Nicolson Papers, FO 800/377.
137 Army Council to FO, 27 February 1915, FO 371/2447/23509.
138 See Hanbury Williams's 'Aide memoire', 27 February 1915, Kitchener Papers, PRO 30/57/67.
139 See Lloyd George to Balfour, 6 March 1915, Balfour Papers, Add MSS 49692, vol. X.
140 'America', 8 March 1915, Wintour Papers, IV, pt II, Mun 5/7/170/25; Morgan to Morgan, Grenfell, 9 March 1915, Mun 4/207.
141 Barker to Zaharoff, 6 March 1913, as cited in Trebilcock, *Vickers*, 121.
142 Owens to Vickers, 27 November 1912, as cited in ibid., 134–5.

143 Sidorov, *Ekonomicheskoe polozhenie*, 262.
144 Buchanan to FO, 9 March 1915, FO 371/2447/27712.
145 Kitchener to Buchanan, 10 March 1915, ibid.
146 Buchanan to FO, private and secret, 12 March 1915, FO 371/2447/29292. See also Blair's dispatch LXX, 15 March 1915, WO 106/994.
147 FO to Buchanan, 13 and 14 March 1915, both in FO 371/2447/29292; an untitled note on Vickers's orders, 31 January 1915, Mun 4/5517.
148 Sidorov, *Ekonomicheskoe polozhenie*, 264–9; Buchanan to FO, 18 and 20 March 1915, FO 371/2447/31924 and 32932; A. L. Sidorov, 'K voprosu o stroitelstve kazenykh voennykh zavodov v Rossii v gody pervoi mirovoi voiny', *Istoricheskie zapiski*, 54 (1955), 158–62.
149 FO to Buchanan, 25 March 1915, FO 371/2447/35305; Buchanan to FO, 30 March 1915, FO 371/2447/37362.
150 FO to Buchanan, 9 April 1915, FO 371/2447/42142.
151 Knox to DMO, 1 April 1915, FO 371/2447/38485; FO to Buchanan, 8 April 1915, ibid.; Buchanan to FO, 14 April 1915, FO 371/2447/44041.
152 A. Nicolson to Hardinge, 21 July 1915, Nicolson Papers, FO 800/378.
153 As cited in Lowe and Dockrill, *Mirage of Power*, II, 169.
154 Knox's dispatch H, 21 December 1914, WO 106/1049.

3
The End of the Promise

Throughout the summer of 1915 the Russian army retreated. Not until the autumn did the Eastern front stabilise, bringing to an end the reverses which had begun with the German offensive at Gorlice-Tarnow on 1 May. The mauling which the Russians took during this period ended any lingering belief that Russia alone could bring about victory for the *Entente*. It became evident that success against the Central Powers would result only from close co-operation between all the Allies in the military, economic and financial spheres.

The Russian collapse forced a re-evaluation of British policies. Essentially the British had two choices with respect to military operations. The first was to concentrate British forces in France and attack vigorously there, forcing the Germans to divert troops from the eastern campaign against Russia. The second was to press on in the Mediterranean, either at the Dardanelles or elsewhere, in the hope of winning a victory sufficient to cause the creation of a Balkan confederation. This confederation would, it was thought, be so powerful as to aid the beleaguered Russians and establish the necessary conditions for eventual Allied victory. Each of these policies had its advocates among the policy-making élite in Britain and debate over them was the essence of wartime politics in 1915.

With respect to finance and supply, the Russian retreat made it evident that more formal methods would have to replace the haphazard dealings between Russia and Britain which had been the norm during the first nine months of the war. However, the problems which the earlier period had thrown up concerning finance and supply remained. The Russians continued to purchase munitions abroad without co-ordinating such purchases with the efforts of Britain and still believed that British financial assistance was niggardly and humiliating. New complications also arose which affected finance and supply. First, the British credit position in the United States began to crumble. Second, the increasing needs of the expanding

New Armies for munitions faced the British with a dilemma: should the requirements of the Russian army take precedence over those of the British army? The answer depended upon the evaluation placed upon the relative fighting strengths of the two forces and their importance to an eventual Allied victory. As was the case about debate over theatres of action, opinions varied. And again, debate over them was central to British policy-making in 1915.

The first manifestation of the new relationship between Britain and Russia showed with respect to munitions. Unable to aid the Russians systematically with supplies, Kitchener dispatched a special envoy to Russia in early May in the hope of arriving at some more productive arrangement.[1] Kitchener's choice of envoy was Colonel W. Ellershaw, an artillery expert at the War Office. Ellershaw arrived at *Stavka* on 14 May bearing with him a letter from Kitchener outlining the British War Office's view of Russia's needs for munitions and the need for co-operation among the Allies.[2] Hanbury Williams presented this letter to the Grand Duke Nicholas, who promptly referred the entire matter to Ianushkevich, the Chief of the General Staff. When informed of Kitchener's attempts to obtain orders for Russia in the United States and of the Grand Duke Sergei's objections to them, Ianushkevich told Hanbury Williams he 'was puzzled as he was under the impression that all necessary orders had been given'.[3] From this, Hanbury Williams concluded that, despite the Emperor's assurance given at Christmas that all red tape would be cut, 'I am under the impression that the "middle men", both military & civil have been too much for the Grand Duke Serge and that he is beat.' This view was overly sympathetic towards the Russians. First, Sergei's exchange of telegrams with Kitchener over the preceding two months had made it clear that it was not misleading commentary or interference by middle men which had led to his rejection of Kitchener's offers. Such rejection was based on Sergei's pique over the failure of foreign manufacturers to fulfil their contracts and his confidence that the Russian shortages would be over by the autumn of 1915. Second, Ianushkevich's puzzlement was obviously feigned. On 13 April the Grand Duke Sergei had written to the Chief of Staff outlining the reasons why Kitchener's offers of munitions contracts were being rejected.[4]

By 19 May 1915 a basic accord was reached by Ellershaw with the Grand Duke Nicholas and the Russian hierarchy at *Stavka*.[5] By this accord, Kitchener was authorised by the Grand Duke Nicholas to act as the purchasing agent for Russia in Britain and the United States. This was in no small part due to Ellershaw's tact and ability. Hanbury Williams found Ellershaw 'excellent' and added, 'I do not think a better officer c[oul]d. have been selected – all the technical knowledge, a pleasant manner, lots of tact, & very hard working.'[6] Upon his return to England in June, Ellershaw played a major role in Anglo-Russian munitions affairs until his untimely death in the *HMS Hampshire* disaster in June 1916.

Despite the signing of the agreement, Kitchener wanted to ensure that there was no misunderstanding about the nature of the British commitment to Russia. A long telegram was sent by him to Buchanan outlining the limits of the aid which Britain would provide in the following months. Kitchener's suspicions of the Russian tendency to blame others for their own problems was evident. As Clerk noted on the draft of this telegram, 'Lord Kitchener is anxious that there should be something official on record, to supplement the discussions which have recently taken place between him and Grand Duke Nicholas. Otherwise, the Russians may try to make us responsible for further retreat on their part, due to lack of ammunition.'[7] The telegram pointedly noted that the Russian government had previously turned down the American Locomotive Company contract which Kitchener had offered.

Such suspicions aside, Kitchener had not flagged in his efforts to obtain supplies for Russia in the United States. Even while Ellershaw was negotiating at *Stavka*, Kitchener had opened discussion with Bethlehem Steel and the Baldwin Locomotive Works for further ammunitions orders for Russia.[8] On 21 May the War Office told their purchasing agents in the United States, Messrs J. P. Morgan, 'For your information, situation is so grave, and supplies of Field Artillery Ammunition for Russia during the remaining months of the year are so vital, we hope some means may be found to meet this extraordinary situation, and obtain substantial supplies say during September and onwards.'[9] In fact the War Office was attempting to organise in the United States a combine to produce Russian shells on a large scale.[10]

As a result of the Ellershaw mission, by the beginning of June 1915 the British government, rather than British private industry, had become responsible for the provision of military supplies for Russia. This obligation had been assumed for purely military reasons, as a strong Russia was essential to victory. The attempt to fulfil this commitment was an important feature of Anglo-Russian relations over the next two and a half years.

While Ellershaw was in Russia, the military impact of the Russian defeats began to make their effect evident on British planning. Combined with the losses at the battle of 2nd Krithia at Gallipoli and the failure of Sir John French's attack on Aubers Ridge, the Russian situation revived Kitchener's fear of a German threat to England. On 14 May Kitchener told the War Council that the latest intelligence from Russia indicated that the Germans had dealt Russia 'the most serious blow' to date.[11] In the light of the Russian disarray and the evident inability of the Allies to break through the German lines in the west, Kitchener felt that the prudent course was 'to maintain the defensive role hitherto imposed on us' and prepare the Home defences. At the same time, Kitchener opposed Churchill's withdrawal of the battleship *Queen Elizabeth* from the Dardanelles. This latter was due to Kitchener's concern with British prestige in the Moslem world and also to the Russian situation. On 12 May Grand Duke Nicholas had asked Kitchener to press for a decision at the Dardanelles in order to release the Russian army of the Caucasus for duty against the German offensive on the Eastern front.[12]

The evident deterioration of the military situation for the Allies, the ongoing quarrel about how to proceed at the Dardanelles, the furore over the shells shortage which Sir John French claimed had sabotaged his offensive at Neuve Chapelle and Asquith's own political calculations all resulted in the collapse of the Liberal government in mid-May.[13] While the first coalition government was forming, however, the debate over strategy continued. On 17 May John French wrote to Kitchener asking for reinforcements.[14] French argued that unless this were done 'it is possible that the German forces in the West will suffice to bring our offensive and that of the French to a standstill.' Carefully tailoring his argument to appeal to Kitchener's concern about Home defence, French added that if Germany had 'further success' against Russia either a major offensive in the west or an attempted invasion of England would be possible. If French were reinforced, he and Joffre could attack in the west and so prevent any possible invasion. Kitchener was not swayed by this argument. He lacked confidence in the Allied ability to pierce the German lines in the west and did not feel that lack of shell or troops had been critical to the failures to do so in the spring. 'We may take it as proved', Kitchener wrote in late May after the French failure to punch through the German defences was evident, 'that the lines cannot be forced.'[15]

On 28 May Kitchener produced a paper clearly outlining his views on the war.[16] Its focus was on the Dardanelles, but the discussion covered the entire British commitment to the Allied cause. Kitchener noted that all the reasons for the initial deployment of British forces at the Dardanelles were still valid, but added that the Russian reverses had placed them in a different light. Only Italy's entry into the war, Kitchener opined, had prevented an even more serious disaster, but Italian aid was not yet certain as a permanent factor. The French and British attacks in France had demonstrated the futility of this course of action and the issue of Home defence was thus paramount. While some military advantage could be gained by reinforcing the Dardanelles, it was not evident that it was of 'permanent benefit' to Britain for Russia to have possession of the Straits after the war. Given that withdrawal was impossible for reasons of prestige, Kitchener concluded that the force at the Dardanelles should be neither withdrawn nor reinforced, but left to 'push on and make such progress as is possible.' What the British policy in the west should be, Kitchener noted in a separate but related paper, was defensive.[17] He was unwilling, even in the face of the need to help the Russians while the Germans were over-extended in Russia, to take the 'colossal losses' which he felt an offensive would entail. In addition, he was not convinced that such losses would be accompanied by any significant gains.

Kitchener's view was not accepted either by the French or by the British Staff in France.[18] A French mission headed by Millerand's *chef du cabinet* came to London early in June in an attempt to bend Kitchener to the French idea of an offensive in the west.[19] The argument turned around the situation in Russia. While Russia could not be permanently knocked out, the French reasoned, she was experiencing great difficulty at present. As a result, by the middle of July the Allies could expect the arrival in the west of large numbers of German troops transferred from Russia. Therefore, '*before that date* we must reach a decision in France. *By that date* we must beat the Germans who are now in France. It is the safest way of beating the Germans who are to come later.' Kitchener replied the following day. His lack of enthusiasm for the scheme was manifest: 'I would counsel you to fight with more prudence than ever', he noted and added that British reserves were unlikely to be available for a summer offensive. If the French were unwilling to wait until the British were ready, the Secretary of State concluded unhelpfully, 'I am sure you will push on and try to get through.'

At the same time, Kitchener sent General Sir Arthur Paget to France to obtain John French's view of the situation.[20] Quite naturally, French concurred fully with Joffre's idea for an offensive. Passive defence in the west, according to Sir John, would permit Germany to defeat her enemies one at a time. Such a policy would be justified only if the German lines in the west could not be broken. French rejected such a view. To achieve a breakthrough what he needed was more men, guns and ammunition. Kitchener was not impressed by such an argument. In rebuttal he prepared a paper which examined French's ideas in some detail.[21] While accepting the force of French's argument about the dangers inherent in passive defence, Kitchener concluded that the proper course was to pursue a policy of small surprise attacks. These attacks would 'induce the Germans to take the offensive wherever possible' and thus suffer the large-scale casualties which resulted only when 'troops are on the offensive'.

By the middle of June it was clear that a decision needed to be made about the direction of the British war effort. The effort to take the Dardanelles was going badly and Churchill now argued that five divisions would be needed there to ensure victory.[22] In addition, the Russian situation was 'rather worse' in Kitchener's words. On 14 June Hanbury Williams informed Kitchener that the Russians could hold Warsaw, Riga and Lemberg 'provided no important reinforcements reach the German troops'.[23] The shortages of munitions were even more pressing than they had been earlier and Knox concluded that 'the situation as a whole in the Eastern Theatre is less favourable than it has been at any time since the commencement of the war.'[24] In Moscow there had been serious public disorders early in June and pressure was growing for the formation of a ministry of confidence to advise the Emperor.

Kitchener had other reasons to worry about the long-term strength of the Russian army. When Ellershaw returned from Russia in early June, Kitchener had formed a special body, the War Office Russian Purchasing Committee (RPC), to deal with Russian munitions. The composition and functions of the RPC will be considered in some detail below; its significance here was what its initial meetings revealed about the state of munitions supply in

Russia. Despite the Grand Duke Nicholas's assurance that complete information about Russian requirements would be given to the RPC, after its initial meeting on 10 June Kitchener found it necessary to write to Hanbury Williams to obtain further details of Russian needs.[25] While the Grand Duke was 'most grateful' to Kitchener for the latter's efforts for Russia, Hanbury Williams found him 'very sketchy' on detailed matters concerning supply and generally 'peevish' about Allied failure to provide munitions in the past. Hanbury Williams belatedly began to realise that the Grand Duke was not capable of dealing with such issues: 'To be quite frank with you he [the Grand Duke] is not of much use on these occasions – his name counts & he "matters" a lot in one way, but he don't "run this show" much *really*.' When Hanbury Williams turned to Ianushkevich about the matter, much the same reaction was encountered.[26] The Chief of Staff said that it was 'useless' to discuss orders which would not produce results before October. Even the urbane and polished Hanbury Williams found this attitude 'madness' and pressed the matter to the point of 'strained relations' with Ianushkevich.

There was also discord in France. Many politicians were concerned over the high casualty figures resulting from the spring offensives and over the British policy of reinforcing the Dardanelles. General Douglas Haig, the commander of the BEF's First Corps, felt that a British failure to 'do something' in the west would mean that 'the "peace party" in France will get the upper hand and peace will be made before the winter!'[27] With the Russian retreat in full swing and French opinion becoming dangerously pessimistic, Kitchener wrote to Sir John French on 22 June asking him both to provide the British government with his strategical views and to arrange a conference with the French to discuss these matters.[28]

This conference was held at Calais on 5–6 July. In the fortnight between the writing of the letter and the opening of the conference, quite divergent opinions about strategy were aired. Generally, these opinions turned about the position on the Eastern front and its implications for the west. French's reply to Kitchener was a detailed argument in favour of an offensive in the west.[29] French argued that the British experience in the spring of 1915 had shown that the German lines could be pierced and that a decisive attack would result if more men and ammunition were provided. A 'further reason' for such an attack was the critical nature of the Russian situation. As the

Germans threatened to obtain a shortened line in the east which would allow the transfer of troops from that theatre, the Allies must strike quickly in the west to forestall such a happening.

Nor did French stop with his letter to Kitchener. On 24 June he held a meeting with the French General Staff at Chantilly.[30] When Joffre was asked if he had 'ever contemplated' a policy of 'passive defence', he replied that he had 'never dreamt' of putting such an idea into practice. The French Commander-in-Chief noted that the Russian situation was such that an offensive in the west was essential if the Russians were to be saved. Having been assured that they had a community of thought about strategy, the two commanders agreed to send letters 'which, to a considerable extent, were identical in tone' to their respective governments calling for an offensive in the west. They agreed that until final plans for a major offensive could be drawn up, 'aggressive, though local' forays should be made along the line to wear down the Germans.

In Britain such a suggestion did not meet with much favour. Both Hankey and Churchill produced memoranda at this time calling for an abandonment of offensives in the west until 1916.[31] Both papers were based on the contention that, since the Russians could not be ready until that year, the Allies must husband their resources in France. At the same time, Russia was to be aided by the Allies continuing vigorously at the Dardanelles. Other key members of the élite shared similar views. While Lloyd George virtually had ceased to take an active role in the formulation of strategy since the inception of the Ministry of Munitions, he played an indirect role in this debate. The meeting at Boulogne on 19–20 June of French and British munitions experts and military commanders – part of the effort of the Minister of Munitions to establish Allied production goals – had concluded that future military offensives if they were to be successful would require more shells and men than would be available until 1916.[32] Balfour also agreed that a policy of the 'active defensive' would be the best course for Britain until 1916.[33]

Few of these views passed unchallenged. John French subjected Churchill's ideas to vigorous criticism. On 26 June he wrote to Kitchener, 'I do extremely trust you will use all your great influence against these fatal proposals.'[34] General William Robertson, the Chief of Staff to the BEF, was even more scathing. As far as he was concerned, 'the whole proposal is based on *ifs* – if Russia recovers – if the Balkan States come in.'[35] Robertson was not convinced that success at the Dardanelles would in any way aid Russia, since her weakness was a result of munitions shortages which were beyond the powers of the Allies to remedy quickly. In any case, he concluded, victory at the Dardanelles 'is the success of a detachment' while a victory in France would mean 'the defeat of our chief enemy in the field and the successful end of the war.'

These were not disinterested opinions. Churchill realised that his career rode with the Dardanelles and French and Robertson had a vested interest in the Western front. The most important opinion was that of Kitchener. For him, the key consideration was the fact that there no longer seemed to be a danger of a major German victory in the west. With the New Armies becoming available for duty, Kitchener was able to consider events without the concern for Home defence which had marked his earlier deliberations about the 29th division. Even so, as he told the Dardanelles Committee on 5 July, the 'next three months' were a 'very vital phase in the war.'[36] The problem lay with the Allies. Russia was in serious difficulty and would require as much aid as could be provided in order to keep her in the war. France was 'sorely disappointed', in the words of Kitchener's liaison officer at French headquarters, about the Russian withdrawals and a 'wave of pessimism' was evident there.[37]

In this circumstance, Kitchener felt that the best policy to pursue was to carry on at the Dardanelles in the hope of helping Russia, while pursuing the 'active defensive' in France.[38] With the New Armies coming into line, Kitchener was willing to divert some troops from Home defence for service at the Dardanelles, since he felt that 'it would make no material difference in our general arrangements in the Western theatre'. On the other hand, Kitchener strongly opposed the French policy of a major offensive in the west. This he felt would lead to high casualties with no accompanying appreciable gain. For the long term, 'a very great industrial effort' would have to be made by the western Allies to repair the deficiencies in Russia's munitions supplies. The difficulty with such a policy, Kitchener opined, was having it accepted by the Allies. While Russia was likely to 'welcome' this policy since she was unable to mount an offensive before 1916, the French would experience a 'great shock' with the realisation that another winter campaign was necessary.

The British position was thus firmly set when the conference between the French and British military authorities opened at Calais on 6 July.[39] Early that morning, Kitchener and Joffre met alone to discuss the military situation. When the conference opened formally later that day, Joffre took little part in the discussions and appeared quite happy with the general acceptance of the English position favouring the active defensive. The following day, an inter-Allied conference was held at Chantilly.[40] At this, Joffre proposed a combined Anglo-French offensive to help the Russians, in direct contradiction to what had seemed to be agreed upon the previous day. Sir John French, for the British, agreed with Joffre's plan; 'it is a duty we owe to the Russians to co-operate.' The two contradictory decisions have suggested that Kitchener at his early-morning meeting with Joffre agreed to British participation, and that the official conference at Calais was merely a smokescreen for the politicians.[41] This was not the case. Kitchener and Joffre had reached an understanding that any major offensive in the west would be undertaken by the French and that the British contribution would be to provide the men necessary to take over the French line. In the interim, Sir John French was instructed to begin staff talks with Joffre in order to co-ordinate the actions of the two Allies.[42]

Kitchener's actions in France seem quite logical if the Russian situation is considered. If the attack at the Dardanelles were to fail and if Russia were to continue her disastrous defeats in the east, it was obvious that some action would have to be taken in the west to alleviate the general weakness of the Allied position. Joffre was persistent in his desire to launch an offensive, French public morale was at a low point and British participation would not require any commitment to join in the attack with the high casualties which the Secretary of State expected. The Kitchener-Joffre compromise was thus a logical and necessary step: whether or not it would be necessary to implement it would depend on the military situation at the Dardanelles and in Russia.

By the beginning of August it was becoming doubtful that the Allied advance at the Dardanelles was going to be successful. In addition, the Russian situation showed little signs of improvement. On 27 July Blair noted that 'it now lies with the Germans to decide when they wish to make their triumphal entry' into Warsaw.[43] A week later Buchanan wrote that in Russia 'feeling against us and France is so widespread that we must lose no time in counteracting [the] impression that we are doing nothing while large numbers of German troops are . . . being transferred from the Western to

Eastern front.'[44] This was a sore point. In the middle of July the Grand Duke Nicholas had written to Kitchener telling the Field Marshal that any effort by the Allies to prevent such transfers of troops 'est d'une grande importance.'[45] At the same time the fear of a separate peace between Russia and Germany led Robertson to call for a major offensive by the British and French in the west.[46] On 9 August Kitchener had a long discussion of the military situation with the King, and seemed to accept Robertson's idea of a general offensive in the west in order to keep Russia in the war.[47]

Such a view was no doubt reinforced by the events in Russia and at the Dardanelles. Warsaw fell on 5 August and by the 10th it was clear that the offensive at Gallipoli had miscarried. On 17 August General Hamilton, the British Commander at the Dardanelles, requested 95,000 reinforcements in order to ensure a victory, and further news from Russia made it clear that the strategic fortresses around Warsaw could not be held.[48] In such circumstances Kitchener abandoned any idea of pressing forward at the Dardanelles and turned instead to carrying out his earlier agreement with Joffre. An offensive in the west was 'necessary to relieve pressure on Russia and keep the French Army and people steady' and not even the reinforcements which Hamilton had requested were certain to 'relieve us of the Dardanelles incubus.'[49]

There remained only to convince the Dardanelles Committee of the need for an offensive in France and a concomitant lessening of the support for the Dardanelles. Kitchener's argument that the Western front was paramount given the situation in Russia was opposed by both Churchill and Lloyd George.[50] The former argued that the Allied strength in France was insufficient for a successful attack; Kitchener replied realistically that 'we had to make war as we must, and not as we should like to do'. While Kitchener felt himself that the 'odds were against' a major victory in France, he noted that the alternative was France or Russia, or both, leaving the war. This bleak assessment was accepted by the Dardanelles Committee and Sir John French was instructed to 'take the offensive and act vigorously' in conjunction with Joffre. In addition, Kitchener informed the Russians that Britain would join with the French in attack 'with all the forces available'.[51]

The decision by Kitchener to commit the BEF to the French attack in September marked the end of the first phase of British strategy. Although it was not evident at the time, the decision not to

reinforce Hamilton and to press on in the west was the beginning of
the period when the Western front was the main concern of the
British. The need to support Russia and France through direct
action in the west had at last forced Kitchener to abandon his waiting
policy. From this point onwards, the New Armies would inevitably
be committed to France.

At the same time as this decision was being made, a major
examination of Britain's total war effort was being made. A War
Policy Cabinet Committee, under the chairmanship of the Lord
President of the Council, Lord Crewe, began to hold sessions on 12
August

> to enquire into the extent to which the existing resources of the
> country are being utilised or can be developed in order to bring
> the war to a successful issue at the earliest possible moment,
> and to ascertain how far new resources can be brought into play
> with the same object.[52]

Many of the arguments which were raised in this Committee
pertained to and centred around Russia. The fact that Russia
represented the superiority in manpower which the Allies enjoyed
over the Central Powers and that she was in need of munitions and
financial support meant that arguments about 'resources' and their
utilisation always needed to be referred to considerations of whether
or not they should or could be placed at Russia's disposal.

In order to set this firmly in the context of events, it is necessary to
go back to June 1915. The long Russian retreats had an effect not
only on Allied planning in the west, but also on the political situation
in Russia. The military failure of the Tsarist government led to the
so-called 'patriotic alarm' in Russia and the formation of a
wide-spread political coalition concerned with the progress of the
war.[53] Its manifestation in the Duma was the creation of the
'Progressive Bloc', a ramshackle collection of parties and individuals
bound only by their demand for a ministry of public confidence and
a more successful prosecution of the war effort. Outside the Duma,
the unhappiness was expressed by the 'public organisations' –
voluntary associations created to assist (or perhaps supplant) the
Tsarist bureaucracy in carrying on the war. The first of these to form
were the Union of Towns and the Union of Zemstvos (normally
referred to collectively by their Russian acronym, *Zemgor*) created in

August 1914 with the original brief of helping the wounded. By the spring of 1915 they had expanded their roles and were acting as an adjunct to the government.[54]

The munitions crisis in Russia, which so concerned the British in their military planning, led to the creation of another of the public organisations, the War Industry Committees (*Voenno-promyshlennye komitety* or VPK).[55] It was the VPK in particular that made its presence felt in British planning and so among the public organisations requires particular examination. The VPK had its origins in the policies followed by the Russian government with respect to munitions production. When the shortages of war material became evident in the autumn of 1914, it was decided by the War Minister, V. A. Sukhomlinov, to fill these shortages by purchase overseas. This policy angered many Russian businessmen who felt that their opportunity to participate in patriotic production, and not incidentally to make substantial profits, was being denied by Sukhomlinov. This policy was made the more politically explosive by the fact that Russia had been divided into a front and rear area, with the former under the command of Grand Duke Nicholas and the *Stavka* and the latter under the regular Russian government, headed by the Council of Ministers. There was little co-operation or co-ordination between these two nearly independent 'governments', a situation made worse by the personal antipathy between Sukhomlinov and the Grand Duke.[56]

The issue of munitions supply thus became both a patriotic and a political issue as well as an economic one. In the autumn of 1914 and over the winter, M. V. Rodzianko, the President of the Duma, and A. I. Guchkov, the head of the Octobrist Party, both travelled to the front to investigate the munitions situation.[57] The Grand Duke Nicholas was only too willing to provide the details of Sukhomlinov's mismanagement to Rodzianko and Guchkov and they were only too willing to use such information to press the Tsarist government for reforms. While such reforms could be justified on patriotic grounds – the need for an improved war effort – it was clear that those involved with the public organisations also intended to use the help that they could provide the Tsarist bureaucracy as a lever for the achievement of political reform.

By January this had resulted in the formation of the Special Efficiency Commission for Artillery Matters under the leadership of the Grand Duke Sergei, as mentioned above, but such a development was not sufficient for Rodzianko. Throughout May he and a cadre of Petrograd-based businessmen and financiers made trips to *Stavka* to confer with the Grand Duke Nicholas. As a result of the retreats of that month, Rodzianko's calls for a change in dealings with munitions were heeded: at the start of June a Special Council for the Examination and Harmonisation of Measures Required for the Defence of the Country (better known as the Rodzianko Council) was set up consisting of representatives from the Council of Ministers and Rodzianko's Petrograd group.[58]

For many Rodzianko's actions were not acceptable. His close collaboration with the government, his clear preference for those industrialists from Petrograd over those from Moscow and the provinces and his assumption that all patriots would follow his lead were galling to many. In particular this was true of the merchants of Moscow. Even in the prewar period, Moscow's *haute bourgeoisie* had formed a unique and special group within Russia, a hard-driving group of entrepreneurs who viewed noble Russia and the government bureaucracy with contempt.[59] This alone meant that the Moscovite *kupechestvo* would resent the Rodzianko Council, but when it was combined with a belief that circles in Petrograd were insufficiently concerned with fighting the war to a finish, the patriotic bourgeoisie of Moscow were incensed. Major industrialists in that city, men like A. I. Konovalov and P. P. Riabushinskii, found themselves hurt both in their patriotic pride and their wallets: the combination was potent.

Early in June Riabushinskii called upon the Ninth Congress of the Association of Industry and Trade to mobilise the economy for the war.[60] The result of this was the formation of the VPK. By the beginning of 1916 there were some 220 VPK across Russia, containing many of the leading lights of liberal Russia, including Guchkov (himself the scion of a Moscovite merchant family), M. I. Tereshchenko, the Kievan 'sugar king' and future minister in the Provisional government, as well as many leading technical and academic men. The VPK soon found allies in the other public organisations. Both the Union of Cities and the Union of Zemstvos were centred in Moscow and their leaders, respectively M. V. Chelnokov (the former mayor of Moscow and a close friend of Bruce Lockhart) and Prince G. E. Lvov, became honorary vice-chairmen of the Moscow VPK. This informal alliance of the public organisations was tied as well to the Progressive Bloc in the Duma and carried with it the potential for political change so long as the Tsarist government showed itself incapable of military victory and organising the war effort.

The reaction of the Tsarist government to the 'patriotic alarm' was a mixture of concession, co-option and, when the military situation stabilised, counter-attack. In mid-June Sukhomlinov was removed as Minister of War and was replaced by A. A. Polivanov, a former Assistant Minister of War who had collaborated with Guchkov prior to the war to reform the War Office. As such, Polivanov was perfectly acceptable to the VPK and to the Grand Duke Nicholas. In addition, when the Rodzianko Commission was legitimised by the Emperor on 20 June as the Special Council on Defence (*Osoboe soveshchanie po oborone*) Guchkov and Konovalov were added to its membership and the number of Petrograders reduced.[61] Finally, and probably most importantly, large numbers of orders for munitions were placed with the VPK as part of the Russian policy of relying primarily on domestic production instead of foreign orders. So much for concession and co-option. In September Nicholas launched his counter-attack. As the military front became secure, the Emperor himself replaced the Grand Duke Nicholas as Commander-in-Chief and ordered the Duma prorogued. With the financial and commercial members of the Progressive Bloc propitiated by lucrative contracts and the Grand Duke in the Caucasus, the political situation seemed securely in the hands of Nicholas and his closest advisers.

Despite the Russian policy of producing her own munitions, foreign supplies were essential in certain key industries. Because of this, the control of overseas purchasing was part of the struggle which the public organisations and the Progressive Bloc waged against the official Russian bureaucracy. Since the Russian Government Committee was controlled by the various ministries in Petrograd, it and its members became the targets of vituperative attack in Russia.[62] None of this was likely to improve the co-ordination of purchasing abroad.

Certainly there was need for improvement. As mentioned above, when Ellershaw returned from Russia in the spring of 1915, a War Office Russian Purchasing Committee (RPC) had been created to deal with Russian munitions. The Russian members of the RPC were Rutkovskii, Major-General E. Hermonius and Colonel N. Beliaev, while the principal British members were Ellershaw,

George Booth, U. F. Wintour (the Director of Army Contracts) and Wyldbore Smith of the CIR.[63] The Russian members of the RPC were also members of the Russian delegation on the CIR (although in practice, they divided up their duties with Rutkovskii dealing mainly with financial affairs at the CIR and Hermonius and Beliaev handling munitions), a fact which sometimes led to confusion over the identity of the two bodies. Rutkovskii, the commercial attaché at the Russian embassy, had been a member of the CIR since its inception, but Hermonius and Beliaev had been sent to London in May as part of the attempt to improve the chaotic purchasing situation there. Hermonius became a key figure in the Russian delegation – he replaced Rutkovskii as head of the Russian Government Committee in December 1915 – and, despite the fact that he spoke no English, was an effective, capable and energetic administrator. His intermediary with the British representatives was Colonel Beliaev (the nephew of General M. A. Beliaev, the Assistant Minister of War under Polivanov), who spoke English fluently. Both of these men were representatives of GAU. Wintour, who began the war at the Board of Trade and was briefly the head of the CIR before becoming Director of Army Contracts (DAC), was the chairman of the RPC. In reality, though, most of the day-to-day work about munitions was handled by Ellershaw who had established a special position of trust with the Russians through his personal mission to the Grand Duke. Wyldbore Smith's presence reflected the fact that the CIR was responsible formally for the financial aspect of all Allied purchasing in Britain.

In some ways, the most important British member of the RPC was Booth. Booth had been involved with munitions work at the War Office since the autumn of 1914 and when the Ministry of Munitions was formed in May and June of 1915, he was appointed one of the three (later four) Deputy Director Generals (DDGs) of the Munitions Supply Department of the new Ministry, under the leadership of Sir Percy Girouard, the Director General of Munitions Supply (DGMS). In addition to being a member of the RPC and the Ministry of Munitions, Booth was also a member of the CIR, and such multiple membership helped to overcome the potential confusion of authority among the three bodies.

In fact, the existence of the RPC independent from the Ministry of Munitions was an anomaly, especially considering that they came into existence roughly contemporaneously.[64] This should be seen as

typical of Kitchener's objection to giving over control of some
aspects of munitions production to Lloyd George and the Ministry of
Munitions. With respect to Russia, Kitchener was able to argue
successfully that his arrangement with the Grand Duke Nicholas was
in the nature of a personal commitment. Thus the RPC was kept
under the jurisdiction of the War Office in direct contradiction to
good organisational logic. It is doubtful that the personal nature of
the link between Russia and Britain provided much in the way of
useful co-operation. Departments like GAU were extremely reticent
to provide information about their requirements; as Knox noted
sarcastically, to get facts and figures one practically required 'an
autograph letter from Lord Kitchener'.[65]

Despite these problems, by the middle of June it had been agreed
that Kitchener was to place an order for 12 millon artillery shells in
the United States for Russia. This purchase was to be done through
the British War Office's purchasing mission which had been
unofficially established in neutral America the previous autumn.[66]
This scheme of purchase had many problems, since all Russian
purchases in the United States were technically under the control of
Hermonius's opposite number in New York, Major-General
Sapozhnikov. The niggling methods of the head of the Russian
Purchasing Committee (*Russkii zagotovitelnyi komitet*) in the United
States were a continual source of difficulty for all concerned, and the
division of authority between Sapozhnikov and Hermonius was a
hindrance to efficiency.

There were British difficulties as well. The search for shells in the
United States by the RPC illustrated the crosspurposes which could
occur between it and the Ministry of Munitions. Wintour had
located offers for some 24 million shells in the United States – while
requiring only 12 million – and the Master-General of the Ordnance
(MGO), Sir Stanley von Donop, had failed to notify the Ministry of
Munitions of the extra offers. As Christopher Addison, the
parliamentary secretary to the Ministry noted, the latter body was
'scouring the country and moving heaven and earth' looking for such
orders and the MGO's oversight led Addison to speculate that von
Donop 'was incompetent or a traitor. I inclined to the latter view.'[67]

At the beginning of July, while the Dardanelles Committee was
discussing the British policy for the Calais conference, efforts were
made to overcome the problems of Russian purchasing in the United
States. A French technical mission, familiar with the details of

Russian artillery specifications, was dispatched to the United States in an attempt to solve the quarrels which had arisen there due to Sapozhnikov's rigidity over specifications.[68] A more far-reaching effort was initiated by Lloyd George as Minister of Munitions. In the middle of July he sent a mission to the United States under D. A. Thomas (later Lord Rhondda) in an attempt to put all of British purchasing in the United States on a more business-like footing. To avoid another shells fiasco, Ellershaw gave Thomas a long summary of the negotiations which the RPC had carried on in the United States on behalf of the Russian government.[69]

Ellershaw's memorandum gave a candid assessment of the problems involved in ordering for Russia in the United States. Sapozhnikov was characterised as 'obstructive', while the four Russian inspectors were apt 'to cause trouble and delay whenever possible.' In Russia itself, Ellershaw noted, there was a conflict between parties, one headed by the Grand Duke Nicholas and the other by the Grand Duke Sergei, a clear reference to the two contradictory policies with respect to munitions which each advocated. The Grand Duke Nicholas was a 'straight strong soldier' but understood 'nothing of business and supplies'; those around the Grand Duke Sergei at GAU were 'past masters in the art of obstruction'. Unless the Grand Duke Nicholas received offers of supply personally, Ellershaw argued, they would be delayed by those at GAU 'for present gains'. This was another echo of the general belief that all Russian bureaucratic dealings were dishonest. As it was put at the Foreign Office, it was 'openly said here that Grand Duke Michael [Mikhailovich, the chairman of the Russian Government Committee in London] & General Yermoloff [Ermolov, the military attaché] are stuffing their own pockets as hard as they can.'[70] Thomas was soon joined in the United States by Hermonius and Ellershaw, the latter pair going to America in order to smooth over the difficulties experienced with ordering in that country.

While these steps were being taken, information from Russia delineating her needs for munitions was still not forthcoming. Knox characterised the attitude of GAU as 'oriental – the kind of atmosphere that one would expect to find in a Bengali artillery department if the English were to evacuate India.'[71] Knox pointed out, however, that the Russian attitude was based on the not unreasonable premise that 'Lord Kitchener had done nothing for

Russia so far'. In the same vein, British requests for information about requirements and offers to examine foreign contracts for feasibility were viewed as an attempt 'to get complete control of American offers.' Blair was told by those at GAU that his continual requests for information 'was like continually checking the score at a game of cards, when no one had any intention of paying.'[72] Even Pares, now returned to England, was aware that the failure of British firms, especially Vickers, had created a poisoned atmosphere so far as cordial relations concerning British assistance with munitions for Russia was concerned.[73]

Such accusations about munitions dovetailed nicely with similar Russian complaints about the military inactivity of the Allies on the Western front. At the beginning of August, with the fate of Poland in the balance, Kitchener submitted a long memorandum to Grey on British efforts to aid Russia with munitions purchases.[74] This was designed to give Buchanan the information necessary to refute the charges that Britain was doing little for Russia but also reflected Kitchener's anger over Russian accusations of British perfidy and neglect. In a section of the memorandum which Grey tactfully excised before sending the substance on to Buchanan, Kitchener stated that the 'real cause' of the Russian retreats was 'the ineptitude of the Russian officials in not obtaining proper supplies of munitions'. Kitchener referred to his telegram in May which had outlined the extent of the British commitment to supply munitions for Russia, and pointed out how Britain had exceeded all prewar expectations of her military commitment to the *Entente*. Despite Kitchener's anger and his attempts to point out the magnitude of the British aid, no doubt the deteriorating position of Russia with respect to munitions helped to influence his decision, discussed above, to commit British reinforcements to France for an offensive to relieve the Eastern front.

The increased Russian munitions orders abroad also had financial repercussions. Early in June 1915 the Russians began exploratory talks for a loan further to that obtained in February at Paris.[75] By the Paris agreement, Russia had been allowed to discount £25 million in Treasury bills in the first half of 1915. As this period was ending, Bark wished to know whether the British Treasury desired to advance Russia the further £25 million due under the Paris agreement or wished her to attempt to raise the amount by a public issue on the London market. The Treasury answered on 18 June that they preferred the former course, but added that due to the 'increasingly difficult' financial situation in Britain further loans would be possible only after an Allied financial conference was held.[76] The Treasury suggested that such a conference be held early in August, but Bark, while agreeing the need for such a meeting, pleaded domestic commitments that left the date of the conference unsettled.[77]

The enormous purchasing programme which Kitchener and the RPC began in the United States quickly brought the financial issue to a head.[78] By the middle of July Bark was faced by an immediate need for £10 million in order to close the shell contracts which had been authorised in June. In an attempt to obtain the money without first attending a financial conference, Bark pretended to misunderstand the terms of the Treasury's telegram of 18 June. He told Buchanan that he assumed that the £25 million which the Treasury mentioned was in addition to the same amount provided for by the Paris agreement and so would not require a financial conference for authorisation. When Buchanan disabused him of this belief, Bark instead asked for an interim credit until he was able to attend the conference.

The need for funds in the United States to cover Russian purchasing there precipitated a mild financial crisis.[79] E. Grenfell, the British partner in Morgan, Grenfell, informed Grey on 23 July of the serious need for British credit in America to pay for the Russian orders. Grenfell felt that 'it was essential' that some gold be shipped to the United States in order to shore up British credit there and that Russia and France should 'be made to do so' as well.[80] McKenna, the new Chancellor of the Exchequer, promptly moved to arrange a credit through Morgans to deal with the Russian needs. This initiated a quarrel between himself and Lord Cunliffe, the Governor of the Bank of England, who felt that his was the responsibility for maintaining credit.[81] The clash between the two was patched up by giving Cunliffe a virtual dictatorship over matters concerning exchange, but the problem of the falling value of sterling was not so easily settled.

This was exacerbated by a contract which Thomas, Ellershaw and Hermonius closed on behalf of the Russian government for 200,000 rifles with the Winchester Repeating Arms Company on 12 August.[82] There was no doubt of the need for this order, but no consideration of Russian credit had been taken by the purchasing trio. As well, Morgans had not been informed of how much credit could be extended to Thomas's mission. Nor had the Russian Government Committee in London been consulted. Complete financial irresponsibility was a possibility unless some regulating mechanism were agreed upon. Morgans was particularly concerned. Despite the interim credit created for Russia in July, by 14 August the exchange rate had fallen from 4.77 1/8 to 4.70 1/4, 'and it is difficult to arrange any considerable amount of Exchange even at the lower figure.'[83] The entire matter was referred to the Treasury, since further large orders of munitions from the United States for Britain and the other Allies were imminent.

After determining the amount for which the Treasury might find itself liable, Bradbury opined that it was 'essential' that the Treasury be kept informed of future purchases if exchange were to be provided.[84] Bradbury further wrote to the Ministry of Munitions and informed it that disadvantageous selling of securities, if not 'actual default', would be the consequence of purchasing done in the United States without giving the Treasury notice.[85] Philip Hanson, the Director of Munitions Contracts at the Ministry, agreed to keep the Treasury informed of events, but requested that decisions be made on a same-day basis for the sake of efficiency. Hanson then inquired as to how much money would be available for purchases in the following months.[86] Bradbury's reply must have been a shock. After agreeing to the idea of rapid decision-making, he noted that 'as regards September payments we shall be very hard put to it to meet *existing* commitments and any considerable addition to September cash liabilities in [the] U.S.A. will make a debacle inevitable.' Since Wintour had written to the Ministry of Munitions that once exchange problems were overcome the Russian government wished to purchase a further £30 million worth of war material, Bradbury's remarks were not comforting.[87] Large-scale purchasing in the United States was revealing the difficulties of the British financial position.

At the bottom of the purely financial aspect of this situation was the question of gold reserves. On 20 August McKenna and Keynes travelled to Boulogne in an attempt to reach an agreement with the French about this matter. Prior to leaving for Boulogne, Keynes set out his views on gold, views which were to guide British negotiations with the Allies on this subject for some time to come.[88] Keynes felt that French and Russian gold was 'wasted' in the vaults. 'The right policy', he wrote, '. . . is to commandeer the gold, in effect, for government purposes and then *use* it.' He dismissed arguments about maintaining a gold reserve for backing currency notes, 'as gold no longer circulates', and advanced the idea that the gold would be better used to protect the exchange rate. This view carried the day at Boulogne. Britain and France agreed each to hold $200 million in gold ready for shipment to the United States should the Bank of England, in consultation with the Bank of France, feel it necessary.[89] A similar course was to be pressed on the Russian government. In addition, a joint Anglo-French financial mission under the Lord Chief Justice, Lord Reading, was sent to the United States in September in the hope of raising more funds for the Allies.[90]

It was these issues of finance and supply, as well as the military situation, which provided the background for the sessions of the War Policy Cabinet Committee. It was the arguments put forward by Lloyd George and the responses to them which most clearly showed the interdependent nature of strategy and supply. When Lloyd George was interviewed on 18 August, he argued that the goals of munitions production should be to equip a British army of 100 divisions as well as to provide sufficient munitions to aid the Russians.[91] If necessary, the Minister of Munitions went on, compulsion should be used to provide the labour necessary for achieving this goal. McKenna did not agree. Using arguments which were largely the work of Keynes, the Chancellor of the Exchequer struck many of the same notes that Walter Runciman, the President of the Board of Trade, also had sounded.[92] Put simply, McKenna suggested that Britain must choose between continuing to finance and supply her Allies and putting a large army in the field. Britain must maintain her exports in order to pay for both her own and her Allies' purchases in America. Further recruitment would mean a drop in domestic production, a decline in exports and a consequent collapse of the exchange rate. The Allies must learn that while the British people were not making 'greater personal sacrifices' than the Allies, the British nation was making 'a greater national effort than any of them'. The reference to Russian and French discontent with Britain was clear if unstated. Nor was this the only opposition to Lloyd George's contentions. Kitchener pointed out that it would be impossible to provide sufficient officers for an army of 100 divisions.[93] The arguments were only partially acceptable. McKenna's argument about the collapse of British credit was rejected, but Lloyd George's call for 100 divisions and compulsion of labour was ignored. The reason for this was political. Conscription was an issue which threatened the political existence of the coalition government; while it was acceptable for some Liberals and called for by most Unionists, there was a large segment of the Liberal party for whom it was anathema.[94]

By the beginning of September it was clear that British policy with respect to Russia would have to await two things, the outcome of the end of the campaigning season for 1915 and discussions with the Russians over the outstanding problems in finance and supply between the two countries. While British military policy for the rest of 1915 had appeared set at the end of August, with the decision not to reinforce the Dardanelles and to join the French offensive on the Western front, this proved not to be the case. The push for a change in policy came from France. In that country there had been a growing disenchantment with Joffre's conduct of the war, with its attendant casualty figures, throughout the summer.[95] The French left had called for his removal as Commander-in-Chief and replacement by General Maurice Sarrail, their own chosen candidate. This, plus the hope that success at the Dardanelles would once again make Russia a potent Ally by allowing a flow of munitions to enter via the Black Sea, made the Mediterranean a more inviting front than before. As a consequence, at the end of August the French government decided that they would send four divisions of troops to the Mediterranean, thus providing Sarrail with a command sufficiently large to satisfy both him and his supporters in the Chamber as well as creating an opportunity to help the Russians.

The British rightly concluded that this decision was primarily a political one. At the Dardanelles Committee of 3 September Kitchener assumed that this meant that the French had decided to cancel their offensive in the west so that a successful attempt could be made at the Dardanelles.[96] This being done, all the forces could be transferred back to the Western front, a move which could 'assist Russia very much'. Lloyd George and Churchill, both of whom were unconvinced of the soundness of an offensive in France, advanced the idea that Kitchener should persuade the French to abandon the attack. Despite his own suspicions, Kitchener would not agree; such a move, he felt, 'would break the Anglo-French alliance'. Obviously, though, it was necessary to establish just what French intentions were, and for this end a conference was set up at Calais on 11 September.[97]

When the conference opened, Joffre made it abundantly clear that he was opposed to sending any French troops to the Dardanelles at least until after his planned offensive.[98] He was not convinced of the 'decisive' results which Sarrail claimed would result from the investment of six divisions there. Joffre also felt that such a diversion of forces might lead to a 'disaster' in France. Millerand, the Minister of War, ignored Joffre's arguments. There were important political ramifications to be considered, and Millerand stated that the decision to send troops to the Mediterranean had already been made and was irrevocable. He turned the conversation to questions of the logistics involved in sending troops to the Mediterranean, effectively preventing the British from discovering just what the overall French policy was. Despite the fact that Millerand had declared the decision final, Joffre did not cease to object to it. At a meeting of the French and British military commanders held at Chantilly on 14 September, Joffre reiterated his view that the position of the Allies at the Dardanelles was a 'morass' and that they should seek only to maintain, not to expand, their position there.[99]

The British attitude at the Calais conference reflected the decisions which had been taken in the latter half of August. It had been decided then that, primarily for the sake of Russia, the BEF should co-operate with Joffre's planned offensive and that Hamilton should not be reinforced at the Dardanelles. The new French policy went against these decisions, but the British did not wish to antagonise their Ally over this matter. Therefore, at Calais Kitchener emphasised only the limited nature of the British commitment at the Straits. He did not foresee any British interest beyond opening up the Straits in order to help Russia with her problems of finance and supply, a subject of particular importance at this time. Joffre had made it perfectly clear that the whole Mediterranean project was a political one, and Kitchener had no desire to appear to be putting pressure on the French government. Besides, should Sarrail's force prove decisive it would end the concerns which Kitchener had long felt about the effect the failure at Gallipoli would have on the British position in the Moslem world. When Kitchener discussed the Calais conference at the meeting of the Dardanelles Committee on 23 September, the general feeling in the Committee was that, if the offensive in France were a success, the situation at the Dardanelles would solve itself. The proper course was to await the outcome of the attack.[100]

This meeting revealed another factor which became an intimate part of strategical decision-making. By this time Bulgarian mobilisation against Serbia had become evident. The fact that Bulgaria was about to declare for the Central Powers underlined another effect which the Russian retreat during 1915 had had upon British policy. As early as 29 May 1915 Grey had attempted to bring in Romania and Bulgaria on the Allied side. As he had told Buchanan, 'their assistance now will enable Russia to check or throw back [the] German advance in Galicia, and should ensure our early success in the Dardanelles.'[101] The question was whether or not the British offer was sufficient for Bulgaria. As far as the British ambassador at Sofia was concerned, the best that Britain could hope for was that Bulgaria would not reject the offer outright; 'more than this, we cannot hope for, in my opinion, in view of the continued non-success of the Russian military operations.'[102] This 'non-success' made Grey less hesitant to push Sazonov for concessions than had been the case in 1914. Early in June the Foreign Secretary suggested major concessions by Russia to Romania since the military position was 'not reassuring'.[103] Despite the fact that the Allies sweetened the offers made to both Romania and Bulgaria over the summer, they refused to accept. The final Allied offers to Bulgaria in early August and mid-September, simply were not sufficient given the lack of success of Allied arms.

The decision of whether or not to send troops to Salonika in order to save Serbia from Bulgaria and the Central Powers served as a focus for the entire issue of the direction of British strategy. At the Dardanelles Committee on 23 September, Lloyd George spoke out strongly in favour of sending a force to Salonika.[104] This he felt would counteract the Bulgarian mobilisation and force Greece to declare herself on the Allied side. The following day, the Dardanelles Committee decided that Britain would associate with France in informing the Greeks that the two Allies would send 150,000 men to Salonika in exchange for a Greek declaration for the Allies. The troops for this expedition were to come from Gallipoli.[105]

The equivocal Greek reply to the Anglo-French initiative was discussed at the Dardanelles Committee on 29 September.[106] Two positions with regard to the Balkans were clear. Grey felt that diplomatic pressure was not an effective tool with which to lever either Greece or Bulgaria into joining the Allies. Only a success in Joffre's ongoing offensive would be efficacious in achieving this end. Lloyd George did not agree. Instead he made a proposal to divert rifles from the British forces to the Russian troops in order to strengthen the Allied presence on the Eastern front where, in any case, he felt a decisive victory could be more easily won.

It was not surprising that the thoughts of the Minister of Munitions had again turned to Russia. For the past six weeks efforts had been made to improve the flow of munitions to that country. First, an appeal had been made to Japan to increase her shipment of arms to Russia.[107] Second, the friction between the War Office and the Ministry of Munitions with regard to purchasing in the United States had been largely overcome by the means described above. While little immediate help could be given to the Russians from British production, efforts had been made to arrange for an Anglo-Russian munitions conference in order to make long-term plans to help Russia.[108] However, the problem which had always soured closer Anglo-Russian co-operation – the Russian tendency to purchase munitions outside the RPC and a disinclination to reveal the exact nature of their needs – continued unabated.[109] The Russians were particularly upset with the British efforts to discover what munitions Russia needed. Blair was told that he and Knox had been getting such information for months 'but no good had come of it.'[110] As far as the Russians were concerned, such requests for information were fatuous as no supplies were forthcoming. Faced with this attitude, even Lloyd George, normally the most fervid proponent of providing supplies for Russia, found his enthusiasm flagging temporarily.[111] This was dispelled by Bark. The Russian Minister of Finance had arrived in Britain in late September for a financial conference and had told Lloyd George that only a shortage of rifles prevented Russia from launching a successful attack.

Despite Bark's support for his argument about rifles, Lloyd George's views were not accepted at the Dardanelles Committee on 29 September.[112] Kitchener promised to try to obtain rifles from other sources (notably China and Italy) for use in Russia, but rejected the idea that British units should be shorted. As to Greece, it was decided that her official rejection of the Anglo-French proposal meant that the two Allies could not send troops there, despite the accompanying unofficial enthusiasm for their dispatch. In essence this was no policy at all, a situation which could only be changed by events.

If British strategy makers found themselves unable to agree on the correct course of action, the same was not true concerning financial relations between Britain and Russia. Since the Boulogne conference, the gap between the Russian and British positions concerning gold had become even more evident. The pressure of Russian purchases in the United States forced Bark, at the end of August, to request an interim credit until he was able to attend the Allied financial conference set for the end of September.[113] He suggested that Russia ship £40 million in gold bullion to the United States in exchange for a credit ten times that size. The Treasury's reply was crisp: an interim credit of £30 million would be extended to Russia, but further credits must await the forthcoming conference.

Bark's belief that shipping gold would create further credit for Russia was a negation of the ideas behind the Boulogne agreement.[114] That conference had in mind the creation of a lump sum of credit in the United States which could be drawn on by any of the Allies, in proportion to the amount of gold contributed by each. If all Russia did were to ship gold to the United States, this would not assist Britain in maintaining the exchange rate upon which Allied credit rested. As Bradbury noted, the shipment of Russian gold to America, 'towards the payment of her own debts', was nearly 'irrelevant' to the establishment of further credits for Russia backed by British funds. At this impasse the matter rested until the financial conference opened.

The Anglo-Russian financial agreement of 30 September (generally referred to as the Treasury Agreement) was a milestone in financial dealings between the two countries.[115] It marked the first time an attempt had been made to establish a comprehensive framework to deal with the problems of regulating Russian finance and to link Russian finance with the purchase of munitions abroad. On the financial side, Britain extended to Russia a monthly credit of £25 million for the subsequent twelve months. Each instalment was to be backed by an equal amount of one-year Russian Treasury bills. For the final six months of the agreement, however, the monthly allotment was to be provisional on 'the ability of the British Government to obtain means of payment in the United States of America'. Russia was to hold ready £40 millon worth of gold for export to the United States, the gold to be used to buy British government Exchequer bonds which were payable in gold and which matured gradually after three years. Russia's commitment to export gold was limited to £20 millions before 31 March 1916, and would not be called for except at the request of the Bank of England.

This aspect of the agreement clearly reflected the Treasury's point

of view. The Russians had conceded that there was not necessarily
any link between the shipment of gold and the creation of an exclusively Russian credit. The principle that gold shipments were a
means of ensuring that Allied – which meant British – credit in the
United States was secure was the keystone of the agreement. Russian
sensibilities about their gold reserve were catered to by the purchase
of the Exchequer bonds, whose later redemption would mean that in
effect Russia had merely lent the gold to Britain.

There was also some provision made in the agreement as to what
purposes the funds made available to Russia could be used. These
credits were to be used 'exclusively' for the following ends: to pay for
contracts in Britain, the United States and Canada (as well as Japan
but to a circumscribed degree) which had been signed prior to the
agreement; to meet payments for contracts in other countries,
provided that these were arranged in the manner called for in the
annexe to the agreement; to provide for the servicing of the Russian
debt held externally except in France; and to pay for new orders
placed to a maximum of £4,500,000 per month. Russia agreed not to
use any of the funds provided for any reason in France or for activity
in the exchange market except as noted above. As compensation for
this latter restriction, the British government agreed to use their
'good offices' to renew £10 million of the Russian government
Treasury bills issued under the February 1915 agreement, and to aid
in solidifying the internal Russian debt and fiduciary issue by
exchanging 'equivalent obligations' of internal debt with Russia to a
value of £200 million over the next year.

In some ways the financial aspects of the 30 September agreement
were less far-reaching than was the accord contained in the annexe to
it. This annexe represented the most comprehensive attempt by the
Treasury to obtain some control over the nature of Russian
spending. All future purchases which Russia made with funds
provided by Britain, either in the United States or in the British
Empire, were to be placed through a group of experts appointed by
the Russian government and sitting in London. This group was to
act in consultation with the British members of the RPC in all
matters concerning war material and through the CIR in all other
matters. To ensure that this procedure was followed, the annexe
provided that no funds would be disbursed for purchases which had
not been approved in this fashion.

Both the Agreement and the annexe were a triumph for the ideas which the Treasury, and especially Keynes, had been putting forward. The shipment of gold was agreed upon, and, in theory at least, the regulation of Russian purchases had been canalised into the existing mechanism provided by the RPC and the CIR. On the other hand, Bark could not have been too displeased with the results of the conference. While he had agreed in principle to the shipment of gold, he had not sent any in actuality. In exchange he had received the assurance of a regular credit as well as a £200 million exchange of securities which would serve as backing for the issuance of further Russian currency notes. He had surrendered Russia's unilateral right to purchase abroad without consultation, but some price had to be expected for what he had gained. In practice, moreover, there would be ways and means of avoiding the more irksome restrictions of the annexe.

While these financial questions were being solved, the Dardanelles Committee had yet to find a policy with respect to strategy. During October and November British war policy was in a period of transition. This largely coincided with the decline of Kitchener's position as the ultimate authority on strategy. The August decision to take part in the battle of Loos rather than send Hamilton reinforcements for Gallipoli was the last decision where Kitchener's voice was dominant. An indication of this was the fact that the Dardanelles Committee had taken advantage of the Field Marshal's absence from its meeting of 22 September to re-establish the General Staff with Sir Archibald Murray as the new CIGS. Murray's appointment did not change the basic situation which faced the Dardanelles Committee, nor alter its options. The question remained as to where to concentrate British efforts. Russia was never far from the minds of those who debated this matter.

On 4 October Murray made his presence felt at the Dardanelles Committee. He presented a major paper outlining the War Office's view of the military situation.[116] This paper came down solidly for a concentration of effort on the Western front. As Murray saw it, the Germans had two options: to cease their present offensive against Russia and retreat to the Vistula, or to continue on until the strategically important Dvina line was reached. In either case, the Germans would soon transfer troops back to France to renew the attack there. Bulgaria's mobilisation against Serbia Murray viewed as a diversion, designed either to facilitate an Austro-Hungarian advance on Serbia or to overawe Romania into allowing free passage of munitions for Turkey across her territory. Both of these considerations were secondary in the War Office's view. Only if the Germans were faced with a 'serious breakdown' in the west could they be deflected from pursuing the achievement of the shorter Dvina line. Therefore Murray felt that the 'main objective' of forcing a decision on the Western front must be paramount. While he realised that the collapse of Serbia would aid Turkey and make the Dardanelles 'extremely precarious' Murray opposed diverting any troops to the Balkans.

Lloyd George's belief in a Balkan attack was not shaken by these arguments.[117] Equally, he opposed Kitchener's contention that the entire issue should be discussed with the French before any decision be taken. The Minister of Munitions was certain that Joffre would never admit that his offensive was a failure nor agree to send troops from France to the Balkans. Since Kitchener already was aware of Joffre's opposition to the Salonika project, it is quite possible that the Secretary of State for War was intent on using French opposition to quash the Salonika project before it gained support.[118] Whatever the case, Kitchener went to Calais and Chantilly, respectively on 5 and 8 October, to meet with the French.

Here he met with a surprise. In an attempt to find a berth for Sarrail far from France and to placate the critics of his western offensives, Joffre argued at Chantilly that sending 150,000 men to Salonika would not put the primacy of the Western front in jeopardy.[119] When Kitchener expressed doubt that such a small force would be adequate, Joffre noted that the terrain at Salonika made taking the offensive impossible in any case and so 150,000 men would be sufficient for the defensive. Three days earlier at Calais, Kitchener had spoken disparagingly of Salonika to the French politicians.[120] He had argued that 150,000 men would not be '*suffisants*' for the task and that any commitment of troops would be the first step in creating '*un autre théâtre d'opérations*'. This he had done in the belief that such an attitude would be supported by Joffre. Faced with the French Commander-in-Chief's new attitude, Kitchener offered three British divisions for Salonika, but did not agree to the French request for a reduction at the Dardanelles.

British policy-makers were faced with three alternatives when Kitchener returned from France.[121] The first was to concentrate on the Western front, the second was to continue the commitment at Gallipoli, while the third was to become involved in the new venture at Salonika. The first alternative was favoured by the General Staff, the second by Churchill and Curzon, and the third by Lloyd George. Other Cabinet figures took up less-defined positions. At the meeting of the Dardanelles Committee on 11 October, Asquith character- istically proposed a compromise solution, wherein 150,000 troops would be sent to Egypt 'without prejudice' to their final destination, pending a clarification of the situation in the Balkans.[122]

Kitchener's opinion was still important if no longer predominant. His lingering hold on strategic opinion at the War Office was evident in a paper prepared to deal with the Prime Minister's suggestion.[123] While the thrust of the paper reflected the General Staff view that neither the adherence of Greece nor that of Romania to the Allied cause was worth sending troops to the Balkans, Kitchener, according to Haig, pressed Murray into adding that eight divisions should be sent to Egypt.[124] This reflected Kitchener's ongoing concern about British prestige in the Middle East, a concern which was to make him a supporter of retaining British forces at the Dardanelles.[125] While Kitchener was at heart a 'westerner', he could not shake his fears for Empire. This division in his thinking gave Kitchener's military pronouncements in October and November an ambiguous tone and led to the final collapse of the government's confidence in his opinions.

Events made this debate academic. By 14 October the Bulgarians had declared war on Serbia, and on 23 October the railway line from Nish to Salonika was cut, effectively preventing Allied reinforce- ments from reaching the Serbs. The reports from Russia were not encouraging, and help for the Serbs from this quarter seemed unlikely. Blair reported that the rifle shortage was acute, and that as a consequence men available for fighting were unable to go forward into the lines.[126] Buchanan was concerned about the internal situation.[127] Only Knox's report that the Germans seemed to be abandoning their attacks against Russia until 1916 offered any cheer about the Russian situation.[128]

By late October Lloyd George was completely isolated in his wish for a Salonikan campaign. The French, however, remained insistent, and Lloyd George did not hesitate to raise the issue. To support his view, he offered the possibility that Russia would be able to send 200,000 men to aid the Serbs as soon as the British were able to provide some 300,000 rifles for the Eastern front.[129] This argument was countered by Churchill, who for his own reasons had no desire to see forces diverted from the Dardanelles to Salonika. The former First Lord contended that the rifles could not reach the front until much too late to aid Serbia, a view reinforced by Blair's assessment of the chaotic state of the Russian railways. No decision was taken at this meeting, but Lloyd George's remarks were lent strength by the fact that Benckendorff presented a note to the British government that day calling for more rifles and heavy guns for Russia.[130]

On 26 October Grey wrote to Lloyd George about Benckendorff's note and asked if the Minister of Munitions could have 'the matter looked into in your Department, and see what can be done?'[131] The opinion of the War Office was in no doubt. As von Donop wrote to Grey, the '*minimum*' needs of the British army for 1916 would occupy fully the entire output of British armament firms.[132] The Master-General of the Ordnance would 'protest most strongly' at any attempt to divert these supplies to Russia. Wintour's views were equally clear, if put less vehemently.[133] No Russian orders could be placed in America since factories there were occupied fully with British orders. In an oblique jab at Lloyd George's decision to prepare sufficient munitions for a 100-division British army despite the War Office's contention that no more than 70 could be put in the field, Wintour suggested that supplies for Russia might be forthcoming from the United States if the Ministry of Munitions would 'limit our orders in the U.S. to what our military authies. considered necessary.' The growing struggle for resources was evident.

When the Dardanelles Committee met again on 27 October, the question of rifles for Russia was raised again.[134] This time it centred around whether the 300,000 rifles should consist entirely of Italian Vetterlis or a mixed batch of Japanese and British types. Kitchener favoured sending the Vetterlis since the others were required for Home defence. Lloyd George demurred. He argued that the limited amount of ammunition available for the Italian rifles made them useless to the Russians and pressed the Committee to take a gamble on Home defence. Kitchener attempted to quash all argument by decreeing 'that the matter had been discussed by the General Staff who had decided it was out of the question.' Such comments no longer had their former force, but did serve to delay discussion of the rifles issue until after Kitchener's departure on 4 November for the Mediterranean.

The British still had no policy about Salonika. From France, Robertson continued to bombard all concerned with letters advocating withdrawal from the Dardanelles and the avoidance of an entanglement at Salonika.[135] Robertson felt that the French examination of the Salonikan expedition had been 'aimless' and conceived only with political considerations in mind.[136] The Dardanelles campaign had failed in its original intent and, Robertson argued, was now in danger of becoming a disaster. Despite the fact that Robertson's arguments were accepted by the majority of the élite, on 29 October the British government reluctantly agreed to send a force to Salonika.

This decision was the result of a personal appeal by Joffre. Having been unable to sway the British military authorities towards a Salonikan campaign at an Anglo-French military conference at Chantilly, the French Commander-in-Chief went directly to London on 29 October to plead his case.[137] The arguments which he put forward were those which had proved unconvincing at Chantilly: a Salonikan landing would, acting in concert with a Russian force poised in Bessarabia, provide the 'element of force' previously lacking in Allied diplomacy.[138] Far more successful was the point made by Joffre that Salonika was essential if the French government were to remain in the alliance. Such an argument struck a responsive note in Kitchener; the Secretary of State had told the Dardanelles Committee just four days earlier that a political crisis in France must be avoided at all costs. Even a Salonikan campaign could be tolerated if the alternative were that the Anglo-French *Entente* were to collapse, since 'if we were to break with France the war would be over.' Grudgingly the British accepted the French proposal for Salonika, but the terms of the British commitment were that should communication with the Serbs be lost, the British forces would be removed. Ironically, as this was being agreed to, the Viviani government in France collapsed, to be replaced by a new regime under the leadership of Auguste Briand.

A limited engagement at Salonika having been agreed upon, the next problem was that of the Dardanelles. Having gotten their way over Salonika, the new French government was much less insistent on the evacuation of the Dardanelles, and the matter became more a purely British concern.[139] The impact of Russia was considerable in this matter. According to Blair, the conditions on the Eastern front were ripe for a Russian success.[140] The Germans were over-extended and experiencing difficulties with their lines of supply and communication. All that was needed for a Russian success was rifles, and Blair recommended shorting the British forces in favour of the Russians. Robertson saw the situation in a different light.[141] Since German troops were being sent from east to west, Robertson argued that no further British troops could be sent to the Dardanelles for fear that a German success would follow in France.

The entire issue of Russia's capabilities and intentions was discussed at a meeting of the War Committee (as the Dardanelles Committee had become) on 6 November.[142] Murray stated that the possibility of a successful Russian offensive in the near future was 'very good indeed', and Asquith opined that the Russians should focus their effort against the Germans rather than consider action in the south near Romania. Murray agreed with this evaluation, echoing Robertson's earlier concern that the Germans might use the forces transferred from the east for an attack in France. For Lloyd George such debate was academic. The Minister of Munitions pointed out that the essential matter was not where Russia attacked, but whether she had the rifles necessary to do so at all. This ended debate over Russia's intentions and talk swung to a general evaluation of the diplomatic situation in the Balkans. George Clerk, who attended the meeting on behalf of the Foreign Office, noted that everything depended on whether or not Russia had military success in that region. The Greeks, he felt, would join the Allies if and only if the Russians were victorious.

On 8 November the question of rifles for Russia was raised once more.[143] Again, as on 27 October, a quarrel arose over which rifles should be sent. Lloyd George wished to send to Russia the 60,000 Japanese rifles which Kitchener had claimed earlier were essential for Home defence, along with about 200,000 British rifles. This, Murray claimed, 'would not paralyze the training of new troops but would interfere with it badly, and would put the onus of home defense upon the Navy.' The choice between British and Russian needs was clear. Balfour, for the Admiralty, characteristically put a foot in each camp. He prefaced his remarks by claiming that 'he belonged to the most forward section in favour of giving the Russians rifles' but then added that if he were a German and heard that Home defence depended solely on the Navy, 'he would at once endeavour to make a landing.' In the debate that ensued, Lloyd George's position was firm: 'the General Staff were quite right to point out the risk, and the Committee ought to take it.' The majority opposed his view, and the final conclusion was that only the 60,000 Japanese rifles should be sent to Russia. Lloyd George 'regretted' this decision, as he felt that 'an extra army to Russia now might make it possible for Russia to break through the line.'

For the next two weeks the debate over Gallipoli and British policy generally went on with no let-up. Robertson called for a concentration in the west and firmer British control of Allied strategy.[144] The Admiralty plumped for an attack to free the Belgian coast and deprive the Germans of their submarine bases there.[145] Murray argued at a meeting of the War Committee on 13 November that the Russians should focus their efforts not against Bulgaria but rather concentrate on the Austro-German forces near Lvov.[146] At the same time Grey was exploring another possibility. On 16 November he probed the probable Russian reaction to a separate peace settlement with Turkey, a move which would solve the Dardanelles in one step but lose Constantinople for Russia.[147] The Russian response was extremely hostile. Arthur Nicolson noted on the Russian reply that a British evacuation of Gallipoli might cause the Russian alliance to be 'lost' or 'certainly jeopardised'.[148] This Russian objection to withdrawal played a prominent part in a memorandum which Balfour put forward on 19 November opposing the evacuation of Gallipoli.[149]

While Grey had abandoned his trial balloon in the face of Russia's negative reaction, it may have had an effect on Russian military plans. On 22 November Hanbury Williams was given a memorandum calling for a joint thrust by the Anglo-French force at Salonika and the Russian forces in Bessarabia.[150] The plan was grandiose. The Anglo-French troops were to occupy Serbia and then drive, in concert with the Russians, into Hungary. This in turn was to 'open a road' for the Italian army to take Vienna! No action was taken on this absurd scheme when it was introduced at the War Committee on 23 November, although Hanbury Williams was instructed to ascertain whether it represented the views of the Russian Chief of Staff, General M. V. Alekseev, and the plan itself was sent to France for evaluation by the French military authorities.[151]

The principal decision taken at the meeting on 23 November was to evacuate the Dardanelles. The impetus for this decision came from Kitchener's telegram of the previous day which recommended such a course as a result of his inspection of Gallipoli and from

Murray's paper outlining the General Staff's view of the situation.[152] This latter paper is interesting in that Murray felt it necessary to discuss the impact that withdrawal would have on Russia. His argument was a direct statement of the purely military point of view. While agreeing that evacuation would have an unfavourable reception in Russia, he added that 'bad military strategy can seldom, if ever, be good policy in the long run.' His views were accepted by the War Committee, but generated opposition outside of it. George Curzon, Lord Privy Seal, and Hankey both wrote papers opposing leaving the Dardanelles.[153] As might be expected from a former Viceroy, Curzon laid great stress on the consequences this would have in the Near East and India. He then added that failure to obtain Constantinople in the near future would create 'the most serious impression upon the Russian army and people [who were] already suspicious . . . of our earnestness, and to a large extent ignorant of our sacrifices'. Hankey made similar points and concluded that if Britain were to leave the Dardanelles she must first discuss it with Russia or else 'lose the co-operation of Russia in this war'.

The whole question of the Balkans was discussed at the War Committee on 1 December, with particular emphasis on the question of Salonika.[154] Lloyd George argued that the Russian insistence on the significance of Salonika made a withdrawal impossible. Others did not agree. Alekseev's plan for a Balkan offensive did not command any respect in military circles. Joffre's evaluation of it was as harsh as that of his British colleagues.[155] Joffre argued that both Salonika and the Dardanelles were secondary theatres and noted that an offensive at Salonika 'in the present situation . . . is not feasible.' Since communication with the Serb army was no longer possible, the War Committee decided to implement the terms of the 29 October agreement with Joffre and advocated a withdrawal from Salonika. Despite Lloyd George's protests this was declared the official British view for presentation to the French at the forthcoming Allied conference at Calais on 4 December.

Meanwhile, the Russians continued their pressure for the retention of Salonika. On 2 December Benckendorff presented Grey with a note stressing the importance which the Russians placed on not allowing the Germans to destroy the Balkan states one by one.[156] To prevent such an occurrence, the note went on, a concerted Allied military effort should be made. In addition Alekseev made a direct appeal to Joffre.[157] The Russian Chief of Staff argued that the maintenance of Allied forces at Salonika forced the enemy to keep forces ready to defend against them, a situation which greatly facilitated the impending Russian offensive in Galicia. Grey was so worried over the effect of British withdrawal on Anglo-Russian relations that he asked Kitchener to inform the Russians of such a move through military rather than diplomatic channels. As Grey put it, the Russians 'will take it much better if they understand it is based solely on military grounds & therefore communicated directly to their G.H.Q.'[158]

At the Allied conference at Calais, Asquith, Balfour and Kitchener were firm in their insistence on the need for withdrawal from Salonika.[159] Among the French opinion was divided. Joffre, for the military, was willing to agree, but Briand and Galliéni, the Premier and War Minister respectively, were not. Even so, by the end of the meetings on 4 December, the British point of view had been accepted. This, however, caused a political crisis within the French government, with strong opposition to such a move from the Left. A similar agitation had been instrumental in bringing down the Viviani government just a month earlier, and Briand was determined that there should be no repetition of this débâcle. To this end, he carefully altered the French version of the *procès-verbal* taken at Calais to suggest that the French delegation had recognised but not agreed to the British position.[160]

When the British government was informed of the change in the French position, the effect was as devastating as it had been in late October. It was again feared that failure to support the French position would lead to a slackening of their war effort and a prolonged political crisis. Such despondency was only intensified by the results of the military conference which was held at Chantilly on 6–8 December.

This conference was the first effort by all the Allies to establish some sort of framework for the future conduct of the war.[161] While it revealed general agreement on many issues, the conference underlined the fact that each of the Allies had interests which were particularly vital to them. This fact became evident on the first day. As hosts, the French went first and presented their views on the proper course of action for 1916. The French plans were based on an examination of the reserves of manpower available to the Allies and the Central Powers. With an approximate parity existing between the two alliances, the French argued that Germany could not be defeated by frontal attacks at present. They therefore recommended that Allies with 'abundant' or 'undefined' resources in manpower should attempt to 'waste' the German army while the French forces were 'husbanded' until a decisive offensive could be launched. Until then, they concluded, every effort was to be made to supply Russia with munitions.

With this broad principle in mind, the French then outlined more specific plans. The ultimate goal was 'the destruction of the German and Austrian armies', a feat to be achieved by concerted attacks on all fronts after the 'wasting' attacks had had their effect. Emphasis was placed on the relative ease with which good results could be had on the Eastern, as opposed to the Western, front and the tone of the presentation was that a Russian offensive should precede a Western one. The second goal was to 'oppose the German plans and endeavour to crush imperialistic attempts in the East', a vague phrase justifying the retention of Salonika as a threat to the flank of any German expansion in the Middle East. In addition, Salonika would help to defend Egypt, whose garrison in any case should be augmented by the British forces which the French wished to have withdrawn fom Gallipoli.

French special interests were clear. There was a desire evident to ensure that their Allies took a full share of the casualties in 1916 while the French forces rested. Salonika was to be maintained (primarily for reasons of domestic politics despite the military points advanced above), and Russia was to be provided with supplies until she was the 'steamroller' which prewar French planning had envisaged. The Dardanelles were to be evacuated. The particular interests of the British and the Russians emerged in the discussion of the French presentation. The British military authorities objected to the Salonika project and stated that it must be considered first by British civilian authorities – an obvious delaying tactic. General Zhilinskii, the Russian representative, did not even mention the French suggestions. His focus was elsewhere. Zhilinskii noted that it must be agreed upon that if any one of the Allies were attacked before '*all*' were ready, then the remaining Allies 'should take the offensive on their respective fronts to help that power which is attacked even if their preparations are not completed.' The Russians clearly were not willing to bear the brunt of German attacks in 1916 as they had in 1915 and be fobbed off with the excuse that the other Allies' plans were not yet formulated.[162]

The Russian view was accepted by the conference as a whole, but when discussion turned to Salonika such unanimity was absent. Murray made it plain that his own view was that the project should be abandoned, and the Anglo-French forces concentrated in France. Murray noted that the position at Salonika was dangerously weak and added that should Greece join the Central Powers the Allied position would be untenable. Nor did he feel that the possible adherence of Romania was worth the immobilisation of 150,000 troops, forces which he felt would be put to better use as an Egyptian garrison. As a final caveat, the CIGS noted that the lines of communication by sea to Salonika were of doubtful security. Zhilinskii opposed Murray's view. Taking a line similar to that which Alekseev had argued previously, the Russian representative said that the Salonikan force offered a threat to the enemy's flank and an 'indirect covering' of Egypt. As Alekseev himself put it, Murray's interpretation was 'a complete misunderstanding of the significance of Romania for the general interest of the Allies'.[163]

The final conclusions of the conference came as no surprise. The principal theatres were recognised to be the Russian, Anglo-French and Italian fronts. It was agreed that every effort be made to co-ordinate attacks against the enemy and that all the Allies must aid any of their number which was attacked separately. It was accepted that the secondary theatres must retain only a minimum of forces in order that every effort could be made on the principal ones. Only over Salonika was no accord reached. Not even a telegram from Alekseev, which Zhilinskii produced after the formal close of the conference, calling upon the British and French to maintain their force at Salonika, was enough to make the British formally agree to do so.[164]

The question of Salonika rested with the politicians. In an effort to sway the British, Albert Thomas, the prominent leftist Minister of Munitions, went to London to talk matters over with Lloyd George. This had its effect. At the War Committee on 8 December Lloyd George made it clear that a break with the French over Salonika was unthinkable.[165] Balfour supported Lloyd George and even suggested that the French be given complete authority over the campaign. Instead Kitchener and Grey travelled to Paris on 9 December to discuss the matter. The fear of joint French and Russian unhappiness with the British proved too much. It was decided, 'for political reasons' as Kitchener wrote to Asquith, to maintain the troops at present in Greece and to delay any final decision about Salonika to the indeterminate future.[166]

Faced with this *fait accompli*, the General Staff turned its attention to stamping out once and for all any consideration of the Russian proposal for a major Balkan offensive. This was necessitated by the ongoing Russian championing of the attack, a campaign which was motivated as much by Russia's fear of losing Constantinople in a postwar settlement as by French efforts to orchestrate a joint Franco-Russian protest over the British proposal to evacuate Salonika.[167] At the War Committee on 13 December Murray presented a paper which outlined the enormous problems inherent with supply and transport in Alekseev's plan.[168] He also pointed out that the time involved to begin such an attack would mean that the enemy would be present in equal strength and strongly fortified. He concluded that Russia would be better served by an Allied offensive on the Western front, a belief with which the War Committee concurred. All that remained for the General Staff was to convince the War Committee to adhere formally to the decisions taken at Chantilly. This was to be the work of Robertson and will be discussed in the following chapter.

At Chantilly there had been general agreement on the need to provide munitions for Russia. Much of the preliminary work required to achieve this had already been accomplished at an inter-Allied munitions conference which had met in London from 23 November to 1 December. The roots of this conference went back to the difficulties which the British had experienced throughout the first eight months of 1915 in obtaining figures from the Russian government of their needs in munitions and to the problems involved with the continued dissatisfaction of the Russian government with the Russian Government Committee in London. In September, the Emperor decided to send a mission to England under the leadership of Admiral A. I. Rusin, the Chief of the Naval Staff, to solve these problems.[169]

Before the Rusin mission could come to grips with these difficulties, the British had to decide what their own policy was with regard to supplying munitions for Russia. During October and November much discussion took place in British munitions circles on this topic. The discussion was set off by a memorandum by Booth.[170] Booth's position was straightforward. He felt that the Ministry of Munitions was aiming at supplying the British army with more equipment than it could utilise. This in turn meant that there was less production available for the Allies. Booth argued in favour of more equitable distribution of orders and a greater degree of centralisation. As he put it: 'we have offered to finance our Allies; we have urged our Allies to put their buying arrangements in our hands; it is unthinkable that at the same time we should inform them that we have monopolised every possible source of production.' Booth wanted to determine the overall extent of British needs and split the rest of British production among the Allies.

Booth's memorandum circulated among the upper echelons of munitions production management. The comments which it drew reflected the very different views which existed concerning the provision of supplies for Russia. The major objection to Booth's suggestions was that Britain could not surrender control of the allocation of munitions which she produced, an argument analagous to the one that the Treasury earlier had produced regarding finance. Eric Geddes, one of the DDGs at the Ministry of Munitions, put the matter clearly. Before one could agree to Booth's proposals 'one must have a statement as to the ultimate aim of the Cabinet. What ultimate forces do they calculate that the country can, if need be, provide and maintain in the Field?' Geddes was sceptical of Booth's proposal to divide up resources among the Allies: 'to pool the resources of the World, is very ideal, but I see great difficulty in arriving at any basis for a pool.' Arthur Lee (later Viscount Lee of Fareham), the head of the Output Department at the Ministry, also had doubts about the practicality of Booth's suggestions.

Lee agreed that Britain must not adopt a 'dog in the manger' attitude towards her Allies, but defended the Ministry of Munitions' 'surplus' policy on three points. First, the War Office might increase its needs in the future; second, contractors might deliver their orders late; third, and most significant, 'whilst we can never lose the War from having too many guns and shells we might easily lose from having too few.' In short, British needs, real and potential, were to have priority over those of Russia.

At the end of October these conflicting views were all sent to Christopher Addison, the parliamentary secretary to the Ministry and its future head, for the consideration of Lloyd George. Addison added his own comments before passing the lot to Lloyd George. In general Addison's sympathy tended to be with Geddes's view, although he agreed that Booth had raised 'some very important points of principle.' Addison's conclusions had the patronising flavour that the Russians grew to resent as the war went on. 'The dominant needs in Munitions are our own and the Russians',' Addison wrote, but 'it is hopeless to set out with the idea that we should aim at equipping the Russian armies throughout on the same scale as is necessary for the French and ourselves upon this side.' The Russians would have to be satisfied with 'what Munitions can be supplied which will have the most useful effect in the shortest time', uniform patterns for ordnance and a single buying organisation in the United States.

There were other problems to be considered. A key point was interdepartmental co-operation. As mentioned, Russian munitions were purchased by the War Office's RPC which lay outside the general stream of Allied munitions buying since the latter were channelled through the Ministry of Munitions. On 2 November a conference was held to consider this matter and others of a similar nature.[171] The split between the RPC and the Ministry with regard to Russian ordering was easily dealt with; it was agreed that some separate meetings between the Russians and the RPC would have to be held apart from the main sessions of the conference. Other matters were not as tractable.

Booth brought up the issue that, although Russian purchases were officially to be funnelled through the RPC, in practice they were still being made directly by the Russian Government Committee in London and the Russian Purchasing Committee in New York. Booth felt that the problem resided in the annexe to the Treasury Agreement of 30 September. He felt that the annexe did not give the British 'any real power of control or veto or even the right to insist that advances made were actually devoted to payment for munitions of war.' Booth wished the British to take control of 'all purchases on behalf of Russia' as well as matters of payment. The conference should be used, he felt, as a means of 'revising' the Treasury Agreement to provide greater British control.

He also found fault with the organisational procedure to deal with orders placed by the RPC.[172] The problem originated in the autumn of 1914 when the department of the Director of Army Contracts at the War Office was split in half. One half, under Wintour, 'retain[ed] the Q.[uarter] M.[aster] G.[eneral] side of things'; the other, under Hanson, 'purchas[ed] for the M.[aster] G.[eneral of the] O.[rdnance]'. When the Ministry of Munitions was formed in

1915, Hanson's department became part of the new Ministry, but Kitchener's insistence on retaining Russian purchasing meant that Wintour still purchased ordnance for Russia, often in direct competition with Hanson. Booth, as a member of both the RPC and the Ministry, had acted as 'Officier de Liaison' between the two, but felt that 'I cannot think that this method is efficient.'

There was yet another problem which Booth outlined. The War Office frequently ordered the same munitions for the British forces as the RPC did for the Russians. When both orders came to the Ministry of Munitions this created a dilemma as 'in most cases help of this sort [for Russia] cannot be given except at the expense of the actual requirements of the War Office, and the Ministry as a Supply Department, is placed in a position of difficulty.' Booth advocated the end of the RPC. Instead, he preferred that the MGO would, jointly with the Russian authorities, draw up one comprehensive list of requirements embodying both Russian and British needs. While Booth did not discuss them, problems also existed between the RPC, the Ministry of Munitions and the CIR. Since the latter body dealt with all materials purchased for Russia other than munitions and warlike stores, there was yet another dimension to the possibility for confusion when dealing with Russian supplies.[173]

Booth's views were eminently sensible, but overlooked several vital points. Hanson pointed them out in a trenchant note written in mid-November.[174] First, the Treasury Agreement of 30 September represented a major concession by the Russians and was achieved only after 'delicate and difficult' negotiation. Second, the annexe did not 'in any way' give the British government control over Russian purchasing, only the right of consultation. While financial support for Russia could be withdrawn under the terms of the Treasury Agreement, such a step would weaken the overall Allied military effort and so remained only a last resort. As Hanson concluded, within Britain itself where the Ministry of Munitions controlled industry the British government had near-complete power over Russian purchasing. In the United States such strictures did not apply and British control was largely nonexistent. If the Treasury Agreement were to be abandoned, as Booth suggested, in favour of complete control by the Ministry, 'there is no reason to suppose' that the latter body would be any more effective in controlling Russian agents in the United States than had the RPC. Besides, as Addison noted in exasperation, the Russians 'generally required three months to make up their minds to anything.' In short the Treasury Agreement, coupled with the existing machinery, was the best compromise solution to a very complex matter.

The conference of the Allies (often referred to within the War Office and Ministry of Munitions as the Conference of the Big Four) opened in London on 23 November.[175] As host, Lloyd George opened the proceedings. His speech delineated the British position clearly.[176] The Royal Navy was at full strength and required little more in the way of supplies; however, the army had undergone and was still undergoing a vast expansion. This expansion had soaked up much of the productive capabilities of the nation, and when dealing with possible aid from Britain 'regard must always be had to this great expansion'. After bland and self-congratulatory speeches by the chief representatives of the three Allies, the haggling began. The Russian demands were outrageous. Perhaps inspired by the frequent British admonitions to quantify their needs, the Russians presented a detailed and formidable shopping list: 1,400 4.8-inch howitzers, 250 8-inch siege howitzers, 90 6-inch howitzers, 54 12-inch howitzers, plus assorted smaller items. In reply Lloyd George stressed the need for Russia to decide on the 'relative importance' of these orders as not all could be fulfilled. Britain could let Russia have a 'fair number, say 200–300' of 4.5-inch howitzers by the spring of 1916, but the General Staff would have to be consulted about the final figure.

Albert Thomas, the French Minister of Munitions, followed Lloyd George's lead. France would give Russia one-third of her production of 4.2-inch field howitzers, but 'while France was making such sacrifices to help Russia, she wished that Great Britain should keep as much of her own heavy artillery as possible for the Western front.' At this point the conference adjourned until the following day.

The British, Russian and French positions had been staked out clearly. Russia had presented a list which had no chance of being filled in the hope of getting as much as possible from her Western Allies. Lloyd George had a strong interest in providing supplies for the Russians, but had to consider his political future. The Welshman had hitched his political wagon to making a success of the Ministry of Munitions, and this success would be measured by whether he was able to supply the requirements of the War Office. British needs would be considered first. France also was willing to aid Russia to a certain extent, but was not willing for Britain to divert more than a certain amount of her output from the Western front. In line with the military position which the French were to take at the Chantilly conference, they desired that the bulk of British production go to equip the British army so that the latter could undertake the majority of the fighting in 1916. The positions adopted by the various Allies at this first session of the conference were to persist for the duration of the talks.

At the second plenary session of the conference on the following day, Thomas introduced a resolution calling for all inter-Allied orders to be approved by an inter-governmental organisation.[177] After discussion it was agreed that in principle all purchases of war material made by one Ally in the country of another should only be done officially. As well, the Ally in whose country the order was placed would be responsible for seeing that the order was carried out. Having settled this, Thomas then introduced a second resolution, one calling for a central inter-Allied body to co-ordinate purchasing and to act as a clearing house for information on production.

Not unexpectedly, Rusin objected. His action was characteristic of the longstanding Russian refusal to allow her independence to be curtailed. While he agreed 'in principle' with the idea, Rusin argued that such an arrangement 'might result in delaying the execution of orders.' He saw it as 'important' that such a body would not interfere with the work of Hermonious and the Russian Government Committee in London. Admiral F. Black, the British Director General of Munitions Supplies (DGMS) at the Ministry of Munitions, offered a compromise between the French plan for a centralised body and the Russian defence of the status quo. He suggested devising some sort of plan whereby co-ordination of English purchasing for the Allies in neutral countries could be achieved. Lloyd George threw his weight behind Thomas. The Minister of Munitions felt that the Allies should pool information on 'all factors influencing production'. Faced with this united front, Rusin managed to give an agreement which was in essence a refusal; he accepted the proposal 'provided that while the details were being arranged existing arrangements were not interferred with.' Rusin had committed himself to little since the Russian government could delay matters indefinitely if it wished through obstruction on the matter of 'details'. The final form of the agreement called for all the Allies to provide a central bureau with details of their industrial capacity and plans for munitions production on a monthly basis. Each of these plans was to be accompanied by an evaluation of its relative importance so that the central body could decide how 'to make best use of the joint resources of the Allies'. In addition, a conference of the Allies was to be held every two months to smooth out any problems which might arise.

These proposals, which in reality never became anything more than pious aspirations, were the first of many similar ideas put forward throughout the war. Such ideas generally foundered on a succession of nationalist shoals which prevented any serious co-ordination from coming about. Not until 1918, when the United States could virtually dictate terms to the Allies, did any sort of overall control of munitions production and distribution occur.

After the second plenary session on the morning of 24 November, the conference broke up into smaller groups in order to consider specific issues. That afternoon the British and French delegates gathered to discuss several matters, including small arms ammunition for Russia.[178] The debate on this issue was instructive, as it emphasised the kinds of disagreements which could arise between the two countries. The British felt that they could offer Russia 10 million rounds a week, but that delivery could not begin for seven months. For France, Thomas felt this was inadequate. France had given Russia cartridges 'at the expense of her own requirements' and he could not see why Britain should not do the same. Thomas emphasised the fact that France had sent Russia almost 400,000 rifles in the last few weeks despite the fact that French production was less than that of Britain and that France held more of the line on the Western front than did Britain. In reply, as he was to do throughout the conference when differences of opinion arose, Lloyd George said that the matter 'was one for the military authorities'. Given the Minister of Munitions' generally low opinion of 'military authorities' such a remark had its ironic overtones, but such an invocation served several useful purposes.

First, it provided Lloyd George with a bargaining counter with which to oppose excessive demands. Second, it separated him from being associated in the minds of the Allies with refusals of their requests; thus he could continue to pose as their champion – a champion regretfully forced to turn down requests by his own War Office. Finally, and most importantly, this was the best practical way to proceed. As noted previously, Lloyd George's first obligation was to provide British needs and he thus had to be careful not to promise to the Allies what was required at home.

After Lloyd George had brought up the need for consultation with the military authorities, the discussion of Russia's small arms needs turned into a technical argument between British and French experts over the correct figure to be used in calculating the number of rounds per rifle per month. The French argued that the British figure was too large by a factor of five, resulting in a corresponding divergence in the totals which the two sides put forward as the overall Russian need. To close the argument, Lloyd George once again mentioned the need to consult the War Office and the matter was not pursued until a joint meeting of the French, British and Russian delegates later that day.[179]

Lloyd George opened this joint meeting by summarising the earlier discussions and asked Rusin for the basis on which Russian requirements were calculated. Rusin's figure nearly approximated the British one, a fact which immediately resulted in the emergence of Lloyd George's caution lest the Russians expect too much. The Minister of Munitions noted that as 'the British output did not reach that [Rusin's] proportion for British rifles . . . the use of this figure would weaken the case for supplying anything to Russia.' In addition, the French continued to argue that the Russian figure for computing their needs was excessive. With nothing being resolved, Lloyd George promised to 'do what he could' to help Russia at the next meeting of the War Committee.

Attention then turned to 'the second Russian requirement in order of importance', the provision of machinery for the manufacture of cartridges. This matter was disposed of quickly. Britain offered a complete factory capable of turning out 10–15 million cartridges per week, with the entire project to begin production within six months' time. At this point talk again strayed to the question of small arms ammunition. Rusin asked Thomas if France were able to provide cartridges for the Austrian rifles which Russia had captured. The French Minister of Munitions' reply that this was 'absolutely impossible' reflected his country's belief that she had done all that could be expected and the issue was dropped.

Rusin then brought up the matter of the supply of howitzers. The original Russian request for 1,400 4.8-inch howitzers was not even mentioned. Hard realism had replaced earlier fantasy. Lloyd George offered the Russians 300 4.5-inch howitzers to be delivered in

100-unit blocks in February, March and April 1916. Thomas promised that one in three of the French production of 105 mm howitzers would be given to Russia, along with two 280 mm guns per month. This was satisfactory to all concerned and the meeting turned to other less vital matters. The session closed with a final French argument for a review of British estimates on small arms ammunition requirements, especially in view of the 'urgent need' of the Russians.

As he had promised, Lloyd George raised the issue of small arms ammunitions at the War Committee on 25 November.[180] Here he was authorised to give 'substantial assistance' to the Russians, no doubt in the hope that such largesse would help to ease their disappointment about the impending evacuation of the Dardanelles. Lloyd George informed the Russian delegates of this decision that afternoon at a meeting of the British and Russian representatives, but added a cautionary note that detailed figures would be available only after he had consulted with the British General Staff.[181] Lloyd George took this opportunity to air briefly the longstanding British unhappiness with the behaviour of Russian representatives in the United States, remarking that they had hindered production of small arms ammunition for Russia in that country. Rusin's agreement allowed the meeting to discuss the means of implementing the British aid to Russia.

After Rusin had raised doubts about his knowledge of the Russian industrial scene by suggesting that skilled labour might be available to come to Britain to work on Russian orders, Lloyd George summarised the position which had been reached. Britain would give up a 'substantial part' of her own production in favour of Russia, the exact details to be worked out after consultation with the General Staff and the departments concerned. This was the last meeting of the British and Russian delegations; the conference adjourned until 1 December when a final session was held to present the full conclusions.[182]

The conference was a success. Everyone was 'immensely struck' by the French, who 'were magnificent to the end' in providing so much for the Russians. The Russians were thought 'an able bunch of fellows', but Addison felt that they were hindered by conditions at home. 'Blackmail and commissions', he noted, 'are the curse of Russia at the present moment.'[183] The conference, like the financial one in September, had been a first step in the direction of creating a regular means of dealing with inter-Allied issues.

By the middle of December 1915 Anglo-Russian relations had

reached a new stage. For the first time since the beginning of the war, agreement had been reached on a majority of the issues between the two countries. First, some effort had been made to co-ordinate the military plans. Second, the Treasury Agreement of 30 September had placed financial relations between the two countries on a regular footing and had attempted to institute some control over the purchase of munitions abroad. Finally, the conference of the Big Four in London had created at least the beginnings of a co-ordinated munitions policy for all the Allies. The contrast between the degree of harmony apparent at the beginning of the 1916 campaigning season and that which had existed a year earlier was evident. The year 1916 was to provide its own problems.

Notes

1 A concise outline of the formation of the Anglo-Russian Committee which grew out of Ellershaw's visit is in *History of the Ministry of Munitions* (12 vols, London, 1922–4), II, pt VIII, 10–12.
2 Kitchener's letter is printed as appendix I in 'Report upon the contracts for munitions placed in Great Britain and America . . .', n.s., n.d. (but prepared for the Anglo-Russian conference of mid-July 1916), Mun 4/1296.
3 Hanbury Williams to Kitchener, 15 May 1915, Kitchener Papers, PRO 30/57/67.
4 Sidorov, *Ekonomicheskoe polozhenie*, 266.
5 Hanbury Williams to Kitchener, 19 May 1915, Kitchener Papers, PRO 30/57/67.
6 Hanbury Williams to Kitchener, 24 May 1915, ibid.
7 See Clerk's note on the draft of FO to Buchanan, private and secret, 21 May 1915, FO 371/2448/64564.
8 Morgan to Morgan, Grenfell and reply, both 20 May 1915, Mun 4/207.
9 Morgan, Grenfell to Morgan, 21 May 1915, ibid.
10 Morgan, Grenfell to Morgan, 29 May 1915 and reply, 9 June 1915, ibid.
11 Meeting of the War Council, 14 May 1915, Cab 42/2/19.
12 See C. F. Aspinall-Oglander, *History of the Great War based on Official Documents by Direction of the Historical Section Committee of Imperial Defence Military Operations Gallipoli* (2 vols, London, 1929–32), II, 5.
13 There are a number of overlapping explanations for the formation of the coalition; the principal variations are found in C. Hazlehurst, *Politicians at War* (London, 1971), 227–82; Pugh, 'First coalition'; P. Fraser, 'British war policy and the crisis of Liberalism in May 1915', *Journal of Modern History*, 54, 1 (1982), 1–26.
14 J. French to Kitchener, 17 May 1915, Robertson Papers I/5/1.
15 Kitchener to Wolfe Murray (the CIGS), n.d. (but late May 1915), Kitchener Papers, WO 159/3. Kitchener's rejection of French's views is in line with recent evaluations of the situation; see D. French, 'The military background to the "Shells Crisis" of May 1915', *Journal of Strategic Studies*, 2, 2 (1979), 192–205.
16 'The Dardanelles. Note by the War Office', 28 May 1915, Cab 37/128/27.
17 'The question of the Germans transferring large forces from the Eastern to the

Western theatre', n.s., n.d. (but late May 1915), WO 106/1524; unsigned (but Hankey) to Asquith, 29 May 1915, giving a report of Kitchener's views on strategy, Kitchener Papers, WO 159/7.

18 Robertson to Callwell, 31 May 1915, Robertson Papers I/8/23; 'Notes from conversations 4th June' taken by Major G. S. Clive, Robertson Papers I/5/13.

19 'Note of a meeting held at War Office', 8 June 1915, n.s., Kitchener Papers, WO 159/7, original emphasis.

20 Reported in J. French to Kitchener, 11 June 1915, WO 158/21.

21 'Reasons for the offensive in Flanders', n.s. (but Kitchener), 12 June 1915, Kitchener Papers, PRO 30/57/58.

22 Meeting of the Dardanelles Committee, 17 June 1915, Cab 42/3/4.

23 Hanbury Williams to Kitchener, 14 June 1915, Lloyd George Papers, D/17/6/17.

24 Knox's dispatch Z, 18 June 1915, WO 106/1063.

25 Hanbury Williams to Kitchener, 13 June 1915, Kitchener Papers, PRO 30/57/67.

26 Hanbury Williams to Kitchener, 16 and 17 June 1915, ibid.

27 Haig diary entry, 23 June 1915, Haig Papers 101; Cassar, *French and the Dardanelles*, 141–42.

28 Kitchener to J. French, 22 June 1915, Kitchener Papers, PRO 30/57/50.

29 J. French to Kitchener, 23 June 1915, WO 158/21.

30 'Notes on Chantilly Conference', n.s., 24 June 1915, Robertson Papers I/5/14.

31 'The future policy of the war', Hankey, 24 June 1915, Cab 37/130/26; 'A further note upon the general military situation', Churchill, 18 June 1915, as cited in Churchill, *World Crisis*, II, 401–8.

32 Edmonds, *France and Belgium, 1915*, II, 115–17.

33 'General situation', Balfour, 2 July 1915, Cab 37/131/4.

34 French to Kitchener, 26 June 1915, Kitchener Papers, PRO 30/57/50.

35 'Notes on W.S.C.'s memorandum', Robertson, 26 June 1915, Robertson Papers I/5/6.

36 Meeting of the Dardanelles Committee, 5 July 1915, Cab 42/3/7.

37 Yarde-Buller to Kitchener, 27 June 1915, Kitchener Papers, WO 159/10.

38 Meeting of the Dardanelles Committee, 5 July 1915, Cab 42/3/7.

39 See Neilson, 'Kitchener', 220–1 for a discussion of the conference.

40 Untitled account of the meeting at Chantilly, n.s., 6 July 1915, Kitchener Papers, WO 159/11.

41 Advanced in Magnus, *Kitchener*, 344–5 and debunked in Cassar, *Kitchener*, 381–2.

42 See the file of letters in WO 158/13.

43 Blair's dispatch LXXII, 27 July 1915, WO 106/996.

44 Buchanan to FO, 3 August 1915, Grey Papers, FO 800/75.

45 Grand Duke Nicholas to Kitchener, 17 July 1915, Kitchener Papers, PRO 30/57/67.

46 'General Staff note on the general military situation. 3rd August 1915', n.s. (but Robertson), 3 August 1915, Kitchener Papers WO 159/4. Evidence for Robertson's authorship in Robertson to Wigram and reply, 6 and 8 August 1915, Robertson Papers I/12/20–1.

47 Wigram to Robertson, 10 August 1915, Robertson Papers I/12/22.

48 Aspinall-Oglander, *Gallipoli*, II, 363; Wilson diary entry, 19 August 1915, Callwell, *Wilson Diaries*, I, 246.

49 Draft of Kitchener to Asquith, 17 August 1915, Kitchener Papers, WO 159/7; see also Haig diary entry, 19 August 1915, Haig Papers, 102.

50 Meeting of the Dardanelles Committee, 20 August 1915, Cab 42/3/16.

51 FO to Buchanan, 20 August 1915, FO 371/2450/116873.

52 'War policy, report, supplementary memoranda, proceedings, and appendices of a Cabinet Committee', Crewe, 30 October 1915, Cab 27/2.
53 My discussion of the political situation in Russia is based, except where otherwise noted, on Pearson, *Russian Moderates*, 28–64; Diakin, *Russkaia burzhuazia*, 72–127, and M. F. Hamm, 'Liberal politics in wartime Russia: an analysis of the Progressive Bloc', *Slavic Review*, 33, 3 (1974), 453–68.
54 On the Union of Towns and Zemstvos, see P. P. Gronsky and N. J. Astrov, *The War and the Russian Government* (New Haven, Conn., 1929), 171–97; A. P. Pogrebinskii, 'K istorii soiuzov zemstv i gorodov v gody imperialisticheskoi voiny', *Istoricheskie zapiski*, 12 (1941), 39–60; W. E. Gleason, 'The All-Russian Union of Towns and the Politics of Urban Reform in Tsarist Russia', *Russian Review*, 35, 3 (1976), 290–302; T. Fellows, 'Politics and the war effort in Russia: the Union of Zemstvos and the organization of food supplies', *Slavic Review*, 37, 1 (1978), 70–90.
55 On the War Industries Committees, see A. P. Pogrebinskii, 'Voennopromysh-lennye komitety', *Istoricheskie zapiski*, 11 (1941), 160–200; S. O. Zagorsky, *State Control of Industry in Russia during the War* (New Haven, Conn., 1928), 97–106.
56 Graf, 'Military rule', 390–411.
57 T. D. Krupina, 'Politicheskii krizis 1915 g. i sozdanie osobogo sobeshchaniia po oborone', *Istoricheskie zapiski*, 83 (1969), 62–3.
58 ibid., 64.
59 L. H. Siegelbaum, 'Moscow industrialists and the War-Industries committees during World War I', *Russian History*, 5, 1 (1978), 64–83.
60 Pogrebinskii, 'Voenno-promyshlennye komitety', 160–1.
61 Krupina, 'Politicheskii krizis', 64–72; Siegelbaum, 'Moscow industrialists', 73–8.
62 D. S. Babichev, 'Deiatelnost Russkogo pravitelstvennogo komiteta v Londone v gody pervoi mirovoi voiny (1914–1917)', *Istoricheskie zapiski*, 57 (1956), 280–5.
63 British membership is listed in *History of Ministry of Munitions*, II, pt VIII, 10–11; the Russian members and problems with the various names given the committee in Sidorov, *Ekonomicheskoe polozhenie*, 285 and the index.
64 See the discussions in 'Correspondence with the Ministry of Munitions of War', p. 4, War Office to Ministry of Munitions, 14 June 1915, Black Papers, Mun 4/524.
65 Knox's dispatch X, 30 May 1915, WO 106/1061.
66 See *History of Ministry of Munitions*, II, pt III.
67 Addison diary entries, 21 and 25 June 1915, Addison Papers, box 97.
68 'Minute of the Sub-Committee on Russian Munitions', n.s., 1 July 1915; 'Instructions for the guidance of Lieutenant Dumontier and M. Lamere . . . in the U.S.A.' n.s., n.d. (but July 1915), both in Mun 7/149.
69 Mun 4/207, entire file.
70 Minute by G. H. Villiers, 31 August 1915, FO 368/1399/121793.
71 Knox's dispatch A1, 4 July 1915, WO 106/1064.
72 Blair's dispatch LXXVI, 26 August 1915, WO 106/999.
73 'Memorandum on Russian munitions', Pares, July 1915, Lloyd George Papers, D/12/2/5.
74 'Memorandum on the steps taken by the British government to assist the Russian government in procuring supplies', Kitchener, 5 August 1915, FO 371/2454/110274.
75 Buchanan to FO, 8 June 1915, FO 371/2452/74462.
76 FO to Buchanan, 18 June 1915, ibid.

77 Buchanan to FO, 5 July 1915, FO, 371/2452/89692.
78 Buchanan to FO, 16 July 1915, FO 371/2452/96486; on the general British financial position in the United States, see two articles by K. Burk, 'The diplomacy of finance: British financial missions to the United States 1914–1918', *Historical Journal*, 22, 2 (1979), 351–3; and 'The mobilization of Anglo-American finance during World War I', in Dreziger (ed.), *Mobilization*, 25–8.
79 Note by E. F. Wise (of the Russian Purchasing Committee) of a conversation with Bradbury, 23 July 1915, Mun 4/5496; H. M. Hyde, *Lord Reading* (New York, 1967), 184–6.
80 Grey to McKenna, 24 July 1915, McKenna Papers 5/6.
81 Asquith to McKenna and reply, 25 and 26 July 1915; Asquith to McKenna, 26 July 1915, all in McKenna Papers 5/8.
82 Morgan to Morgan, Grenfell, 12 August 1915 and the attached note from Wise to Wintour, 12 August 1915, Mun 4/5500.
83 Morgan, Grenfell to Kitchener, 14 August 1915, Mun 4/5496.
84 'Memorandum' of a conversation with Bradbury, n.s., 20 August 1915, ibid.
85 Bradbury to Ministry of Munitions, 27 August 1915, Bradbury Papers, T 170/73.
86 Hanson to Bradbury, 31 August 1915, ibid.
87 Bradbury to Hanson, 31 August 1915, ibid.; Wintour to Sir F. Black (the DGMS), 18 August 1915, Mun 4/1369.
88 'A summary of the gold position', Keynes, 19 August 1915, Johnson (ed.), *Keynes*, XVI, 109, original emphasis.
89 'Protocol – Boulogne, August 22, 1915', n.s., T 172/256.
90 Burk, 'Diplomacy of finance', 353–4.
91 Lloyd George's testimony, 18 August 1915, Cab 37/132/28.
92 McKenna's testimony, 23 August 1915, Cab 37/133/9; Runciman's testimony, 19 August 1915, Cab 37/132/1. On Keynes's authorship of McKenna's position, see Johnson (ed.), *Keynes*, XVI, 110–15.
93 Kitchener's testimony, 24 August 1915, Cab 37/133/10.
94 Fraser, 'British war policy', 6–11.
95 Cassar, *French and the Dardanelles*, 151–2, 163–71; Tanenbaum, *Sarrail*, 59–63.
96 Meeting of the Dardanelles Committee, 3 September 1915, Cab 42/3/32.
97 A rumour was current at the time that the French had decided to abandon or postpone their attack; see Wigram to Robertson, 8 September 1915, Robertson Papers I/12/25.
98 'Proceedings of a meeting held at Calais', n.s., 11 September 1915, WO 158/13. For a general account, see Hankey, *Supreme Command*, I, 411–12.
99 'Proceedings of a meeting at Chantilly', n.s., 14 September 1915, WO 158/13.
100 Meeting of the Dardanelles Committee, 23 September 1915, Cab 42/3/28.
101 Grey to Buchanan, private and secret, 29 May 1915, FO 371/2448/67703.
102 Bax-Ironside to Grey, 4 June 1915, as cited in Lowe and Dockrill, 'Mirage of Power, II, 194.
103 Buchanan to Sazonov, 3 June 1915, as cited in Rieber, 'Russian diplomacy', 259.
104 Meeting of the Dardanelles Committee, 23 September 1915, Cab 42/3/28.
105 Meeting of the Dardanelles Committee, 24 September 1915, Cab 42/3/30.
106 Meeting of the Dardanelles Committee, 29 September 1915, Cab 42/3/34.
107 Grey to Sir C. Greene (British ambassador to Tokyo), 17 and 24 August 1915, Cab 37/132/24 and Cab 37/133/11.
108 Wintour to Addison, 9 September 1915, Addison Papers, box 9, file 'Russia – Munitions'; Lloyd George to Russian War Office, 11 September 1915, Lloyd George Papers, D/19/15/1.

109 Wintour to Addison, 9 September 1915, Addison Papers, box 9, file 'Russia – Munitions'; 'Memorandum', Kitchener, September 1915, especially 5–10.
110 Blair's dispatch LXXVI, 26 August 1915, WO 106/999.
111 Addison diary entry, 19 September 1915, Addison Papers, box 97.
112 Meeting of the Dardanelles Committee, 29 September 1915, Cab 42/3/34.
113 Buchanan to FO, 30 August 1915, FO 371/2452/122285; Buchanan to FO, 6 September 1915, FO 371/2452/126556.
114 'Russian credits', Bradbury, 16 September 1915, Bradbury Papers, T 170/73.
115 The text of agreement is in T 172/255. The conference itself is discussed in B. E. Nolde, *Russia in the Economic War* (New Haven, Conn., 1928), 146–51; Sidorov, *Finansovoe polozhenie*, 259–76.
116 'Appreciation by the General Staff of the actual and prospective military situation in the various theatres of war – 2nd October 1915', A. Murray, Cab 42/4/2, annexe 1.
117 Meeting of the Dardanelles Committee, 4 October 1915, Cab 42/4/2.
118 Esher to Kitchener, 3 October 1915, Kitchener Papers, PRO 30/57/59.
119 'Proces verbaux Conference de Chantilly', n.s., 8 October 1915, Kitchener Papers, WO 159/7.
120 'Conference de Calais du 5 Octobre 1915', n.s., 5 October 1915, ibid.
121 Aspinall-Oglander, *Gallipoli*, II, 382.
122 Meeting of the Dardanelles Committee, 11 October 1915, Cab 42/4/6.
123 'A statement of the views of the General Staff on a question raised at the War Council . . . in regard to . . . the Balkan situation', A. Murray, 13 October 1915, Kitchener Papers, WO 159/4.
124 Haig diary entry, 17 October 1915, Haig Papers 103.
125 Magnus, *Kitchener*, 356–7 and Callwell to Robertson, 23 October 1915, Robertson Papers I/8/30 for Kitchener's 'obsession' with Egypt.
126 Blair's dispatch LXXX, 4 October 1915, WO 106/1003.
127 See the exchange of telegrams between Buchanan and Grey in mid-October 1915, Grey Papers, FO 800/75.
128 Knox's dispatch G2, 12 October 1915, WO 106/1071.
129 Meeting of the Dardanelles Committee, 25 October 1915, Cab 42/4/7.
130 Blair's dispatch LXXXI, 22 October 1915, WO 106/1004; Benckendorff to FO, 25 October 1915, FO 371/2457/159969.
131 Grey to Lloyd George, 26 October 1915, Grey Papers, FO 800/99.
132 Von Donop to Grey, 27 October 1915, Nicolson Papers, FO 800/380, original emphasis.
133 As contained in A. Nicolson to Grey, 28 October 1915, ibid.
134 Meeting of the Dardanelles Committee, 27 October 1915, Cab 42/2/18.
135 Robertson even asked Haig to speak to the King; Haig diary entry, 24 October 1915, Haig Papers 104.
136 Robertson to Callwell, 23 October 1915, Robertson Papers I/8/29.
137 Cassar, *French and the Dardanelles*, 209.
138 Meeting of the Dardanelles Committee, 25 October 1915, Cab 42/4/17. On the French political crisis, see D. J. Dutton, 'The union sacrée and the French Cabinet crisis of October 1915', *European Studies Review*, 8 (1978), 411–24, and M. M. Farrar, 'Politics versus patriotism: Alexandre Millerand as French Minister of War', *French Historical Studies*, 11, 4 (1980), 602–5.
139 Kitchener to Asquith, 5 November 1915, Kitchener Papers, PRO 30/57/76.
140 Blair's dispatch LXXXII, 1 November 1915, WO 106/1005; Buchanan to FO, 30 October 1915, FO 371/2457/161373.
141 Robertson to A. Murray, 3 November 1915, Robertson Papers I/9/23/1.
142 Meeting of the War Committee, 6 November 1915, Cab 42/5/4.

143 Meeting of the War Committee, 8 November 1915, Cab 42/5/15.
144 'Memorandum on the conduct of the war', Robertson, 5 November 1915, Cab 24/1/G 33.
145 'Project for combined naval and military operations . . . with a view to preventing the enemy using Ostend as a submarine base', General Staff, WO and Admiralty War Staff, 12 November 1915, Robertson Papers I/9/25/2.
146 Meeting of the War Committee, 13 November 1915, Cab 42/5/10.
147 Grey to Buchanan, private and secret, 16 November 1915, Grey Papers, FO 800/75.
148 Buchanan to Grey, private and secret, 17 November 1915; minute by A. Nicolson, 20 November 1915, ibid.
149 'Gallipoli', Balfour, 19 November 1915, Robertson Papers I/9/29.
150 Untitled memorandum, 22 November 1915, Robertson Papers I/9/33.
151 Meeting of the War Committee, 23 November 1915, Cab 42/5/20. The plan was seriously meant by the Russians as a means both of aiding Serbia and strengthening Russian claims to Constantinople; see V. A. Emets, 'Pozitsiia Rossii i ee soiuznikov v voprose o pomoshchi Serbii oseniu 1915 g.', *Istoricheskie zapiski*, 75 (1965), 132–6.
152 'Summary of arguments for and against the complete or partial evacuation of Gallipoli', A. Murray, 22 November 1915, Cab 42/5/20.
153 Untitled memorandum, Curzon, 25 November 1915, Cab 37/138/12; 'The future military policy at the Dardanelles', Hankey, 29 November 1915, Cab 42/5/25.
154 Meeting of the War Committee, 1 December 1915, Cab 42/6/1.
155 Translation of a paper by Joffre, 30 November 1915, WO 158/13.
156 Untitled note, Benckendorff to FO, 2 December 1915, FO 371/2457/184297.
157 Captain Doumayrou (the French liaison officer assigned to Kitchener) to Kitchener, n.d. (but early December 1915), Kitchener Papers PRO 30/57/57. On Alekseev's new military plans, see Emets, 'Pozitsiia Rossii', 138–9.
158 Grey to Kitchener, 4 December 1915, Kitchener Papers, PRO 30/57/77.
159 D. J. Dutton, 'The Calais Conference of December 1915', *Historical Journal*, 21, 1 (1978), 144–50; Cassar, *French and the Dardanelles*, 230–2; Tanenbaum, *Sarrail*, 81–3.
160 Dutton, 'Calais Conference', 151–2.
161 My account of the conference comes from 'Meeting at Chantilly 6 December 1915', n.s., n.d., WO 106/1454; 'Dossier de la conférence entre les représentatants des Armées Alliées (tenus à Chantilly les 6, 7 et 8 Décembre 1915)', n.s., n.d., WO 106/391; and Edmonds, *France and Belgium 1916*, I, 5–11.
162 Rostunov, *Russkii front*, 279–82.
163 As cited in V. A. Emets, 'Protivorechiia mezhdu Rossiei i soiuznikami po voprosu o vstuplenii Rumynii v voinu (1915–1916 gg)', *Istoricheskie zapiski*, 56 (1956), 60.
164 See Emets, 'Pozitsiia Rossii', 141–5 for the Russian insistence.
165 Cassar, *Kitchener*, 434; Dutton, 'Calais Conference', 154–5. Meeting of the War Cabinet, 8 December 1915, Cab 42/6/6.
166 Kitchener to Asquith, 10 December 1915, Kitchener Papers, PRO 30/57/76.
167 Cassar argues that the campaign for a Balkan offensive was orchestrated by the French, see *French and the Dardanelles*, 234, an argument supported by Tanenbaum, *Sarrail*, 82–3. The Russians had their own motives; see Emets, 'Pozitsiia Rossii', 144–5.
168 'A note by the General Staff on General Alexeieff's suggested plan of campaign', A. Murray, 10 December 1915, Cab 42/6/7.

169   The Rusin mission is discussed in A. L. Sidorov, 'Missiia v Angliiu i Frantsiiu po voprosu snabzheniia Rossii predmetami vooruzheniia', *Istoricheskii arkhiv*, 4 (1949), 351–86.

170   Untitled memorandum, Booth, 22 October 1915, Mun 5/136/1010. All comments are attached to the memorandum.

171   'Memorandum', n.s., 2 November 1915, Llewellyn Smith Papers, Mun 4/7054.

172   'Confidential' memorandum, Booth, 2 November 1915, Black Papers, Mun 4/533.

173   See the explanation of the procedure for buying supplies for Russia in Mun 7/149.

174   'Note on memorandum on munitions contracts for the Allies', n.s. (but Hanson), n.d. (but seen by Ellershaw, 20 November 1915), ibid.

175   The minutes of the conference are in Mun 4/5068.

176   'Conference between the representatives of the Allied governments', 23 November 1915, ibid.

177   Second day, 24 November 1915, ibid.

178   Meeting of the British and French delegates, 24 November 1915, ibid.

179   'Discussion between British, French and Russian delegates', 24 November 1915, ibid.

180   Extract from meeting of the War Committee, 25 November 1915, Cab 37/138/4.

181   'Discussion between British and Russian delegates', n.s., 25 November 1915, Mun 4/5068.

182   'Summary of conclusions', 1 December 1915, ibid.

183   Addison diary entry, 25 November 1915, Addison Papers, box 97.

4

The General Staff and Russia

By the end of 1915 the transitional period in British strategy was complete. Throughout 1916 the British were to be committed to a policy which called for the defeat of the Central Powers by means of an offensive in France. Russia was no longer the saviour which would prevent the invasion of Britain and win the war single-handedly. However, the basic importance of Russia to the *Entente* and her influence on British strategy remained substantial.

Much of the strategic debate of 1916 had been foreshadowed the previous autumn. In 1915 the debate over Serbia had been not simply a matter of that country alone, or even of the Balkans. It had involved an evaluation of whether or not military action (or inaction) was acceptable in Petrograd on a diplomatic level and likely to aid Russia on a military one. It had been only the added diplomatic pressure from Russia which had decided the British to maintain their force at Salonika. Arguments as to the adverse impact of withdrawal from the Dardanelles on Russia had played a major role in strategic discussions. In 1916 similar arguments centred around Romania.

In some ways, the argument between Lloyd George and the General Staff reduced itself to a dialogue concerning the most effective means of helping the Russians to help the Allies win the war. Both sides in the debate recognised the need for Russia to acquire the requisite munitions and supplies to renew the offensive, but they varied both in their belief as to the impact that this offensive would have on the course of the war and on the role that the other Allies should play in co-operation with the Russians. Lloyd George felt that if the Russians were resupplied they could win a decisive victory over the Germans in the east. The British could best contribute to this by attacking through the Balkans, detaching the German allies by such means and hence avoiding bloody and useless battles in France. Men like Robertson did not share Lloyd George's beliefs. The CIGS did not feel either that Russia could win a decisive victory by herself in the east or that a Balkan offensive by the western Allies would hinder Germany's war effort seriously. In the General Staff's view, only a concerted attack on the main fronts by a British army in France and by a resupplied Russian army in the east would yield the desired victory against the Central Powers.

The views of the General Staff were largely dominant throughout 1916, the first year of what one historian has called 'the age of Robertson'.[1] When he became CIGS on 23 December 1915, Robertson inherited a situation completely different from the one which had been left to Kitchener in August 1914. By the beginning of 1916, the British army was on a par with that of its continental Allies. No longer were France and Russia the dominant partners on land, with Britain serving only as an adjunct to their forces. In a contradiction of Admiral Fisher's well-known prewar remark, Britain had managed to create an equivalent to the German army as well as having the Royal Navy. In fact, considering that Britain had reserves of men and financial resources as yet uncommitted to the war, her strength in the *Entente* was waxing. With respect to strategy, this meant that Robertson was no longer bound to follow the Russian lead as slavishly as had Kitchener. Given a freer hand by the increased British military strength, the CIGS's primary concern was to ensure that the efforts of all the Allies were co-ordinated carefully. This concern was shared by the Russians. The major quarrel which emerged between Robertson and the Russians during 1916 was over the Balkans. The ongoing Russian support for an attack at Salonika irritated the CIGS and provided support for his political critics.

Robertson's first task as CIGS was a domestic one. It was evident to him that the government must accept the decisions taken at Chantilly as official policy before anything could be undertaken in 1916. At the meeting of the War Committee on 23 December, Robertson called for an immediate evacuation of the Dardanelles in line with the Chantilly proceedings.[2] Balfour objected to such a course. The First Lord argued that Russian opinion about withdrawal should be determined prior to a British decision, given the concern that Russia had evinced about the Balkans generally. Robertson pointed out that the Russians had agreed at Chantilly to the British leaving the Dardanelles, but little store was placed on the value of the opinion of the Russian representative at that meeting. Balfour asked Robertson what the 'real opinion' of Russian military authorities was about evacuation and the CIGS was forced to reply that he 'did not know'. It was indicative of the new driving power in the War Committee which Robertson personified that it was decided that a purely British decision would be reached on the Dardanelles and that this would then be communicated to the Russians. Old habits died hard, however; Balfour sent a note to Hankey outlining his objections to the War Committee's decision.[3] At the next meeting of the War Committee on 28 December, Robertson tried to commit the government further to the Chantilly decisions. In a paper prepared by Murray just before he resigned as CIGS, the General Staff's view was placed clearly before the War Committee.[4]

Murray's paper was an examination of all the possible fronts where British efforts could be made in 1916. Its conclusion was that the most promising location was in France. It pointed out that the Western front was where the British could strike the heaviest blow, and that the Russians, 'strained to their utmost power to hold their own main front if seriously attacked', could not spare forces to co-operate with the Allies in secondary theatres such as the Balkans. In fact, in the opinion of the General Staff the Balkans were best avoided altogether. By following this latter course, Murray argued, the army of Bulgaria and that of Romania (should the latter become hostile) could be kept isolated in the peninsula. Such a view was not acceptable to Balfour. Balfour argued, as Robertson wrote to Haig a few days later, that the Western front was 'so strong that we should transfer all possible troops to co-operate with Russia on the Eastern front'.[5] This scheme, the CIGS noted in the same letter, was so irritating to him that 'words failed me, and I lost my temper.' Despite such opposition the General Staff's view was triumphant. The final conclusions of the War Committee on the 28th were a recognition of France as the main theatre for the British, an acknowledgement that 'every effort is to be made to prepare for carrying out offensive operations' in the coming months and an acceptance of the idea that secondary theatres were to be maintained only with forces large enough for defensive purposes.

Having achieved this, Robertson turned his attention to Russia. The key to the General Staff's plan was co-ordination with and accurate information about Russia. As Haig wrote to Robertson, the 'actual date' of the British offensive in France 'depend[ed] on the date when Russia can act', and the British commander went on to say that Robertson therefore needed to 'take the required steps to get a *true* statement of the Russian situation.'[6] To do so, Robertson sent

General Callwell, who had just been replaced as DMO by General
Maurice, to Russia. As the CIGS wrote to Haig, Callwell's mission
was to discover the 'real state of affairs' in Russia as well as to obtain
some 'good and useful' information about Russia's intentions.[7] To
date, Robertson had found the Russian General Staff 'tiresome' in its
continuing concern over the Balkans. General Alekseev, the Chief of
Staff, continued to press for a joint Allied offensive in the Balkans,
while the Grand Duke Nicholas, now commanding the Russian
forces in the Caucasus, advocated a combined Anglo-Russian action
in Persia. Robertson naturally opposed both of these plans, and
hoped that Callwell could determine just how seriously they were
proposed by the Russians.

Meanwhile, Robertson was experiencing difficulties in keeping
the government committed to the plans agreed upon on 28
December. McKenna, the Chancellor of the Exchequer, raised a
series of economic and financial arguments which threatened the
plans for the Western front in 1916.[8] McKenna was concerned about
the costs of the equipment necessary for the New Armies as well as
with the related issue of the effect on the economy caused by the
withdrawal of so many men from industry for the army. A further
argument was made by Balfour. At the War Committee meeting on
13 January, the First Lord introduced a memorandum calling for a
delay of any offensive until the summer at which time the Russians
would be prepared fully and the British forces entirely equipped.[9] In
the discussion which followed, the overall question of Russian
munitions was aired, with concern voiced that until some accurate
estimate of Russian production and needs was obtained it was
impossible to know how much Russia could be counted on militarily
in 1916. The final decision of the meeting reflected the concern of
the War Committee. The resolution of 28 December 1915 that 'every
effort is to be made to prepare for carrying out offensive operations
. . .' was modified by adding the phrase 'without necessarily
committing ourselves to offensive operations'. This of course made
the original resolution meaningless, and Robertson wrote to Haig
that 'in general there is a good deal of wobbling'.[10]

In addition to the concerns of the British politicians not to attack
before the Russians were ready, Joffre was exhibiting a similar
tendency to delay the French attack. What the French commander
preferred was that the British begin wearing down attacks while the
French prepared their major blow.[11] Both Robertson and Haig

opposed such an idea. They feared that Germany might turn against Russia before the latter was prepared and that the sooner Britain and France were both ready, the sooner they could counter such action.[12] In order to sort matters out a conference with Joffre was arranged by Haig for 22 January. Robertson for his part managed to win over Balfour, his most severe Cabinet critic, to an acceptance of making preparations for an advance on the Western front. To do so, Robertson had to agree that no advance would take place before all preparations were complete unless it became necessary to save Russia from a German attack.[13]

At the conference between French and British military representatives which was held on the 22nd, Robertson pressed Joffre to explain why the latter felt that the Russians would not be able to mount an offensive until July.[14] The CIGS pointed out that Knox was certain that the Russians would be prepared much sooner. Joffre said that his opinion was based on considerations of climate and transportation, and that he felt that the Russians could be ready no sooner than June. When Robertson mentioned his belief that the Germans might attack Russia prior to this date, Joffre replied that such an occurrence would be '*très avantageuse*' for the Allies. '*Les allemands*', Joffre went on, '*ne pourraient obtenir en Russie de succès décisifs et nous prendrions l'offensive avec toutes nos forces sur notre front.*' To prepare for such an eventuality, Joffre considered that the Anglo-French forces must be ready to attack by the end of April.

While the British were no doubt pleased to hear that Joffre agreed on the course of action to be taken should Russia be attacked, Robertson felt that there was a possibility of friction in the Allied plans.[15] The decisions of Chantilly had called for all of the Allies to be ready for a simultaneous offensive in March. Joffre now wanted British and Russian 'wearing-down attacks' in April to precede a main French offensive. Robertson favoured a further conference to work out a new plan of action. He preferred that all of the Allies should prepare for an early offensive in case of the pre-emptive German attack, with the date of the Allied offensive (in the absence of a German blow) to 'depend mainly upon when Russia is ready'. The British and French component of this offensive, Robertson felt, should begin about a month before the Russian one. This he held for two reasons: first, the two western Allies could be ready before the Russians and second, the 'wearing-down attacks' should be planned as a logical precursor to and initial component of the main attack.

Haig accepted Robertson's views and advocated such a plan to Joffre on 1 February. For his part, Joffre largely agreed with the CIGS's plan, but preferred to maintain the 'wearing-down attacks' as an element independent of the main attack.[16]

Early in February the two related issues of Romania and Salonika were raised again.[17] Since the collapse of Serbia, the Central Powers had put pressure on Romania to join them. Bratianu, the Romanian Foreign Minister, insisted that Russia dispatch troops to the Danube in order to protect Romania from possible Bulgarian attack before Romania would accept any sort of military arrangement with Russia.[18] Alekseev opposed such a move. The Russian Chief of Staff preferred that Romania remain neutral since 'the burden of defending Romania will fall on us.'[19] Should Romania not be satisfied with this and threaten to join the Central Powers, Alekseev planned to concentrate his army in Moldavia against the Austro-German flank. Romania's forces could then concentrate in the south in conjunction with the Allied forces at Salonika.

Robertson proposed to discuss the entire issue with Joffre at a meeting of the British and French high commands at Chantilly on 14 February. Joffre felt that Salonika was a political and not a military issue.[20] The French Commander-in-Chief noted that a further 100,000 troops sent to Salonika (making a total of 400,000) might serve to induce Romania to join the Allies. Robertson demurred and argued that Romania could best be protected against the Germans by a British and French attack on the Western front. A few days later, Robertson wrote to Hanbury Williams to 'do all you can' to point out to Alekseev the problems inherent in a Balkan offensive.[21] While the Salonikan-Romanian issue remained undecided, the other results of the Chantilly conference were in line with Robertson's earlier proposals. Joffre agreed that the British concept of the 'wearing-down attacks' as an integral part of the main offensive should be adopted and the offensive itself was scheduled to begin about 1 July 1916.[22] Ironically, while it was agreed formally that a German offensive against Russia must be met by an immediate Anglo-French attack in the west, no discussion occurred as to the best course of action should a German thrust occur in the west. A letter from Haig to Joffre raising this very point was not sent until 20 February, too late to influence the battle of Verdun which began the following day.[23]

The Russians still did not accept the idea that an Allied offensive in the west would be the best aid for the Balkans. Alekseev, wrote Hanbury Williams, still preferred to clear the Balkans rather than have the Allies attack in France, and was encouraged in this contention by the French. Robertson should, Hanbury Williams advised, inform the Russians clearly that British aid would be forthcoming only in France, ending all the speculation concerning a Salonikan offensive.[24] At this same time, Robertson attempted to settle the Salonikan issue by other means. At the War Committee meeting of 22 February, he proposed that Britain make a separate peace with Turkey, ending the need for Allied involvement in the Balkans while at the same time opening the Straits.[25] Grey rejected such a course. In his view Russia remained in the war only in the expectation that she would obtain Constantinople. To deny her this prize, Grey opined, would be 'fatal'. Balfour concurred with this evaluation and Grey pointed out that of all the Allies only Britain could not end the war at present on 'tolerable' terms. He put the matter clearly when he stated that '[we are] therefore dependent upon the Allies for our safety to a greater extent than they are upon us.'[26] Grey also made it plain that there was more involved than just Salonika. In a letter to Kitchener, written a week after the meeting of the War Committee, the Foreign Secretary noted that it was essential to attempt to supply Romania in order to counteract German attempts to win her over to the side of the Central Powers.[27] Since Russia was attempting to negotiate a military convention between herself and Romania, any idea of a separate peace with Turkey would undermine all the Allied efforts in the Balkans.[28]

The attack on Verdun changed the entire situation. Desperate for assistance, the French cast around for a means to divert enemy troops from the Western front. Suspecting that the Russians were being too difficult in their negotiations with Romania, the French began supporting the Romanian position. At the same time, Sarrail was instructed to hold as many of the enemy at Salonika as he could by feigning preparations for an offensive.[29] The French interference infuriated the Russians. On 8 March a conference held at *Stavka* under the chairmanship of the Emperor decided that the solution to the Romanian issue lay in the defeat of the Central Powers.[30] This in fact dovetailed nicely with the views of Joffre and the British, although not with those of many high-ranking French politicians who still favoured the eastern approach. For Robertson, Joffre's abandonment of any support for Salonika was amusing, but the

CIGS was pleased that it had occurred.[31] On 12 March the Allied representatives met at Chantilly and agreed that all forces possible should be concentrated in the main theatres.[32]

Within the British government, there was great worry that there would be no co-ordination between the Allied offensives which had been agreed to at Chantilly. This was particularly worrisome with respect to Russia, since the War Committee felt that General Zhilinskii 'knew nothing' of the Russian plans.[33] The general impression gathered at Chantilly by the British was that the Russians were anxious to get an offensive underway, an impression reinforced by reports from Knox that the situation on the Russian front was much improved with respect to both munitions and morale.[34]

On 18 March the Russians began their ill-fated offensive at Lake Narotch. This attack was a direct result of the decision taken at *Stavka* ten days earlier to pursue direct efforts against the Central Powers in an effort to ease the pressure on the French. Since the British had not been informed in advance of the offensive at Lake Narotch, it served to confirm the fears of those who had warned that the Allies would fail to co-ordinate their efforts in 1916.[35] Both Balfour and Lloyd George urged the War Committee on 21 March that every effort was to be made to ensure closer co-operation between the Allies in the future.[36] The entire question of inter-Allied co-operation was raised at a meeting of military representatives held in Paris a week later. At Paris the British representatives again pressed the French for a withdrawal from Salonika or at least an end to any talk of an offensive there. In addition, Robertson pressed for the acceptance of Joffre's proposals for a combined offensive by all the powers on the major fronts. The problem, as Robertson explained to the War Committee a week later, was Russia.[37] Despite numerous telegrams which the CIGS had sent to Alekseev via Hanbury Williams, the Russian Chief of Staff had been unwilling to specify that Russia would not undertake an advance before the other Allies were ready.[38]

Throughout April the War Committee remained concerned about Russia's intentions. The Russian feeling was that it was best to attack now while their limited amount of munitions lasted; any delay would make an offensive impossible due to the losses in supplies caused by normal wastage. In fact, such arguments were more in the way of an excuse than anything else. Lake Narotch had dealt a paralysing blow to the confidence of *Stavka* and many of those there now believed that victory could be achieved only if an overwhelming superiority in material existed on the Russian side.[39] Despite this, the War Committee was concerned that Russia might collapse if nothing were done to aid her. Major efforts, which will be discussed in detail in the following chapter, were made to provide supplies and financial aid to Russia. In addition, on 28 April the War Committee asked Robertson to investigate the possibility of giving Russia military assistance in theatres other than the western should Russia undertake an independent premature advance.[40]

Robertson put his views to a meeting of the War Committee on 3 May.[41] He stated that Alekseev proposed to begin his offensive about the middle of May, and that a plan for a British attack must be decided 'at once' if it was to be carried out in time to help the Russians. The possible theatres where the British could aid the Russians Robertson saw as five: Mesopotamia, Syria, the Balkans, the German coast and France. The first alternative, Mesopotamia, Robertson dismissed due to the problems of 'defective communication', while the second, Syria, required a force of eight divisions which the British did not have to spare. In addition, a Syrian campaign would require 'many months' of organisation and put a 'greater strain' than could be borne on shipping. The idea of an assault on the north German coast Robertson objected to as 'hazardous', leaving only the Balkans and the Western front for serious consideration. The value of a Balkan attack Robertson thought was its effect on Bulgaria and Romania. Russia would be aided only if such an attack prevented Bulgaria from attacking Russia on the main Eastern front or if it would induce Romania to join the Allies, and as far as this latter was concerned Robertson felt that the possibility of it was 'problematical'. The best course of action, Robertson argued, was an attack in France which would ensure that the Germans were not able to transfer troops to the east and might even 'compel' them to shift troops from Russia to France. Should Germany risk transferring troops to the east, the British and French would make 'her pay for denuding the Western front by attacking her with all the force with which we are capable.' These arguments were not accepted unreservedly by the War Committee. It instructed Robertson to examine again the feasibility of a Balkan offensive in conjunction with Joffre before it was excluded as an alternative to an offensive in France.

Such hesitation as the War Committee displayed was evident as

well in Russia. During the first week of May, Alekseev and Joffre
agreed to delay the Russian offensive, the former without informing
the British of this decision.[42] Robertson's reaction to this indicated
both his irritation with his Allies and the lack of co-ordination which
existed between Britain and Russia. As Robertson wrote to Hanbury
Williams on 8 May, the Russian action 'affords a further proof that
neither our general contribution to the war which far exceeds that of
any other Power, nor the necessity for co-operation with us are
sufficiently recognised by Russian GHQ.'[43] The reason for the
Russian decision, Hanbury Williams replied, was evident. Since the
'menace of [an] enemy offensive on [the] Russian front [was] now
considered less immediate . . . [the] Russians themselves feel the
necessity before taking the initiative of accumulating [a] greater
supply of heavy shell.' As to why the British were not informed
separately of this decision, Hanbury Williams wrote that 'there is
undoubtedly a feeling prevalent here that Joffre is commanding both
[the] French and British forces and that in consequence it is
unnecessary to repeat to [the] British French Army information as
they [the British] will obtain it from French sources.'[44]

Robertson's reaction to the Russian decision should not be taken
as resulting from any desire to launch an offensive in the west
prematurely. Haig was opposed to taking the initiative in the west
until the British were 'quite ready' and the CIGS shared these
sentiments.[45] When Joffre wrote to Robertson on 10 May, outlining
the reasons for Alekseev's delay, Robertson's reply made it clear that
his earlier anger was merely a result of not being consulted about or
informed of the Russian decision.[46] In fact, the CIGS was worried
that his agreement to delay the offensive in the west until the
Russians were ready might disturb Joffre and so, as he told Haig, the
CIGS had couched his agreement in mild terms so as not to 'frighten
the old man'. Haig replied that he, too, did not wish to begin
prematurely; when the Allied blow fell it was essential that it was a
'real one'.[47]

Meanwhile, in line with the War Committee's decision of 3 May,
the matter of a Balkan offensive had been discussed with Joffre at
Chantilly on 15 May.[48] At this meeting, the French Commander-in-
Chief made his support for an attack at Salonika evident. Political
pressure had been brought to bear on Joffre throughout the last ten
days of April, and Briand, the French president, had convinced
Joffre that support for Sarrail was essential for both their careers.[49]

The British did not agree. The Director of Military Operations, General Maurice, pointed out to Joffre the difficulties in transportation involved in maintaining the British forces at Salonika but met Joffre at his most uncooperative. Not even when Maurice pointed out that shortages of tonnage would require that shipping found for Salonika would have to come from that allotted to France and Russia for the transport of munitions would Joffre budge from his position. The French Commander-in-Chief was adamant on two points. First, a Balkan offensive was necessary in order to bring in Romania on the Allied side. Second, an offensive in the west must occur, beginning around 1 July in co-ordination with the Russian attack in the east.

Robertson was not taken by this Balkan suggestion, nor by the initiative put forward by the French government suggesting that divisions from Egypt, ticketed for France, be diverted to Salonika.[50] In a paper which he prepared for the War Committee, the CIGS rebutted Joffre's arguments, and made his support for an attack in the west clear.[51] On 17 May the War Committee accepted Robertson's arguments and made it evident that the French proposals were unacceptable. Romanian intervention was deemed to be uncertain, Bulgarian collapse unlikely and the best course of action was said to be the diversion of the bulk of the Allied forces at Salonika to the Western front.[52] Despite this categorical rejection, the matter of a Balkan offensive continued to be raised until the beginning of June when Robertson again attempted to dampen any lingering Russian enthusiasm for such a project.[53]

While the wrangling over the Balkans continued, final plans were being made for what became the Somme offensive. By 24 May the readiness of the Russians to begin the offensive and the damage being done to French morale and manpower at Verdun made Joffre suggest that the summer offensive should begin early in July.[54] Two days later, Joffre formally proposed beginning on 1 July. Haig noted that he would prefer to wait until August, but when Joffre exploded that 'the French Army would cease to exist, if we did nothing till then', the British commander agreed to the earlier starting date.[55] On 31 May Joffre, accompanied by Poincaré, the French President, Briand, the Prime Minister, and General Roques, the Minister of War, again visited Haig, and the latter once more stated that he would be willing to join in a joint offensive on 1 July.[56]

A further Russian suggestion of a Balkan offensive and the intricacies of French internal politics led, early in June, to a

conference in London between the British and French. When this
meeting opened on 9 June, Briand and Joffre pointed out that both
Italy and Russia were willing to provide some troops for an offensive
at Salonika.[57] They laid stress on the fact that a failure by the Allies
to take the initiative would allow the Bulgars to choose the place and
time for an attack, and noted that an Allied success might bring in
both Greece and Romania on the side of the *Entente*. The British
were not impressed by such arguments. As Robertson wrote to
Hanbury Williams the following day concerning a Balkan attack,
'our Government and General Staff have consistently objected from
the first to a Balkan campaign, and [have never] agreed either
directly or indirectly to co-operate in such a campaign.'[58]

With the unexpected success of the Brusilov offensive and the
beginning of the Somme attack, British concern with Russia during
the rest of June and early July centred mainly around issues
involving munitions. However, by the end of the first week of July,
the question of a Salonikan offensive was raised yet again. A note by
the French ambassador in London, Paul Cambon, called for an
offensive at Salonika designed to draw in Romania. General Alekseev
and Cadorna (the Italian Commander-in-Chief), the note pointed
out, both favoured such a course. Robertson's rebuttal at the
meeting of the War Committee on 6 July was concise.[59] In
Robertson's opinion the situation had not changed since his
memorandum of 16 May which had pointed out how unlikely a
Balkan success was. 'I am convinced', wrote Robertson, 'that if
Romania can be induced to come into the war on our side this year it
will be because of the successes obtained by the Russians and not
due to any efforts at Salonika.' A Balkan offensive would be, in the
CIGS's words, 'useless and unjustifiable'; a waste of troops and a
drain on resources. Robertson's arguments carried the day at the
War Committee. A reply to Cambon's note was drafted which said
that the Allies should attack at Salonika when and if Romania's
armed forces took the field. This attitude found its parallel in
Petrograd, where the French ambassador was informed that
Romanian entry after Russia had won a 'victory over Austria-
Hungary at great cost [would] be not only superfluous but
undesirable'. Robertson was satisfied with this decision, very
optimistic in general about the course of the war, but unhappy with
the continued French insistence about Salonika.[60] Such unhappiness
was bound to increase.

On 18 July the French suggested that a military convention be signed with Romania. This suggestion was taken up at the War Committee the same day with discussion soon turning to the related question of providing supplies for Romania.[61] Lloyd George attempted to introduce his Salonikan project indirectly by wondering whether a direct supply route to Romania could be created militarily by advancing through Bulgaria. In reply Robertson again paraded his familiar arguments. He felt that the possibility of piercing the Bulgarian lines was 'very problematic', that the French suggestion was based on a desire to create a combined Anglo-French force under Sarrail's command, and that the Romanians would not be able to take the field until after the 1 August date stipulated by both the French and the Russians. In short, he felt that the British must stick by the decision of 6 July not to begin any advance until the Romanians actually committed themselves. Others were not convinced. Andrew Bonar Law, the leader of the Unionists and Colonial Secretary in the coalition government, felt that it was not wise to delay a decision on the matter since 'Romania might be of great importance to Russia.' Robertson added, in light of the recently concluded inter-Allied conference on munitions, that to supply the Romanians and to mount an offensive in the Balkans would put an enormous strain on the available tonnage. With no set agreement, it was decided by the War Committee to authorise talks about Romania with the French, to approve in principle a loan to the Romanians and to investigate the matters concerning tonnage which Robertson had raised.

All of these points were discussed again two days later.[62] At that time Robertson found himself with increased support. Balfour pointed out that if Romania were to be supplied at the expense of Russia 'the less Russia would be able to do on the Eastern front'. Lord Curzon, who now headed the Shipping Control Committee which dealt with the allocation of tonnage for the Allies, noted that all this 'merry' talk about Salonika had occurred before the question of transport had been discussed. He projected a need for a hundred extra ships at Salonika in order to make an offensive possible. Given such discouraging technical opinion, the War Committee decided that Robertson should go to Paris the following day to discuss the proposed Romanian military convention, but that the British position should be based on the decision reached on 6 July.

While Robertson attended the meetings in Paris, he characterised his stay there as 'wasted' time in his report to the War Committee on 28 July.[63] The Romanians were unwilling to be committed to a definite attack, and Robertson was not hopeful of their doing so in the future. As Robertson telegraphed to Hanbury Williams, for transmission to Alekseev, 'firm language' with Romania was more likely to obtain results than 'undignified begging and haggling over details'.[64] Alekseev, too, was tired of dealing with the Romanians. He had long argued that Romanian intervention must be tied to an attack by them against Bulgaria, but by the end of July had decided that further negotiations were unnecessary provided that Romania agreed to enter the war immediately.[65]

It should not be inferred from Robertson's remarks that he was opposed in principle to aiding Romania. As he wrote to Grey on 1 August, what the CIGS wished to avoid was committing the Allies to aiding Romania 'before Roumania *definitely* comes in [since] until the Bulgars reduce their forces we have *no* prospect of doing any good.'[66] Like Alekseev, the CIGS wanted something on paper from the Romanians. Until this was to occur, Robertson suggested that diplomatic means be used to solve the Balkan imbroglio.[67] In suggesting that Bulgaria be separated from the Central Powers, Robertson returned to a theme which he had pursued as early as 22 February.[68] At that time he had argued that a separate peace with Turkey would end the difficulties in the Balkans, and the Bulgarian proposal was simply a variant on the theme. As Robertson had written in May, 'The part played by diplomacy during the present war is not as good as it might have been'.[69] Grey did not accept Robertson's Bulgarian argument any more than he had accepted the CIGS's earlier proposal about Turkey. The Foreign Secretary opined that such an attempt would be a confession of weakness and would irritate the Romanians as well as the French. Instead he offered a proposal, authored by Lloyd George, that Russia assemble 150,000 men on the Bulgarian border. This manoeuvre, it was hoped, would yield Romanian intervention as well as Bulgarian capitulation, thus opening up a direct line for the supply of Russia. Robertson was surprisingly mild in his reaction to this plan; he agreed that an Allied offensive at Salonika should occur 'provided that the British Government were satisfied before the offensive began that Roumanian intervention . . . was definitely secured.' It was agreed that Lloyd George should go to Paris the following week to discuss the entire issue with the French.

While the debate over Romania went on, the War Committee was becoming a 'little uneasy', as Robertson wrote to Haig, with respect to the mounting casualties and apparent lack of success of the Somme offensive.[70] The difficulty of Robertson's position and an indication that his relationship with Haig was not quite as harmonious as generally believed was shown clearly by this letter. Robertson pressed Haig to keep him informed of events on the Western front. The CIGS noted that if he were forced to rely on press communiques for his information, '[my] opinion is regarded as not much more valuable than that of anyone else' by the War Committee.[71] Haig's marginal note on this letter showed that the Commander-in-Chief was not pleased by less than complete support from Robertson: 'not exactly the letter of a CIGS. . . . He ought to take some responsibility also!' The timeliness of Robertson's request was evidenced at the meeting of the War Committee on 5 August, when Churchill's biting attack on the Somme offensive was discussed.[72] Haig's letter in response to Robertson's request was, in Curzon's words, a 'real rejoinder' to Churchill's view.[73] Haig argued that the Somme offensive had lifted the pressure on Verdun and prevented the successes of the Russians in the east from being checked by the transfer of troops from the west. He felt equally that the Somme had inflicted heavy casualties on the Germans and had demonstrated to the Allies the British will to fight. Haig ended his letter with a call for the continued focusing of every effort in the Somme attack, noting that failure to do so would prejudice, 'probably fatally', the Russian attacks in the east. This latter point he reiterated a few days later.[74]

The relationship between the two fronts remained an issue of discussion throughout August. While Haig was forced to justify his offensive to the War Committee, General Foch told the British Commander-in-Chief that the Russians were 'crying out' for activity in the west.[75] Robertson had difficulty believing this. A memorandum prepared by Alekseev for Hanbury Williams (who was returning to England for a brief leave) made no mention of any desperate Russian need for activity in the west. After outlining the nature of the Russian attacks, Alekseev noted that 'if the English and French armies act also with tenacity, I am convinced that our enemies' capacity for resistance will be substantially weakened, will begin breaking and that the war will begin to approach its end.'[76] Despite this, with Romania's agreement to enter the war on 17

August there was increased pressure on the British to make a major commitment in the Balkans.

The plan which Lloyd George had generated for a major Russian commitment against Bulgaria was soon raised again by the French. There was little support for such a plan among the Allied military staffs. Alekseev told General W. H.-H. Waters (Hanbury Williams's temporary replacement at *Stavka*) that Russia had sent all the troops to Dobrudja that she could and that any who were sent would be put under Romanian commanders 'who might keep them inactive and prevent them from assisting in a possible crushing blow against the enemy on the SW front'. In fact, Alekseev made it clear that he objected 'strongly to diplomatists interfering with purely strategical questions' and dismissed all such diplomatists as 'foul people'.[77] British and French opinion was equally certain. Haig wrote to Robertson on 23 August that his views on future policy were unchanged from those expressed on 1 August, while Joffre informed Haig two days later that the present offensive must be maintained in order to wear down the German resistance further and to aid the efforts of the Russians and Romanians.[78] Supported by such a unanimity of military opinion, Robertson felt confident of his ability to control the War Committee and told Haig that the latter should plan his actions as he saw fit, since the War Committee supported him wholeheartedly.[79] Robertson also advised Haig to carry on his attacks all winter; 'if we do not do this the Germans will be taking troops over to the Eastern Front and Alexeieff is already beginning to call out.'[80]

The strategy advocated by the General Staff for the final months of 1916 was outlined formally in a paper prepared in early September.[81] According to the General Staff, the most likely line of attack for the Central Powers to adopt in the autumn of 1916 was an offensive against Romania. Faced with this, the Allies could either send troops to Salonika or continue their offensive in the west. To settle on the former would be, in the words of the General Staff, 'a flagrant and inexcusable surrender of the initiative to the enemy'. Such a course would involve the abandonment of 'our own carefully considered plan of campaign' which was based on the idea of vigorous simultaneous offensives on the principal fronts. With the ongoing collapse of the Romanian army, the General Staff argued that the only support which could be given her was through the continuation of Russia's offensive in the south. Should this be successful, the Carpathian passes could be taken and Russia's forces thus linked with those of Romania. This paper was discussed at the War Committee meeting of 12 September.[82] The meeting decided that the British role at Salonika should be to pin down, not attack, the Bulgars, while in France the Somme attacks should be continued as long as Romania were menaced. Ironically, on this same day the forces under Sarrail at Salonika began their long-awaited offensive against the Bulgarians.

Despite Robertson's optimism that he could control the War Committee, the autumn of 1916 found a growing disenchantment with a policy of continuing the offensive in the west.[83] The failure of Sarrail's offensive and the collapse of the Romanians became a matter of concern by the end of September. On 28 September Robertson asked Waters to outline the British fears to Alekseev. While 'it would not be appropriate' for Waters to suggest that Russia make a special effort to help Romania, Robertson telegraphed, Waters should find out Alekseev's opinion about the topic at the 'first opportunity'.[84] For his own part, Robertson felt that much of the problem with the Romanians was due to their own ineptitude. As he told the War Committee on 3 October, when the crucial battle of Turtuku began, the Romanian commanding general 'was playing bridge in Bucharest.'[85]

To Lloyd George the situation in early October was reminiscent of that of a year earlier. The only difference, he felt, was that in 1916 it was Romania and not Serbia which was collapsing without Allied aid. At the meeting of the War Committee of 9 October, the entire question of support for Romania was discussed.[86] Lloyd George argued that the crushing of another small Balkan ally would have a bad effect both on opinion in Greece and on British prestige generally. While Robertson continued to lay the blame on the 'very indifferent' strategy of the Romanians and argued that only Russia was in any position to do anything directly to help Romania, Lloyd George did not agree. The Secretary of State for War felt that the Allies could not expect Russia to solve all their problems and what was needed was all the General Staffs of the Allies to 'collaborate and put up some definite concerted plan to the execution of which they could all contribute, for the relief of Roumania.' Robertson's arguments were supported by Curzon. The head of the Shipping Control Committee pointed out that any aid Britain and France could send to Romania would arrive too late to be of assistance.

Robertson reinforced his position by reading a telegram from the
commander of the British forces at Salonika, General Milne. Dated 8
October, Milne's telegram made it evident that no successful
advance could be contemplated without a vast infusion of troops.
Despite this, Lloyd George remained insistent that something be
done and the War Committee agreed to seek further information
from Milne as well as from Joffre and Briand about the possibility of
a Balkan attack. In the mean time, Curzon suggested that Russia
might be 'induced' to offer Romania some extra aid in exchange for
some of the large-calibre artillery which they had requested from the
British. Lloyd George was not to be put off by this proposal and
pointed out that the lateness of the shipping season made it
impossible to deliver guns to Russia until the spring of 1917. The
meeting concluded with a decision to await the arrival of further
information about the situation at Salonika.

The reports from Joffre and Milne were discussed on 12
October.[87] Milne argued that it would require at least ten and
preferably fifteen divisions, plus more artillery, for the Allies to
push back the Bulgarians. Joffre, on the other hand, felt that two
British divisions along with two Italian ones could, in league with the
Russians, 'co-operate' to defeat the Bulgarians. To these conflicting
views, Robertson added his own. In his paper on the subject, the
CIGS stated that to depart from the agreed policy of pinning down
the Bulgarians was folly.[88] Robertson felt that Joffre's suggestion of
four divisions was inadequate; such a force could 'do no more' than
the forces at present in Salonika. Reinforcements on the scale which
Milne suggested, the CIGS argued, could not possibly arrive before
Romania fell. He reiterated his view that only Russia could help
Romania directly and pointed out that the combined Russian,
Romanian and Serb forces in the area enjoyed a marked numerical
superiority to those of the enemy. While Robertson managed to
prevent either Milne's or Joffre's advice from being adopted – the
War Committee decided to send only about a division of replace-
ments to Salonika – it 'was only with the greatest difficulty' that he
had managed to do so. The CIGS realised that he was 'handicapped',
as he wrote on 16 October, by the fact that Lloyd George favoured a
Balkan attack, and had gone so far as to indicate to the Secretary of
State that he could 'no longer carry on unless my advice was
accepted.'[89]

Although Robertson was convinced that nothing could be done to help Romania, he realised clearly that there was need for discussion between the Allies before the campaigns for 1917 were decided upon. One of the key issues which needed to be discussed was the allocation of resources. As Robertson wrote to Haig in the middle of October, Russia's shortage of heavy artillery had blunted her offensive.[90] While reassuring Haig that no guns would be taken from the Western front in the next little while, Robertson added that 'we must decide what will be the best thing to do early next year with the heavy artillery then forthcoming.' Robertson had his own particular reasons for wanting to ensure that Russia would be ready to begin the offensive as early as possible in 1917. The CIGS felt that if Russia were ready this would deny Joffre any reason to delay a French offensive in the west. Any such delay, Robertson felt, would allow the German to 'pull himself together' after the batterings of 1916, to the detriment of the Allies.

Once again the issue of Salonika became the pivot of Allied strategy. Sarrail's lack of success and his involvement in Greek politics had eroded Italian and Russian confidence in him. The Russians, in particular, were concerned that the general's support for Eleutherios Venizelos would both weaken the royalist elements in Greece and promote an aggressive Greek foreign policy which would threaten Russia's acquisition of Constantinople and the Straits.[91] On 20 October a conference was held at Boulogne between British and French political and military figures in order to discuss Salonika.[92] Three days earlier Robertson had managed to solidify British opinion in the War Committee behind a policy of sending no further troops to Salonika, and at Boulogne, in Haig's words, 'for once the British Govt. stood firm and refused to be black-mailed by the French.'[93] At the conference it was decided not to send any reinforcements to Salonika. Instead the General Staffs of the Allies were to examine the military situation there to ensure that the forces already deployed were secure and to investigate the possibility of a joint offensive with the Russians.

When the British representatives returned to London, the results of Boulogne were scrutinised carefully. The War Committee was unanimous that, in Asquith's words, 'something curious' was going on in France.[94] Lloyd George noted that some members of the French government wanted the British to press for Sarrail's removal, presumably to shift the responsibility for his dismissal to the Allies. Despite the general disgust with the French, it was decided that a further British division should be sent to Salonika for political reasons. It was felt that this would soothe both the French and the Russians and give moral support to the Romanians. Such a move was opposed, naturally, by Robertson, but he was joined, surprisingly, by Lloyd George: the latter argued that the Romanians would probably capitulate before the Allied forces arrived.

While French influence in this decision was evident, the major reason for the British change of heart was Russia. As Robertson wrote to Joffre, the Russians repeatedly had insisted over the past month that the Balkans must be treated as a 'main theatre'.[95] If the British had refused to send any troops to Salonika, Robertson pointed out to Haig, they would have been the only Ally which had done so. Such an attitude was impossible considering the political pressure being exerted by 'Poincaré, the Czar, and the French and Russian Governments, to say nothing of the Roumanians.'[96] Faced with this opposition, Robertson began to look for support within the French high command. In a letter on 27 October the CIGS attempted to enlist Joffre in the ranks of those opposed to making Salonika a major theatre. Robertson hoped that Joffre would oppose the 'great pressure' which the Russians and Romanians would exert at the forthcoming Allied military conference at Chantilly. Joffre's reply to Robertson's appeal was cautious.[97] While the French commander agreed with Robertson that it was dangerous to denude the Western front of troops in order to support a Balkan theatre, Joffre added that he felt Romania must be supported as well in order to crush Bulgaria and support the Russians. Much of Joffre's attitude was based on Russian opinion. Alekseev informed the French commander that both 'military and political considerations' made a strong effort in the Balkans essential.[98] Robertson's disgust was manifest; as he wrote to Haig on 4 November Joffre was 'most hopeless'.[99]

While Robertson was preparing his arguments for Chantilly, Lloyd George was attempting to make that conference superfluous by arranging for a political conference to precede it, a conference to determine Allied strategy for 1917. At a meeting of the War Committee on 3 November, at which no military or naval members were present, Lloyd George stated that it was time to realise that the attacks in the West had failed and to 'get on' with a new policy.[100] The Secretary of State cited Alekseev's opinion that a major effort in the Balkans was a 'strategic and moral duty', and called for a conference of all Allied political representatives to convene before the opening of the Chantilly gathering on 15 November. As Lloyd George noted a few days later, such a political gathering was necessary in order that the military staffs would not be able to devise some 'line of military trenches' at Chantilly in order to thwart any proposals which ran counter to their plans.[101]

When it became apparent that a meeting could not be called at short notice, Grey proposed that a conference should be held in Russia to ensure that the Eastern and Western fronts were co-ordinated fully in 1917. This idea was avidly agreed to by both Curzon and Lloyd George, but some were not as enthusiastic. McKenna, the Chancellor of the Exchequer, observed that such a conference would mean that the Russians would have an opportunity to 'open their mouths very wide for financial and other assistance, and the people who represented us must be prepared to say that they would have very little to give.' Grey pointed out that the political situation in Russia was not good and that such a conference might serve to settle the present unstable situation there. Grey's fears undoubtedly had been raised by an evaluation of the situation in Russia prepared by the Director of Military Intelligence.[102] In it, General Macdonogh noted a growing discontent with Britain among Russians. Many Russians, he felt, resented Britain's control over Russia's external purchasing, feared the spread of 'democratic ideals' in Russia and some even favoured a separate peace with Germany. While Lloyd George supported Grey's call for a conference in Russia, the Secretary of State for War objected to letting the Chantilly conference proceed before the proposed Russian meeting could take place, lest the generals adopt positions from which they 'might be unwilling to depart'.

When Robertson discovered Lloyd George's efforts to forestall the Chantilly conference, he reacted swiftly. The CIGS sent an envoy to Joffre, informing the latter of the plot.[103] Joffre did not appear to share the CIGS's alarm. After keeping the envoy waiting overnight, the French Commander-in-Chief replied only that he was opposed categorically to any delay of the conference. By 10 November the Chantilly conference had been saved, and Robertson could write to Haig that the two of them might have 'a chance' to change Lloyd George's views when the latter visited the British front during the next week.[104]

On 15 November the Chantilly conference and an equivalent political conference in Paris opened simultaneously.[105] The decisions taken at Chantilly in 1916 paralleled closely those taken at the same location a year earlier. It was agreed that in 1917 the Allies would continue their offensives on the main fronts (defined as in 1915), that they would commence simultaneously at a date to be decided later, that the Germans should be harassed over the winter to the extent that climate permitted, and that all the Allies should come to the aid of any one of them which was attacked by the enemy. The political meeting was much less predictable. Briand opened the conference by enquiring rhetorically whether the civilian governments of the Allies should 'let go out their hands altogether the conduct of the campaign?' Briand then went on to suggest that over the winter the British, French and Russians should combine in a major Balkan offensive to defeat Bulgaria. The British refused to be drawn on this point. Asquith, in reply to Briand's remarks, did not take up the French premier's proposal, but instead called for a conference of all the Allies to be held in Petrograd. This conference, Asquith stated, should settle three questions: '(1) what it is possible to do on the Eastern Front; and (2) as to the nature and degree of help which the Western Powers could give to Russia and Roumania.' The Russian ambassador to France, Count Izvolskii, agreed that a conference in Russia was necessary, but stated that 'all information' possessed by the Russian government led it to consider a Balkan offensive of 'capital importance'.

The positions of the three major Allies were clear and the British found themselves isolated in their opposition to a Balkan offensive. Briand attempted to take advantage of this isolation by trying to turn the discussion directly to the consideration of actual plans of campaign in the Balkans. Lloyd George spoke against this attempt. It was necessary, he felt to hold a conference in Petrograd first, in order that all aspects of the situation, political, economic and military, could be examined simultaneously. Faced with such opposition, Briand turned the talk to a discussion of the Greek situation and no further attempts at military planning were essayed. At a second session of the conference the following day, it was agreed that until a meeting could be held in Petrograd the main concerns for 1917 must be a continuation of the attacks on the Western front in close co-ordination with those on the Eastern front, an effort to help Russia obtain sufficient munitions, and an attempt to knock out Bulgaria.[106] These decisions were in reality no more than aspirations, since the conference had made little attempt to examine the means by which these things might be achieved simultaneously. The real significance of the Paris conference was that it evidenced the dissatisfaction of the politicians with the military's handling of the war and that it showed clearly the difference of opinion about Salonika between Britain and the other Allies. This latter difference was in some ways more a matter of timing than a major disagreement; the British wished to ensure that Russia was consulted fully through a conference in Petrograd rather than continue to make decisions exclusively in the west. The question of Salonika, it was felt, could best be decided in Russia.

While Lloyd George and Asquith attempted unsuccessfully to persuade Robertson to become the British representative to the Petrograd conference, the latter endeavoured to justify a military policy dominated by the Western front.[107] Such an endeavour was made more difficult by the continuing succession of military setbacks experienced in the late autumn of 1916. The collapse of Romania added further gloom to the situation, and Robertson's exasperation with the attitude of his political colleagues was plain. As the CIGS wrote to General Murray in Palestine on 1 December, 'I wish you success in what you are now undertaking and hope you will have a good show and give us something to cheer up these London pessimists a little. They have been very bad lately as though the world was coming to an end because Roumania has made a fool of herself.'[108] This was an unusual position for a man who had endeavoured for the past year to keep efforts on secondary fronts to a minimum.

The fall of the Asquith government in early December and the creation of a new one with Lloyd George as Prime Minister was not designed to reassure the CIGS about the continuing commitment of the government to his policies. Lloyd George had been the strongest proponent in the War Committee of the eastern approach and his elevation to the political leadership made his voice all the more important. The CIGS was not swayed from his beliefs, however, and at the first meeting of the newly created War Cabinet on 9 December, argued strongly against a new French proposal to send two further British divisions to Salonika.[109] While Robertson was able to forestall this French initiative, the attitude of the new Prime Minister made it unlikely that the CIGS could continue indefinitely to deflect all schemes for new fronts. The key issue remained that of Salonika. By the end of December there was another demand from the French and the Russians for a resumption of the offensive at that location. In a letter to the War Cabinet Lieutenant-General Dessino, the head of the Russian military mission in Britain, explained that the Russian General Staff felt that as it was impossible to strike a 'swift and decisive blow' on either the Western or the Eastern fronts against the Germans, an effort should be made in the Balkans.[110] In fact, Dessino was suspicious of both Britain and France; he felt, as he informed *Stavka* in December, that the Western Allies preferred to let the bulk of the fighting in 1917 fall on Russia.[111] Joffre, now superseded in all but title by General Nivelle, also insisted that the British transfer troops to Salonika for an offensive. The matter was discussed by the War Cabinet on 26 December at the same time as an Anglo-French conference opened in London.[112]

Robertson was adamant in his opposition to the Balkan plan, as well as what he had described to Haig a few days earlier as a 'very dangerous tendency . . . for the War Cabinet to direct military operations.'[113] He pointed out to the War Cabinet that to divert forces to Salonika meant lessening the chances of victory in France in 1917 without creating the possibility of victory in the Balkans since it was impossible to send sufficient troops there to do anything but remain on the defensive. He stated further that transportation sufficient for such a transfer of troops was impossible to procure unless the government were willing to abandon other shipping programmes such as that for coal to Italy. The CIGS found Joffre's conduct in the matter of Salonika 'peculiar' and his arguments inconsistent. As to the Russian arguments, the CIGS felt that they were all things to all men. General V. I. Gurko, who was temporarily in charge of the Russian armies while Alekseev was incapacitated by illness, had

> telegraphed this week saying we ought to reinforce Salonica in order to safeguard ourselves in Mesopotamia and Egypt. He has telegraphed to Cadorna saying that he ought to reinforce Salonica in order to safeguard Italy; and now he writes that everybody should reinforce Salonica in order that a decisive result may be sought in the Balkans.

At the next meeting of the War Cabinet on 27 December, the Balkans were discussed once more.[114] Robertson presented a statement to the meeting calling upon the War Cabinet to adopt a defensive role at Salonika. The CIGS emphasised strongly the supply problems which the near-closure of the Mediterranean due to increased submarine activity would mean for the forces at Salonika. No decision was arrived at until the following day when it was agreed that the entire issue of Salonika must be discussed with the Italians at a conference of the Allies to be held early in January in Rome.[115]

While the debate over Salonika took place, a new departure occurred in the strategy for the Western front for 1917.[116] At the end of November 1916 Haig had outlined a major British assault in Flanders designed to clear the coast of German submarine bases. Joffre had agreed to this plan on 8 December, viewing it as part of his own wider offensive plans for 1917. Five days later, however, Joffre had been removed as commander of the French forces in France and resigned on 26 December. General Nivelle, his successor, put forward his own plan for 1917 at the end of December. Nivelle revealed his plans to Haig on 21 December, plans which called for Haig to take over large amounts of the French line in order to free French troops for the offensive. Haig's reluctance to do so led Nivelle to attempt unsuccessfully to pressure the British government in to forcing the British Commander-in-Chief to comply.

Nivelle's promise of a decisive victory made the conference at Rome a difficult one for Lloyd George. The Prime Minister had seen this conference as an opportunity to meet General Sarrail and to promulgate his own concepts of strategy, support for which was so lacking in British military circles.[117] In Rome Lloyd George displayed his lack of sympathy for the ideas agreed on at Chantilly and called for a unified Allied command, a greater focus on Salonika and an increased supply of heavy guns for Italy in order that a major offensive could be launched from that country against Austria-Hungary.[118] To his surprise, Lloyd George found little support for his plans. Cadorna, the Italian commander, was not enthusiastic about undertaking an offensive and deprecated the need for artillery on the Italian front. The French, on the other hand, were committed to Nivelle since Joffre had been deposed with the promise that Nivelle could provide victory. For their part, the British military representatives put forward concerns about the transportation problems involved in a Balkan offensive, effectively shelving such an idea for the time being. The principal conclusion of the conference was that every effort must be made in 1917 to equip the Russian

army and that all matters should be discussed at the forthcoming
Petrograd conference.

Thwarted at Rome in his attempt to create an alternative strategy
to that of Haig and Robertson, Lloyd George took up Nivelle's plan
with apparent enthusiasm, and Haig agreed reluctantly on 15
January to co-operate with it. Robertson did not fail to point out to
the War Cabinet that Lloyd George's support for Nivelle was
contradictory.[119] The Prime Minister had professed to espouse the
belief that all offensives should be co-ordinated among the Allies, the
CIGS noted, yet the early date which Nivelle projected for his attack
precluded the possibility of Russian and Italian support. Therefore
the instructions which the War Cabinet had given to Lord Milner,
the chief British delegate to the Petrograd conference, that he was to
make every effort to see that Russia's 'offensive capabilities' were
developed as fully as possible in order that they could participate
fully in a concerted Allied offensive were vitiated by the decision to
go along with the Nivelle plan. Obviously the Petrograd conference
would have much to discuss.

By the end of January 1917 a new era was emerging in British
relations with Russia. A change of Prime Ministers in Britain and the
deposition of Joffre in France had opened up new strategical vistas
which were to have repercussions in Anglo-Russian relations.
Throughout 1916 the Anglo-Russian alliance had had two main
focuses. The first was the British desire to ensure that all Allied
actions were pursued simultaneously. Considerations of Russia had
much influenced the British to begin the Somme offensive as early as
they did. Providing support for the flagging Russian offensive in the
south was the primary reason for the decision to maintain the British
attacks in France in the autumn. The second focus had been
Salonika. Supported by the French, the Russian belief that Salonika
must be considered a major front was a continual source of irritation
to the British military establishment and a continual source of
support for those politicians, like Lloyd George, who supported a
Balkan offensive. By the opening of the Petrograd conference at the
end of January 1917 a full-scale examination of this issue and a
discussion of plans for 1917 was highly desirable. Agreement would
be another matter.

Notes

1 Rothwell, *British War Aims*, 8.
2 Meeting of the War Committee, 23 December 1915, Cab 42/6/13.
3 Balfour to Hankey, 24 December 1915, ibid.
4 Meeting of the War Committee, 28 December 1915, Cab 42/6/14; 'An examination by the General Staff into the factors affecting the choice of a plan of campaign; together with a recommendation as to the best plan to adopt', A. Murray, 16 December 1915, ibid.
5 Robertson to Haig, 31 December 1915, Haig Papers, 104.
6 Haig to Robertson, 3 January 1916, Robertson Papers I/22/6.
7 Robertson to Haig, 3 January 1916, as cited in W. S. Robertson, *Soldiers and Statesmen 1914–1918* (2 vols, London, 1926), I, 256; Callwell's mission is in Callwell, *Experiences of a Dug-Out*, 237–52.
8 Kitchener to Asquith, 11 January 1916. Kitchener Papers, PRO 30/67/76; Robertson to Wigram, 12 January 1916, Robertson Papers I/12/30 and Kitchener to Haig, 14 January 1916, Kitchener Papers, PRO 30/57/53.
9 Meeting of the War Committee, 13 January 1916, Cab 42/7/5; untitled memorandum, Balfour, 27 December 1915, ibid.
10 Robertson to Haig, 13 January 1916, Haig Papers, 104.
11 Haig diary entry, 14 January 1916, ibid.; Robertson to Haig, 16 January 1916, Robertson Papers I/22/16.
12 Haig diary entry, 18 January 1916, Haig Papers, 104; Haig to Kitchener, 19 January 1916, Kitchener Papers, PRO 30/57/53.
13 Balfour's views are in his 'The present military position, and opinions in the War Committee', 21 January 1916, Cab 37/141/7. For Robertson's influence on this paper, see 'Notes by the Chief of the Imperial General Staff on Mr. Balfour's memorandum of 18th January 1916', 20 January 1916, Balfour Papers, ADD MSS 49726, vol. XLIV.
14 'Procès-verbal de la conférence du 22 Janvier 1916', n.s., 22 January 1916, WO 106/393.
15 Robertson to Haig, 28 January 1916, Haig Papers, 104.
16 Haig to Joffre, 1 February 1916 and reply, 6 February 1916, both in ibid.
17 Robertson to A. Murray (now commander of British forces in Egypt), 10 February 1916, Robertson Papers I/32/1; Grey to Kitchener, 10 February 1916, Kitchener Papers, PRO 30/67/77.
18 Lowe and Dockrill, *Mirage of Power*, II, 202–3.
19 Alekseev to Sazonov, 8 February 1916, as cited in Rieber, 'Russian diplomacy', 267.
20 Robertson to Grey, 10 February 1916, Kitchener Papers, PRO 30/67/77; 'Conversation tenu entre le Général Joffre et le Général Robertson', n.s., 14 February 1916, WO 106/396.
21 Robertson to Hanbury Williams, 16 February 1916, Robertson Papers I/35/57.
22 The results are outlined in Joffre to Haig, 18 February 1916, WO 158/14; Edmonds, *France and Belgium 1916*, I, 28–9.
23 Haig to Joffre, 20 February 1916, WO 158/14.
24 Hanbury Williams to Kitchener, 19 and 24 February 1916, Kitchener Papers, PRO 30/57/67.
25 Meeting of the War Committee, 22 February 1916, Cab 42/9/3.
26 'The position of Great Britain with regard to her Allies', Grey, 18 February 1916, ibid.

27 Grey to Kitchener, 28 February 1916, Kitchener Papers, PRO 30/67/77.
28 Buchanan to FO, 6 March 1916, FO 371/2748/43676.
29 Tanenbaum, *Sarrail*, 89–90.
30 Emets, 'Protivorechiia mezhdu Rossiei i soiuznikami', 62–5.
31 Robertson to A. Murray, 15 March 1916, Robertson Papers I/32/12.
32 Haig diary entry, 12 March 1916, Haig Papers, 105.
33 Meeting of the War Committee, 21 March 1916, Cab 42/11/6.
34 Buchanan to FO, very secret, 7 and 14 March 1916, FO 371/2748/44349 and 49413; Knox's dispatch I2, 9 March 1916, WO 106/1073.
35 Scott diary entry, 22–24 March 1916, Wilson (ed.), *Scott diaries*, 182.
36 Meeting of the War Committee, 21 March 1916, Cab 42/11/6.
37 Haig to Robertson, 4 April 1916, WO 158/21; meeting of the War Committee, 7 April 1916, Cab 42/12/5.
38 ibid., and Robertson to Haig, 7 April 1916, WO 158/21.
39 Stone, *Eastern Front*, 222–31.
40 Meeting of the War Committee, 28 April 1916, Cab 37/146/22.
41 Meeting of the War Committee, 3 May 1916, Cab 42/13/2; 'Military assistance for Russia', Robertson, 1 May 1916, ibid.
42 Haig diary entry, 2 May 1916, Haig Papers, 106.
43 Robertson to Hanbury Williams, personal and secret, 8 May 1916, Robertson Papers I/14/12.
44 Hanbury Williams to Robertson, most secret, 10 May 1916, Robertson Papers I/14/13.
45 Haig to Kitchener, 5 May 1916, Kitchener Papers, PRO 30/57/53.
46 Robertson to Joffre, 13 May 1916, Haig Papers, 106.
47 Robertson to Haig, 13 May 1916 and reply 16 May 1916, Robertson Papers I/22/34 and 35.
48 'Summary of discussion at Chantilly, 15th May 1916', n.s., 15 May 1916, WO 106/394.
49 Tanenbaum, *Sarrail*, 92.
50 Robertson to Haig, 18 May 1916, Robertson Papers I/22/36.
51 'Offensive operations in the Balkans', Robertson, 16 May 1916, Cab 42/14/1.
52 Meeting of the War Committee, 17 May 1916, ibid.; Tanenbaum, *Sarrail*, 93–4.
53 Robertson to Hanbury Williams, 10 June 1916, Maurice Papers, WO 106/1510.
54 Haig to Kiggell, 24 May 1916, Kiggell Papers II/3; the readiness of the Russians in Buchanan to FO, secret, 17 May 1916, FO 371/2748/94914.
55 Haig diary entry, 26 May 1916, Haig Papers, 106.
56 Haig diary entry, 31 May 1916, ibid.
57 Tanenbaum, *Sarrail*, 96–7.
58 Robertson to Hanbury Williams, 10 June 1916, Maurice Papers, WO 106/1510.
59 Meeting of the War Committee, 6 July 1916, Cab 42/16/1. Cambon's note was dated 1 July. 'Note', Robertson, 5 July 1916.
60 Robertson to Haig, 11 July 1916, Robertson Papers I/22/54.
61 Meeting of the War Committee, 18 July 1916, Cab 42/16/8. The note from the French ambassador and the test of the proposed convention are included.
62 Meeting of the War Committee, 20 July 1916, Cab 42/16/10.
63 Meeting of the War Committee, 28 July 1916, Cab 42/16/11.
64 Robertson to Hanbury Williams, personal and secret, 31 July 1916, Robertson Papers I/14/26b.
65 Rieber, 'Russian diplomacy', 270.
66 Robertson to Grey, 1 August 1916, Robertson Papers I/21/34, original emphasis.

67 Meeting of the War Committee, 10 August 1916, Cab 42/17/5. Robertson's paper, 'Note on the position of Bulgaria', 4 August 1916, is included.
68 'Note prepared by the Chief of the Imperial General Staff . . . on the assistance that diplomacy might render to naval and military operations', Robertson, 12 February 1916, Cab 42/9/3.
69 Robertson to Duff, 18 May 1916, Robertson Papers I/32/27.
70 Robertson to Haig, 29 July 1916, Robertson Papers I/22/61.
71 Robertson to Haig, 1 August 1916, Robertson Papers I/22/62.
72 Meeting of the War Committee, 5 August 1916, Cab 42/17/3; Churchill's memorandum, 1 August 1916, Cab 37/153/3.
73 Haig to Robertson, 1 August 1916, Cab 42/17/3.
74 See Edmonds, *France and Belgium 1916*, II, 180 for Haig's remark of 9 August 1916.
75 Haig diary entry, 12 August 1916, Haig Papers, 107.
76 Alekseev's memorandum, 15 August 1916, WO 106/1144.
77 Waters to Robertson, 27 August 1916, Robertson Papers I/14/30; W. H-H. Waters, *'Secret and Confidential' The Experiences of a Military Attaché* (London, 1926), 328.
78 Haig to Robertson, 23 August 1916, Haig Papers, 107; Joffre to Haig, 25 August 1916, ibid.
79 Haig to Robertson, 27 August 1916, referring to Robertson's letter of 25 August, Robertson Papers I/22/71. Robertson to Haig, 29 August 1916, Haig Papers, 108.
80 ibid.
81 'Possible action of the Central Powers during the autumn and winter of 1916', General Staff, WO, 9 September 1916, Maurice Papers, WO 106/1510.
82 Meeting of the War Committee, 12 September 1916, Cab 42/19/6.
83 See P. Guinn, *British Strategy and Politics 1914 to 1918* (Oxford, 1965), 165–7 for a discussion of this occurrence.
84 Robertson to Waters, 28 September 1916, Robertson Papers I/14/43.
85 Meeting of the War Committee, 3 October 1916, Cab 42/21/1.
86 Meeting of the War Committee, 9 October 1916, Cab 42/21/3.
87 Meeting of the War Committee, 12 October 1916, Cab 42/21/6.
88 'Further reinforcements for the Allied forces at Salonika', Robertson, 11 October 1916, ibid.
89 Robertson to A. Murray, 16 October 1916, Robertson Papers I/32/48.
90 Robertson to Haig, 16 October 1916, Robertson Papers I/22/83.
91 Tanenbaum, *Sarrail*, 117–18; 121–2.
92 'Conclusions of the Anglo-French Conference held at Boulogne on October 20, 1916', n.s., 20 October 1916, WO 106/395; Tanenbaum, *Sarrail*, 129–32.
93 Haig diary entry, 20 October 1916, Haig Papers, 108.
94 Meeting of the War Committee, 24 October 1916, Cab 42/22/5.
95 Robertson to Milne, 27 October 1916, Robertson Papers I/34/34; Robertson to Joffre, 27 October 1916, Haig Papers, 109.
96 Robertson to Haig, 25 October 1916, Haig Papers, 108.
97 Robertson to Joffre, 27 October 1916 and reply, 3 November 1916, Haig Papers, 109.
98 Alekseev to Joffre, 14 November 1916, as cited in Rostunov, *Russkii front*, 332.
99 Robertson to Haig, 4 November 1916, Robertson Papers I/22/88.
100 Meeting of the War Committee, 3 November 1916, Cab 42/23/4; Hankey, *Supreme Command*, II, 556.
101 Handwritten note by Lloyd George, 7 November 1916, Cab 42/23/5.

102 'The situation in Russia', G. M. W. Macdonogh, 30 October 1916, Maurice Papers, WO 106/1511.
103 See the account in Robertson Papers I/6/6/2.
104 Robertson to Haig, 10 November 1916, Robertson Papers I/22/89.
105 The results of the military conference are in Edmonds, *France and Belgium 1916*, II, 532. The political conference can be followed in 'Minutes of the proceedings of a conference held at Paris', n.s., 15 November 1916, WO 106/397; see also Hankey, *Supreme Command*, II, 558–62.
106 'Proceedings of a conference held at Paris on Thursday, November 16th, 1916', n.s., 16 November 1916, WO 106/397.
107 See Cab 42/25/2,8,10 and Haig to Kiggell, 25 November 1916, Kiggell Papers II/6; Robertson to Lloyd George, 24 November 1916, Robertson Papers I/6/7.
108 Robertson to A. Murray, 1 December 1916, Robertson Papers I/32/49.
109 1st meeting of the War Cabinet, 9 December 1916, Cab 23/1.
110 'Letter from Lieut. Gen. Dessino to the Chairman of the War Cabinet', Dessino, 22 December 1916, Cab 17/180.
111 See his letter to *Stavka* as cited in Rostunov, *Russkii front*, 332–3.
112 18th meeting of the War Cabinet, 26 December 1916, Cab 23/1.
113 Robertson to Haig, 24 December 1916, Robertson Papers I/22/97.
114 19th meeting of the War Cabinet, 27 December 1916, Cab 23/1.
115 21st meeting of the War Cabinet, 28 December 1916, ibid.
116 Outlined in Edmonds, *France and Belgium, 1917*, I, 18–43.
117 Hankey, *Supreme Command*, II, 605.
118 Accounts of the conference are in ibid., 606–12; 'Conclusions of a conference of the Allies, held at the Consulta, Rome on the 5th, 6th and 7th January 1917', n.s., n.d., Cab 28/2 I.C. 15; Callwell, *Wilson Diaries*, I, 307–9.
119 'Note by CIGS on Nivelle's Plan', Robertson, 24 January 1917, Maurice Papers, WO 106/1511.

5
Russian Desires; British Capabilities

In 1916 the limits of Britain's ability to provide munitions and finance for Russia became evident. With respect to finance, the British dependence on American credit became absolute and the increasing Russian need for funds to spend in the United States continued to be a contentious issue, both between the British and Russian governments and within the British government itself. The Russian government kept up its policy of avoiding whenever possible any restrictions on how it was to spend the monies it had borrowed as well as delaying any shipment of gold to Britain. Russia felt that Britain's credit was inexhaustible and only the entrance of the United States into the war in April 1917 was able to resolve the disparity between Russian demands for credit in America and the British ability to provide it.

A similar problem existed with regard to supplies. Despite some major reforms in the organisational aspects of providing munitions for Russia, close Anglo-Russian co-operation did not come about. The difficulty lay in the fact that there existed a fundamental difference of viewpoint between the two countries. Russia, faced with a rapidly expanding economy, required a large amount of goods seemingly unrelated to the production of war material lest the failure of some aspects of her economy choke off the growth in the military sectors. Britain, on the other hand, faced with a growing dependence on the United States for many war goods, increasing difficulties in providing shipping for goods purchased abroad by Russia, and the burgeoning needs of her own army, did not see the situation in the same light. Russia, Britain felt, should be provided only with those goods directly necessary for the war effort and which were likely to have an overt influence on Russia's military performance. To the Russians, convinced that Britain's industrial output was limitless, this attitude was parsimonious. To the British, the huge Russian demands for goods of all sorts reflected the latter's inability to differentiate between the essential and inessential needs of the Russian war economy.

The longstanding problem with Russian inspection of munitions ordered in the United States became an issue again late in November 1915, just before the opening of the inter-Allied munitions conference in London. Philip Hanson put forward the familiar catalogue of Russian obstructionism: specifications and drawings were usually absent from orders and when they were not they were 'incomplete', 'inaccurate' and 'nearly always' in need of modification.[1] The Russian inspectors showed 'no desire or willingness to cooperate', were 'deliberately obstructive' and resented the War Office's 'encroachment' on their prerogatives which they felt included placing orders independently. None of this was news, but the Ministry of Munitions concluded that two steps must be taken to resolve the matter. In the short run, Ellershaw and Hermonious should travel to the United States in order to straighten out the existing difficulties. As the beginning of a long-term solution, the Ministry recommended that Asquith should send a 'strongly worded' telegram to Petrograd about the situation in the hope that a permanent solution could be worked out. On 24 November, the same day as the inter-Allied conference opened, and no doubt to reinforce the similar firm stand which the British government planned to adopt at the conference, the main points of the Ministry's complaints were sent to Petrograd.[2]

The Russian Minister of War, A. A. Polivanov, replied to the criticisms in uncompromising terms.[3] He welcomed the idea that Ellershaw and Hermonious should travel to America in an attempt to ease the frictions which existed there, but denied that the delays experienced in the United States were caused 'by any fault of Russian inspectors'. In Polivanov's opinion such problems were due to 'the fact that American factories had accepted more orders than they were able to execute.' Polivanov acknowledged that there had been shortages of trained Russian technical personnel in America which had caused some delays, but noted that General Sapozhnikov had been sent an additional sixty men in October to remedy this problem. In Polivanov's view what was most urgently required to ensure smooth co-operation was a permanent British member on the Russian Purchasing Committee in New York to act as a liaison between it and the British purchasing missions in the United States.

Polivanov concluded by stating that the Russian government would do its best to ensure cordial working relations existed in the future, but added 'unfortunately information received by [the] British Government, probably from Morgan's, gives a different impression to that received by the Ministry of War from reports sent by General Sapojnikoff.'

While Eustace Percy at the Foreign Office minuted on this telegram 'a pretty weak defence of indefensible scandals', there was much to be said for Polivanov's contentions.[4] Many of the problems experienced in the United States were, as they were in Britain, due to firms taking on more orders than they could handle. On the other hand, Sapozhnikov had been at fault in all the ways the British claimed and his incompetence, or scrupulosity, was harmful to the fulfilling of the Russian order placed in the United States.[5] The British reply to Polivanov implicitly recognised the justice of his remarks as well as reflected the fact that little could be done to force the Russians to press the matter further. The British suggested only that Ellershaw, already destined to go to the United States with Hermonious, become the British member of the Russian Purchasing Committee in New York. The Russians agreed.[6]

The difficulties with Sapozhnikov's position in the United States did not end with this. His continued placing of orders against the advice of the British purchasing agents in America led to the Treasury's refusing to provide credit for his orders. In London, Rutkovskii's sympathies in this matter lay entirely with the Treasury. As he wrote to Ramsay, the Joint Permanent Secretary at the Treasury, 'my impression is that General Sapojnikoff has not shown any capacity for making purchases of supplies in the United States.'[7] Rutkovskii was even more cutting when writing to his own government. As he sent to Bark in mid-December, Sapozhnikov had made contracts with '*personnes irresponsables*' and with firms lacking the necessary organisation to fulfil them.[8] Rutkovskii recommended to both Ramsay and Bark that Hermonious be permitted to examine all of the dubious contracts placed in America by Sapozhnikov in an attempt to end the chaos which existed there.

One of the contracts '*désastreuse*', to use Rutkovskii's term, which Sapozhnikov had placed in America was a further one with the Canadian Car and Foundry Company (CCFC), the firm which had taken over the contracts for 5 million 3-inch shells placed with Colonels Allison and Mackie in February and March 1915.[9] When Ellershaw arrived in New York one of the major problems he had to deal with was these shell contracts. While his firm dealing had temporarily resolved the problems with the CCFC by early 1916, the CCFC's dealings with the Russians were typical of the problems which had been experienced in North America by the Russians. While the CCFC undoubtedly suffered from mismanagement and while there were well-founded suspicions that the company had used large advances from the Russian government to finance expansion in other areas of the company's activities, the CCFC had excellent grounds to complain of Russian inefficiency and obstructiveness. Such situations could be overcome with goodwill, but by the end of 1915 there had built up such a legacy of ill-feeling on both sides that goodwill had become a scarce commodity. Outside intervention by men like Hermonious and Ellershaw could patch over many such matters but once they were to leave things tended to revert to the old pattern of mutual distrust and recrimination.

There were other problems for Russian purchasing in the United States. In the middle of November 1915 Edward Stettinius, who handled all of Britain's purchasing in the United States for J. P. Morgans, suggested that no further British orders be placed in America. As he pointed out, 'the chances are dead against' further orders being fulfilled since all manufacturing capacity in the United States was occupied fully.[10] There were financial reasons for such caution as well. At the beginning of 1916 the Chancellor of the Exchequer, McKenna, wrote to Lloyd George to ask if Russian needs could be provided out of the production of the Ministry of Munitions, rather than be ordered in the United States.[11] McKenna pointed out that Russia was near to exceeding the credits due to her under the provisions of the Treasury Agreement of 30 September 1915 and that he did not wish to extend further credit for purchases overseas. Lloyd George's reply is worthy of quotation in full:

> If you will come over here now – and if you like bring the Lord Chief Justice with you if you can manage it – I could show you the whole of our big gun and ammunition programme as I have the figures by me at the present moment; and unless I can convince you that we shall have nothing to spare for anybody except the Germans I am prepared to undertake to swallow the largest gun with its quota of ammunition![12]

While Lloyd George was able to sidetrack McKenna for the moment with this reply, there were others whom he found less easy to get around.

When Robertson took over as CIGS in December 1915 one of his primary concerns was to concentrate the British effort in 1916 on the Western front. Lloyd George's promise of 300 4.5-inch howitzers for Russia at the inter-Allied conference in November was greeted with hostility by both Robertson and the new Commander-in-Chief of the British forces in France, Douglas Haig.[13] On 20 January the Army Council wrote to the Ministry of Munitions that 'in view of [the] deficiencies' in the British army's supply of 4.5-inch howitzers, they hoped that there was to be no diminution of the 100 howitzers promised for France in January.[14] The reason for Lloyd George's evasive reply to McKenna cited above became clear when the ministry replied that due to the Russian commitments the British army would receive only fifty-one howitzers in January.[15] The Minister of Munitions was caught between his desire to provide armaments for Russia and the promises which he had made with respect to creating an abundance of munitions for the British army. Robertson suspected Lloyd George was 'beginning to see that he will not turn out in time the enormous amount [of munitions] about which he has talked so much' and so was looking for excuses to avoid any summer offensives as a consequence.[16]

The War Office immediately began a campaign to oppose sending the howitzers to Russia. At the War Committee meeting of 26 January Lloyd George defended his actions.[17] The Minister of Munitions laid particular stress on the fact that Russia had 'no heavy guns', that British and French artillery experts now felt that 'the 4.5-inch was not as good as formerly', and that the Russians 'were relying' on these guns and had in fact asked for more than they were to receive. The objections raised were twofold. Balfour stated that the shipping situation was such that there was 'no chance' of the guns being delivered by the promised date. Robertson noted that 'if this material was sent to Russia our Army would be lower than it ever had been in France in the matter of 4.5-inch ordnance.' Lloyd George still contended 'that we could not go back on our promise' and the matter was not resolved, Robertson grudgingly agreeing only 'to consider' the Minister of Munitions' argument.

The division between the two camps was clear. Robertson wished to focus the British effort for 1916 along the lines which had been agreed to at Chantilly. This meant a reduction of the secondary theatres and a concentration of men and supplies in France. On the other hand, Lloyd George wished to strengthen the Russians in the hope that they would be able to achieve the decisive result which the Minister did not believe was possible in the west. In addition, he felt that a strengthened Russia would be able to turn the Balkan situation to the Allies' advantage, an occurence which the British withdrawal from the Dardanelles and grudging commitment to Salonika made unlikely.

Lloyd George was essentially alone in his belief. Robertson was quick to marshal expert opinion which showed Lloyd George's ideas to be technically unfeasible and this opinion proved decisive. The War Office argued that no 4.5-inch ammunition could be spared for Russia and 'therefore for that reason, as well as the urgency of our own requirements, it is very desirable that no howitzers be sent there for the present.'[18] At the War Committee meeting of 3 February, Lloyd George managed to beat a retreat which kept open his options for the future.[19] After noting that, as 'Archangel would not be open until May', it was impossible to ship either the howitzers or the machinery for producing rifles and cartridges, Lloyd George agreed that the supplies would be used for British needs until the Russian transportation situation could be resolved. Faced with strong opposition in the War Committee, the Minister of Munitions had been forced to bide his time.

The problem of shipping and transportation in general was not one which permitted such delaying tactics. Britain had been involved in the transport of Russian supplies since the beginning of the war.[20] In 1914 the Russian Government Committee in London had chartered shipping to carry its purchases to Russia. This was handled through the firm of R. Martens and Co. Ltd.[21] By June 1915 sufficient shipping was unavailable by charter and the British government was approached to provide requisitioned tonnage for the shipment of coal to Russia. This was granted, but by the autumn of 1915 a shortage of tonnage for Russian goods was manifest.[22]

Discussions about shipping were a specific instance of the general argument which existed between Russia and Britain. With shipping, as was the case in matters dealing with finance and supply, the Russian government resented any British efforts which seemed to curtail Russia's independence; however, the exigencies of war forced Russia into surrendering some of her prerogatives. By the beginning of December 1915 discussions were opened between representatives of the Russian Volunteer Fleet and the British War Office on the growing problem of finding sufficient transport for Russian munitions purchased in the United States.[23] The Admiralty explained that ships would be 'exclusively under' the control of the company from which they were chartered, save that 'they would receive instructions as to sailing and as to cargo from the British Admiralty'. On 20 December a reply was received from the Russian Special Council for Defence, enquiring about the conditions which would be imposed in exchange for Admiralty provision of shipping and as to how much shipping Russia could expect to receive in 1916.[24]

The Admiralty's response to these enquiries was not encouraging. The Admiralty was 'not aware' that the British government had agreed to take over the transport of supplies for Russia and until this was the case the matter could be not discussed 'with advantage'.[25] As the Admiralty informed the War Office, their lordships 'deprecated' any move which might encourage the Russians to assume such a thing possible. The enormous size of the Russian requirements made it, in the Admiralty's opinion, 'open to doubt' that they could be dealt with in any case. The entire matter was discussed in the War Committee on 13 January in conjunction with the related issue of whether or not the British could count on Russia being able to join in a summer offensive.[26] As Balfour, the First Lord of the Admiralty, pointed out, the matter which needed to be discussed was whether or not transport was available to satisfy the Russian requirements. Robertson agreed, although the CIGS was undoubtedly more concerned about forestalling the shipment of 4.5-inch howitzers to Russia than he was about the First Lord's concern with available tonnage. Further discouraging news was forthcoming from New York, where Ellershaw wired that the problem of finding tonnage for Russian munitions purchased in the United States was 'becoming critical'.[27] Ellershaw concluded that unless the 'British Admiralty [would] undertake the transport of all Morgan orders' sufficient transport for Russian purchases would be unavailable.

At the end of January, the entire matter was referred to General Hermonious. The latter replied that the Russian government awaited an answer to its queries of 20 December.[28] As a result the Russian Purchasing Committee again questioned the Admiralty as to its attitude towards providing tonnage for Russia. In the Admiralty's reply of 2 February they refused to go beyond the cautious position they had taken above.[29] Since the question of whether or not transport for Russia would be provided was being discussed by Lord Curzon's Shipping Control Committee and the CIR, the Admiralty felt that these two bodies should be consulted instead. While all of this buck-passing was taking place, the shortages of tonnage had serious consequences for Russia. As pointed out above they had led to a delay in shipping of the 300 4.5-inch howitzers promised to Russia and a large reduction in Russian orders for explosives was necessitated as well.[30]

Robertson favoured adopting a firm line with Russia over the shipping issue. It was necessary, he felt, to indicate to Russia that the tonnage available to them in the following months was 'limited and may become still more limited in the future.'[31] Equally, the 'invariable vagueness' of the Russian figures as to their requirements for tonnage made it imperative, in the opinion of the CIGS, that the British government press the Russians more closely for information.[32] Despite advocating firmness with Russia, Robertson was aware of her military significance for the Allies, especially in the light of the 'heavy fighting' around Verdun which made it 'more necessary' than before to do 'everything possible' to help the Russians get supplies.[33]

The matter of tonnage was a key issue within Russia as well as in Britain. While Rusin had suggested to the Russian government that Hermonious be given authority to conclude an arrangement with the British Admiralty, and Hermonious could write to Wintour that the Council of Ministers had agreed tentatively to such a course, there were many objections within Russia to handing over control of transport to the British.[34] Rodzianko, the President of the Duma, argued that to do so 'might serve to certify the bankruptcy of the Russian government' and would be insulting 'to the national pride'.[35] Just as the financial agreement had reduced Russia's sovereignty compared to the wealthy nations, Rodzianko contended, the transport agreement would do likewise with respect to the nations strong in maritime transport.

By the end of February the issue was discussed once more in Britain. At the meeting of the War Committee on the 29th, Curzon and Balfour pointed out the problems involved in the Russian requests for tonnage.[36] Russian demands for 3 million tons of shipping were 'absolutely impossible' in Curzon's words, and the head of the Shipping Control Committee added that it was necessary to find out exactly what were the Russian tonnage resources since Russian information about this point was 'never honest'. Despite this, Curzon added, a key consideration was Russia's *amour propre*. The Russians were sensitive about appearing to be reduced to the position of beggars and the British should consider the issue carefully from this point of view. While Russian members of the CIR had agreed to let Britain take control of the arrangements for Russian shipping, Curzon was cynical about their motives. He felt that they favoured such a course 'chiefly . . . because it presented a way out of the difficulty for the Russians and threw the onus of responsibility on to the British.' For the Admiralty, Balfour concurred. The First Lord said that 'his own instinct' was against accepting such a responsibility, a responsibility which the Admiralty 'could not fulfil'. In any case, Balfour added, since the Russians would be responsible for removing the material delivered to their ports to the front, only a 'very small proportion' would ever reach the fighting lines. Faced with such a unanimity of opinion, the War Committee decided to defer any decision until Curzon was able to obtain full information about Russian shipping resources.[37]

Meanwhile Wyldbore Smith of the CIR was attempting to achieve a *démarche* with the Russians about transport. In a paper for the War Committee he pointed out that unless some sort of plan for transport were arrived at, the White Sea ports would be 'entirely blocked' by all sorts of goods, including non-military ones, when the season opened in the spring.[38] The Admiralty, Wyldbore Smith argued, must be allowed to handle the situation as 'the Russian government show no signs of attempting to deal with the question'. To such end, he outlined the points of agreement reached by the Russian members of the CIR and representatives of the Admiralty at a meeting on 19 February.[39]

However, the problem of Russian shipping had to be considered within the wider context of the matters dealt with by the Shipping Control Committee. By the beginning of 1916 the total of Allied demands on the tonnage requisitioned by the British government exceeded supply by more than 3.25 million tons. To deal with this Curzon's Committee had to formulate a policy of import restriction in order to provide extra tonnage for essential war needs.[40] This meant a careful balancing between Allied needs and British commercial needs (or, as Curzon had put it earlier, between 'the Foreign Office point of view, and the Board of Trade point of view').[41] At the meeting of the War Committee on 8 March, Curzon's arguments were made plain in a note which he prepared for the Committee:

> if as I understand the Russian Government are now themselves agreeable to hand over control of the Archangel Transport work to us, and assume that of Vladivostock themselves it might be worthwhile to pursue this suggestion [that Britain take over providing transport for Russia] . . . but should the balance of shipping with which my Committee is to be empowered to deal be reduced in the manner which I understand is favoured by the Board of Trade, it must be realised that the satisfaction of the Russian demands can only be accomplished at the probable expense of those of Italy and France.[42]

At the War Committee Balfour pointed out that the Admiralty could meet the Russian demands only by resorting to requisition, a move which would interfere with the workings of Curzon's Committee.[43] Kitchener then made it clear that purely military considerations far outweighed Balfour's caveats. The Secretary of State pointed out that 'this shipment of munitions was essential' and argued that Britain should tell Russia that the Admiralty would assume control of transport with the understanding that it might prove impossible to fulfil the Russian demands in their entirety. His advocacy of taking on such a further commitment firmly establishes the significance he gave to Russia's contribution to the *Entente*, and shows how unjust were the criticisms which the Russians had heaped upon Kitchener over the past year. After discussion in the War Committee, Kitchener's suggestion was agreed on and a telegram embodying his main points was sent to the Russian government.

British discussions about providing transport for Russia were influenced not only by considerations of available tonnage, but also by evaluations of the capacity of the Russian White Sea ports to handle goods received.[44] A particularly sensitive related issue was the problem experienced in building the railway designed to service these ports. The building of the line from Kem to Kandalaksha had been entrusted to Paulings, a British firm, and the failure of that company to complete its obligations had proved to be a disaster on a par with Vickers's default. The cancellation of Paulings's contract by the Russian government had been achieved with mutual recriminations and had dealt, in the words of the Admiralty's representative in Russia Admiral Phillimore, 'a severe blow . . . to British Commercial Prestige in Russia.'[45]

By the end of March, with fears growing that Russia's offensive at Lake Narotch would presage a season of uncoordinated thrusts by the Allies, Curzon's Committee reached a decision that Russia be allotted 100 ships for the White Sea summer programme.[46] Despite objections from the Board of Trade, the War Committee approved the Shipping Control Committee's recommendation.[47] This meant that Britain was responsible for providing Russia with 2 million tons of shipping in order to transport to Russia all the Morgans orders placed in the United States in addition to those placed in Britain.[48] There still remained, however, the need to obtain the agreement of the Admiralty to administer the programme. After much negotiation the Admiralty agreed to do so on 5 May.[49] By a memorandum of agreement, the Admiralty took responsibility, not only for providing 2 million tons of shipping for the Russian government in the twenty-five weeks following 15 May, but also for the control of all shipping in the White Sea, the arrangements for all on- and off-loading at Archangel and the clearing and marking of a channel in the White Sea. For their part, the Russian government promised to close the White Sea to all but CIR-approved shipping, to provide labour, storage and rolling stock at the ports and to ensure that adequate material for the transport inland of supplies was available.

While the prolonged negotiations over transport were taking place, the British government had other dealings with Russia. One such concerned rifles. The Russian need for rifles illustrated just how much British decisions on Russian requests for munitions rested increasingly on factors outside direct British control.[50] The War Office initially was sympathetic to providing rifles for Russia out of the surplus left over from British orders in the United States; however, when production figures in the United States failed to meet Ministry of Munitions projections, the War Office balked at losing their own supplies to Russia.[51] Despite the fact that there was apprehension lest the disastrous failure at Lake Narotch dishearten the Russians, and despite the fact that the War Office was 'fully in agreement with the principle of rendering every possible assistance to Russia', the War Office argued that a definite promise of rifles to Russia would be 'premature'. The War Office suggested that it would perhaps be better to investigate whether plants in the United

States could re-tool to produce rifles of Russian-calibre instead of sending those of the British model, a proposal which the Ministry of Munitions pointed out would take until mid-1918 to implement.[52] While the American production figures improved somewhat in May of 1916, allowing Russia to be supplied from British surplus, the question of rifles made clear two important points. First, it showed the constant competition between the British and Russian military establishments for a limited resource, and second, it pointed out the effect which industrial shortages in the United States could have on munitions supply for both Allies.

An unresolved issue after the shipping agreement had been signed was that of obtaining exact information about Russian requirements for munitions. While negotiations about shipping were progressing, a conference about munitions needs had been held in Paris on 27–28 March. The fact that the Russian delegate to the conference, General Zhilinskii, had little information about Russian needs meant that all that was achieved was an exchange of platitudes.[53] In the United States something more was accomplished. At the end of March a reorganisation of the purchasing system in that country was instituted along the lines which had been suggested by the Russian government in December 1915. By the terms of the reorganisation, the Russian Government Committee in New York was connected formally with the British purchasing mission in that city by placing two British members on the Committee and by defining the respective spheres of authority of the two bodies.[54] While this reform was useful, by the end of May 1916 the need for clear and concise information concerning Russian munitions requirements was one of the major reasons behind the push for sending Kitchener to Russia on a special mission.[55]

The other was finance. After the signing of the 30 September Treasury Agreement, a long negotiation had gone on between Bark and the British Treasury. This negotiation had centred on the expenditure of funds from the Agreement for the maintenance of the Russian exchange, a matter which Bark attempted to tie to the gold shipments provided for in the Agreement.[56] The Treasury was unwilling to provide additional funds to Bark for the matter of exchange, but was forced by circumstances to be more helpful about other matters. In the face of rising Russian purchases in the United States which threatened to exceed the £4.5 million per month limit of Russian credit provided by the Treasury Agreement, the Treasury assured Bark at the end of 1915 that they would 'do all they can within the limits of their resources' to ensure that Russia could continue to finance her essential military purchases.[57]

A month later, on 20 January 1916, the Treasury further evidenced its conciliatory attitude towards Russia. It was decided to grant a further £2 million per month of discretionary credit to the Russian government.[58] Far from being satisfied by this gesture, Bark pressed for further concessions, including permission to use remaining credits to pay for new orders and lump sums to settle certain outstanding debts in countries not covered by the provisions of the Treasury Agreement. Bark also argued that he would never be able to ship more than the £40 million worth of gold called for in the September pact, since the maintenance of the exchange was crucial to good relations between the two countries.[59]

The Treasury's response to Bark's demands made clear their opposition to his efforts to maintain the exchange rate at British expense. At the bottom of this opposition was the Treasury's belief that foreign exchange was being used both for the importing of luxuries, a practice which 'ought to be discouraged', and for the dishonest ends of certain Russian businessmen.[60] On the issue of letting Bark spend funds in other countries, the Treasury was less dogmatic but still opposed to providing any funds beyond the new £2 million monthly discretionary credit.

With respect to Russia's spending funds abroad, the matter of Russian purchasing in Japan became a central issue. In mid-February the Treasury agreed to let Russia ship an extra amount of gold to Japan in order to finance purchasing there but cautioned against over-purchasing.[61] By the beginning of March Sazonov had indeed asked for further credits for purchasing in Japan. The Treasury preferred to offer the offices of the British government to aid Russia in obtaining credit in Japan on their own.[62] The War Office, concerned about the collapse of the Lake Narotch offensive, pushed the Treasury to reconsider their views, arguing that 'every assistance should be rendered to Russia in her efforts to obtain munitions from the Japanese Government.'[63] This matter was resolved in July 1916 when the Russian government concluded a 70 million yen loan from the Japanese government, but it was typical of the niggling points which divided British and Russian financial thinking.

So, too, was the fact that Bark continued to request small sums from the British for various expenditures abroad. In mid-March the Treasury extended the Treasury Agreement to the end of 1916, thus providing a further three months' worth (or £13.5 million) of free credit to Russia. The Treasury hoped that this gesture of goodwill would show Bark that the Agreement was not being interpreted 'in any grudging spirit', but private opinion in the Treasury was not so conciliatory. As Keynes told the Board of the Admiralty, Britain's Allies, exclusive of France, were all 'mercenaries'.[64]

Other issues divided Russian and British financial opinion. Early in April the Russian Minister of Ways and Communications, A. F. Trepov, put forward a request for a special credit of approximately £12 million for the purchase of rolling stock, an order which he characterised as 'absolutely essential'.[65] Since the matter was put forward as being of major significance for the Russian summer campaign, it was referred by the Treasury to the War Office, the CIR and the Ministry of Munitions. Their replies reflected the differing departmental responsibilities involved. The War Office's view was that, while 'the question of supplying a blank cheque' to Russia was the Treasury's affair, 'from the strategical point of view' compliance with the Russian request was 'most desirable'.[66] The Ministry of Munitions was less happy about the Russian suggestion. In their view large independent orders of rolling stock in the American market by the Russians would be 'disastrous', and the Ministry suggested that they be allowed instead to buy the goods for Russia.[67] The Treasury was pleased with the Russian suggestion that they try to raise the money themselves on the American money market. Contrary to Russian suspicions that the British wished to have exclusive control over Russian finances abroad, Keynes noted that 'it is clear that we have everything to gain from the Russian Government having some funds at their disposal other than those which they obtain from us.'[68]

The continuing problems over Russian finance led the Chancellor of the Exchequer to bring the matter before the War Committee on 4 May.[69] In a paper prepared for that body, McKenna noted that the funds granted Russia under the Agreement of 30 September were 'exhausted' and that a further £25 million could be spent almost instantly if more credit were granted.[70] McKenna pointed out if that were the case, the Russians must be made to put priorities on their demands since the total of them was impossible to meet. At the meeting of the War Committee itself, McKenna was more far-reaching in his remarks. If the Allied demands on British credit continued unabated, he stated, 'the time will come when I shall have to state to this committee that in three or four months' time we must make peace.' In his view what was now necessary was to send a mission to Russia to determine exactly what were Russia's needs and to regularise Anglo-Russian finance. Kitchener pointed out the vital need to continue to supply Russia and suggested that a committee be formed to evaluate Russia's requests. McKenna felt that matters had gone too far for this expedient to work. Instead, he put forward the idea that Kitchener himself head a mission to Russia. Kitchener asked for time 'to think it over', but by the end of May it was decided that he should go to Russia, with one of the main objects of his mission being to explain 'the essential connection between British finance and the cause of the Allies as a whole' to the Russians.[71]

By June 1916 there was a real need for such a mission. The previous arrangements regarding co-operation in finance and supply either had proved themselves inadequate or had been overtaken by events. The financial Agreement of 30 September 1915 had been stretched beyond recognition. The unexpectedly large Russian expenditures in the United States had made it necessary to create further credits. As well, Bark's efforts to get funds free from British scrutiny and the continued Russian practice of placing independent orders in America had made a mockery of the attempts to gain control over Russian purchasing abroad. Most important, the deterioration of British credit in the United States was beginning to undermine the entire structure of Allied credit in the United States.[72] This latter problem was compounded by the needs of an expanding Russian war economy which required large amounts of goods not exclusively military.

Similar problems existed with munitions. Despite a strengthening of Russia's representation overseas and organisational changes in Anglo-Russian bodies dealing with munitions, there was not a significant improvement in the amount of supplies which Russia received from overseas. The reasons for this were varied. The demands of the British army for munitions had multiplied enormously and occupied the majority of British plants. The American orders had not for the most part yet begun to be fulfilled. The American war industry had taken on more contracts than it could handle and the Russian orders, hampered by financial and technical problems, were assigned a low priority. Further, the problem of tonnage became more serious, and this meant that shipping was not available for all the Russian orders from America, even if they should be completed. Linked with this, the Russian internal transportation system had demonstrated itself incapable of moving goods from the ports to the front even in the limited amounts which were delivered. Clearly the time had come for a new departure to attempt to solve some of these problems which threatened to choke off British aid to Russia in both finance and supply.

The tragic sinking of *HMS Hampshire* and the death of Kitchener put an end to the hope that the Secretary of State's mission would provide a solution. But even before Kitchener's death, the matter of Russian orders in Canada and the United States had become a critical issue once again. As before, it was the CCFC orders which touched off the crisis. On 3 June the vice-president of the Russian Purchasing Committee in New York telegraphed that the CCFC refused to honour the penalty clauses in its contract. He pointed out that the CCFC's arguments were 'legally worthless' and that the company must be held to its contracts lest any compromise 'encourage complete laxity' in similar orders held in America.[73] Given the serious consequences of any disruption in the flow of supplies from Canada and the United States, the Ministry of Munitions immediately investigated these charges through the agency of the Canadian Imperial Munitions Board (the Canadian branch of the Ministry, or IMB).[74]

Perry and Gordon, two members of the IMB, examined the CCFC problem.[75] Essentially nothing had changed since Ellershaw's visit in December 1915–January 1916. Bitterness and distrust between the Russians and the CCFC meant that little could be accomplished. More seriously, in the view of Stettinius, situations comparable to the CCFC's position existed with regard to other firms which held contracts for the Russian government.[76] Stettinius felt that this problem called for 'prompt and energetic action' in order to head off further problems. It was suggested that Perry be appointed as a trustee on the board of the CCFC in order to lessen the tension between the company and the Russians. In addition the appointment of a British representative of 'high position' competent to deal both with technical matters and arbitration between the Russians and American contractors was suggested in order to ease the strained relations existing in the United States. Any decision was delayed until the middle of June by the death of Kitchener and the end of his mission.

While the shock caused by Kitchener's death subsided, discussions occurred concerning the problems of inspection of Russian orders in the United States. Sapozhnikov and Hermonious favoured the idea of Perry's becoming a member of the board of the CCFC, but no agreement was reached on the issue of inspection.[77] General Minchin, the Inspector-General of the British purchasing mission in the United States, felt that the problem was due 'partly to the language difficulty and partly to the difference between autocratic and democratic ideas' and argued that only a fundamental reorganisation of inspection procedures would solve the problem.[78] Russian *amour propre* and a lack of British inspectors in America made this solution unlikely. Even so, both Stettinius and Minchin were convinced that major changes had to be made, not only in organisation but also in personnel. As they pointed out, the Russian inspectors in the United States were rejecting munitions on 'frivolous grounds' to the detriment of all concerned.[79]

In a letter to Lloyd George on 21 June Minchin reviewed the entire issue which the CCFC imbroglio had brought to light.[80] Before writing to Lloyd George, Minchin had discussed the matter with a wide range of people including Stettinius, General Gonelin (of the French purchasing mission in the United States), and Grace (the president of Bethlehem Steel Company). All agreed that the case of Bethlehem Steel's contract for Russian shells was typical of the problems experienced in the United States. The Russian inspectors, hampered by difficulties of language and differences of temperament, had rejected shells which both the French and British government found acceptable. Moreover, the legal position surrounding these orders was delicate. While the Russian inspectors had the final say on the acceptability of production standards, the British government was legally responsible for the contracts. Thus, Minchin wrote, 'if the arbitration which is mentioned in the contracts is called into effect, it will be arbitration between the contractors and the British Government.' Given the financial dependence on the United States which McKenna had pointed out in May, any such arbitration was to be avoided. In addition, such an occurrence could put the British government at loggerheads with both the Russian and American governments simultaneously, an unenviable position. In Minchin's view the matter could only be eased by a British takeover of inspection. This, he felt, could be accomplished by utilising the capacity of the IMB's Canadian personnel, augmenting the British organisation already in the United States with further personnel from England and retaining a 'small number of expert Russian officers'.

A great deal of discussion also centred on the idea that the problem could be met by the creation of a new committee in the United States.[81] This committee, it was proposed, would consist of the president and one other member of the Russian Purchasing Committee in New York and of two British representatives. This new body would be empowered to deal with all matters concerning manufacture and inspection and would make final decisions on all points of contention. As usual, the Russian objection to any suggestion of British control over their independence of action in the United States was marked. Sapozhnikov wrote a memorandum on the situation rebutting the British proposal.[82] There was no need for a new committee, he argued, as the provisions of the annexe to the Treasury Agreement of 30 September 1915 already had authorised a body capable of taking such decisions. Sapozhnikov further opined that the principle must be maintained that orders could be placed in the United States either directly by the Russian government or through joint endeavours. Finally, he stated that all decisions of any committee created must be 'carried unanimously' and be binding on both sides. Sapozhnikov's remarks illustrated the intransigent position of the Russian government, for the annexe of 30 September had proved itself woefully inadequate as an instrument for regulation. Separate Russian ordering in the United States was what had caused the difficulties in the first place and the principle of 'unanimity' meant that nothing could be achieved.

While such discussion took place, the financial position of the CCFC became precarious, carrying with it the threat that all Allied orders in the United States would be jeopardised.[83] As had been foreseen, the continued Russian niggling over inspection had caused difficulties for firms other than CCFC. Both Bethlehem Steel and Westinghouse were demanding large advances respectively on their shell and rifle contracts in order to overcome shortages of cash caused by the extended production time which the finickyness of Russian inspection had caused. At the Treasury Keynes felt that the Bethlehem advances should be given, but did not favour giving money to Westinghouse as the latter also wished for an extension in the delivery dates for the rifles contracted.[84]

By the end of the first week in July the talks between the British and Russian representatives reached an impasse. Hermonious put the Russian position clearly in a letter to Wintour dated 7 July.[85] Hermonious averred in this letter that it was essential for the working of any agreement between the two countries 'to avoid in one way or another interfering with the independence of either parties [*sic*] to the Agreement.' While he recognised that the Treasury should have partial control over purchasing in America and 'the direct control of expenditure', Hermonious did not agree that Britain should have control of inspection in the United States. Such a move, he felt, would weaken 'the mutual trust' between the two countries as differences of opinion over technical matters might result in 'petty' and 'cumbersome' delay. While consultation with the British on such matters would be 'carefully considered and taken into consideration with gratitude', Hermonious would not accept final authority over inspection passing from the exclusive control of the Russian representatives.

As Booth wrote on the same date, the situation was such that three alternatives existed.[86] The first was to leave things as they were; the second was to set up a new Anglo-Russian committee to deal with orders and inspection, and the third was to remove inspection from Russian hands entirely. Lloyd George, Booth noted, favoured the latter, but Booth felt that the second alternative was best. As Booth saw it, the Secretary of State for War's preferred line of action was impossible since the Russians would never agree to such a diminution of authority. In addition, Booth felt that the formation of a new committee held out some promise since in the past the committee approach had worked well, if sporadically, the few times that it had been tried. The major problem with such an approach had been that no effort had been made to put consultation on a regular basis. Only the two joint visits by Hermonious and Ellershaw had taken place, but they had resulted in problems being ironed out, albeit temporarily. A new solution, Booth concluded, had other considerations as well: it had to be worked out in the context of an overall evaluation of Anglo-Russian supply and finance. The opportunity for this would be the conference scheduled to begin 12 July 1916 in London between high-ranking members of both the British and Russian governments.

There were other reasons necessitating such a conference. Both Lloyd George and Albert Thomas felt that the Russians were coming to depend too much on the Allies for aid, at the expense of their own domestic production. Lloyd George raised this point at the War Committee meeting of 6 June, a meeting held in the shadow of the death of Kitchener. His point was taken by the Committee and a telegram was sent to Russia emphasising the need for her to produce as much as she could with her own resources.[87] As the telegram made clear, any impression that the Russian government had that the British preferred them to purchase overseas was false. In fact, such purchase was 'to be regarded only as a regrettable necessity to be ended as soon as possible.' As well as this growing disillusionment with Russia's war effort with respect to munitions, there were other points which needed to be resolved. One involved railways.

By the middle of June the Treasury had ready a reply to Trepov's request of 6 April for £12 million to purchase railway material.[88] The Treasury informed the Foreign Office that the Russian overture was 'quite beyond what it is possible for Their Lordships to meet.' Not only was the sum required too great, the Treasury felt, but also there was insufficient transport available to ship such orders as the Russians wished to make. While shipping for goods worth £5 million might be available, the Treasury went on, the Russians had already expended all the credits due to them. In fact, it was concluded, 'it is probable that Their Lordships will be forced by financial considerations to adopt the policy that no more orders of any kind must be placed in America except in quite exceptional circumstances.'

This warning had little effect on the Russians. Throughout June they continued undaunted in their negotiations in the United States for railway material, to the detriment of their stock with the British Treasury.[89] Early in July before the conference opened, McKenna sent a testy telegram to Petrograd stating that he presumed that the Russians were not relying either on British finance or on British transport for the rail orders in the United States, as neither would be forthcoming.[90] The Russian reply emphasised the disparity between the British and Russian positions.[91] The Russian government had waited 'in vain' for a reply to their earlier request for credits with which to purchase railway goods. As the American firms had demanded 'immediate' replies, the Russian government had had no alternative but to place the orders on their own initiative since the receipt of these goods 'was necessary if the war was to continue.'

According to Keynes, who reviewed Russia's requirements for war in a trenchant paper prepared for the forthcoming conference, the railway orders 'much prejudiced' any discussions which would be held in London.[92] As far as Keynes was concerned, the Russian efforts to place such orders in the United States, 'in the hope that the British Government will provide the necessary credits and necessary freight', were an attempt to force the British hand.

Railway issues were not the only other reason why a conference was required. Equally important was a decision by Haig that the requirements of the British army for heavy artillery in 1917 were to be increased substantially.[93] This clashed with a similar Russian demand for 6- and 8-inch howitzers; a demand accompanied by the allegation that their offensive could be continued successfully only if the weapons 'specially necessary in Siege warfare' were provided.[94] The attitude of the War Office to the Russian requests was surprisingly obliging. At a conference held on 5 July, Robertson showed himself to be ready to accommodate Lloyd George's suggestion that the British provide the Russians, in the manner of the French, with one in three of the British production of 6-, 8- and 9.2-inch howitzers.[95] The CIGS stipulated only that the levels of heavy guns projected in Lloyd George's own programme of the previous September be reached before guns were sent to Russia. A similar conference, held the next day, agreed that Russian needs in rifles, machine guns and small arms ammunitions could also be met without serious damage to British requirements.[96]

Such a congenial attitude was not found at the Treasury, where concern with the British financial position in America was paramount. Lloyd George refused to accept such an argument. At the meeting of the War Committee on 29 June 1916 he presented a note which rejected McKenna's contention that the United States might cut off supplies to the Allies.[97] As Lloyd George argued, 'in my opinion if the American manufacturers are faced with the alternative of losing the very lucrative orders which the Allies give them or of making their own arrangements for financing these contracts on the joint credit of the three Allied countries. . . . They would prefer the latter alternative.' He also felt that President Wilson would be unwilling to create massive unemployment on the eve of the presidential election by stopping the Allied contracts. After all, he concluded, if American firms could do annually $20,000–30,000 million worth of orders on a credit basis, then they would not balk at doing $800 million worth for the Allies backed by the credit of all three. In any case, Lloyd George noted, Russia had been denied munitions already on financial grounds and thus 'a victory which would with proper equipment be assured for 1917 is thus put off for another year.'

The entire issue of credit for Russia was discussed in detail at the meeting of the War Committee the following day.[98] The difference of opinion between Lloyd George and McKenna was marked. Lloyd George, supported by Balfour, pressed for a concerted approach to be taken toward the Russian demands for funds. What Lloyd George called for was a conference to precede the Anglo-Russian financial meeting tentatively scheduled to begin when Bark and General Beliaev arrived in Paris. This conference would determine the dimensions of all the Russian needs in munitions as well as the British ability to provide both them and the tonnage necessary to transport them. McKenna was skeptical about the value of such a conference. He affirmed that 'what they could spend, they would spend. A Conference might be held to determine the maximum of Russian requirements, but had nothing to do with the maximum of spending.' Besides, McKenna said that he would have little time to participate in a long conference before he attended the Allied financial meetings in Paris. Lloyd George, however, was insistent and pointed out that a conference would require only two days, and the Chancellor of the Exchequer admitted that he could spare that much time. Agreement was widespread that Russia should be encouraged to develop her own munitions industry as far as possible and to quantify the exact nature of her needs.

A final position was adopted on the following Monday at a meeting of the Cabinet Finance Committee.[99] Lloyd George's proposal for a conference to precede the inter-Allied meeting in London was accepted as the best course of action. This preliminary conference was to discuss Russia's war needs, to determine to what degree these needs could be fulfilled in the Allied countries and to establish what transport was available for these supplies. It was agreed as well that it was 'essential' that Russia be equipped if victory was to be assured. The Treasury's arguments were not, however, overlooked. Russia was to be encouraged to produce as much as possible for herself and what had to be purchased abroad should be found, as much as was feasible, in Britain and France where Allied credit would not be endangered. Also, 'pressure should be put' on Russia (and France) to get them to co-operate with the Treasury's plans to finance purchases in the United States. As to the nature of the purchases which the Allies were to make abroad, 'the War Committee hold that the British Government is entitled and indeed, bound, to satisfy itself as to the degree of urgency of the various Allied requirements (the principal of which are the Russian) from America, from the point of view of the effective prosecution of the war.' No greater contrast could have existed between this latter position and that held by Russia. The London conference was to make this point very clear.

Despite the conclusions which the Cabinet Finance Committee reached, there was not unanimity among the British policy-makers about the financial situation. Lloyd George's arguments about the availability of American credit did not sit well at the Treasury. Keynes produced a memorandum for McKenna which served as a rebuttal to Lloyd George's arguments, and these are worthy of close examination for they underline just how Russia's needs for credit and munitions were intimately linked with the entire prosecution of the war.[100] Through McKenna, Keynes argued that Lloyd George was wrong to assume that American contractors would create their own credit for Allied orders. He challenged the Secretary of State for War to arrange any contracts on that basis since such a move would 'greatly relieve' the financial situation. As to the notion that cancellation of contracts would result in massive unemployment in the United States, McKenna was dismissive. The Americans had far more orders, both domestic and foreign, than they could handle and the 'labour shortage is acute'. Keynes was equally contemptuous of Lloyd George's argument that as the Americans annually did $30,000 million worth of business on a credit basis they would not hesitate to do $800 million worth for the Allies on a similar basis. This argument, Keynes stated, showed a misunderstanding both of the word 'credit' and of American banking law. The large figures used by Lloyd George as representing the work done on 'credit' in the United States applied only if 'credit' were understood to mean either 'cash transactions . carried out for convenience by the intermediary of a cheque or Bank note' or 'a transaction in which the borrower possesses goods the sale of which at an early date will furnish funds for repayment of a loan.' The kind of credit that Lloyd George envisaged getting in the United States was of another sort, the sort 'where the borrower gives no immediate return, but only a promise to pay in the future.' Such an unsecured credit was, Keynes said, different both legally and economically. American banks were not permitted by law to lend money against such unsecured credit, even should they so wish, and this legal restriction posed an insuperable barrier against the kind of 'credit' financing which Lloyd George proposed.

Keynes was even more biting about Lloyd George's contention that Russia had been denied supplies in the past because of the penny-pinching attitude of the Treasury. In a passage which McKenna tactfully excised before printing, Keynes stated that any stinting of Russia had been due to the War Office's placing (through Lloyd George's Ministry of Munitions) excessive orders for Britain in the United States.[101] McKenna instead countered that since he had become Chancellor of the Exchequer the Russians had spent £300 million of British credit and that the forthcoming conference was designed to provide her with further credits. He also pointed out that the Treasury had made great efforts to co-ordinate Russian purchasing with that of the other Allies and to ensure that she bought at the most favourable prices in America. Finally, McKenna noted that Lloyd's George's argument had missed the central point entirely. The problem of procuring Russian munitions in America was not simply a matter of whether or not to go another £100 million into debt in the United States, but rather whether or not America was *'prepared'* to lend such a sum. McKenna's advisers both 'here and in America' did not feel confident that such was the case.

While there was still sharp debate about Britain's financial policy, other departments of state established less contentious positions in the week before the conference with the Allies opened. W. T. Layton, the Director of Munitions Requirements and Supplies (DMRS) at the Ministry, made clear that body's attitude towards Russia in a memorandum which he prepared for Edwin Montagu, Lloyd George's successor as Minister of Munitions.[102] This memorandum emphasised the limiting nature of the tonnage available to ship Russian orders. By Layton's calculations the tonnage available for Russia was 'largely taken up already' by present orders and further orders, which were 'very greatly in excess' of available tonnage, had therefore to be presented by the Russians in order of priority if any of them were to be fulfilled. This need for priorities was made even greater by the limited capacity of Russia's ports. While this capacity was to be expanded by 0.5 million tons by 1917, proposed new orders for Russia were more than double this figure. In such circumstances the British would have to impress upon the Russians the close relationship between transportation and ordering abroad.

The inter-Allied conference opened at the War Office on the morning of 13 July.[103] Lloyd George began the conference with a speech to the Allies which put the British position nicely. In his diary Addison caught the flavour of the Secretary of State's remarks:

> [It was] a statement to them generally that the business was to make a summary of their different requirements, which practically resolved themselves to demands by the Russians and Italians and L.[loyd] G.[eorge] took the occasion to rub into the Russians that it was absolutely up to them to make a better use than they had up to the present of their own machinery and manufacturing capacity. He did this tactfully but firmly.[104]

The Russian reply was given by General Beliaev. The general made it clear that Russia's primary requirement was for heavy artillery, as she was now able domestically to provide for the most part the necessary rifles and shell. Beliaev was quick to link the provision of heavy artillery with Russia's military contribution to the *Entente* and, by doing so, exert pressure on the other Allies to ensure that Russia's needs were fulfilled. 'The need for heavy artillery [within the Russian army] at present is so great', Beliaev told the conference, 'that, if they cannot get it, it will put an end to success.' He emphasised that 'the unsatisfactory results' of the previous winter's offensive had been caused by a lack of heavy artillery and explained the success of Brusilov's offensive as being 'due to the concentration there [on the Russian south-western front] of all the resources which Russia has in heavy artillery and shells.' While the accuracy of both of these assertions was doubtful, the line of the Russian argument was evident: if the Allies expected the Russian offensive to continue then they must provide her with the heavy artillery that she desired.[105]

Beliaev then turned to the question of transport. He outlined the enormous difficulties involved for Russia in transporting imported goods – for example, the 300 4.5-inch howitzers which Britain had sent in May – to the front. For this reason railway material was the second priority among Russian needs; if Russia did not receive railway supplies then her transportation system would be inadequate to handle the other things which the Allies sent to her. After completing his list of Russian requirements by discussing matters for which the need was less urgent, Beliaev concluded his speech with a further reference to the urgent Russian need for artillery. Unless he were able to obtain some solution to this matter, Beliaev remarked, he would 'dare not face Russia again'.

Lloyd George's response to these demands was cautious. He pointed out that, in view of British requirements, heavy artillery was in short supply and would be unlikely to be available in any large amount until 1917. He also pressed Beliaev closely about the latter's seeming unconcern about rifles. The general was not to be sidetracked by such questions. He reiterated that rifles were no longer a matter of the first importance since orders placed abroad had begun to arrive in Russia and domestic production had increased. This brought the morning session of the conference to an end. In his concluding remarks to this meeting, Lloyd George was not optimistic about the possibility of fulfilling Beliaev's demands for heavy artillery. Pointing out that heavy artillery for Russia would have to be drawn from British requirements and 'not out of a surplus', Lloyd George told his audience that he would have to consult with the British military authorities before he could promise anything specific to Russia. The Secretary of State for War also noted that there would have to be decisions taken as to what campaigns were to be undertaken in 1917 before it could be resolved as to what would be the munitions requirement of each front. Until such matters were determined, he warned, the best course for the Russians to follow was to produce as much from their own resources as possible. Thomas seconded Lloyd George's remarks, and noted obscurely that Britain and France 'do not know how to give anything to Russia, and yet something must be given to Russia.'

The bargaining positions of the various Allies having been staked out in broad outline in the morning, the conference reassembled that afternoon at the Ministry of Munitions for some hard bartering.[106] After an opening speech by Asquith and some prefatory remarks by the chairman of the session, Edwin Montagu, Lord Curzon gave an outline of the transportation situation as viewed by the British. Curzon's evaluation of the White Sea ports was pessimistic. The main port of Archangel, he said, was receiving more cargo than could be removed from it, necessitating much storage of imports for shipment to the interior in the winter when the port was closed. As a result of this congestion, Curzon pointed out, over the following year 'Archangel will only be available for new orders for a brief space'. As to the port of Kola, by Admiralty estimates the railway line connecting it with the interior would not be finished until March of 1917 making assumptions of its capacity during the following year problematical at best. On this basis, Curzon estimated that the White Sea routes taken together could carry new orders up to a maximum 'of (say) 110,000 tons'. Vladivostock would be able to handle a further 390,000 tons of new orders, making the total amount of tonnage available for new orders up to the middle of 1917 500,000 tons in round figures.

Beliaev's reply to Curzon's remarks was not recorded, but the import of it was evident from Curzon's rejoinder. Beliaev's figures on transport, Curzon said, were 'in excess' of any British estimates, and he added that, 'while the General was speaking, I was wondering whether he was sometimes moving perhaps in the region of hope rather than in the region of recognizable fact.' At this awkward point, Montagu tactfully changed the subject from transportation to a consideration of Russia's needs for railway material 'really necessary for the conduct of the war.'

Given this opportunity Beliaev went on at length about the internal problems of transportation in Russia and the need for enlarged rail capacity to speed the offensive. He then asked for 1,300 locomotives, 30,000 wagons and 'about' 300,000 tons of rails to be delivered to Russia by the spring of 1917. Since these figures were obviously impossible to fulfil due to considerations of tonnage, Montagu decided to approach them obliquely. He pointed out that there was 'considerable difficulty' with Russian orders already placed in the United States due to the matter of inspection. Thus, he said, American manufacturers would 'look with great reluctance' on further large orders being made unless some new method of inspection were agreed to. Montagu then linked Beliaev's request for railway material to a resolution of the issue of inspection: 'this question is immediate and must govern any decision with regard to either railway materials or any other goods which we may order from America on behalf of Russia.' With the ball clearly in Beliaev's court, Montagu then offered the general a copy of one of the various proposals on inspection which Booth and Wintour had worked out with Hermonious over the course of the preceding month.

Put on the defensive, Beliaev agreed that these proposals seemed sound, but Thomas took the opportunity to interject his own ideas into this exchange. The French Minister of Munitions revived the concept of an inter-Allied purchasing commission to deal comprehensively with supplies. Montagu pleaded a lack of familiarity with Thomas's ideas and refused to be drawn on the subject, despite the latter's continued insistence to get some accord on it. When the matter was dropped, Montagu offered a counter-proposal to Beliaev's demands for railway supplies. The Minister of Munitions suggested that Britain might be able to supply 500 locomotives, 7,000 wagons and 100,000 tons of rails to Russia. He accompanied this offer with a warning which expressed the longstanding British irritation with Russia's tendency to order independently abroad: a Russian attempt to buy rails in the United States might 'prejudice' all Allied attempts to purchase steel goods in that country.

In bringing the afternoon session of the conference to an end, Montagu was scarcely less cautious than Lloyd George had been in the morning. Montagu reiterated Lloyd George's remarks about the need to consult with British military authorities before the issues of heavy artillery and shell could be resolved and added that Lloyd George would discuss the matter further the next day. The Russian needs for machinery and transport were then turned to and the British delegates raised doubts about whether either tonnage or money for them could be found. The Russian domestic production of rifles, field guns and small arms ammunition was the only point which gave rise to much satisfaction as far as the British were concerned, Addison noting in his diary that the Russians had done 'infinitely better' with regard to these matters than had been anticipated.[107]

The following day, 14 July, two meetings were held at the Treasury to discuss financial issues. At the morning session McKenna emphasised that there was a need to establish in advance the need for credit which each Ally might require in a given time period.[108] The Agreement of 30 September 1915 had now been abandoned, McKenna noted, and there was a pressing need for a new arrangement to replace it. At present each order placed by the Allies had to be considered individually, resulting in a situation where the British Treasury never knew for exactly how much it would be responsible. To this end, McKenna suggested to Bark that Russia make her requests for funds, within the context of a fixed overall limit, on a monthly basis. Thomas suggested that no obligations should be taken which extended beyond July 1917, a proposal which McKenna accepted as a working proposal. Discussion then turned to the amounts that Russia should be permitted to owe abroad until the end of July 1917. No ready agreement was found. Debate quickly bogged down over whether the sum allotted to Russia should be that sufficient to pay for the maximum orders which Beliaev had put forward the day before or that capable of meeting the amount of orders which Curzon's figures concerning tonnage had suggested were possible.

Opening the afternoon session at the Treasury, Montagu summed up what the munitions and supplies portion of the conference had agreed upon.[109] He outlined the difference of opinion between Curzon and Beliaev on tonnage and put forward the differing figures on railway goods which the Russian and British governments had presented. He pointed out that an agreement had been struck concerning the vexatious matter of the inspection of goods ordered for Russia in the United States, since Beliaev had agreed that a joint Anglo-Russian Sub-Committee was to be set up in New York to deal with all such matters.[110] Thomas's plan for a common purchasing bureau, however, had been shelved pending further study. Informal discussion had reduced the Russian demands for metals by two-thirds and some promises had been made to supply Russia with shells in 1917. Other, less pressing, matters had been resolved as well, leaving outstanding only the matter of heavy artillery, a matter which could not be decided until British military figures were consulted.[111]

After Montagu's speech, Bark, McKenna, Beliaev, Ribot and Thomas continued their discussion of financial matters. In his remarks McKenna attempted to shift the responsibility for a reduction of credit to be given Russia away from his own department. 'The question of money', he told Bark, 'does not stop us. . . . The limit which is imposed on you is not a limit of credit but a limit of manufacture and of transport.' As evidence for this contention, he pointed out the discrepancy which existed between the Russian demands for material and the amount of tonnage which was available to ship it. As well, McKenna suggested that the order which Russia had placed recently in the United States for 200,000 tons of rails was apt not to be fulfilled as there was a steel shortage in that country caused by the heavy demands on supply for the manufacture of shells.

The Russians did not accept either argument. Concerning transport, Beliaev noted that improvements would be made which would permit greater amounts to be moved than was thought possible at present. He did not, however, provide any concrete explanation of how such improvements would be accomplished. Instead he stepped into the realm of the metaphysical; as he put it, 'the need is so great that we must surmount all obstacles and we shall suceed[sic] in doing it.' As to the implied rebuke of independent orders which McKenna had made concerning rail orders, Beliaev made it clear that such orders were a military necessity. 'Without rails', the general argued, 'our army will receive neither reinforcements nor munitions.' Bark addressed the same topic with a somewhat minatory attitude. Rejecting McKenna's argument that Russia should limit herself when ordering abroad if the orders seemed likely to be unfulfilled the Russian finance minister stated

> The equipment of the Russian Army is in all respects very inferior to that of the Allies; it must be improved at all costs, even at the price of entrenching upon the more generous equipments of the English and French Armies. It is not to the interests of the Allies that the Russian offensive and the possibility of future offensives should be rendered impossible.

The French delegation attempted to bridge the gap between the British and Russian positions by turning the discussion to the question of co-ordination. The key thing, they advanced, was to be able to present Lloyd George as Secretary of State for War with a clear outline of the needs of the Russian army in order that some agreement could be reached as to what the British could spare out of their own production. As to matters in the United States, they emphasised the need, as Thomas put it, to find 'the means of organising that [American] production for our own benefit.' At this uneasy juncture, the discussion turned to the raising of a new Allied loan in America and the conference was adjourned until the following day, when smaller meetings and a final plenary session were held.

Despite the closure of the conference on 15 July, the two major issues discussed at it, the supply of heavy artillery to Russia and more finance for her, had not been settled. Both became matters of long debate within the British government, and both found opinion divided within the élite. The arguments proceeded along familiar paths.

With respect to artillery, at the conference Beliaev had requested 600 4.5-inch howitzers, 100 6-inch howitzers and as many larger howitzers as available.[112] Lloyd George had offered to provided 200 medium and heavy howitzers by the spring of 1917, but had promised no deliveries before the beginning of the new year. His position was at best a compromise one since General Haig was opposed even to this amount being shipped to Russia. Haig's position was based upon his evaluation of the military situation. The commander of the BEF felt that a German attack on Russia in the autumn of 1916 was unlikely and therefore that 'the most patriotic and the wisest policy is to provide all that we require ourselves before we give to others.'[113] The issue became one for the War Committee.

On 28 July Montagu circulated a memorandum to the War Committee calling for Russia to be supplied with some 376 guns and howitzers of 4.7-inch calibre and larger by the end of September 1917.[114] Montagu argued, in his memorandum, that such a move should be undertaken for several reasons. First, Russia was sceptical of Britain's contribution to the alliance, and this gesture would show just how highly Russia was valued by Britain. Second, unless Russia were aided it was unlikely that she could take part in the concerted offensives necessary to defeat the Germans. Finally, without receiving assistance, Russia's effective value to the Allies would diminish forcing the British forces to take on the bulk of the fighting and suffer the casualties which this would entail. At the War Committee's meeting, Lloyd George argued against these proposals.[115] The Secretary of State for War raised the arguments which Haig made concerning sending guns to Russia and Montagu's point of view was not accepted by the War Committee. No doubt influenced by the size of the commitment to supply Romania with arms as part of that country's preconditions for joining the *Entente*, a matter which was considered the same day, the War Committee decided that before any guns were sent to Russia it was necessary to determine exactly what use had been made of the 300 4.5-inch howitzers already dispatched there. In fact, as Lloyd George told Beliaev, the final figures as to how much heavy artillery Britain could provide for Russia could not be made until after the General Staffs of the Allies had met to determine the military plans for 1917.[116] In the face of British requirements and the dubious ability of the Russians to provide immediate transport for goods sent to Russia, the War Committee had decided to defer Russian demands until the following year.

The financial matters discussed at the conference were not settled until the end of October. The real stumbling block in the talks which followed was the export of gold and, to a lesser extent, the related issue of the exchange value of the rouble.[117] At the July conference the Treasury had offered the Russians a credit of £25 million per month, for six months, with £4 million of this amount to be a free credit at Bark's disposal for 'miscellaneous purposes and partly for support of exchange.'[118] In addition to the monthly credit, military orders to a value of £63 million could be placed at once and a further £31.5 million of such orders could be made in each of October and November. In exchange, Russia was to agree to ship Britain up to a maximum of £40 million in gold, in two £20 million instalments. The first instalment was to be shipped if the British gold reserve fell below £80 million and the second was to be sent if the levels went below £70 million. If Russia would agree to ship the £20 million in gold which was still outstanding from the amount owed under the Agreement of 30 September 1915 – £20 million having already been shipped – then none of the £40 million due under the proposed new agreement would be called for until 1917.

Buchanan informed the Russian government of this offer, but told the Foreign Office that the Russians were not happy about the proposed shipment of gold and that rumours were circulating alleging that Britain was denying Russia the credit necessary to buy arms.[119] On 14 August Benckendorff offered the Russian government's counter-proposal that Russia send two £10 million instalments of gold, each to be paid only if British reserves dipped below £70 million.[120] In an accommodating mood the Treasury agreed that, if the £20 million due under the 30 September 1915 Agreement were paid, then the new Russian commitment could be reduced to a further £20 million as the Russians suggested, although in view of the 'very grave risks' involved, the Treasury would require 'full discretion' to call for this £20 million any time after 1 January 1917 'irrespective of the precise amount of the British gold reserves at the moment.'[121]

Bark was not pleased with this formula, as he disliked the stipulation that gold should be available on demand.[122] While this concept was at the bottom of the Treasury's willingness to accept a reduced amount of gold from Russia, Buchanan pointed out that the entire issue had political ramifications. The delay in coming to terms with Russia over the loan was, in the ambassador's words, 'creating a bad impression' in Russia and he suggested that the Treasury accept the Russian proposal of two £10 million shipments linked to a drop in British reserves below £70 million. Since Buchanan's suggestion was echoed by a formal note from the Russian government, the Foreign Office forwarded the matter to the Treasury for a decision on 2 September.[123]

The Treasury's attitude to the Russian modifications was much the same as it had been to proposals which the French had put forward in the latter part of August with respect to credit overseas. Prior to the Anglo-French financial conference held in Calais on 24 August, the French had suggested that the Allies should not undertake any independent borrowings in the United States but rather should act in concert with one another.[124] The Treasury viewed this as an attempt to take control of Allied finance out of British hands and objected to it strongly. At a meeting of the War Committee on 22 August, McKenna pointed out to his colleagues that as Britain was the financial mainstay of the alliance and often had to raise large sums in the United States at short notice, she could not afford to give up control to a joint Allied body which would be unable to deal rapidly with such situations.[125] He met with little objection from the War Committee. The real issue, as Asquith pointed out, was one of the maintenance of the gold standard and the Allies must be prepared to ship gold to preserve it.

When the Russian arguments were brought before the War Committee on 12 September, McKenna approached them as he had those of the French.[126] Since the French had agreed at Calais to send £50 million of gold on the demand of the Bank of England, the Russians could do no less. This line was agreed to and a telegram outlining it was sent to Bark the following day.[127] Faced with such an attitude, Bark resorted to several ploys in order to make his position stronger.[128] First, he replied that he personally accepted the British argument, but that the finance committee of the Council of Ministers felt that France was sending less gold than Russia. Second, he noted that the finance committee also believed that Russia needed to husband her gold to provide backing for her paper currency. In shifting the responsibility for protracting the negotiations, Bark was following the course which Lloyd George had employed so successfully at inter-Allied conferences, where the Welshman had used the British military establishment as his stalking-horse in discussions. By the beginning of October Bark's arguments of political opposition to his negotiations and Buchanan's warnings of 'bad impression[s]' in Russia were confirmed. General Waters reported on 3 October that the Russians were making threatening noises that failure to sign a financial agreement at once would prevent Russia from continuing the war.[129]

The problems which McKenna experienced in getting the Russians to accept the British terms reflected the different considerations which determined the financial conditions of the two countries. The Russians were irked by what they construed as the 'too grasping' attitude of the British, and were trying by means of private American loans to free themselves both from dependence on and control by the British Treasury.[130] On the other hand, the British were faced with an increasing squeeze on their credit, a squeeze made tighter by competing demands for manpower from industry and the army. By the end of September, as a report of the Manpower Distribution Board made clear, a shortage of manpower within British industry threatened to make Britain even more dependent upon the United States for manufactured items.[131] Thus the Treasury had to insist that the Russians ship the gold on demand in order to maintain the lines of British credit. In rebuttal to the Russian arguments, the Treasury pointed out that France had already shipped £63 million of gold and was being asked for only a further £40 million.[132] Despite some futile attempts by the Russians to budge the Treasury from this position, on 27 October a final agreement was signed which embodied the British position with respect to gold shipment. The signing of this financial accord marked the true end to the conference of 13–15 July.[133]

While it had taken to the end of October to complete the negotiations begun at the conference, the event itself had en-compassed some worthwhile achievements. At an organisational level a means had been found to ease the longstanding problem of the placing and the inspection of Russian orders in the United States. A joint Anglo-Russian Sub-Committee was set up in New York to deal with all aspects of Russian orders in the United States.[134] The terms of the agreement, signed 14 July 1916, which created this Sub-Committee gave the British members on it a veto over the placing of new orders, a move which promised to prevent orders being placed for which financial backing had not been arranged. Also, a 'protocol' had been signed on 15 July by the financial representatives of all the Allies which bound them to confer with each other before placing orders in neutral countries or negotiating loans on foreign markets.[135] As will be seen, this 'protocol' was often ignored by the Russian government, but its very signing was a measure of the British concern with the issue.

Other changes of an administrative nature concerning the supply of munitions for Russia also took place around this time. When Kitchener died early in June 1916, the activities of the War Office's Russian Purchasing Committee also came to an end. The anomalous position of that body in relation to the Ministry of Munitions and the CIR made reorganisation of the bureaucracy for Russian supply essential, now that Kitchener's feelings no longer had to be considered. It was decided at the end of June that the functions, as well as the majority of the staff, of the RPC should be transferred to the CIR where a special section was created under General Callwell to deal with Russia.[136] At the Ministry of Munitions an equivalent body was set up under Booth to procure the Russian orders approved by the CIR. The Treasury ensured its control of these contracts by having its representative, a Major Montfries, sit both on the Russian department of the CIR and on Booth's Russian Supply Committee (RSC) at the Ministry of Munitions. This entire shuffle was more amalgamation than reorganisation, but the elimination of the RPC brought Russian purchasing more into the mainstream of Britain's dealings with Allied purchase and made one less step for Russian orders to take before they might be fulfilled, never an unimportant consideration.

Despite all attempts – the Anglo-Russian Sub-Committee in New York, the 'protocol' of 15 July, and the creation of the RSC – to ensure efficient handling of and co-operation concerning Russian orders, not all went smoothly. One matter in particular exacerbated Anglo-Russian relations with respect to supply: the issue of independent Russian negotiations in the United States for railway material. On 27 July Buchanan reported that Russia was attempting to buy 1,300 locomotives in the United States, an effort to which the Treasury objected 'strongly' as a violation of the agreement of 14 July.[137] Even before news of the Treasury's unhappiness had reached Russia, the Russian Minister of Ways and Communications,

Trepov, had told Buchanan that Russia had placed the order in violation of the agreement only because 'if we wanted to win Russia must have rails and rolling stock and we had up to now failed to get any through regular channels'.[138] When informed of the Russian attitude, the Treasury rejected it, pointing out that the Russian order would not be completed in any case 'as it would be physically impossible to secure delivery in Russia of reported order for rails.'[139] This reaction reflected only the difficulties of delivery and not any objection by the British to the need for the order itself. When the Russian need for rails to complete the Murman railway was discussed at the War Committee on 10 August, Robertson presented a paper strongly endorsing providing sufficient funds for this task, arguing that the cost was 'small when compared with the military advantages to be obtained by the completion of the line.'[140] McKenna pointed out that he also believed in the importance of completing the line and noted that the Treasury had never refused any funds for the purpose.

Robertson's argument was reinforced by an interview which Trepov gave to Waters the following day. In it, the Minister of Ways and Communications stated that the 'provision of rails at the present moment [was] more important than that of shells, [and] that without them [the] Russian Army would not be able to advance and that [a] defensive attitude would have [the] worst possible results for [the] Allied cause.' This was discussed at the War Committee meeting of 18 August.[141] It was decided that, in view of the urgency of the Russian needs and of the significance of the Russian effort for the Allies, 400,000 tons of rail supplies would be expedited to Russia within the next eight months. This 400,000 tons did not include, however, those orders which Russia had placed independently in the United States, but rather was composed of that material which had been approved at the July conference. Although the War Committee was very much aware of Russia's value as an ally, there was no thought that the hard-won agreements on control of purchasing should be abandoned. The decision of the War Committee to provide rails for Russia merely indicated a shift in shipping priorities; now most of the 500,000 tons of shipping available for Russian supplies up to mid-1917 were to be taken up with railway goods.[142]

While the War Committee had decided to provide Russia with rail material, there were some practical difficulties in carrying out this resolution. The first was financial. The continuing negotiations with the Russians over the terms of further loans as discussed above made it difficult for the Ministry of Munitions to make definite plans for the purchase of Russian needs abroad.[143] The second concerned conflicting demands for railways supplies. The increased utilisation of Britain's west coast ports for trade with the United States meant that domestic needs for rails were heavy.[144] Also, the needs of the British army in France for railway equipment increased sharply at this time as a result of the efforts of Eric Geddes. Geddes, who had accompanied Lloyd George to the War Office from the Ministry of Munitions, was sent to France by the Secretary of State for War to examine rail transport there. Geddes requested so much rail material for France that wagons were everywhere in short supply by the autumn of 1916 and the shortage remained acute throughout the following year.[145] The building programme which he established in order to end this shortage illustrated the impact which one sector of the war economy could have on another; it was a major cause of the steel shortage which occurred during this time. In addition to these practical matters, there was another point which soured discussions about railway supplies. Early in October a series of reports came to the Foreign Office of Russian railway building in the Urals and Central Asia. As Hankey wrote to Hardinge, there was suspicion that these lines were not 'really required for the purposes of the war. If they are not, it is a great shame that Allied resources . . . be utilized for the construction of new railways not essential to the conduct of the war.'[146] In such circumstances, Hankey felt, Russian orders must necessarily take a back seat to the British needs for military lines in France.

Railways were not the only problem for close Anglo-Russian relations. In the United States the newly created Anglo-Russian Sub-Committee was faced with a whole series of matters to resolve as soon as it was established. The majority of them dealt with the outstanding orders, such as those of the CCFC, for Russian supplies of which deliveries had been delayed so long. This problem was a vexatious one, for the payment of these orders was causing many difficulties for the Treasury. The latter body hoped that most of these contracts could either be terminated or have 'break' clauses inserted in them which would cancel the order after a set period of non-fulfilment. However, to cancel some of the Russian orders would put the contracting firms in severe financial difficulties and this would jeopardise their production of other munitions for the Allies and strain relations with the American financial and economic community.

The first order of business for the Sub-Committee was to investigate the outstanding CCFC orders which were both the largest and the most expensive. The general conclusion reached was that while the Russians had adopted a 'reasonable' attitude, and while the CCFC's management was 'inefficient', it was best to continue the orders rather than cancel them.[147] This decision was taken on the wholly practical grounds that to bring in another firm at this late date would lead only to further delay in delivery. Even the much-maligned Sapozhnikov, the British members of the Sub-Committee felt, should be retained, as he had full knowledge of the old contracts and spoke English well. This feeling led to an awkward situation, as General Zalubovskii had been sent from Russia to replace Sapozhnikov, and the British mission in Russia was placed in the curious position of having to ask for the retention of a man whose activities they had criticised consistently for the preceding year.[148] This oddity aside, a solution was reached with respect to the CCFC on 19 August. The company was advanced money against deliveries made, easing the Treasury's worry that 'very large payments' would be made to the CCFC 'without producing any apparent results.'[149]

The CCFC's orders were not the only ones which were potentially troublesome for the Treasury. In mid-August it was calculated that as much as $100 million might have to be found if all the contracts in arrears had to be paid. Investigations were launched to find out how much of the material ordered in these contracts actually still was needed by the Russian government and by what means unnecessary contracts could be stopped without angering the American contractors.[150] These contracts were dealt with by the Sub-Committee one at a time, and while this prevented them from becoming critical, the matter remained a potentially explosive one well into 1917.

While Lloyd George had told General Beliaev at the end of July that there could be no final decision about providing artillery for Russia until after the Allied General Staffs had decided on the direction of the campaign for 1917, the matter continued to be discussed within the British government. The Ministry of Munitions suggested to the War Office that in order to provide adequate ammunition for the 300 4.5-inch howitzers which had been sent to

Russia (and a potential 100 more about which a decision was pending), a week's supply of shells originally slated for France be diverted to Russia.[151] At the same time, Callwell tested the water at GHQ about the possibility of diverting substantial amounts of heavy artillery from France to Russia. In a letter to Kiggell, Callwell argued that the Russians had 'for practical purposes failed entirely to do any good against the Germans . . . [and stated that] this is almost entirely due to the lack of heavy artillery.'[152] After noting deferentially that 'I am rather butting into General Staff questions which are not my concern', Callwell added, 'but to my mind 100 of our 6 inch howitzers in Russia would be worth 300 of them in France at the present time or during the next six months.' Not unexpectedly, Kiggell's response to such an idea was cool, but by the end of September the Army Council authorised the sending of further 4.5-inch howitzers to Russia.[153]

While debate occurred within the hierarchy of the British army about whether Russia should receive arms, towards the end of October a more ominous situation arose, one which concerned the entire Allied war effort. At this time the dangers inherent in the British financial situation in the United States became apparent.[154] Ongoing negotiations by Morgans for further loans to Britain were not progressing well. One of the difficulties was that of the outstanding contracts for Russia. McKenna pointed out to the War Committee on 18 October that, unless some satisfactory arrangements could be reached with regard to the Winchester and Westinghouse contracts, Morgans were certain that it would be 'quite impossible' to secure further loans in the United States.[155] McKenna felt that the American position was one of 'blackmail', but added realistically that while the Americans were 'holding a pistol to our heads we might tell them to do their worst, and their worst would be that we should get neither rifles nor money.' This placed the War Committee in a quandary. On the one hand they agreed that it was necessary 'in the wider financial interests of the Allies' to reimburse the American firms involved at least to some extent, while on the other they refused to agree to the 'altogether unacceptable' principle that the British government should have to rescue American firms that had entered into unprofitable contracts. As Balfour typically put it, he 'thought that there must be some third course short of acknowledging that we were so dependent on the United States, that they could do anything they pleased.'

A week later McKenna made it clear that there was no 'third course'. In a paper for the War Committee he demonstrated that the British dependence on America for war material was essentially absolute.[156] McKenna's paper had been triggered by the findings of a joint Anglo-French financial committee which had met early in October to discuss the Allied financial reliance on the United States.[157] McKenna prefaced his remarks by noting dourly that he felt it unlikely that further gold could be obtained from the Allies, but that their demands for credit would continue to increase. He then outlined how precarious the British position was in the following words:

> There are two sets of circumstances, and in my opinion two only, which may deprive us of the liberty to fix for ourselves the time and terms of peace. One is the inability of a principal ally to continue. The other is the power of the United States to dictate to us. . . . If things go on as at present, I venture to say with certainty that by next June or earlier, the President of the American Republic will be in a position, if he wishes, to dictate his own terms to us.

In 1917, McKenna went on, five-sixths of the money Britain would spend in the United States would have to be found in that same country. This fact made it necessary, in Keynes's words, 'not only to avoid any form of reprisal or active irritation [towards the United States] but also to conciliate and to please.'[158] The Treasury's assessment of Britain's dependency was underlined by a series of papers prepared by other departments and presented to the War Committee early in November.[159] These papers illustrated the reliance of Britain on the United States for almost all goods necessary to maintain the war effort. In such a situation the cancellation of the delinquent Russian orders placed in the United States became a matter with wide implications for the entire Allied cause.

Despite their importance, the delinquent contracts were not discussed at the inter-Allied munitions conference held 8–10 November 1916 in London. Instead, the conference focused its attention on determining what the Allied needs for munitions would be for the 1917 campaign.[160] Russia's requirements were outlined by Colonel Beliaev. By 1 July 1917 Russia would require the following items: 562 6-inch howitzers, 100 4.2-inch guns from France, 199

60-pounders from England, 200 8-inch howitzers and 30 9.2-inch howitzers. The size of this order was imposing and, with atypical understatement, Lloyd George termed it 'very formidable'. On the other hand, Lloyd George felt that such a demand was not 'wholly beyond' the ability of the Allies. For France, Thomas was not so sanguine. He emphasised that France, as well as Russia, had call on the British production of artillery, and added that Russia's needs could not be examined 'alone nor apart' from other considerations such as the ability to provide ammunition for guns requested or indeed possessed. Arguments also were raised that the large Russian demands for artillery could be met only if all else were not shipped to Russia since tonnage considerations placed an upper limit on the total possible.

The problems which had been so evident at the July inter-Allied conference had resurfaced here in November. The Russian requests, despite Lloyd George's remarks, bore little resemblance to any figures which might conceivably have been fulfilled, considering either production or shipping. In addition, the French attitude was now less accommodating than before. Thomas made it clear, after the hard-fought campaigns of 1916, that France expected her fair share of available guns.

The inter-Allied conference did not resolve these matters. Instead, they became a matter of debate within the British government throughout November. As Lloyd George had noted at the conference, the success of the British gun programme did not make the carrying out of the Russian requests a complete impossibility. The issue was whether or not such a total commitment should be made. The entire matter was summarised ably in a memorandum prepared for Lloyd George at the end of the month by his military secretary, Arthur Lee.[161] Lee pointed out that the levels of artillery which the War Office had requested for the British forces would be reached early in 1917. While the Master-General of the Ordnance had subsequently argued that the supply of artillery to the Allies must be restricted severely, none the less Lee concluded that Britain could give one-half of her future production to Russia, providing that it was considered sound policy to do so. This would mean Russia receiving by 31 March 1917 170 6-inch, 102 8- and 9.2-inch howitzers and a further 200 4.5-inch howitzers. Both on strategic and moral grounds, Lee argued, the best policy would be to 'give with both hands.'

The key to such plans was transport. On 17 November Trepov announced to Buchanan that the Murman railway would open at the beginning of 1917, but tried to link this welcome news with other matters. The Russian minister asked that Russia now be permitted to place her own orders in the United States for rail materials, as the British control had resulted, he alleged, in 'constant difficulties and delays'.[162] While Buchanan supported Trepov's proposal, and despite the impressive fact that the Murman line was to open much earlier than predicted by the Admiralty's agents, a meeting held at the Foreign Office on 20 November argued against such an idea.[163] Both Keynes and Booth felt that letting Trepov do his own ordering would be counterproductive: Keynes because it would undermine the principle of Treasury control of foreign ordering by presenting the British with a series of *faits accomplis;* Booth because he felt that Trepov was incompetent to place such orders. Despite this, the Foreign Office formally suggested that Trepov be given this privilege, a suggestion based on Buchanan's arguments that such a course was politically advantageous.

Replies to the Foreign Office's proposal were forthcoming from both the Treasury and the Ministry of Munitions. For the most part, the former body merely reiterated the points which Keynes had made earlier, but added the further comment that, as 'the total requirements of the Allies both for railway material and for steel products generally are substantially in excess of the American market', it could see no justification for Trepov to wish to place independent orders.[164] Such remarks, with which the Ministry of Munitions concurred, were sent to Buchanan on 12 December. When the ambassador conveyed them to Trepov and pointed out the difficulties with internal transportation in Russia, the latter was not dismayed. His reply to Buchanan's second point illustrated just how far apart were Russian and British estimations of the situation. Many of the problems experienced by Russia in her internal transport, Trepov argued, were due to the inefficiency of Romania's railroads and this could be solved only by Russia's taking them over. Given the notorious incompetence of the Russian lines, Oliphant minuted sarcastically, such a move would necessarily be a *'pis aller'.*[165] Despite such opinion and despite the growing worry over tonnage shortages, the need for a strong Russian military effort in 1917 had had its influence. The War Committee had ruled on 13 November that the White Sea route should be allotted an extra three ships in order to meet some of the Russian needs.[166]

In addition to these problems over transportation and artillery, by the end of November there were also discussions once more about finance. Less than a month after it had been signed, Bark began to seek to go beyond the financial accord of 27 October. In requesting further loans, Bark added that both the Duma and the finance committee of the Council of Ministers had 'categorically pronounced' against any further shipment of gold from Russia.[167] Such a request could not have come at a less propitious time. In an article inspired by President Wilson, the American Federal Reserve Board had warned American investors about the danger of lending too much abroad, a warning which triggered off a serious run on British funds in the United States.[168] It was clear to the British that the question of finance, along with those of supply and transportation, could not be resolved simply. By the beginning of December 1916 it was decided that only a major inter-Allied conference, such as the one scheduled to be held in Petrograd early in 1917, would suffice to deal with the complicated issues of Anglo-Russian relations.[169]

This being said, however, there still remained some pressing matters which could be dealt with in the interim. The first was the relatively minor one of working out improved procedures to deal with Russian orders; the second was the major matter of terminating the overdue contracts placed by Russia in the United States. The deteriorating credit position of the British government in the United States made an equitable solution to this latter imperative.

There were two delinquent contracts in particular which were sore points. The first was for 4 million complete rounds of 3-inch shell placed with Bethlehem Steel, a contract with a final delivery date of 27 January 1917; the second was for 1.8 million rifles (in two separate contracts) placed with Westinghouse, with delivery to be completed by 31 March 1917.[170] The first contract had a value of $64 million and the second was worth just over $48 million. Just prior to the serious run on British credit in the United States, the Treasury offered to advance Westinghouse 20 per cent of the total value of the rifles on terms which reflected the British concern with maintaining their credit abroad. To protect the exchange rate, payment was to be in one-year Treasury Bills, while to ensure that further delay was not encouraged no further advance would be provided until 480,000 rifles were delivered.[171] For the Russians Zalubovskii felt that these terms were too generous; he preferred to advance Westinghouse only

10 per cent.[172] All of this changed with the credit crisis. By 20 December the Treasury felt that even Zalubovskii's reduced offer was too much for Westinghouse and that no deliveries of 3-inch shell from Bethlehem would be accepted after the final delivery date.[173]

These two decisions were not well received in American circles. At Keynes's suggestion Booth was sent to the United States in January in the hope that he could alleviate the situation. His mission was outlined in a letter of 11 January.[174] Christopher Addison, the Minister of Munitions, told Booth to make 'every effort' to cancel contracts of which Russia was 'no longer in need'. Compensation was to be offered the firms involved, but the main objects to be pursued were to 'save our dollar exchange' for other acquisitions and to free the manufacturing capacity tied up with useless orders at the same time as easing the competition for scarce raw materials and labour in the United States. This was not to be an easy task.

Cancellation of the Westinghouse and Bethlehem contracts, and others like them, was made even more difficult by the usual reticence of the Russian government to disclose which, if any, of the contracts were still needed.[175] The British did not wish Booth to cancel any but superfluous contracts; however, the information which they received from the Russian Government Committee in London did not tally with that which was sent by the British mission in Petrograd. This difference was of particular significance with respect to rifles. By the middle of March 1917 Booth had effected a settlement with Westinghouse which extended the final delivery date until the end of 1917 and provided for payment in two-year Treasury Bills.[176] The Treasury immediately queried the need for this settlement, since the figures which the Russian War Office had given the British delegates to the Petrograd conference indicated that the rifles could be provided from other sources.[177] Booth had been negotiating on the basis of the assurances given him by Colonel Beliaev of the Russian Government Committee who had 'no doubt whatever' that it would be correct to extend the contract to the end of 1917.[178] When Beliaev and Hermonious were questioned about this discrepancy, Beliaev answered that he had received 'no information as to this effect' and that as far as the Committee was concerned 'all rifles possible' were to be found for 1917.[179] While it was possible that the impact of the revolution on the bureaucracy of the Russian War Office in Petrograd was responsible for this mismanagement, this was merely an extreme case of the kind of muddle which the incompetence of the Russian administration had caused throughout the war.

Similar mismanagement also caused problems for Booth's negotiations with Bethlehem Steel. The Russian government gave no clear directive as to how important the 3-inch shell contracts were and as a consequence, Booth was unable to make any arrangements concerning them until mid-February.[180] The deal which Booth did strike was typical of those which he made in the United States and for that reason deserves to be looked at in detail. Simple cancellation of the contracts would provide minimal saving as more than 75 per cent of the value of the shells had already been advanced.[181] The best solution was to accept late deliveries and get a token reduction on the final payment per shell, a move which would ensure that something was obtained for the moneys already advanced as well as save a small amount of precious dollars. Such an arrangement was as favourable as could be expected. In the case of Bethlehem, the final delivery date was extended to 31 July 1917, a reduction of one dollar per shell (a saving of $4 million) in the final price was accepted and Bethlehem agreed to receive all further payments in two-year 5 per cent Treasury Bills.[182]

Both the Westinghouse and Bethlehem Steel contracts, as well as many similar but less important ones, illustrated one of the difficulties which faced Britain at the beginning of 1917. The amount of aid which could be given Russia was circumscribed ever more tightly by the growing financial dependence on the United States, but efforts to ease this squeeze by the cancellation of excess and in arrears contracts contained their own dangers. First, to do so unilaterally would offend the American business community to the further detriment of British credit. Second, the Russian government was not eager to co-operate in the cancellation of orders for its own supplies, and the British government did not wish either to offend Russia, or, particularly, to weaken her military effort in 1917 by doing so in gratuitous fashion.

As mentioned, there was another aspect of Anglo-Russian dealings besides the matter of cancellation of contracts which could be dealt with outside the context of the Petrograd conference: this was the issue of organisation. Early in January 1917 Hermonious wrote two letters to the Ministry of Munitions citing the clumsiness of the procedure for placing new Russian orders as one of the principal reasons for the inability of the Russian government to make long-term plans.[183] He pointed out that nearly 50 per cent of the 1,713 applications which his committee had made in the last four months of 1916 had 'neither been sanctioned or refused'. This, Hermonious felt, was due to the twenty-five step procedure which all applications underwent. After this paper chase, which required around twenty-two days to complete, there was need for at least two weeks of discussion which meant that the Russian Government Committee 'cannot under the most favourable conditions expect to get an answer in less than five or six weeks, and this conclusion is confirmed by actual experience.' The 'most rational' answer to this problem, Hermonious felt, was to allow his committee to place the orders themselves and then refer them to the Ministry of Munitions.

This proposal could be seen as part of the long Russian effort to free themselves of British control, but deserves closer scrutiny. Hermonious was not alone in his displeasure over the means of placing Russian orders. Sir Edmund Wyldbore Smith, the chairman of the CIR, wrote a long memorandum to the Ministry of Munitions which called for the abolition of Booth's department there, a department which Wyldbore Smith felt acted as a barrier between the CIR and the Ministry.[184] While Addison felt that there was some truth in this assertion, much of Wyldbore Smith's argument seems to have been based on a personal dislike of Booth and a mis-conception of the latter's role in the procurement of Russian supplies.[185] However, there was little doubt that the sluggishness of the mechanism for dealing with Russian supplies was an irritant to good relations between the British and the Russians. This irritation, coupled with suggestions for change which emanated from the Petrograd conference, led to the formation of a new committee to deal with Russian supplies, a matter which will be dealt with in some detail below. The significant point was that nearly two years had elapsed since Britain had begun to be responsible officially for Russian purchasing and still there was no effective organisation.

Despite the problems which continued to dog Anglo-Russian co-operation in finance and supply throughout 1916, this period was one of major importance and significant achievement. The achievements were evident. The Admiralty agreement of 5 May placed control of and responsibility for White Sea transport in British hands. While this arrangement was not perfect, it was certainly an improvement on the chaos which had prevailed before. The series of conferences held in July 1916 linked for the first time the problems of finance, supply and transportation, although the effect of this was scarcely evident at the London conference in November. The Treasury agreement of 14 July which created the Anglo-Russian Sub-Committee in New York and the formation of the RSC at the Ministry of Munitions underlined the British attempts to create a rational and effective means whereby Russian affairs could be dealt with. Despite criticism of these organisational reforms, the bureaucracy which was established was reasonably effective and not any more complicated than could be expected of an apparatus which had to deal with three independent countries and a plethora of government departments.

Regardless of these very real achievements, the verdict on this period must be one of failure. From the point of view of the supplies delivered to and the financial aid provided for Russia, 1916 was not a banner year. This failure was, of course, relative only to the needs of Russia and did not reflect a British lack of goodwill or concern. Rather, the failure was caused by a number of things largely outside the control of the British government. The underlying reason for much of Britain's inability to aid Russia to the extent she desired was the former's dependence on the United States. By the end of 1916 Britain needed to raise 40 per cent of her daily expenditure on the war by means of loans in America and her munitions production, and that of the Allies, was tied to American manufacturing industry. Thus, instead of having the inexhaustible credit and infinite manufacturing capacity which Russia believed she possessed, Britain found herself depending on what seemed to be an uncertain source – the United States – for both credit and supplies. The British efforts to deal with this situation often meant that Russian demands went unanswered, an occurrence which the Russians put down to Britain's insensitivity rather than to the facts.

Other factors complicated the unbalanced equation between what could be provided for Russia and what could not. The increasing requirements of the British army had to be weighed against the effect which it was supposed that giving these same supplies to Russia would have. Here widely differing opinions were held among the élite. Equally important was transportation. While tonnage was in short supply in 1916, by the beginning of 1917 the shortage was becoming acute. Matters like a poor wheat harvest in North America which necessitated shunting shipping to the longer Australian run meant that competition for tonnage would increase. Russian needs had to be examined in the total context of the Allied effort. In addition, despite the opening of the Murman line in January 1917, the capacity of the Russian ports by no means matched the size of the orders which she wished to place abroad. And there were questions about the capability of Russia's internal transportation system.

Clearly there were matters affecting Anglo-Russian relations with regard to finance and supply which mere organisational changes could not mask. Only a fundamental alteration in the situation, such as the entry of the United States as an active participant in the war, could hope to resolve the issues of March 1917.

Notes

1 'Difficulties of inspection in connection with the contracts placed in America on behalf of the Russian Government', n.s. (but Hanson), 15 November 1915, marked 'referred to P.M. 20/11', Mun 7/149.
2 FO to Buchanan, 24 November 1915, FO 371/2584/177109.
3 Buchanan to FO, 5 December 1915, FO 371/2584/184996.
4 ibid.
5 A low opinion of Sapozhnikov was held not only by the British. In the words of the Russian naval attaché in Washington, who worked with Sapozhnikov in procuring supplies, the latter 'had done a great deal toward lowering Russian prestige in the United States by his entire lack of *savoir faire,* his outrageous nepotism, and friendships with some of the shadiest characters among the munitions crowd.', D. Fedotoff White, *Survival Through War and Revolution in Russia* (London, 1939), 56.
6 FO to Buchanan, 11 December 1915 and reply of 26 December 1915, in FO 371/2584/189394 and 198875.
7 Rutkovskii to Ramsay, 20 December 1915, Mun 7/149.
8 Rutkovskii to Bark, 15 December 1915, ibid.
9 See Neilson, 'Russian foreign purchasing', 578–85, for a discussion of the CCFC.
10 Bradbury to Wintour, 18 November 1915, Mun 4/5506.
11 McKenna to Lloyd George, 5 January 1916, Cab 1/15/5.
12 Lloyd George to McKenna, 6 January 1916, ibid.
13 Haig diary entry, 21 January 1916, Haig Papers, 104; the sheaf of letters marked 'Correspondence between the War Office and the Ministry of Munitions regarding the supply of 4.5″ howitzers to Russia', Cab 17/183.
14 R. H. Brade (Secretary to the War Office and Army Council) to Ministry of Munitions, 20 January 1916, ibid.
15 H. Llewellyn Smith to Brade, 25 January 1916, ibid.
16 Robertson to Haig, 14 January 1916, Robertson Papers I/22/15.
17 Meeting of the War Committee, 26 January 1916, Cab 42/7/13.
18 'The supply of guns, howitzers, and artillery ammunition to the Russian army', WO, 31 January 1916, Cab 42/2/G 53.
19 Meeting of the War Committee, 3 February 1916, Cab 42/8/1.
20 C. E. Fayle, *History of the Great War based on official documents by Direction of the Historical Section Committee of Imperial Defence. Seaborne Trade* (3 vols, London, 1920–4), II, 122–5.

21 E. W. Haig (of R. Martens) to FO, 30 June 1915, FO 368/1404/88343.
22 Martens was blamed for shortages and accused by public opinion in Russia of being German agents. Quite probably these attacks were part of the campaign to discredit the Russian Government Committee in London, as Rutkovskii said that he had 'every confidence' in Martens. The 'Martens affair' can be followed in Sidorov, *Ekonomicheskoe polozhenie*, 295–7 and FO 368/1404/107069, 109903, 112602 and 175701.
23 'Memo. of conference held in D.A.C.'s room on the 6th December', n.s., 6 December 1915, Mun 4/5497.
24 Special Council for Defence to Timchenko-Ruban, 20 December 1915, forwarded to the Admiralty via the War Office, 5 January 1916, ibid.
25 W. Graham Greene (Secretary to the Admiralty) to Cubitt, 9 January 1916, ibid.
26 Meeting of the War Committee, 13 January 1916, Cab 42/7/5.
27 Morgan (Ellershaw) to Morgan, Grenfell (War Office), 25 January 1916, Mun 4/5496.
28 Note by E. N. R. Trentham (Secretary to the RPC), 26 January 1916, ibid.
29 Admiralty to Wintour, 2 February 1916, ibid.
30 See the correspondence in Cab 1/15/33.
31 'The ignoring of the freight problem on the part of the Russians', WO, 3 February 1916, Cab 1/23/13.
32 'Memorandum on Russian shipping requirements from the United States', Robertson, 16 February 1916, Cab 42/9/3.
33 'Note prepared by the Chief of the Imperial General Staff for the War Committee, on the question of the shipping of Russian munitions', Robertson, 28 February 1916, Cab 17/183.
34 Sidorov, *Ekonomicheskoe polozhenie*, 291–3; Hermonius to Wintour, 4 February 1916, Mun 4/5496.
35 As cited in Sidorov, *Ekonomicheskoe polozhenie*, 294.
36 Meeting of the War Committee, 29 February 1916, Cab 42/9/7.
37 Conclusion 6 of the War Committee, 29 February 1916, Cab 42/7/16.
38 'The transfer of war material to Russia', E. Wyldbore Smith, 2 March 1916, Cab 42/10/3, paper G 53.
39 'Transport of war material for the Russian government', n.s., 19 February 1916, Cab 42/10/3, paper G 63.
40 Hankey to Curzon, 6 March 1916, Cab 17/182; Fayle, *Seaborne Trade*, II, 231–4; 261–5; 314–16.
41 Meeting of the War Committee, 29 February 1916, Cab 42/9/7.
42 Curzon to Asquith, 7 March 1916, Cab 42/10/8.
43 Meeting of the War Committee, 8 March 1916, ibid.
44 Stone, *Eastern Front*, 157–9; reports 3, 18 and 20 of Admiral Phillimore (the Admiralty's liaison officer in Russia), 20 October 1915, February 1916 and 17 March 1916, all in Adm 137/1389; Blair's dispatches XCI and XCVI, 16 January 1916 and 30 March 1916, WO 106/1013 and 1018; Fayle, *Seaborne Trade*, II, 118–26.
45 Phillimore's report 20, 17 March 1916, Adm 137/1389. Paulings's failed attempt in Adm 137/1390.
46 'Report of Shipping Control Committee', n.s., 31 March 1916, Cab 37/144/46.
47 'Memorandum', Board of Trade, 4 April 1916, Cab 37/145/8; Hankey to C. Jones (Secretary to the Shipping Control Committee), 11 April 1916, Cab 17/182.
48 Morgan, Grenfell to Morgan, 7 April 1916, Mun 4/5497; meeting of the War Committee, 28 April 1916, Cab 42/12/2.

49 'Memorandum of agreement between the Russian and British Governments as to the necessary procedure to be established in order to ensure transport of munitions to Russia', signed by Benckendorff and Grey, 5 May 1916, Layton Papers, Mun 4/372. The most comprehensive account of the problems and negotiations leading to the signing of this agreement is M. A. Stoliarenko, 'Anglo-Russkie soglasheniia o severnykh portakh Rossii v gody pervoi mirovoi voiny', *Vestnik Leningradskogo Universiteta*, 16, 8 (1961), 46-58.
50 The Russians asked for 2.7 million rifles to cover their needs up to mid-1917. Cubitt to Ministry of Munitions, 21 March 1916 (misdated 1917), Lloyd George Papers D/12/3/3.
51 Cubitt to Ministry of Munitions, 27 April 1916, Lloyd George Papers D/12/3/7.
52 Ministry of Munitions to WO, May 1916, ibid.
53 'Procès-verbale of the Paris Conference', n.s., 27 March 1916, Cab 37/145/39; 'Conference of the Allies. 3rd Session, Tuesday, March 28th, 1916', n.s., 28 March 1916, Kitchener Papers, WO 159/5.
54 'Statute governing the Russian Supply Committee in America', n.s., 31 March 1916, Mun 4/6254.
55 See the note prepared for the mission, 'Visit of special mission to Russia. Enquiries to be made concerning Russian output &c', n.s., n.d. (but late May 1916), Black Papers, Mun 4/533.
56 See the long correspondence during November and December 1915, FO 371/2456/163140; 174042; 175743; 183548; 183460; 192823.
57 Bradbury to FO, 24 December 1915, FO 371/2456/198495.
58 FO to Buchanan, 20 January 1916, FO 371/2743/9738.
59 Buchanan to FO, 16, 29 and 30 January 1916, FO 371/2743/9589; 18708; 18871.
60 Treasury to FO, 7 February 1916, FO 371/2743/24495; the comments on Russian dishonesty were not sent on to Russia.
61 FO to Buchanan, 19 February 1916, FO 371/2743/32805.
62 Sazonov's memorandum of 2 March 1916, FO 371/2743/21223.
63 War Office to FO, 28 April 1916, FO 371/2743/81189.
64 Treasury to FO, 11 March 1916, FO 371/2743/47761. Keynes's opinion was given in a speech to the Board of the Admiralty, 15 March 1916, in Johnson (ed.), *Keynes*, XVI, 187.
65 Buchanan to FO, 6 April 1916, FO 371/2846/65905.
66 Ellershaw (WO) to FO, 21 April 1916, FO 371/2846/76616.
67 Ministry of Munitions to FO, 18 May 1916, FO 371/2846/95022.
68 Keynes to A. Nicolson, 18 April 1916, FO 371/2848/73831.
69 Meeting of the War Committee, 4 May 1916, Cab 42/13/4.
70 'Russian credits', McKenna, 2 May 1916, Cab 37/147/5.
71 Conclusion of the War Committee, 26 May 1916, Cab 37/148/36.
72 Burk, 'Diplomacy of finance', 355; Burk, 'Mobilization of Anglo-American Finance', 30–2.
73 Morgan (Golezhevskii) to Morgan, Grenfell (Ellershaw), 3 June 1916, Mun 4/5460.
74 Ministry of Munitions to IMB, 5 June 1916, ibid.
75 IMB (Perry and Gordon) to Ministry of Munitions, 11 June 1916, ibid.
76 Morgan (Stettinius) to Morgan, Grenfell, 9 June 1916, ibid.
77 Morgan, Grenfell (Whigham) to Morgan (Stettinius), 21 June 1916, Mun 4/5490, part I.
78 Morgan (Stettinius) to Morgan, Grenfell (Whigham), 19 June 1916, ibid.
79 Spring-Rice to FO, 20 June 1916, FO 371/2852/119312.
80 Minchin to Lloyd George, 21 June 1916, Black Papers, Mun 4/533.

81 Well summed up in a note from Wintour to Creedy, 26 June 1916, accompanying a 'Memorandum', n.s., n.d., prepared for Asquith outlining the problems of Anglo-Russian supply in the United States, Mun 4/6524.

82 Untitled memorandum, Sapozhnikov, n.d., accompanied by a note from Hermonius to Wintour, 30 June 1916, ibid.

83 IMB (Perry) to R. H. Brand (IMB's representative in London), 30 June 1916; reply of 30 June 1916; Morgan to Morgan, Grenfell, 6 July 1916, all in Mun 4/5460.

84 Untitled memorandum, Keynes, n.d., accompanied by a note from G. L. Barstow (Treasury) to Booth, 3 July 1916, Mun 4/5490.

85 Hermonius to Wintour, 7 July 1916, Mun 4/6524.

86 Booth to Minchin, 7 July 1916, ibid.

87 Meeting of the War Committee, 6 June 1916, Cab 42/15/4; the text of the telegram, sent to Buchanan 8 June 1916, is in Lloyd George Papers D/16/17/11.

88 Bradbury to FO, 10 June 1916, FO 371/2846/112730.

89 Buchanan to FO, 20 June 1916, FO 371/2846/119157. Oliphant noted on this telegram that 'I fear the action of the Russian Govt. in going behind the back of our Treasury in this matter will render the latter less accommodating than ever.'

90 FO (McKenna) to Buchanan, 5 July 1916, FO 371/2846/130829.

91 Buchanan to FO, 8 July 1916, FO 371/2846/132844.

92 'Analysis of Russian requirements', Keynes, 11 July 1916, Cab 17/182.

93 Haig to War Office, 24 June as cited in *History of Ministry of Munitions*, X, 28–9.

94 Hermonius to Wyldbore Smith, 3 July 1916, Mun 4/3006.

95 'Minutes of a conference held in the minister's room at the Ministry of Munitions at 5 p.m. July 5th 1916', n.s., Mun 4/2696; these conclusions were accepted at a conference held 6 July 1916, attended by Lloyd George, Col. A. Lee, Montagu and other munitions officials, see Black Papers, Mun 4/533.

96 'Minutes of a meeting . . . with regard to the supply to Russia of machine guns, rifles and small arms ammunition . . .', n.s., 6 July 1916, Mun 4/2696.

97 'Note', Lloyd George, 29 June 1916, Cab 42/15/14.

98 Meeting of the War Committee, 30 June 1916, Cab 42/15/15.

99 'Draft conclusion of a meeting . . . on Monday July 3rd 1916, at 4:30 p.m.', sent by Hankey to Lloyd George, Mun 4/2696.

100 'Memorandum on Mr. Lloyd George's proposals', McKenna, 5 July 1916, Johnson (ed.), *Keynes*, XVI, 188–95.

101 See the editor's comments in ibid.

102 'Memorandum for discussion at conference – Thursday Afternoon', n.s. (but Layton), n.d. (but prepared for the meeting of 13 July 1916), Black Papers, Mun 4/533.

103 'Report of proceedings at a conference between the Secretary of State for War and representatives of the French, Italian and Russian governments', n.s., 13 July 1916, Mun 4/5068.

104 Addison diary entry, 13 July 1916, Addison Papers, Box 97.

105 Stone, *Eastern Front*, 229–31; 237–40.

106 'Minutes of proceedings at a conference on Russian requirements', n.s., 13 July 1916, Black Papers, Mun 4/533.

107 Addison diary entry, 13 July 1916, Addison Papers, Box 97.

108 'Finance Conference – Treasury', n.s., 14 July 1916, Mun 4/3007.

109 'Conference at the Treasury', n.s., 14 July 1916, 'after luncheon', ibid.

110 See Brand to Perry, 15 July 1916, Mun 4/5460 for details.

111 Von Donop wrote to Haig on this matter, 15 July 1916; see the latter's reply of 18 July 1916, Kiggell Papers V/28.

112   'Memorandum of the allocation of heavy artillery to Russia', E. S. Montagu, 17 July 1916, Cab 42/16/11.
113   Haig to von Donop, 18 July 1916, Kiggell Papers V/28.
114   See note 112.
115   Meeting of the War Committee, 28 July 1916, Cab 42/16/11.
116   Beliaev to Lloyd George and reply, 28 and 31 July 1916, Lloyd George Papers E/3/22/2 and 3.
117   Hardinge, reflecting the desire of the Foreign Office to maintain good relations with Russia, considered McKenna's attitude to the latter issue 'narrow-minded and pedantic'; Hardinge to Buchanan, 27 July 1916, Hardinge Papers, 23.
118   A concise outline of the negotiations at the July conference with the Russians is in Treasury to FO, 1 August 1916, FO 371/2750/152550.
119   Buchanan to FO, 8, 9, 11 and 12 August 1916, FO 371/2743/157199; 156932; 158672 and 159726.
120   Benckendorff to Grey, 14 August 1916, FO 371/2750/160298.
121   Bradbury to Hardinge, 18 August 1916, FO 371/2750/163510.
122   Buchanan to Hardinge, private, FO 371/2750/173073.
123   Benckendorff to FO, 1 September 1916, FO 371/2750/173363.
124   'Rapport de Monsieur le Ministre des Finances au Conseil des Ministres du 19 Août, 1916', presented to the British government by the French ambassador as a note, 21 August 1916, Cab 42/18/4.
125   Meeting of the War Committee, 22 August 1916, ibid.
126   Meeting of the War Committee, 12 September 1916, Cab 42/19/6.
127   FO to Buchanan, 13 September 1916, FO 371/2750/182282.
128   Buchanan to FO, 15 and 21 September 1916, FO 371/2750/184618; 190208.
129   Waters (Hanbury Williams's temporary replacement at *Stavka*) to War Office, 3 October 1916, Cab 42/21/2.
130   Waters to Robertson, 30 September 1916, Robertson Papers I/14/42. On American loans, see an untitled memorandum, F. O. Lindley, 30 September 1916, FO 371/2743/20482 and R. Sh. Ganelin, 'Politika tsarizma i Amerikanskii kapital vo vremia pervoi mirovoi voiny (konets 1915-nachalo 1916 g.)', in G. P. Tsifrinovich (ed.), *Vnutreniaia politika tsarizma* (Leningrad, 1967), 321–62.
131   'First report of the Man-Power Distribution Board to the War Committee', A. Chamberlain, 29 September 1916; see the discussion of this report at the meeting of the War Committee, 5 October 1916, Cab 42/21/2, for the fear that manpower shortages would throw Britain completely into America's arms.
132   FO to Buchanan, 29 September 1916, FO 371/2750/192156.
133   The negotiations are in the series of telegrams and notes exchanged in October 1916, FO 371/2750/197895; 199706; 201934; 203681 and 203710. The text of the agreement is in FO 371/2750/211427.
134   See Mun 4/5460. The minutes of the initial four meetings of the Sub-Committee are in Mun 4/6254. The role of the Sub-Committee is defined in an agreement signed by Grey and Benckendorff, 14 July 1916, Mun 4/4866.
135   'Protocol', signed by Bark, McKenna, Ribot and others, 15 July 1916, T 172/385.
136   'Russian government supplies', n.s., 27 June 1916, Mun 4/140/1013; Callwell, *Experiences of a Dug-Out*, 293–7; 'Procedure in regard to Russian government applications', Duke, 15 August 1916, Mun 4/5504.
137   Buchanan to FO 27 July 1916, FO 371/2846/146988; Bradbury (drafted by Keynes) to FO, 4 August 1916, FO 371/2846/152563.
138   Buchanan to FO, 1 August 1916, FO 371/2846/150715.
139   Bradbury to FO, [11] August 1916, FO 371/2846/156908.

140 Meeting of the War Committee, 10 August 1916 and 'The completion of the Murman railway', General Staff, War Office, 9 August 1916, Cab 42/17/5.

141 Meeting of the War Committee, 18 August 1916, Cab 42/17/11; FO to Buchanan, 18 August 1916, FO 371/2846/160646.

142 FO 371/2846/175484.

143 Ministry of Munitions to Treasury, 18 August 1916, Mun 4/3009.

144 Railway Executive Committee to Board of Trade, 19 August 1916, Cab 42/18/3.

145 A. M. Henniker, *History of the Great War based on official documents by Direction of the Historical Section Committee of Imperial Defence. Transportation on the Western Front* (London, 1937), 242–7; P. K. Cline, 'Eric Geddes and the "Experiment" with businessmen in government, 1915–22', in K. D. Brown (ed.), *Essays in Anti-Labour History: Responses to the Rise of Labour in Britain* (London, 1974), 80; *History of Ministry of Munitions*, VII, 15–21; 5th meeting of the Russian Supply Committee, 11 October 1916, Mun 4/6254.

146 Hankey to Hardinge, 11 October 1916, Cab 17/182.

147 Minchin, Crease and Sampson (the British members of the Sub-Committee) to Duke, 16 August 1916, Mun 4/6254.

148 War Office to Knox, 30 September 1916, Mun 4/5490; Blair's surprised reply in his dispatch 10, 6 October 1916, WO 106/1027.

149 See Booth to Brand for the Treasury's concern, 3 August 1916, Mun 4/5460. The details of the CCFC settlement are in Gordon to Perry, 19 August 1916, ibid.

150 Bradbury to Morgan, Grenfell, 23 August 1916, Mun 4/4866; Morgan to Morgan, Grenfell and reply, 15 and 16 August 1916, Mun 4/5490; the comments of Montagu at the meeting of the War Committee, 18 August 1916, Cab 42/17/11.

151 Layton to Montagu, 'Note on 4.5" ammunition for Russia', 29 August 1916, Mun 4/3009.

152 Callwell to Kiggell, 30 August 1916, Kiggell Papers V/36.

153 Kiggell to Callwell, 13 September 1916, Kiggell Papers V/42; 4th meeting of the Russian Supplies Committee, 27 September 1916, Mun 4/6254.

154 Burk, 'Diplomacy of finance', 355–8; Burk, 'Mobilization of Anglo–American finance', 31–3.

155 Meeting of the War Committee, 18 October 1916, Cab 42/22/2.

156 'Our financial position in America', McKenna, Cab 24/2/G 87.

157 'Report to the Chancellor of the Exchequer of the British members of the Joint Anglo-French Financial Committee', Lord Reading, R. Chambers, B. Cockayne (Deputy Governor of the Bank of England), and Keynes, 18 October 1916, Johnson (ed.), *Keynes*, XVI, 201–9. The Cabinet version in Cab 24/2/G 87 is an extract.

158 'The financial dependence of the United Kingdom on the United States of America', Keynes, 10 October 1916, Johnson (ed.), *Keynes*, XVI, 198.

159 Cab 42/33/7.

160 'Summary of the proceedings of the Inter-Ally Munitions Conference held in London November 8th, 9th, and 10th, 1916', Mun 4/5068; a fuller version is in Lloyd George Papers E/7/3/7.

161 'Supply of artillery to Russia', A. L.[ee], 27 November 1916, Lloyd George Papers E/5/2/6.

162 Buchanan to FO, 17 November 1916, FO 371/2752/232510.

163 'Report on Murman railway and certain White Sea ports', Cmdr. G. Eady, RN (assistant naval attaché, Petrograd), 20 November 1916, Layton Papers, Mun 4/372; untitled summary of a meeting, 20th November 1916, FO 371/2752/234004.

164 Treasury (Chalmers) to FO, 30 November 1916, FO 371/2752/242446.
165 Buchanan to FO, 16 December 1916, FO 371/2752/255075; Oliphant's minute is attached.
166 Meeting of the War Committee, 13 November 1916, Cab 42/24/5.
167 Buchanan to FO, 23 November 1916, FO 371/2750/236800.
168 Burk, 'Mobilization of Anglo-American finance', 32–3.
169 Balfour to Bonar Law, 3 January 1917, Balfour Papers, FO 800/205.
170 'The D.G.M.S. the Minister', W. J. Benson (the acting DDG(B) in Booth's absence), 22 February 1917, Mun 4/5490.
171 'Notes on discussions with Col. Belaiew', n.s., 22 November 1916, Mun 4/5510.
172 ibid., 29 November 1916.
173 9th meeting of the Russian Supplies Committee, 20 December 1916, Mun 4/6254.
174 Addison to Booth, 11 January 1917, as cited in Crow, *Push and Go*, 143–44.
175 Benson to Booth, 31 January 1917, Mun 4/5490.
176 Booth to Benson, 16 March 1917, T 172/441.
177 Bonar Law to S. Hardman Lever (the Treasury's representative in the United States), 14 March 1917, ibid.
178 'Colonel Belaev', n.s., 22 February 1917, Black Papers, Mun 4/533; 12th meeting of the Russian Supplies Committee, 21 February 1917, Mun 4/6254.
179 'Notes on discussions with Col. Belaev', Layton and Benson, 21 March 1917, Mun 4/5510.
180 Benson to Booth, 31 January 1917, Mun 4/5490; 'Memorandum of a conference on contracts for Russian requirements in U.S.A.', n.s., 3 February 1917, Black Papers, Mun 4/533.
181 Booth to Benson, 17 February 1917, Mun 4/5490.
182 'The D.G.M.S. the Minister', Benson, 22 February 1917, ibid.
183 Hermonius to Ministry of Munitions, 8 and 10 January 1917, Black Papers, Mun 4/533.
184 'Memorandum on Commission Internationale de Ravitaillement. Ministry of Munitions Procedure', Wyldbore Smith, 20 January 1917, Mun 5/137/1010.
185 Addison diary entries, 12 and 15 January 1917, Addison Papers, Box 98; but see the correspondence between Wyldbore Smith and Benson, Black Papers, Mun 4/533 and the letter, Black to Sir L. Worthington Evans (the parliamentary secretary to the Ministry of Munitions), 16 February 1917, ibid.

6
The Petrograd Conference

The Petrograd conference represented the last major attempt during the war to ensure close Anglo-Russian co-operation.[1] While its origin may have owed something initially to Lloyd George's desire to get Robertson out of the way by sending the latter to Russia – what the CIGS referred to as 'the K[itchener] dodge' – it also reflected Lloyd George's longstanding conviction that Russian finance, supply and military co-operation must be dealt with in a concerted fashion.[2] Although the agreements of the conference were soon invalidated by the events of March 1917 and the first Russian revolution, the Petrograd conference was a major event in Anglo-Russian relations during the First World War.

The conference was an attempt to solve the problems which had impeded close relations between the two Allies throughout the war. While the acceptance of the Nivelle plan by the western Allies had put constraints on the military talks at Petrograd, there still remained the matter of a Salonikan offensive to discuss and the opportunity for the British to get a fresh perspective on the capability of the Russian army. With respect to finance, Russian requests for further loans needed to be evaluated, while a whole complex of issues surrounding supply and transport could be threshed out by experts on a personal basis. For the first time, all three matters – strategy, finance and supply – which were the essence of the alliance were on the same agenda. This was to ensure close co-ordination. Despite this new approach, the conference foundered on the problem which had scuttled previous meetings: the difference between the capacities of Britain and Russia and the expectations which each had of the other.

The first suggestion for a conference in Petrograd was made by Lloyd George in late September 1916. Citing the growing Russian dissatisfaction with Britain over supply and an increasing pro-German sentiment in Russia, Lloyd George advised Asquith that 'a person or persons of high standing and influence in this country'

should be sent to Russia.[3] Lloyd George suggested Robertson as one
of these men, since military men 'for the moment . . . are the only
people who count in Russia'. For the other, Lloyd George advanced
Lord Reading, Lord Chief Justice, since the latter possessed the
financial expertise necessary to deal with Bark as an equal.
Robertson refused. The CIGS argued that he could not go to Russia
'without losing entire control over the war', and began a concerted
campaign to resist any further efforts to make him go.[4]

Faced with such adamant opposition, Lloyd George allowed his
proposal to drop until November. However, during the debates over
strategy in that month, the idea gained new impetus. Grey, no doubt
alarmed by the rumours of a separate Russian peace with Germany,
the Russian unhappiness with the British rejection of a Salonikan
offensive and a growing anti-British sentiment in Russia, suggested
that a conference be held in Russia in order to calm the growing
political unrest there.[5] The idea of a major conference with the
Russians to discuss strategy for 1917 was broached to the French at
the Paris conference on 15–16 November, and Lloyd George even
offered at this time to accompany Robertson to Russia in order to
allay the latter's fears that Lloyd George would indulge in 'mischief'
during the absence of the CIGS.[6] While this offer was not taken up,
both the French and Russians agreed to the holding of a conference
in Petrograd sometime in the near future. The Petrograd conference
had been born.

Once the conference had been agreed to, the British began the
difficult search for the right representatives. It was accepted that the
conference was to be held at the highest level possible, that is, as
Hardinge explained to Bertie, 'excluding Ambassadors and
confining the discussion to Ministers'.[7] Initially it was assumed that
Robertson and Grey would be the British representatives, but this
reckoned without the CIGS's absolute refusal and the fall of
Asquith's government. The search for a military representative
became somewhat comic and the Cabinet finally settled upon
General Sir Henry Wilson, the prewar DMO and subsequent liaison
officer attached to French headquarters, who had just returned from
commanding the British IVth Army Corps in France.[8] The civilian
head of the British mission was just as difficult to find, with Balfour,
Austen Chamberlain and Hardinge all rejecting the post before it
was accepted by Lord Milner. And even Milner was said to be
'sticking his toes into the ground' before he finally acquiesced.[9]

Milner requires additional space, for he was to become the minister most intimately connected with Russia in 1917. His selection for the War Cabinet in December was a surprise to most political observers, for Milner, as C. P. Scott observed, 'spoke of himself as outside party – almost it would seem outside politics.'[10] However, Milner had been an early advocate of the need to reform government in order to prosecute the war more effectively and this, combined with the strong support that he received from prominent Unionists, may have convinced Lloyd George that the former High Commissioner to South Africa would be the man most useful practically and least threatening politically. Milner is best known as the apostle of Imperial federation and for the Kindergarten of similar-minded young men which formed around him while he was in South Africa, but despite such a background his views of Russia prior to 1917 are not clear.[11] Given his views on race and empire, however, it seems safe to assume that Milner had no fond feelings for Russia, long Britain's colonial rival in Asia. Why then did Milner accept Lloyd George's offer of the mission to Russia, especially when friends had warned that the Prime Minister was attempting to get rid of him?[12] The answer lies in the war and Milner's commitment to its efficient running. As A. M. Gollin notes in his study of Milner's political career, Milner 'realised how important was the Russian mission as part of Lloyd George's entire strategic outlook.'[13]

While finding military and political representatives to go to Russia had been difficult, it was a much less onerous task to find representatives in the fields of finance and supply. Lord Revelstoke, the chairman of the firm (Baring Brothers) which handled Russia's finances in Britain and a director of the Bank of England, was chosen as the head of the British financial mission. While he had his own sources of information about Russia, Revelstoke acted only as a spokesman for the Treasury. As Balfour wrote to Bonar Law, Revelstoke

> expressed to me [Balfour] the earnest hope that he will be furnished with very full and precise instructions as to the lines he is to adopt, and that all the information in the possession of the Treasury which can be of any assistance to him may be placed at his disposal.[14]

The principal members of the supply contingent were W. T. Layton, the Director of Munitions Requirements and Statistics

(DMRS) at the Ministry of Munitions, and Major-General John Headlam, formerly the commander of the British 5th Artillery Division in France and now one of the War Office's artillery experts.

The inclusion of an artillery expert in the Petrograd entourage reflected the longstanding political argument in Britain over the wisdom of sending heavy guns to Russia. Robertson suspected that one of Lloyd George's reasons for wanting the Petrograd conference was the latter's wish to divert guns from France to Russia. The CIGS had good reason for such a belief. At a meeting of the War Committee on 21 November which Robertson did not attend, Lloyd George stated that the 'great question' to be discussed with the Russians was whether or not they should get a 'spearhead' of 500–600 guns, a course which he supported strongly.[15] This issue of guns for Russia was made even more contentious by a report from Knox, discussed at the War Cabinet on 3 January 1917, that the 400 4.5-inch and the 32 5-inch howitzers sent to Russia in 1916 had not been utilised due to problems in training men in how to use the new weapons.[16] Clearly a man of Headlam's ability was necessary if any accurate appreciation of Russia's needs and capabilities with respect to artillery was to be achieved.

The instructions given the various members of the British mission reflected the disparate views of the government. Once Wilson had been chosen as the military representative he was instructed by Robertson to become familiar first with the conclusions of Chantilly and second with 'other information', presumably about Russia.[17] Robertson's priorities reflected clearly his concern that Lloyd George planned to use the Petrograd conference as a means of overturning the conclusions of Chantilly. For his own part, as early as 21 November 1916 the CIGS had made it clear that 'he had no question of strategy which he wished to discuss with General Alexeieff'.[18] Even the official instructions which were given to Wilson on 17 December reflected the determination of the CIGS not to permit Petrograd to be an opportunity for formulating new strategic plans. According to the War Cabinet, Wilson's brief was to determine the aid necessary to improve the fighting capacity of the Russian army and not to discuss new military adventures.[19]

In fact, the matter of supply was the overriding concern for all members of the British delegation. Milner's official instructions, given at the meeting of the War Cabinet on 18 January, made it evident that the principal task of the British members was to determine whether or not 'Russia could make use of a greater quantity' of guns in particular and munitions in general.[20] While this was to be the guiding principle of the delegation, informed British opinion in Russia was not optimistic either that giving Russia war material or even that holding the conference itself would be of much use. Buchanan was worried about the technical competence of the Russian army to fight a 'modern scientific war', noting that 'even if we gave them heavy artillery and aeroplanes I doubt whether they are capable of using them properly'.[21] While the technical competence of the Russians was far better than Buchanan believed, there were other problems which were quite pressing. One was the Russian attitude towards British aid. As a British officer returning from Russia noted, the Russian concept of British help 'seems to be a sort of fairy gift of unlimited guns and equipment, of the most modern type'.[22] Another problem was the value of the conference itself. Knox was concerned that the political situation in Russia might vitiate any achievements of the conference. While he hoped that the meetings in Petrograd would be valuable, his own opinion was that they would not. 'We only require', wrote Knox, 'a dictator who would choose a strong ministry and do a little hanging.'[23]

This was typical of Knox's blunt views and reflected the frustration of one who had had to deal with the irritating ineptitude of the Russian bureaucracy throughout the war: it was, however, simplistic. At the same time as Knox was writing his pessimistic views, the British mission was on its way to Russia, having sailed from Oban aboard *HMS Kildonan Castle* on 21 January. The British party arrived at Port Romanov (now Murmansk) four days later. The Milner mission entered a Russia in which the political atmosphere was highly charged. Since the prorogation of the Duma in the autumn of 1915, the Tsarist government had grown progressively more reactionary, as the successes of the Russian army in 1916 encouraged Nicholas II to dismiss his more liberal ministers.[24] In July B. V. Stürmer was made a sort of 'civil dictator' by Nicholas and Sazonov was dismissed as Minister of Foreign Affairs. Such changes were greeted with dismay by the British. Buchanan viewed Stürmer as 'a second-rate intelligence, without any experience of affairs, a sycophant, bent solely on the advancement of his own interests and extremely ambitious' and once remarked that he 'utterly despise[d]' the former Minister of the

Interior.[25] Sazonov's dismissal had triggered off fears that Nicholas planned on negotiating a separate peace with the Germans and Hardinge wrote to Buchanan that 'when we first heard the news [of Sazonov's fall], we had a feeling of despair'.[26]

By the autumn of 1916 the political situation had deteriorated further. While there was a 'greatly diminished' fear that Russia would conclude a separate peace and indeed an improvement in Russian attitudes towards Britain, there was mounting pressure for change emanating from the liberal elements – the Progressive Bloc – of the Duma.[27] When the new session opened in the middle of November, Miliukov, the head of the Cadet party, set the tone with his 'Stupidity or Treason?' speech in which he harangued the Stürmer government for its opposition to any collaboration in public affairs by the liberals and for its reactionary policies generally. Despite the fact that, due to censorship, this speech was not reported in the newspapers, everyone of political consequence knew of it, and Buchanan made it clear to the British government just how chaotic the Russian political scene had become.[28] While the storm caused by Miliukov's speech resulted in Stürmer's dismissal and his replacement by the more moderate A. F. Trepov, the political respite was only temporary. In December and early January there was a wholesale reshuffling of the Council of Ministers, with more liberal members removed en masse. At the end of this shuffle, as one writer has put it, 'the Council of Ministers was left to reactionaries, conscripts and incompetents.'[29]

Faced with the obvious reluctance of Nicholas to accommodate any reform of a progressive sort, many in Russia began to turn to extra-legal means of achieving change. For example, A. I. Guchkov, the leading light of Moscow's public organisations, had begun a long correspondence with prominent military figures in the autumn of 1916 with an eye to a possible coup against Nicholas. Talk of revolution was everywhere when Milner arrived and he noted the 'astonishing frankness' with which even members of the royal family spoke concerning the political situation.[30] The murder of Rasputin at the end of December caused shock waves within Russia and showed the kinds of tactics which political impotency had forced upon those in opposition to the government.

Nor was this feeling confined to political life. While Guchkov's proposals had found only a tepid reception within *Stavka* – many were willing to accept a coup; few were prepared to help with it – the attitude of the troops deteriorated with the long, hard end of the

Brusilov offensive.[31] In December Major J. F. Neilson, who was attached to the Russian armies on the South-west front, sent a long report to the War Office detailing the growing unrest in the Russian army. This report was taken quite seriously in London. As one senior British officer wrote:

> The report admirably describes what I understand to be the state of affairs in Russia, & the real feelings of the Russian Army & people. While Col. Knox's Reports give the views of the Court, & of the higher strata of society both military & civil, I think it probable that Major Neilson gives more accurately those of the great mass of the people – i.e. of the non-Guards officers & rank & file, of the merchant class & of the peasantry.[32]

While Neilson was certain that the Russian army 'is determined to continue the war', he noted that 'the lower classes, with true Russian apathy seem to be indifferent as to who wins this war.' Moreover, he detected a change in the attitude of the officer corps, where he now heard frequently expressed a belief that the Emperor had to be removed: 'all this is a sign of the times, for the Officer class is of course the firmest supporter of the Sovereign.' Perhaps more ominous, as far as prosecution of the war was concerned, was Neilson's strong opinion that 'there is no doubt that to-day the Army is on the side of the people. If 1905 repeats itself, and it will, the Army will be one with the people, and who can then stop the movement?' As far as Neilson was concerned, the increasing respect for the British military effort which he saw developing in Russia had to be encouraged and nurtured for the Russian army would play a decisive role in Russia's future development both during and after the war. The army's opinion would be vital for 'however carefully the feelings of the [Russian] nation may be tuned [in Britain's favour], the passage of the Russian Army across the keys will play the tune the Army wishes.' These were prophetic words, and while more applicable after the March revolution, reflected the serious problems within the Russian army.

Buchanan was fully aware of these problems. As Lindley wrote in his dispatch of 18 January, 'as regards the future, the Ambassador's telegrams will have shown what the feeling in the country is. For my own part, I never hear anyone say a good word either for the Emperor or Empress, and their assassination is quite openly discussed by persons in responsible positions.'[33] Just a few days before, on 12 January, Buchanan had spoken so frankly to the Emperor about the internal situation in Russia that the latter had been offended.[34] While the domestic political situation was not a matter of formal discussion at the conference – indeed, the Emperor made it clear that it was not a matter for discussion at all[35] – it no doubt had an influence on those who attended. G. R. Clerk, who attended the conference on behalf of the Foreign Office, reflected this point clearly in a letter which he wrote on the mission's first full day in Petrograd, 30 January. The Russians, Clerk felt, 'moved perhaps by an impulse they scarely understand' would see the war through to a finish, 'but what will happen politically, God knows.'[36] Clerk's optimism that the war would be fought through before a revolution would occur, a view shared by others in Russia, no doubt reflected as much his hopes as his judgement. The need for a militarily strong Russia in the struggle against the Central Powers made everyone close his eyes to the distressing thought of a Russian defection.

When the mission arrived in Petrograd its various members set to work. Milner spent his first day meeting with Buchanan and Sir Samuel Hoare, the latter the head of the British intelligence mission in Russia. Meanwhile Revelstoke and Bark held their first financial discussion and the opening meeting on '*ravitaillement*' began with a session discussing transport.[37] At this latter meeting, the Russian attitude which was to characterise their position throughout the conference quickly emerged. This attitude reflected a series of meetings and decisions which had taken place during the last month.

After Alekseev's call for a joint Allied offensive in the Balkans was rejected at Chantilly, various Russian generals were polled during early December 1916 to determine their views about future strategy. This culminated in a conference of generals held at *Stavka* on 30–31 December with the Emperor in the chair.[38] With General V. I. Gurko acting as Chief of Staff while Alekseev was on sick leave in the Crimea, the generals decided to reject the Allied decisions at Chantilly. There was no intention to take the initiative on the Russian front over the winter and, even if the Allies did achieve something during that period, Russia would only, in Gurko's words, 'prepare for active operations on every front, but comparatively small in extent, and with small forces.'[39] Instead, it was decided to focus all efforts on a major thrust on the South-west front in the spring, a decision which the Emperor gave final assent to on 6

February after consulting the convalescing Alekseev. Even as the French and British adherence to the decisions of Chantilly had, in Wilson's phrase, 'for the most part fallen to the ground' due to the acceptance of the Nivelle plan, so too had the Russian.[40]

Another conference had taken place at *Stavka* just before the military one. Beginning on 27 December, Gurko had chaired a discussion of economic and supply problems. This had been brought about in part by a demand of some senior generals that the vexatious problem of food supply be solved and in general by the fact that 'the machinery of government was breaking down and that the ship of state was tossing on a sea of troubles.'[41] While no concrete solutions were attained at the conference, it was decided that better co-ordination between supply ministries must be achieved and to this end Gurko went to Petrograd early in 1917. Here he had a series of discussions with D. S. Shuvaiev, the Minister of War, where the two decided that the key issue to be discussed at Petrograd was supply, not strategy, and that the Russian policy must be to get all that she could from the Allies.[42] Obviously there was not much likelihood of such an attitude finding acceptance with the British delegation.

The first session on '*ravitaillement*' was opened by Trepov, the latter acting more in his former capacity as Minister of Ways and Communications than as President of the Council of Ministers.[43] Trepov outlined the estimated capacity of the major Russian ports – Archangel, Romanov and Vladivostock – for the period of the next eighteen months. According to him, this capacity was 9.5 millon tons and General Beliaev, who had replaced Shuvaev as Minister of War on the eve of the conference, implored the British and French representatives to provide that amount of tonnage for Russian use during the next year and a half. After a query by General Janin, one of the French delegates, as to whether the Russians could transport such amounts from the ports to the front, to which Beliaev replied, '*facilement*', the meeting adjourned until the following day. The British representatives at this meeting, Hanbury Williams, Knox, Headlam and Layton, had made no comments on the Russian requests, undoubtedly being shocked by their magnitude. Layton in particular was amazed by the Russian figures and expressed his surprise to Wilson the following day, resulting in the whimsical Ulsterman noting of the Russian delegates that 'they are difficult gentlemen!'[44]

Such a remark also was prompted by Wilson's own dealings with Gurko on 31 January. While Milner journeyed to Tsarskoe Selo to see the Emperor, Wilson had a long talk with Gurko from which the British general emerged 'very dissatisfied' with the acting Russian Chief of Staff.[45] Wilson's dissatisfaction did not stem from any arguments over grand strategy. With the collapse of Romania and the Anglo-French acceptance of the Nivelle plan, neither Gurko nor Wilson had any interest in maintaining the fictions of Chantilly. Indeed, they were generally in accord over military matters, although Gurko favoured Sarrail's taking strong action against the Greeks in order to force the latter to commit themselves to the Allied cause: Wilson did not. The problem was supply. Gurko was insistent about the need for massive shipments of military supplies to Russia. Wilson attempted to put the Russian off by stating that matters of supply were dependent on factors concerning transportation, but Gurko clung tenaciously to his demands. Wilson was not impressed by Gurko's arguments and the future CIGS wrote in his diary afterwards that 'I must get a hold of the man and shake him into some practical frame of mind.'[46]

That same day a similar argument occurred, this time at the second meeting on supplies.[47] When the Russian artillery needs were presented by Grand Duke Sergei, *Stavka*'s representative with the Artillery Department, Colonel Remond, the French artillery expert, exclaimed that the size of the Russian requests made him feel '*dépourvu*'. Remond pointed out that the French did not have enough guns to satisfy their own needs, let alone these large Russian demands, but the Grand Duke Sergei countered that the Russian front had to be supplied with artillery more in line with the scale provided on the Western front.[48] Only if greater amounts of artillery were provided for Russia, the Grand Duke went on, could an offensive be made '*non seulement efficace, mais possible*.'[49] This point was reiterated by Beliaev who, half-threateningly, indicated that any Russian offensive in 1917 would be guided by the amount of artillery provided by the Allies. Beliaev then asked Layton if Britain were prepared to furnish part of her production of heavy artillery to Russia. Layton agreed that Britain would do so, although the DMRS hedged his reply by noting that no final decision about amounts could be reached until the figures presented by the Grand Duke were examined carefully.

On 1 February the conference opened officially.[50] In his

introductory remarks Gurko again stressed the supply needs of Russia, noting that Russia's own industries were unable to provide all the material necessary to permit the launching of a large-scale offensive. This plenary session was attended by so many people that is was impossible to do any serious work, but it did decide to split the remainder of the conference into a series of sub-committees to deal separately with the military, political, financial and supply issues. The lack of organisation manifest at the opening session was typical of the entire conference and was a sore point throughout, as far as the British were concerned.[51] In part this was due to the rapid change of ministers in the Russian government over the preceding few months, an occurrence which meant that ministers 'had to begin by learning the duties they were supposed to perform'.[52] There was also the matter of interdepartmental rivalries, as various departments strove to maintain their positions of influence within the Russian bureaucracy at the expense of the overall efficiency of the conference. The net result was to reinforce the general British belief that the Russians were incapable of sound organisation.

The day after the conference opened, Milner went to see the Emperor in the morning and returned in the afternoon for the first political meeting.[53] The centre of discussion was Greece. The Russians, and in particular the ubiquitous Gurko, wanted to let General Sarrail force the Greeks to declare war using military action if necessary. As this course of action had been rejected already by the other Allies at the Rome conference of 5–6 January, the British and French could not agree, and the discussion in Milner's words was 'long and animated'.[54] It was decided that this issue could not be resolved without reference to the Allied governments and, despite the matter being raised again by the Russians at the second and third political meetings on 4 and 6 February respectively, the final conclusion of the conference was only that the Allies must take all actions towards Greece in concert.[55]

While Milner was engaged in the fruitless discussion of Greece, the supply sub-committee was further examining the Russian artillery demands.[56] Layton opened the session of 2 February by asking the Grand Duke Sergei to provide the basis upon which the Russian artillery requests were calculated. The latter, promising to provide the information the next day, promptly switched the topic to the provision of shells. After the Grand Duke had presented figures commensurate with his earlier artillery orders, Layton decided to interject a note of realism into the discussions. The DMRS suggested that as a first step in facilitating shell supply from abroad, the Russian representative in New York, General Zalubovskii, be advised to co-operate closely with Booth in the latter's efforts to improve Russian purchasing in the United States. Beliaev quickly turned discussion away from this sore point, which involved the longstanding quarrel about Russia's right to place orders abroad independently of Britain, by describing it as being of secondary importance which could be dealt with later. After an examination of some of the specific Russian demands, the Grand Duke Sergei noted that the figures for machine guns which he had given at the first meeting were too low and had to be revised upwards to a figure in excess of 90,000. In massive understatement, Layton and Remond found this new figure '*très considérable*'. The size of this order, and of the complementary one for small-arms ammunition, reintroduced the question of Russia's making further purchases in the United States, as neither Britain nor France could provide the amounts requested. Layton pointed out the barriers in both finance and transportation to such further orders, but Beliaev insisted on the Russian need, and the session closed on that note.

Already the chief features of the conference were emerging. The military and political talks, aside from the arguments over Greece, were concerned mainly with confirming that Russia and the other Allies were fully aware of each other's intentions and were working in co-operation. As Milner was to state later, most of the formal conference was a 'shell' and truly important work was carried on in the sub-committees, particularly the one dealing with supply.[57] It was this latter issue which was most contentious. The Russian policy was similar to that followed at the conference in London in July 1916. Every effort was made to obtain as much as possible in the way of supplies, while at the same time to avoid having restrictions placed upon Russia's right to purchase them unilaterally in the United States. The British, on the other hand, wanted to determine the exact size of Russia's requirements and to correlate them with what Britain could provide, what could be transported, and what effect they would have on Russia's military effort. These two approaches were not compatible. The Russian policy was regarded by the British as involving presenting 'an exhaustive list of all Russian wants . . . and ask[ing] us to foot the bill', while the Russians viewed the British opposition to their demands as taking a '*point de vue commercial*' and failing to recognise the Russian military effort.[58] With such opposing ideas, the likelihood of agreement was slight.

There were also problems with respect to finance, despite the fact that one of the major difficulties involved with it had been resolved on the eve of the conference. In January the Treasury had responded in sharp fashion to Russian complaints that Britain was not justified in requesting shipments of gold under the terms of the agreement of 27 October 1916. The Treasury pointed out that new contracts for Russia had been placed in the United States to a value of nearly $50 million since the middle of November and that Britain was entitled to call for Russian gold as reserves had fallen below the level specified in the agreement. The Russian government, in response to the Treasury's censures, agreed to ship a further £20 million worth of gold on 27 January 1917. The bullion was sent via Vladivostock and Japan to Canada, where it was kept as collateral for British loans to maintain credit in the United States for the Allied war effort.[59]

With this troublesome issue out of the way, the financial discussions at Petrograd should have proceeded smoothly. This was not the case. At the major financial meeting on 7 February the British delegation made it clear that they were not authorised to negotiate a further loan, but were in Russia only to 'examine thoroughly the needs of Russia in a most sympathetic spirit, and to advise such means of meeting them as were likely to be most acceptable to the British Treasury.'[60] This was not what the Russians wanted to hear. Bark pointed out that the value of the rouble had declined by 41.9 per cent on the London market since the beginning of the war, and argued that Britain must provide Russia with more credit in order to counteract this depreciation.[61] As usual, Gurko added his views. The General called for a common Allied financial as well as military policy, but Milner avoided any comment on this matter by pleading the need for further study. Gurko continued to press his point, causing Milner to note in his diary that 'Gurko (the General) was lengthy & irrelevant.'[62] Bark reiterated his opinion that funds must be given to support the exchange rate, and Milner replied that while this and other Russian financial problems were appreciated by the British delegation, '*Hélas! les Anglais ne sont pas des magiciens.*' The Russian hopes of unlimited credit were unlikely to be realised.

While there were further financial discussions between Bark and the British delegation on 15 and 20 February, the basic financial positions of both sides had been taken at the meeting of 7 February. The British delegation's final recommendations reflected the Treasury policies which had been established as early as 1915. These recommendations gave approval to a continuation throughout 1917 of the provisions of the financial agreement of 27 October 1916 with respect to the payment of goods ordered through the Russian Government Committee in London and to the servicing of the Russian debt abroad. However, the contentious issues of the maintenance of the value of the rouble and the provision of a free credit for Russia to spend abroad at her discretion were treated less favourably. The delegation said that they would recommend the supply of only £12 million for the rouble exchange and would make no commitment whatsoever to the Russian request for an increase in the free monthly credit to £5.5 million.

The basic political, military and financial decisions had been reached by 7 February. The political decisions were not startling. The decision with respect to Allied policy towards Greece has been described above, and in addition it was agreed only that Japan should be pressed to give Russia more aid and prisoners of war, such as the Czechs, might be enrolled in the war effort.[63] The military decisions were no more novel. They merely confirmed what both sides had decided before the conference had opened. Despite heavy French pressure, the Russians refused to commit themselves to an attack in concert with Nivelle's offensive, and it was agreed that there would be no large Russian attack in Romania, that the Anglo-French force at Salonika should act purely on the defensive, while all other secondary theatres should have their forces reduced to a minimum.[64] Faced with totally opposed views, the conference had plastered over the differences with a do-nothing pronouncement.

With the conference at this stage Wilson and Milner left Petrograd. Having dealt with the military and political matters, Wilson went to visit the front while Milner travelled to Moscow to sample opinion there. Before they left the capital, however, they sent interim reports to England.[65] These reports contained several suggestions for the improvement of the bureaucratic mechanisms of Anglo-Russian co-operation and these require some examination as most were actually implemented. The suggestions dealt mainly with munitions matters, although some related to the delineation of the duties of the various British representatives in Russia.[66]

Wilson proposed that a British Military Equipment Section (BMES) should be set up in Russia under direction of Brigadier-General F. C. Poole, an artillery expert who had served under Wilson in France and had accompanied the mission to Russia at the latter's request.[67] Poole's organisation was to ensure that British munitions sent to Russia were utilised fully, reflecting the British concern. For his part, Milner suggested that the Ministry of Munitions should have a body of representatives in Russia to provide an element of co-ordination between the various Russian departments in Petrograd. Echoing the sentiment which British representatives in Russia had expressed since the beginning of the war, Milner noted that there was at present 'very little' such co-ordination. In addition, such a body could keep the Russians fully advised of the munitions situation in England, thereby stopping 'unreasonable demands at the source', and could investigate the possibilities of increasing Russia's domestic production.

Suggestions for the improvement of Anglo-Russian co-operation also came from other sources. Layton was concerned that some new British representation be introduced in Russia since co-ordination between the various Russian departments was, in his view, 'appalling'. Both Knox and Hanbury Williams were out of touch with British developments with respect to munitions and had 'in fact said so as soon as I [Layton] arrived.'[68] Given such circumstances, Layton suggested that a Ministry of Munitions body be set up in Petrograd, although he warned that this body should be placed, at least ostensibly, under Poole lest the confusion in Petrograd be expanded rather than contracted. On 24 January Hoare wrote to Alfred Herbert, one of the Deputy Director Generals of the Ministry of Munitions, calling for the establishment of a machine tools department of the Ministry in Russia.[69] This proposal was forwarded to the Minister of Munitions on 13 February with a recommendation for its implementation, a recommendation which Addison minuted three days later, 'I agree'.[70] Before setting anything in motion, on 17 February Addison telegraphed Milner to determine the latter's views about the wisdom of such a project, a telegram which undoubtedly only reinforced Milner's own belief that some new body dealing with British supplies should be set up in Petrograd.[71] Surprisingly, considering the general dislike which the Russians usually displayed towards any initiative which seemed to encroach upon their prerogatives, Russian opinion also favoured such suggestions. Milner found the Emperor 'quite sympathetic' with the proposals for Poole's mission, and General Beliaev 'warmly welcomed' the idea of British representation in Russia.[72]

Such unanimity led to results. By the end of March staff for Poole's BMES had arrived in Russia and it began to function early in April. In addition, after a 'long talk' on 8 March between Layton and Addison, when the former returned to England after the Petrograd conference, it was arranged that a Colonel F. Byrne should go to Russia as the Ministry's representative.[73] Addison was concerned that Byrne was 'too big a man' to send to Russia, reflecting his high opinion of the latter rather than a low opinion of the Russian post, but concluded that the Russian situation demanded a man capable of organising matters on a large scale.[74] Byrne's mission officially was to be under Poole, but was to act independently on matters of supply. Indeed, there were plans for this autonomy to be enlarged should Byrne's mission prove efficacious in improving the speed of supply. As a memorandum prepared for Milner later noted:

> It is probable . . . that the work of munitions representatives may rapidly grow in importance if it secures the good-will of the Russian authorities, and that it may be subsequently desirable to arrange for its complete separation from General Poole's organization, which would concern itself with tactics, training, the use of munitions and questions of policy as to the best form of assistance in completed munitions that can be given to Russia.[75]

The formation of two new bodies under Poole and Byrne was a step in the right direction. Not only did it began to clear away the welter of confusion surrounding munitions ordering in Petrograd, but also it freed Knox and Blair from the work, 'giv[ing] us more time to work at purely G.[eneral] S.[taff] stuff.'[76]

But this is to anticipate. When Wilson and Milner departed Petrograd at the end of the first week of proceedings, they had left the British munitions experts to wrestle with their Russian counterparts. While the basic shape of the conference had been established by the time the senior personnel had left, in Layton's opinion the 'crux' of the discussions at Petrograd had not been broached. This central issue was, as Layton wrote to Addison on 8 February, 'the scaling down of these [demands for supplies by the

Russians] to the available means of transport.'[77] The matter of tonnage had been raised on 6 February at a meeting held to discuss Russian needs for railway material.[78] The discussion led to a consideration of the capacity of the Russian ports, and Trepov again put foward his estimate of 13 million tons as the combined capacity of the three major harbours. Hanbury Williams pointed out that as the Admiralty was going to allocate only about 4 million tons of shipping for Russia in 1917 '*il faut classer les commandes par ordre d'importance*'. Beliaev was in opposition to this view, but the discussion of tonnage was deferred until a later unspecified date, reflecting the reluctance of the Russians to consider the matter.

The question of allocations arose again on 11 February, this time as part of a meeting held to discuss Russian needs for strategic metals.[79] When the Russian requests for metals were totalled they came to just short of 1.9 million tons, and Layton judged the time appropriate to reintroduce the question of tonnage. The DMRS pointed out that British and French transportation experts had determined that Russian ports were capable of disembarking only 3.4 million tons of supplies during the 1917 shipping season. Since, at an earlier meeting, it had been agreed already that 1.5 million tons of coal were to be provided for Russia in 1917, there remained only 1.9 million tons for all Russian orders. Did the Russian government wish to employ all of this tonnage for metals? This remark produced, rather than a sober re-evaluation of Russian needs, impassioned defences of all proposed orders for metals by the Russian delegates. Layton then poured further cold water on Russian hopes. There were, he pointed out, shortages of metals in all the Allied countries and Russia must increase her own production instead of relying upon foreign supply. In any case, he added, the Russian demands for steel were '*la moitié de la production anglais*'. The need for putting Russian orders in some order of priority was evident.

Such advice ran counter to all the intentions which the Russians had for the conference, and resulted in an immediate barrage of argument. The Russians alleged that the British did not appreciate the military necessity of their orders, a necessity which made every order crucial. Layton was not intimidated by this line of argument. In rebuttal he contended that his reasoning was indeed based upon sound military principles for '*le matériel qui rest pendant des mois dans les docks du Londres ou à Arkhangelsk, parce qu'il ne peut être transporte est entièrement perdu pour les Allies.*' Unable to counter the

logic of this statement, the Russian delegates turned the discussion
to less global matters: the consideration for small orders of zinc and
tin.

The Russian reluctance to consider restrictions upon tonnage
continued until the end of the conference. As a consequence of this,
Layton and Headlam drew up their own list of Russian priorities and
presented it to the Russian delegation on 18 February at the final
session dealing with Russian orders abroad.[80] Layton and Headlam's
list was compiled on purely military grounds; it had been guided by
'Wilson's judgement of [the] capacity and needs of the Russian
army as far as he has been able to gauge them by visits to the front.'[81]

In fact, Wilson was quite impressed by the Russian army. He
noted that it had recovered entirely from the defeats of 1915 and was
'a fine fighting machine better in every respect than it was at the
beginning of the war.' Wilson felt that the chief weakness of the
army was its 'deplorable' railway transport and that its major
munitions requirements were heavy artillery and aircraft. As to
military capacity, Wilson suggested that 'with luck' Russia might
achieve 'great things', but he was convinced that she would be
unable to launch a large offensive in 1917 and would be able to
contribute only small local attacks in support of the Nivelle
offensive.[82] In short, Wilson's opinion was one not far from that of
the Russians themselves.

The final plenary session of the conference was held 20 February
and reflected the displeasure of the Russians with the final amounts
of munitions which they were to receive.[83] Gurko – 'that vain,
talkative devil' as Wilson characterised him – alternately complained
of British indifference towards Russia and threatened that the
reductions made in Russian requests would result in a weakened
military effort on the Eastern front.[84] Gurko's curmudgeonly
behaviour was so marked that it resulted in a public reprimand from
Beliaev, but while this rebuke ameliorated Wilson's anger with
Gurko, it did not end the latter's resentment of the British. Nothing
could bridge the gap between Russian expectations and British
capacities.

On 21 February the British delegation left Petrograd for
Murmansk whence they embarked on 25 February for Scapa Flow.
Five days later they were back on British soil, having spent just over
a month in Russia. Opinions as to the success of the conference were
varied. Hoare, who returned home with the British party, felt that

the Milner mission had been a waste of time. The Russians had not wanted politicians and advice, Hoare felt, only munitions.[85] Buchanan struck a more balanced note. The ambassador felt that a 'good deal of useful work' had taken place, particularly with respect to finance and munitions, but was not optimistic that the present Russian government would be able to utilise the aid given due to its unpopularity and incompetence.[86] Headlam, who remained behind in Russia to visit the artillery positions at the front, was in no doubt that some good work had been done at the conference, and added that Layton 'has been really *the* success of the whole proceedings. I am sure that our colleagues and the Russians would all agree to this.'[87] This latter opinion was shared by Knox, who felt that Wilson had made an excellent impression on the Russians.[88]

Upon their return to Britain, Wilson, Layton and Milner gave their final reports to the War Cabinet on 6 March.[89] Milner's report was filled with pessimism. While he stated that a revolution was not imminent Milner was not blind, as Lloyd George was to suggest later in his memoirs, to the political unrest in the country. The conversations which Lockhart had arranged for Milner in Moscow with Chelnokov and Prince Lvov, two of that city's leading liberal lights, had made the British envoy sensitive to the twists and turns of the Russian political scene.[90] The Byzantine nature of Russian politics coloured Milner's presentation to the War Cabinet. In a remark undoubtedly reflecting his long experiences in the Empire, Milner noted of the Russians that 'they are, in fact, orientals to a large extent – very suspicious and sometimes shifty, but willing to be led by capable leadership.'[91] This observation also had implicit within it the condescension which many British officials felt towards the Russians, an attitude which could not have helped make for good relations.

Milner felt, as did Knox, that the major work accomplished at the conference concerned munitions. In a supplementary note to his report on the conference, Milner stated that he attached 'very much greater importance to this work than to all the other Petrograd proceedings put together.'[92] Milner's greatest worry about Russia, even exceeding that of revolution, was concerned with munitions and their administration. As he put it, what had to be feared was 'not so much deliberate revolution as chaos resulting from the confusion into which a badly organized administrative system has been thrown by the strain of war.' He was not optimistic that these problems could be any more than ameliorated by the Allies: 'all we can do is to send out a few competent technical experts and . . . to see that these experts get a fair chance'. Certainly Milner was not biased in favour of the existing government, however much his remarks could be interpreted as a 'do-nothing' policy. While by 18 March Milner was convinced that the revolution had 'wasted' much of the work of the conference, he felt that the British must continue to do 'everything in our power' to aid the new Provisional government as it consisted 'mainly, perhaps entirely, of our friends'.[93]

What did the Petrograd conference achieve? While it represented a new approach by the British – an attempt to deal with all matters concerning Anglo-Russian co-operation in a concerted fashion – it experienced the same problems which had hindered earlier, less comprehensive, conferences. At Petrograd the Russians felt, as they had at the conference in London held during July 1916, that British arguments about finance, transport and shortages of supplies and tonnage were only excuses to cover up an unwillingness to provide Russia's needs. For their part, the British viewed the Russian refusals to scale down their needs to fit the means available as characteristic of the bureaucratic incompetence which was a standard feature of Russian life.

The advent of the March revolution just two weeks after the conference closed makes any judgement of its achievements difficult. The chaos which ensued after the fall of Nicholas would have made even a perfect agreement at Petrograd difficult to implement. However, it was unlikely even before the revolution occurred and, in fact, even before the conference itself took place, that any great improvement would transpire in Anglo-Russian co-operation. There are several reasons for this conclusion. The first is that the positions taken by both sides before the conference began made any agreement nearly impossible. With the British interested in providing support for Russia only in direct proportion to what its assumed effect would be on Russia's military capacity and the Russians interested in obtaining 'the largest possible amount of war materials of the very best quality', disharmony was near inevitable.[94] The second reason is that many of the factors which limited the support which Britain could offer Russia were not directly controlled by Britain. Many of the restrictions placed on finance and supply were determined to a large extent by considerations in the United States. Even had the British wished to fulfil Russia's most extravagant demands, it is unlikely that they could have done so given the degree of dependence on America which existed. A final reason has to do with transportation. While the allocation of tonnage was under British control, a decision to provide more ships for the Russian runs did not occur due to the inadequate internal transportation system in Russia herself. A change in this policy after Petrograd was made even less likely by the German declaration of unrestricted submarine warfare on 1 February 1917 and the subsequent enormous increase in British shipping losses. While these reasons made success unlikely, the Petrograd conference was not a complete failure. The new organisations to deal with supplies which resulted from it were a distinct improvement on what had gone before; however, no innovations of this sort could overcome the practical difficulties which were at the base of the problems with the supply of munitions. The March revolution served to make the probable outcome the inevitable one.

Notes

1 There is no English-language study of the Petrograd conference. The best Soviet accounts are M. M. Karliner, 'Angliia i Petrogradskaia konferentsiia Antanty 1917 g.', in *Mezhdunarodnye otnosheniia politika diplomatiia XVI–XX veka* (Moscow, 1964), 322–58; A. V. Ignatev, *Russko-angliiskie otnosheniia v 1917 g.* (Moscow, 1966), 102–22; V. A. Emets, 'Petrogradskaia konferentsiia 1917 g. i Frantsiia', *Istoricheskie zapiski*, 83 (1969), 23–37.
2 As cited in Roskill, *Hankey*, I, 320.
3 Lloyd George to Asquith, 28 September 1916, Lloyd George Papers E/2/23/5.
4 Robertson to Lloyd George, 29 September 1916, Lloyd George Papers E/1/5/2; Roskill, *Hankey*, I, 316–20; Hankey, *Supreme Command*, II, 556–7; Haig to Kiggell, 25 November 1916, Kiggell Papers II/6.
5 Grey's fears were probably raised by a memorandum given to him by the DMI, entitled, 'The situation in Russia', Macdonogh, 30 October 1916, Macdonogh Papers, WO 106/1511. Grey's suggestion was at the meeting of the War Committee, 7 November 1916, Cab 42/23/9.
6 Robertson to Haig, 10 November 1916, Robertson Papers I/22/89. 'Minutes of the proceedings of a conference held at Paris', n.s., 15 November 1916 and 'Proceedings of a conference held at Paris on Thursday, November 16th 1916', n.s., 16 November 1916, both in WO 106/397.
7 Hardinge to Bertie, 14 November 1916, Bertie Papers, FO 800/178.
8 Haig to Kiggell, 25 November 1916, Kiggell Papers II/6.
9 Hardinge to Bertie, 21 December 1916, Hardinge Papers, 28.
10 Scott diary entry, 19–21 April 1917, Wilson (ed.), *Scott Diaries*, 278–9.
11 P. A. Lockwood, 'Milner's entry into the War Cabinet, December 1916', *Historical Journal*, 7, 1 (1964), 120–1; J. A. Turner, 'The formation of Lloyd George's "Garden Suburb": "Fabian-like Milnerite penetration?" ' *Historical Journal*, 20, 1 (1977), 165–6. Milner's biographer, A. M. Gollin, does not make Milner's views on Russia clear in *Proconsul in Politics: a study of Lord Milner in opposition and in power* (New York, 1965).

12   ibid., 403. Lloyd George appears to have used missions as a convenient means of ridding himself of awkward personalities; see J. M. McEwen, 'Northcliffe and Lloyd George at war, 1914–1918', *Historical Journal*, 24, 3 (1981), 666–7.

13   Gollin, *Milner*, 403.

14   Balfour to Bonar Law, 3 January 1917, Balfour Papers, FO 800/205.

15   Robertson to Haig, 10 November 1916, Robertson Papers I/22/89; meeting of the War Committee, 21 November 1916, Cab 42/25/2.

16   26th meeting of the War Cabinet, 3 January 1917, Cab 23/1.

17   Robertson to Wilson, 19 December 1916, Robertson Papers I/35/119; Callwell, *Wilson Diaries*, I, 303–14.

18   Meeting of the War Committee, 21 November 1916, Cab 42/25/2.

19   Cab 37/162/15.

20   37th meeting of the War Cabinet, 18 January 1917, Cab 23/1.

21   Buchanan to Hardinge, 30 December 1916, Hardinge Papers, 28.

22   Brig.-Gen. L. Jackson to Addison, 13 January 1917, Addison Papers, Box 29, 'Russia'.

23   Knox to Buckley (M.I. 3), 22 January 1917, WO 106/5128.

24   See Pearson, *Russian Moderates*, 65–139; Diakin, *Russkaia burzhuazia*, especially 128–311, for an examination of Russian politics in this period.

25   Buchanan, *Mission*, II, 3; Buchanan to Hardinge, 5 December 1916, Hardinge Papers, 28.

26   Hardinge to Buchanan, 26 August 1916, Hardinge Papers, 24.

27   Hardinge to Bertie, 14 November 1916, Bertie Papers, FO 800/178.

28   Buchanan to Grey, 5 December 1916, Cab 1/21/33.

29   Pearson, *Russian Moderates*, 127.

30   Milner diary entry, 25 January 1917, Milner Papers 280.

31   Wildman, *The End of the Russian Imperial Army*, 105–20.

32   Note by Agar (M.I. 3) to D.M.I., 29 December 1916, accompanying Neilson's 'The outlook of the Russian army', n.d. (but 16 December 1916), both in WO 106/1125.

33   Dispatch 15, 18 January 1917, FO 371/2995/23644.

34   Buchanan, *Mission*, II, 41–50.

35   Callwell, *Wilson Diaries*, I, 315.

36   Clerk to T. Russell (Balfour's political secretary), 30 January 1917, FO 800/383.

37   'Conférence des Allies à Petrograd. Commission de Ravitaillement', 1st session, 30 January 1917, Cab 28/2 IC 16(B). Hereafter cited only as *Ravitaillement* along with the number and date of the session.

38   Rostunov, *Russkii front*, 333–8.

39   V. I. Gurko, *Memories & Impressions of War and Revolution in Russia 1914–1917* (London, 1918), 217.

40   Wilson diary entry, n.d. (but written while on the way to Russia aboard *HMS Kildonan Castle*), Callwell, *Wilson Diaries*, I, 312.

41   A. A. Brusilov, *A Soldier's Note-book 1914–1918* (London, 1930), 279–80.

42   The economic conference is discussed in Sidorov, *Ekonomicheskoe polozhenie*, 311, and the same author's, *Finansovoe polozhenie*, 416.

43   *Ravitaillement*, 1st session, 30 January 1917.

44   Wilson diary entry, 31 January 1917, Callwell, *Wilson Diaries*, I, 314.

45   Milner diary entry, 31 January 1917, Milner Papers 280.

46   Wilson diary entry, 31 January 1917, Callwell, *Wilson Diaries*, I, 314.

47   *Ravitaillement*, 2nd session, 31 January 1917.

48   Emets, 'Petrogradskaia kontferentsiia', 35–6. For example, the Russians wanted 4,964 3-inch guns and 1,424 4.5- and 4.8-inch howitzers. These figures are in 'Conference of the Allies at Petrograd January–February 1917. Documents

Relating to the Sub-Commission on Munitions.' Headlam and Layton, 16 February 1917, pt IV, 2 and pt V, 8. Cab 28/2 IC 16(i). Hereafter DRSCM.

49 *Ravitaillement*, 2nd session, 31 January 1917.

50 'Procès-verbaux, Petrograd. Première Séance, tenue le 19 Janvier/1ᵉʳ Février, 1917 au Palais Marie, dans la salle de Departement du Conseil de l'Empire', Cab 28/2 IC 16. (Hereafter cited as *Procès-verbaux*, with the number and date of sessions.)

51 Milner diary entry, 1 February 1917, Milner Papers 280.

52 Brusilov, *A Soldier's Note-book*, 278. Organisation problems were due also to interdepartmental rivalries within the Russian government; see Sidorov, *Ekonomicheskoe polozhenie*, 311–13.

53 *Procès-verbaux*, 1st political session, 2 February 1917.

54 Milner diary entry, 2 February 1917, Milner Papers 280.

55 *Procès-verbaux*, 2nd and 3rd political sessions, 4 and 6 February 1917. The final decisions are in 'Séance du Clôture, tenue le 7/20 Février, 1917 au Ministère des Affaires Etrangères', Cab 28/2 IC 16.

56 *Ravitaillement*, 3rd session, 2 February 1917.

57 'Allied Conference at Petrograd, January–February 1917. Further confidential note by Lord Milner dated March 13, 1917', Milner, 13 March 1917, Cab 24/3/GT 131.

58 ibid.; see the argument between Layton and the Russians in *Ravitaillement*, 10th session, 11 February 1917.

59 FO to Buchanan, 19 January 1917, FO 371/2997/13524; Buchanan to FO, 27 January 1917, FO 371/2997/21976.

60 'Financial questions raised at the conference', n.s., 7 February 1917, Cab 21/42; 'Procès-verbal of the Allied financial conference at Petrograd, February 7 1917', n.s., 7 February 1917, Cab 28/2 IC 16(a). Unless otherwise noted, my discussion of financial matters is drawn from these two sources.

61 Sidorov, *Finansovoe polozhenie*, 430.

62 Milner diary entry, 7 February 1917, Milner Papers, 280. The 'other' Gurko was Vladimir I. Gurko, a member of the State Council and a brother of General Vasilli I. Gurko.

63 *Procès-verbaux*, 2nd and 3rd political sessions, 4 and 6 February 1917.

64 Emets, 'Petrogradskaia kontferentsiia', 29–37.

65 Milner to FO, 9 February 1917, FO 371/3004/32539; Wilson to Robertson, 5 February 1917, Cab 17/197.

66 I have discussed other aspects of the bureaucratic reforms elsewhere, Neilson, ' "Joy Rides"?', 888–9.

67 The origin of Poole's section is in 'Report of the work of the British Military Equipment Section in Russia', Poole, 17 January 1918, WO 106/1145. Poole later commanded the British interventionary force at Archangel and served as the British representative to the White commander, General Denikin.

68 Layton to Addison, 8 February 1917, Addison Papers, Box 29, 'Russia'.

69 Hoare to Herbert, 24 January 1917, Layton Papers, Mun 4/360.

70 Black to Addison, 13 February 1917; minute by Addison, 16 February 1917, ibid.

71 Addison to Milner, 17 February 1917, ibid.

72 Callwell, *Wilson Diaries*, I, 315; 'Notes of interview with General Belayeff', Milner, 19 February 1917, Addison Papers, Box 29, 'Russia'.

73 Addison diary entry, 8 March 1917, Addison Papers, Box 98.

74 Addison diary entry, 12 March 1917, ibid.

75 'Mr. Layton's Papers. Representation in Petrograd', n.s., 15 March 1917, Layton Papers, Mun 4/360.

76   Knox to Buckley, 27 February 1917, WO 106/5128.
77   Layton to Addison, 8 February 1917, Addison Papers, Box 29, 'Russia'.
78   *Ravitaillement,* 5th session, 6 February 1917.
79   *Ravitaillement,* 10th session, 11 February 1917.
80   *Ravitaillement,* 15th session, 18 February 1917; Milner diary entry, 16 February 1917, Milner Papers, 280. The final allocations are in DRSCM, pt II, 2.
81   Milner to Lloyd George, 22 February 1917, FO 371/3005/40885.
82   'Report on Petrograd', Wilson, 3 March 1917, Cab 17/197; Callwell, *Wilson Diaries,* I, 320.
83   'Séance de Clôture, tenu le 7/20 Février, 1917 au Ministère des Affaires Etrangères', Cab 28/2 IC 16; *Ravitaillement,* 16th session, 20 February 1917.
84   Callwell, *Wilson Diaries,* I, 321.
85   Sir Samuel Hoare, *The Fourth Seal* (London, 1930), 203–4.
86   Buchanan to Hardinge, 21 February 1917, Hardinge Papers, 29.
87   Headlam to Addison, 21 February 1917, Addison Papers, Box 29, 'Russia', original emphasis.
88   Knox, *With the Russian Army,* I, 516–17.
89   88th meeting of the War Cabinet, 6 March 1917, Cab 23/2.
90   Lockhart, *British Agent,* 163–64; Milner described his long meeting with Chelnokov on 11 February as 'a most interesting talk about the Russian situation'. Milner diary entry, 11 February 1917, Milner Papers, 280. Clerk's impressions of the talk are in Lloyd George, *War Memoirs,* III, 1589–95.
91   Addison diary entry, 6 March 1917, Addison Papers, Box 98.
92   'Further confidential note by Lord Milner dated March 13, 1917', Milner, 13 March 1917, Cab 24/3/GT 131.
93   Untitled note by Milner, 18 March 1917, Cab 21/42.
94   Gurko, *Memories & Impressions,* 242.

7
Between the Revolutions

The abdication of Nicholas II and the collapse of the Russian army changed the nature of the alliance between Britain and Russia. Russia went from being a powerful ally potentially capable of winning the war to being a dubious ally potentially a liability to the Allied cause. This change in status immediately affected Anglo-Russian relations. For the remainder of 1917 the British treated Russia much more cautiously than before, always aware that Russia could soon drop out of the war. Such a concern gave British policy towards Russia in 1917 a tentative quality which was evident in several areas.

After the failure of the Nivelle offensive to provide a decisive victory in the west, the situation in Russia became one of the major issues in the debate over strategy within the British government. Most agreed that Russia was unlikely to help the Allies in 1917, but there were sharp divisions over what this meant for Allied strategy. Those who favoured a continued emphasis on the Western front argued that only such a course would allow Russia to regroup her forces before the Germans could crush her. Those who inclined to an alternative strategy claimed that the collapse of the Russian army invalidated the decisions taken at Chantilly for a concerted Allied offensive in 1917 and necessitated a change away from a concentration on the Western front. Russia became the focal point for the wider debate over war strategy.

Despite this division of opinion about strategy, Russia still was considered an important ally, if not for what she could do in 1917 then for what she might do in 1918 or for what her continued presence in the war meant that the Central Powers could not do. Such considerations were reflected in the British attitude towards providing war supplies to Russia. With the collapse of the Russian war effort and the administrative disruption caused by the March revolution, the British had second thoughts about sending to Russia war material which could be used by British forces elsewhere. On the other hand, the British had no desire to weaken the Russians fatally by failing to provide munitions necessary to her long-term contribution to the war. As a result, supplies were sent to Russia in a piecemeal fashion, each new shipment triggered either by a fear that failure to do so would result in a complete Russian collapse, or by the fond hope of a Russian military success.

The British concern about Russia's contribution to the Allied cause had other effects on the alliance. The attempts of the Provisional government to strengthen itself through a re-examination of Allied war aims were largely rejected by the British because it was felt that such a move would weaken the *Entente*. The fact that this contributed to the demise of the Provisional government was not anticipated by the British, but would not have been decisive in any case. Any government in Russia was judged primarily, if not solely, by its ability and will to carry on the war. This explains British actions and attitudes in two significant cases. First, in their desire to create a new Russian military power the British government gave tacit support to men like General Lavr Kornilov who seemed to promise a functioning military effort at the expense of maintaining the Provisional government. Second, the need for a Russian army on the Eastern front accounted, in large part, for the British attitude towards the Bolsheviks after the latter seized power in November 1917. The support which the British gave to the various White movements, as the counter-revolutionary forces were known, can be explained more by the fact that these promised to carry on the war than by any political antipathy to the new Bolshevik regime. Even the signing of the armistice of Brest-Litovsk in December 1917 did not turn the British irrevocably against the Bolsheviks, for the British continued to negotiate with the new regime in the hope that it could be induced to carry on the war. While the war gradually became a matter of importance for the Russians only as it affected the revolution, for the British the reverse was true. Such reversed priorities meant that Anglo-Russian relations from March 1917 until the end of the year would not be smooth.

On 9 March, just three days after the War Cabinet had met to hear the final reports on the Petrograd conference, Buchanan informed the British government of an outbreak of public disorder in Petrograd. While the ambassador characterised it as 'nothing serious', he did note that the strikes which accompanied the unrest were popular: '[the] sympathy of [the] population is entirely on

[the] side of [the] workmen.'[1] In the following days it became obvious that the strikes and rioting were of a serious nature, and as always the British concern was with the impact this would have on the war. On 12 March Knox spoke directly to this concern. Knox felt that '[the] movement which was at first economic is now anti-Government but it is not directed against the war', and cited the contention of Guchkov and Polivanov 'that there is general dissatisfaction among workmen at the slackness with which [the] Government is waging war.'[2] By that same afternoon, opinion had shifted. The commander of the Petrograd district told Knox that the city's garrison troops were no longer reliable and the military attaché informed the British government that 'there seems every reason to believe that all [the] depot troops in Petrograd will go over to the people.'[3] Buchanan pointed out that 'mutinies had broken out in several regiments' and added that he had been informed by the Russian minister of foreign affairs that in order to restore 'order and discipline' in the army 'it would be necessary to appoint at once a General who possessed the confidence of the Army as dictator'.[4] By 14 March Buchanan sent that the revolution was 'now an accomplished fact' but added, happily, that 'whether the Emperor remains on the throne or not there seems to be no longer any danger as regards [the] vigorous continuation of the war.'[5]

Robertson was not optimistic about the state of affairs in Russia. On the same day that Buchanan announced that the revolution was a *fait accompli*, the CIGS wrote to the commander of the British forces in Egypt that

The news from Russia is bad and goodness knows what will happen. There is bound to be a revolution sooner or later, and the only thing one can hope for is that it will not greatly affect the war, but of course it will affect it to some extent.[6]

Others were less pessimistic. Reflecting the concern that he had for an improved co-operation between Britain and Russia with respect to providing munitions for the latter, Addison noted in his diary that the revolution 'may be an enormous help to us. We should at last get cooperation there, although it will mean that they will expect even more help from us.' As far as the Minister of Munitions was concerned, if the revolution meant that 'efficient people' took charge of the Russian war effort, 'it is the biggest blow to the Germans since

the beginning of the War'.[7] Despite the differences in their
assessments, at the bottom of both Robertson's and Addison's
opinions lay a concern with the war, and this concern was shared by
all Allied decision-makers.

On 16 March the War Cabinet decided to follow Buchanan's
advice and recognise the new Russian government. Buchanan was
given discretionary power to extend Britain's blessings to the
Provisional government, with the proviso that 'Doubtless your
action in this matter will largely depend upon the attitude of the new
Government towards the War. All your influence should be thrown
into the scale against any Administration which is not resolved to
fight to a finish.'[8] In France similar concerns were voiced. There it
was believed that the change of governments would result in a 'more
vigorous' war effort, but that the improvement would take time.[9]
The Provisional government realised the significance which the
Allies placed on the continued Russian participation in the war, and
hurried to confirm their active allegiance to the Allied cause. On the
other hand, the new government refused to attempt to reinstitute
discipline – shattered by the issuing of Order No. 1 by the Petrograd
Soviet on 14 March – as demanded by the British government.[10]
Already the dichotomy between the military requirements of the
foreign policy which the Provisional government wished to follow
and its ability to fulfil them had become evident.

Robertson attempted to point out to the War Cabinet the
implications of the rampant disorganisation in Russia. The CIGS
wrote on 17 March that any transfer of troops from the Western
front to Italy would pivot upon the result of the Nivelle offensive and
'the developments of the unfortunate Russian situation'.[11] A few days
later the problem was placed in wider context in a major examination
of the British military situation prepared by the War Office.[12] As far
as the General Staff were concerned, despite the averred intention of
the Provisional government to carry on the war and the seeming
'welcome' with which the Russian army greeted the new government, the least impact that the revolution would have on Russia's
military effort would be a disruption of the production of war
material due to industrial unrest. More seriously, while the General
Staff had not anticipated that Russia 'would be able to do more than
keep the German and Austrian divisions, now on the Eastern Front,
fully employed' in 1917, the revolution made even this 'uncertain'.
As far as they were concerned, the entire question in the west was

now one of manpower, and the best course for the Allies to adopt was to ensure that they maintained sufficient troops there to gain victory. This was the 'westerner' point of view at its most uncompromising. While all members of the War Cabinet did not believe this line of reasoning, all were aware that the Russian revolution meant that Allied plans would have to be reconsidered. On 21 March Curzon was commissioned by the War Cabinet to investigate the 'probable effect' of the secession of 'one or more' of Britain's allies from the *Entente*.[13]

By the end of March any optimism that the revolution would result in an improved Russian war effort was dashed by the collapse of discipline within the Russian army and the deterioration of industrial production. On 26 March Alekseev made this point clear in a memorandum which he telegraphed to Robertson.[14] The Russian commander pointed out that the loss of morale and discipline in the Russian army made any large-scale operations by the Russians before June or July unlikely. Because of this, Alekseev felt that there should be a delay in the Nivelle offensive until the Russians were able to come in wholeheartedly, and that the British and French should follow up the German retreat to the Hindenburg line 'prudently'.

Robertson outlined his opinion of this suggestion in a letter to Haig asking the latter for his views.[15] Robertson professed that he was not surprised by Alekseev's comments. The CIGS stated that he had never expected Russia to do much more in 1917 than hold the enemy forces at present on the Eastern front. 'The new factor', he wrote, 'is whether she will be able to do even this much, or indeed whether she may not drop out of the war altogether, in practice if not in theory.' Being unconvinced that Russia might never be ready to support the Anglo-French offensive, the CIGS felt it 'most unwise' to delay and added that 'it seems to me that the sooner we get going the better'. After this letter, Haig's reply of 1 April was not surprising.[16] In it the British commander stated that any delay in the Nivelle offensive would be 'unwise' and that Russia should be 'urged' to assume the offensive as soon as possible.

Meanwhile Robertson put forward some ideas concerning non-military means of dealing with the new situation. In two related papers the CIGS pointed out that should Russia negotiate a separate peace, it would be possible to detach Bulgaria or Turkey from the Central Powers.[17] While Robertson was aware of the 'great objections'

which such a course would raise, since to do so would involve breaking many of the existing agreements concerning the postwar settlement of Europe, he observed that 'the greatly increased burden'
which the revolution had put on the British army made the military
attainment of the projected settlements 'very doubtful' in any case.

Everything hinged on the success or failure of the Nivelle
offensive, and the War Cabinet came to no decision on Robertson's
suggestions. Robertson, however, had no intention of awaiting the
outcome of the attacks in France before he determined what might
be expected militarily from the Russians in the near future. On 14
April the CIGS telegraphed to Hanbury Williams and Knox asking
them for their opinions about the possibility of a Russian offensive in
the spring. Robertson's typically blunt and practical approach to
matters was evident. Knox and Hanbury Williams were, he stated,
to 'divest [their] minds of claptrap such as determination to win and
fighting for freedom and so forth, remembering that without
discipline and reasonable administrative efficiency, an army is
merely a leaderless armed mob.'[18] The replies were gloomy. Knox
rejected any idea of an attack as 'most improbable' while the most
that Hanbury Williams could add was that Alekseev felt that the
Russian army was 'still useful' for the offensive and that an attack
against the Germans was set for mid-May.[19] Despite Alekseev's
reported ray of hope, Knox's more pessimistic view was accepted by
the War Cabinet, resulting in a decision not to ship heavy artillery to
Russia 'for the present'.[20]

Even before he received the replies from Russia, Robertson was
not sanguine about Russia's offensive capabilities. In a letter to
Haig, Robertson argued that future British plans would have to
consider three factors: submarines, Russia, and the return of control
of British armies from the French.[21] Without Russian co-operation,
Robertson wrote, the Nivelle offensive would not achieve the
decisive results at which it aimed. In addition, a dangerous situation
might be created in the west; as Robertson opined, 'I am inclined to
think Germany will allow Russia to stew in her own juice and will
bring over as many divisions as possible from the East Front.' This
was the fear which had been at the back of Kitchener's mind in 1914
and 1915, but Robertson did not share the late Field Marshal's belief
that a Russian collapse necessarily meant disaster in France. Buoyed
by the increased strength which three years of frenzied activity had
given the British army, the CIGS argued that Haig should attack,

'for if these [German] reinforcements are to come [from the Russian front] the more vigorous we act before their arrival the better.' All would be determined by the fate of the Nivelle offensive, which began on 16 April.

While the military implications of the revolution were being determined, work was underway on the problems which the Petrograd conference had made clear with respect to munitions. At an inter-departmental conference held on 14 March to consider supplies for Russia, it quickly became apparent that the first order of business was bureaucratic.[22] After objections had been raised to the sending of artillery and aircraft to Russia by the military representatives, and representatives of the Shipping Controller had warned that tonnage for Russia might not be available, the Minister of Munitions proposed that the War Cabinet create a special interdepartmental committee to deal with Russian supplies.

The need for reorganisation had been evident for some time. In January and February, while suggestions for reform emanated from Petrograd, a clash between the Ministry of Munitions' Russian Supply Committee and the *Commission Internationale de Ravitaillement* developed over the role of George Booth in ordering supplies for Russia in the United States.[23] While much of this quarrel was a conflict of personality between Booth and the head of the CIR, Sir E. Wyldbore Smith, it did underline the confused nature of the tangled bureaucracy surrounding the provision of supplies for Russia. Even when no differences of opinion separated the CIR, the RSC and the Russian Government Committee in London, decisions took about six weeks to be made due to the unavoidable shuffling of paper.[24] Thus, when Poole suggested on 22 March that he set up in Petrograd a committee of 'leading Russian and British business men' to help increase Russian munitions production, the production of raw materials and railway efficiency as well as to ensure that goods sent to Russia were used effectively, his telegram triggered off a complete restructuring of administration in Britain to deal with Russian supplies.[25]

Late in March a second inter-departmental meeting was held at which a committee under the chairmanship of Lord Milner was created to act as a permanent co-ordinating body for Russian supplies.[26] This body, whose official title was the Committee on Russian Supplies (but was generally referred to at the time as the Milner Committee and will so be called here), was sanctioned officially by the War Cabinet on 4 April. Its mandate was 'to examine and decide upon Russian applications [for supplies] in accordance with the decisions of the Petrograd Conference.'[27] In practice the Milner Committee tended to have a wider range of activity. While final decisions about Russia remained with the War Cabinet, the Milner Committee held the bulk of the discussions about Russia. Only when that body was unable to arrive at a decision itself were matters referred to the War Cabinet for resolution.

The composition of the Milner Committee reflected the diverse nature of the departments involved in, and the previous history of British dealings with, Russian supply.[28] Milner was, of course, chairman of the Committee but he was normally represented at meetings by his parliamentary private secretary, Captain W. Ormsby-Gore MP (later Baron Harlech). In Milner's absence, the meetings were chaired by the parliamentary secretary of the Ministry of Munitions, Sir L. Worthington Evans. Keynes, for the Treasury, acted as secretary to the Committee, while the War Office was represented by General Callwell. Kemball Cook served as the representative of the Ministry of Shipping, B. H. Dobson as the liaison with the CIR, Captain Grant, RN, brought the Admiralty's point of view to the Committee while Booth and Layton represented the Ministry of Munitions. In addition to these members, the Milner Committee had several assistant secretaries and some lesser lights too numerous to mention.

Once the Committee was created its relation to the CIR and the RSC had to be defined. W. J. Benson, acting as the DDB(B) at the Ministry of Munitions while Booth was in the United States unravelling Russian contracts, felt that the RSC should be dissolved and its functions taken over by the Milner Committee.[29] His suggestion was adopted, and the Russian Supplies Section of the Ministry of Munitions was renamed the Russo-American Supplies Section while the Anglo-Russian Sub-Committee in New York, formerly responsible to the RSC, was placed under the Milner Committee. For the CIR, Wyldbore Smith felt that the Milner Committee should confine itself to being a decision-making body and leave the execution of these decisions to the machinery already in existence at the CIR.[30] Wyldbore Smith's suggestions became the basis for the relationship between the Milner Committee and the CIR.

While these matters of organisation were relatively straightforward, the relationship of the Milner Committee to the Russian Government Committee in London was not. Even before the creation of the Milner body the members of the RGC were 'getting restive' about the position of their committee as they had not been informed by either side of the result of the negotiations at Petrograd.[31] The RGC had long been a target for criticism in Russia: it had been castigated by the opponents of Tsarism as being typical of government inefficiency and it had been criticised and ignored by various departments within that government itself.[32] Despite this, Wyldbore Smith felt that the RGC was useful and should be retained. Russian complaints about it, he felt, were only natural as it was the body which relayed British decisions unfavourable to Russian demands and thus, illogically, was held responsible for the decisions. Further, the RGC had been often an embarrassment to the Russian government as it revealed the incompetence of Russian administration in Petrograd. As far as Wyldbore Smith was concerned, the new committee of businessmen which Poole suggested creating in Petrograd 'should supplement rather than replace the existing organization.' Other than being 'unduly numerous', he opined that the RGC had been quite effective and doubted whether the Russian government would be willing to give up their representation in Britain as a matter of pride.[33]

Poole's suggestion for a Petrograd committee was discussed at the War Cabinet on 11 April, with the result that the matter was referred to the Milner Committee. The latter body decided that same day to establish a body under Byrne in Petrograd rather than accede to Poole's suggestion.[34] The Byrne organisation, discussed above in Chapter 6, was to ensure the close co-operation of the Russian government and the Milner Committee. In addition, the Milner Committee asked Poole to discuss with the Russians whether or not the RGC should be dismantled. At the same time, as secretary to the Committee, Keynes wrote to General Hermonius, the head of the RGC, to inform him of the formation of the Milner Committee and of Byrne's mission to Petrograd.[35] Naturally Keynes did not inform Hermonius of the query to Poole about the fate of the RGC and, as it turned out, the RGC was not dismantled. Although the RGC was maintained, it did not establish the close relationship with the Milner Committee which Hermonius suggested in a response to Keynes's letter; rather, the role of the RGC diminished sharply during the rest of 1917.[36]

By the end of March, even before the Milner Committee had been sanctioned officially, decisions about munitions for Russia had to be made. Since there was yet no definitive opinion about Russia's military value for 1917, these decisions tended to be tentative, and illustrated the difficulties which providing supplies for Russia was to involve. On 22 March the War Cabinet decided to honour a pledge made at Petrograd to provide 800 aircraft for Russia, although shipment was prudently delayed until July in order to ensure that British requirements had been met.[37] Two days later, the interim report on shipping resources, presented by the First Lord of the Admiralty, created another problem for Russian supplies.[38] Since the report projected that from April through August of 1917 only 60–70 per cent of the tonnage required would be available, all shipping programmes had to be reviewed. For Russia the tonnage reductions were highly significant. On 27 March Booth was informed that no new orders for the Russian government could be placed in the United States and the following day Poole was instructed to tell the Russian government that the tonnage allotted to them for 1917 at Petrograd was a maximum figure and that reductions might become necessary.[39] With the possibility of reductions in mind, the principle was laid down that no machine tools should be shipped to Russia unless they were 'definitely' for the production of munitions, needed for plants already existing in Russia and not to be found in that country already.[40] To the British, the need for belt-tightening was evident.

The question of further orders for Russia introduced the matter of how such purchases were to be financed. Keynes was quick to point out to Lord Cunliffe, when the latter was to depart with Balfour on a financial mission to the United States in April, that any credits which the United States might see fit to advance to Russia must be tied firmly to the available tonnage.[41] In the event, such a warning was unnecessary. While the Americans did agree to finance British and French purchases in the United States, such an arrangement was not made with Russia. Britain continued to finance Russian purchases abroad, albeit in the expectation of being reimbursed eventually from credits which it was felt the Americans would extend to the Russians in time.[42] Until such an event should occur, however, the Treasury decided to extend the free monthly credit of £4 million indefinitely and noted that Russia still had ample credit left over from the agreement of October 1916 to finance her present purchases in the United States.[43]

By mid-April the issue of supplies for Russia awaited the outcome of military events in the west. No military plans for 1917 could be considered before the success or failure of the Nivelle offensive was clear; no major decisions could be taken about supplies until these military plans were made. On 18 April the War Cabinet decided to delay shipping any heavy artillery to Russia 'for the present', while a week earlier the Milner Committee was asked to investigate the 'question of what freight for Russia was awaiting shipment in America, and decide what portion of it was imperative.'[44] Until a full examination of the shipping programme was completed, the War Cabinet decided on 20 April, 'tonnage for the Russian Programme should be postponed as much as possible without calling attention to the delay.' In line with this decision, in New York Booth was instructed to make a more accurate evaluation of the essential items which were to be shipped to Russia.[45]

There were even suggestions that supplies be used as a lever against the Provisional government in order to force it to follow the lines which the Allies favoured. On 21 April Buchanan informed the Foreign Office that the French ambassador had suggested that a joint note be presented to the Provisional government stating that unless 'Socialist agitation in the army and peace talk' were suppressed, no more munitions would be sent to Russia.[46] Buchanan rejected such a line. He contended that such an attitude would be 'playing into the hands of the Socialists' as the latter would argue that such a policy left Russia no alternative but to make peace. Instead Buchanan suggested that it would be better to try to get the Provisional government to agree to the neutralisation of Constantinople and the Straits as a means of improving the Allied position, as this step would open the way to a possible separate peace with Turkey. To weaken the Russian army by refusing it supplies, the ambassador argued, would gain the Allies nothing. Robert Cecil, in charge of the Foreign Office during Balfour's absence in the United States, agreed completely with Buchanan's advice. 'I believe this is eminently sound advice', the Minister of Blockade wrote, for 'the Provisional Government may make mistakes but they are less likely to do so than we are.'[47] This was 'eminently sound', but the French proposal demonstrated the close linkage between Russian military capability and the provision of supplies.

On 16 April the Nivelle offensive began. Three days later it was clear that the massive success which Nivelle had predicted for his attack was not to be. The failure of the French plan meant that the situation in Russia was of prime importance and made it the centre of strategic debate in Britain. On the same day Haig outlined his views on future military policy in a letter to Robertson.[48] The British commander was convinced that neither the French setback nor the inability of the Russians to participate in an offensive should be allowed to delay his proposed offensive in Flanders. Such a policy of delay, he felt, would be 'most unwise' since the best course of action was to continue the offensive in France in order to prevent the Germans from regaining the initiative and recovering from the batterings which the Allies had inflicted in 1916.

The same view was echoed, but with less optimism, by Robertson. While the CIGS had discounted Russia entirely by the latter half of April (Russia 'is no use to us this year'), he felt that 'Things will still go all right notwithstanding the collapse of Russia if only our side will set their teeth.'[49] Sudden and decisive victory, the CIGS opined, had to be discounted; what the Allies had to do was cease thinking of breaking through the enemy's lines and concentrate instead on 'breaking down the enemy's army'. Even Lloyd George was persuaded by the CIGS's line of argument. At a meeting held in Paris with the French authorities on 20 April to discuss the situation in the aftermath of Nivelle's débâcle it was agreed that Haig's offensive should be continued.[50]

While this seemed a victory for the General Staff's ideas, the dismissal of Nivelle and the continuing gloom over the situation in Russia led to a further Anglo-French discussion of strategy in Paris on 4 May. Although Robertson optimistically informed Haig that the conference would not 'unduly interfere' with the latter's plans for an offensive, the CIGS made every effort to convince the War Cabinet of the soundness of the High Command's position prior to the Paris meeting.[51] At the secret session of the War Cabinet on 1 May, Robertson clearly outlined his views on strategy. The CIGS categorised the French concepts of 'active defensive' and 'offensive defensive' as 'words without any meaning in practice.' Robertson's arguments for a continuation of the offensive were not full of promise of decisive victory; rather he believed that only this offensive would prevent Germany from crushing either Russia or Italy. Since 'when all is said and done there is no satisfactory alternative to continuing the battle we and the French have started', Robertson believed that the British must bear the brunt of the fighting while Russia and France were unable to continue effectively.[52]

To support his position, Robertson gave the War Cabinet a memorandum which Haig had drawn up.[53] Haig's views were more optimistic than those of the CIGS. While Haig also emphasised the beneficial effect for Russia and Italy that a continuance of his offensive would have, the commander of the BEF was sanguine that both powers would soon recover. Once Italy and Russia were ready to begin the offensive, Haig noted that he would turn his attention to clearing the Belgian coast. This latter project also required French participation both in taking over some sections of the British line and in launching a limited offensive to pin down German forces. The combined arguments of Robertson and Haig were accepted by the War Cabinet, although not without demur. Lloyd George pointed out that both the French and the Russians suggested a defensive stance for the Allies. None the less the Prime Minister eventually agreed to put forward the General Staff's view at Paris.[54]

The Paris conference of 4–5 May was a complete victory for British military ideas and marked the last time that British military and political leaders were as one in their views on the subject. In a statement to the political session of the conference, Robertson outlined the new Allied policy. It called for the continuation of the 'wearing down' attacks which Robertson had advocated earlier and for the abandonment of plans envisaging breakthroughs to 'distant objectives'. The ascendency of Robertson and Haig was at its zenith.[55]

The situation in Russia was a prime factor in the breakdown of the consensus over military strategy. The beginning of May saw a continuation of bad news from that country. Knox pointed out that discipline no longer existed in the army, that all officers were elected by the troops without any concern as to their ability and that fantastic rumours were accepted at face value by the credulous troops. Improvement seemed unlikely: 'it is no use appealing to higher feelings [of duty and patriotism] which should exist but do not.'[56] Buchanan found that varied opinions existed among the ranks of the Provisional government as concerned the internal situation in Russia, but the ambassador made it clear there was 'apathy about the war and [a] general desire for peace . . . [along] with [an] unsatisfactory state of the army'. As Oliphant concluded gloomily, the situation in Russia was 'parlous'.[57]

As a result of such information the War Cabinet began to reconsider Russia's position in the alliance. On 8 May Curzon was asked, 'in view of the fact that news from Russia continued to be of an unsatisfactory nature', to complete his report on the military situation should one or more or the Allies secede from the war.[58] Such a probability was discussed in detail at a secret session of the War Cabinet the following day. At this meeting, Robertson argued that the defection of Russia would have serious consequences indeed. After pointing out that Russia's withdrawal could have some positive aspects (the possibility of detaching Austria from Germany or the negotiation of a separate peace with Turkey), the CIGS stated that 'the moral and material effects of the withdrawal of Russia from the war would be so serious that we should not only take every precaution to mitigate its effects but should also take every possible step to prevent its occurrence.'[59]

Robertson outlined what the loss of Russia to the Allies would mean in military terms.[60] His arguments were doubly important as they contained the essentials of all the salient points he was to make about Russia in 1917. If Russia left the war, the CIGS wrote, the Allied numerical superiority would vanish and it would become necessary to abandon all secondary theatres in order to strengthen the forces in France. Any offensive against Turkey would be impossible and Egypt would have to be defended at the Suez canal. In addition, the impact of the blockade against Germany would be lessened. Despite such dolorous remarks, he was not entirely pessimistic. If the Allies concentrated their forces on the French and Italian fronts, the withdrawal of Russia 'need not entail disastrous consequences' in either locale. However, Allied victory would necessarily be delayed until the Americans took the field. In order to prevent Russia from leaving the war, Robertson argued, 'no military methods . . . better than those agreed upon at the recent Paris Conference can be suggested, but every military success which we gain should be made the occasion for friendly advice and diplomatic pressure designed to bring Russia into line.'

Lloyd George agreed with Robertson's analysis. In the War Cabinet the Prime Minister noted that if Russia dropped out the best course to follow would be to get a separate peace with Austria, despite Italian objections, or if this were not possible, to get the Germans to evacuate Belgium in exchange for the return of the German colonies. This was a far cry from the 'knock-out blow' of

1916 and reflected the pessimism which infected thinking in the aftermath of the events of the spring of 1917. If neither of these possibilities could come about, Lloyd George went on, then Britain should make every effort to put Turkey out of the war. Here his ideas met with opposition from Robertson. The CIGS indicated that if Russia left the war, any decisive attack on Turkey would be impossible as every man would be needed in France. The final conclusion of the War Cabinet, that if Russia went out of the war 'every possible effort' should be made to get Austria to agree to a separate peace, reflected the views of the CIGS and indicated just how few options existed and how bleak the future seemed should Russia collapse.

Five days later, on 14 May, a further discussion of the options available to the Allies should Russia leave the war took place at the War Cabinet.[61] At this meeting Curzon presented the conclusions of the report on the subject which the War Cabinet had commissioned on 21 March. His report was essentially a summary of the views of Robertson and the First Sea Lord, Admiral Jellicoe.[62] After weighing the reasons for and against Russia's making a separate peace, Curzon concluded that what seemed most probable was that Russia might remain indefinitely 'both in the War and yet outside of it', paralysed by the effects of the revolution. British policy, Curzon felt, should be a waiting one. British leaders should support moderate elements within Russia, listen to peace proposals and encourage Allied socialists to meet in London rather than Stockholm, the latter in an attempt to block the influence of extremist groups within Russia. Finally, Britain must be willing to accept less than absolute victory in the war.

While such pessimistic discussions were taking place in London, shifts were occurring in French military opinion. The mutinies and indiscipline in the French army led, by the middle of May, to second thoughts among French leaders as to the wisdom of supporting the course of action agreed to at Paris.[63] Haig had no such doubts. In a letter to Robertson on 16 May, Haig evinced unconcern about the French lack of support and stated that his attack was ready to procede: 'the only question I have to consider now, therefore, is how far, if at all, the situation in Russia . . . may necessitate any alteration or modification in my plans'.[64] While he considered it unlikely, Haig was prepared to cancel his attack should the Russian situation necessitate it.

Such confidence was not enough for Robertson. Faced with a War Cabinet which was growing steadily more concerned about Russia and the state of affairs in France, the CIGS asked Haig to determine the views of the new French Commander-in-Chief, General Pétain.[65] Haig did so and reported them directly to Lord Derby, the Secretary of State for War, when the latter travelled to France. After he returned to England, Derby told the War Cabinet on 23 May that Haig had assured him that the French would join unhesitatingly in the British offensive as agreed to earlier at Paris, an assurance which had been repeated by the French War Minister, Painlevé.[66] While this was comforting news, it did not appear to quiet Robertson's concern about the effect which the collapse of Russia would have both on Allied plans and on French attitudes. To this end, he wrote to General Foch, the French Chief of the General Staff, suggesting a meeting 'to discuss the general situation'.[67] In this letter the CIGS stated his belief that no active support could be expected from the Russians in 1917 and that as a consequence the British and French must decide on a concerted plan of action to deal with the new situation.

The conference which Robertson proposed did not take place until 7 June at Abbeville. In the interim, opinion in France moved steadily towards a policy of 'waiting for the Americans', while news from Russia was not encouraging.[68] Robertson made plain his lack of confidence in Russia. To General Wilson, the chief British liaison officer at French headquarters, Robertson wrote that 'On the Russian Front the war seems to be practically over', while at the War Cabinet on 5 June he persuaded that body to delay sending any further heavy artillery to Russia until it could be determined whether that already sent was being utilised properly.[69]

Robertson's concerns were not eased by his meeting with Foch.[70] Robertson opened the meeting at Abbeville by pointing out that Allied plans for 1917 had been devised before the advent of unrestricted submarine warfare, prior to American entry into the war and previous to Russia having 'practically dropped out' of the war. In such circumstances, the CIGS hoped that this meeting could arrive at a 'basis for our general military policy for the future.' Foch replied that with Russia out of the war it was 'inadvisable' for an offensive to be launched on a large scale. He advocated a defensive posture; waiting for the Americans to arrive in order to achieve the necessary numerical superiority for a successful attack. Given such an overall view, Foch felt that Haig's attack on Zeebrugge should be cancelled unless the submarine threat from the ports there should become critical. For the present, Foch suggested that the British and the French should encourage the Russians to attempt an attack in the east. Robertson agreed that General Brusilov should be chivvied to do 'something', although the CIGS was not optimistic about Russia's capacity to achieve any great success. Foch was more sanguine about the Russian chances, particularly against Austria, but was firm that French policy in any circumstances would be to engage in no great offensives. Instead, it would be to 'attack seriously at a number of points at various periods during the summer'.

The situation in Russia and the French attitude had a strong effect upon Robertson. When the CIGS visited Haig at British headquarters in France, Robertson suggested that the Allies might concentrate efforts against Austria in Italy instead of carrying on with attacks in France.[71] Robertson pointed out to Haig the 'difficult situation' which would result in Britain if the latter carried out 'large and costly attacks without [the] full cooperation by the French.' Haig 'did not agree' and found Robertson's views generally 'unsound', but the CIGS was quite in tune with the opinion of the War Cabinet. In a note which was circulated only to members of the War Cabinet, Milner called on 7 June for a 'fresh stocktaking' of the military situation.[72] Milner's views echoed Robertson's concerns. The Minister pointed out that military plans for 1917 had been based upon co-operation among the Allies and had held out 'good prospects' for success: 'the defection of Russia has completely destroyed these prospects.' On 8 June, with Robertson still in France, the War Cabinet decided to set up a War Policy Committee to investigate the overall naval, military and political situation.[73]

Much of Milner's concern about Russia and his belief in the need for a re-evaluation of military plans was based upon matters dealing with munitions. May had seen little change in the British lack of confidence in Russian ability to utilise supplies sent to them, although the mechanism to deal with supplies had been improved substantially. In Petrograd, Poole had established a close working relationship with the new Mikhelson committee which the Provisional government had created to deal with 'all questions of supply from abroad.'[74] Poole, showing what Knox described as a 'frequent tendenc[y] to try his hand at everyone else's [business]', hoped the Milner Committee would delegate to himself and the Mikhelson Committee the authority necessary to decide on all orders, arguing that otherwise 'our labour would only be wasted if the necessity of all orders is again discussed by you and [the] present system with long delay will be accentuated.'[75] Such an argument was not acceptable in Britain.

Keynes's reply to Poole's request illustrated clearly the fact that questions of Russian supply had wider ramifications than could be dealt with from Petrograd. Keynes pointed out that decisions about Russian supplies were not based merely on whether a Russian request was needed or reasonable, but on '(a) priority of need, (b) capacity to supply (c) transport' as well as a consideration of the uncertain financial position of Russia.[76] Evaluation of these required the full scrutiny of the appropriate departments in England. Further, Keynes remarked, such decisions required 'advice from the Naval and Military experts in London'. As a consequence Keynes informed Poole that such powers as the latter requested were not possible to grant, and official relations with Russia must be carried on through the Russian Government Committee in London until the Provisional government stated otherwise.

The discussions which the War Cabinet held early in May about the impact of Russia's withdrawal from the war also had an influence on the provision of supplies for that country. On 8 May, the same day that Curzon was asked to finish his report on the effect of Russia's leaving the war, it was decided to extend the decision of 20 April to cut back the tonnage provided for Russia.[77] The following day, after the secret session on strategy had concluded, Buchanan was asked to investigate 'any reasonable likelihood' of heavy artillery shipped to Russia being utilised as the need for these guns on the Western front was 'urgent'. Buchanan's reply mirrored the conflicting factors which played on such decisions. The ambassador pointed out that Alekseev was 'trying his hardest' to prepare an offensive and that to deny him the guns was not 'fair on him'; however, because guns already at the White Sea ports could not be conveyed to the front for some time, Buchanan stated that further shipments could be delayed as long as one month.[78] As usual, the practical requirements of the war were deemed to outweigh any symbolic value that might accrue from continued support.

In Britain there was strong doubt that any good might come from the British shipments of munitions to Russia. On 15 May Milner wrote to Buchanan that the revolution 'naturally knocks the bottom out of all our plans. The work which our Mission tried to do at Petrograd, and which was of course based on the hypothesis that Russia would continue to be an effective member of the Alliance, is all as dead as Queen Anne.'[79] Although Milner felt that Britain would uphold her end of the bargain, he considered that soon the 'futility' of shipping to Russia arms needed in the west would cause a 'breakdown' of the entire agreement.

The British policy of reducing the flow of munitions to Russia did not pass unnoticed. By mid-May General Hermonius was fully aware that delay over the shipment of machine tools to Russia 'rests entirely with the Milner Committee.'[80] After pointing out just how significant these orders were for Russia, Hermonius told Addison angrily that 'you will therefore appreciate how deeply in Russia's present strenuous times, my Government resents these unexpected difficulties.' Machine tools were not the only cause of friction. On 17 May the Milner Committee decided to discontinue the manufacture of certain cartridges for the Russian government, a decision taken because the Committee felt that 'ample reserves' of the cartridges existed in Russia.[81] Once Hermonius had been informed of this fact, he expressed both his irritation and anger with the Milner Committee. Hermonius was 'extremely sorry' that such a decision had been taken without consultation and added that the Russian government believed the continued production of the cartridges to be 'imperative'.[82] While Hermonius received a soothing reply to his irate letter, it was obvious that British interests and needs were to take precedence over those of Russia, given the latter's inability to provide a major military effort.[83] And other factors began to intrude as well.

By the end of May the increasing shortage of tonnage meant further cuts in the Russian programme.[84] The June shipments to Russia from both Britain and the United States were slashed ruthlessly. The Russian requirements of some 164,400 tons was to be met with only 47,563 tons, a deficit of just over 71 per cent of the total. In addition there was already a shortfall of approximately 125,000 tons carried over from May on the American routes and there was a projected shortage of 50 per cent in the collier tonnage of 252,000 promised Russia for June.[85] Such shortages were crippling, and when the Milner Committee met on 31 May to consider them it was decided to send a letter to Hermonius 'emphasiz[ing] the

shortage of ships owing to submarine activity; and . . . stat[ing] that
everything possible will be done to supply tonnage to Russia to the
utmost of our capacity.'[86] This was the sugar coating. More
practically, Hermonius was told to draw up new lists of priorities to
meet the projected tonnage situation.

The events of June and early July made it clear that concerns
about tonnage were little more than a cloak to disguise the British
reluctance to send badly needed tonnage and munitions to Russia
when chances of a successful military operation there looked slight.
At the War Cabinet on 5 June, Robertson argued that heavy artillery
shipments for Russia, already delayed since early May, should be
put off further in view of British requirements. Before this was
agreed to, the CIGS was instructed to ask Poole and Knox 'whether
there was any reasonable prospect of the guns supplied by us to the
Russians being used against the enemy.'[87] Replies from Russia were
unanimous in suggesting that no more guns be sent unless the
projected Russian offensive in July should prove successful and this
led to Derby writing a memorandum arguing that in such
circumstances the needs of the British army were paramount.[88] This
issue was discussed at the War Cabinet on 2 July where the
relationship between tonnage, supplies and military success was
made explicit. The meeting decided that while 'the present moment,
when the Russians were apparently reassuming the offensive[, would
be a bad time definitely to refuse to furnish any more armament', the
policy to be adopted until the results of the offensive were evident
was one of 'temporisation'.[89] As always, military success was the
prerequisite for the supply of munitions.

Such a cautious evaluation of Russia was also evident with respect
to calls by the Provisional government for a re-examination of war
aims. Such calls were a product of the tension between the 'dual
powers' in Russia: the Provisional government and the Councils of
Workers and Soldiers Deputies (CWSD).[90] The foreign policy of the
Provisional government initially was largely the work of P. N.
Miliukov, nicknamed 'Dardanellski' by his opponents for his strong
conviction that Russia must adhere to the secret treaties with the
Allies which would give her Constantinople and the Straits.
Miliukov made this policy clear as early as 20 March and held to it
tenaciously despite the calls of the CWSD for 'peace without
annexations'. While an uneasy compromise was reached on 10 April
between the Provisional government and the CWSD over this

contentious issue, it continued to divide the two groups fundamentally. The entire matter came to a head at the beginning of May when the Provisional government issued a note calling for a decisive victory in the war. Such a call obviously rejected the idea of peace without annexations and any idea of a negotiated peace. Such a policy was unacceptable to the CWSD whose ranks were badly split between those who believed that a defensive war was just and those who rejected the war entirely. The resulting political turmoil (known as the 'April crisis' according to the Russian calendar) ended in the formation of a new coalition government and the end of Miliukov's domination of Russian foreign policy. With a new War Minister, the moderate socialist A. F. Kerensky, and with M. I. Tereshchenko as Foreign Minister, there was a renewed interest by the Provisional government in a revision of war aims.

The British were well aware of the connection between the stability of the Provisional government and the issue of war aims. When Buchanan had attempted on 15 April to discover exactly what 'peace without annexations' meant, the Prime Minister, Prince G. E. Lvov, had told the ambassador 'not [to] be alarmed by a phrase which in no way modified their original programme. If [the] war went well for us those who now spoke of permanent occupation of Constantinople, Galicia etc. as annexation would regard it as liberation from enemy yoke.' A minute on this telegram reflected the Foreign Office's appreciation of Lvov's position: 'this confirms the opinion that the present public declarations of the Provisional Govt., forced from them by political exigencies, must not be taken at their face value. "Liberation from enemy yoke" certainly sounds better than "annexations" & can have the same meaning.'[91]

The collapse of Lvov's government over the issue of war aims and negotiated peace brought an immediate response from Buchanan. In a telegram which was circulated to the War Cabinet, the King and leading military figures, the ambassador pointed out that the new coalition government 'offers us [the] last and almost forlorn hope of saving [the] military situation of this side.'[92] While Buchanan felt that Kerensky was not 'an ideal Minister of War in normal times' his support from the CWSD and oratorical powers made him 'perhaps [the] only man who . . . can galvanise [the] army into new life.' Therefore, Buchanan argued, the British government must 'face [the] fact that Socialism is now dominant factor [in Russia] and . . . try to win its sympathy.' To do so, the ambassador felt that the Allies should issue a statement pointing out that agreements concerning war aims in places like Asia Minor were designed only to block German advances in that area and were not a barrier to peace.

Such an interest in Asia Minor was due to the attempts by the Italians to garner vast areas in Turkey as part of their share of the postwar settlement.[93] In April Lloyd George had offered the Italians Smyrna, but the Italian appetite grew with the eating and the summer of 1917 was filled with increased demands. Such demands cut across the position which the British wished to adopt with Russia. The British were quite willing to provide the Provisional government with a statement on war aims which would strengthen the latter's hand against the anti-war elements in Russia, and to agree to a peace based upon President Wilson's fourteen points.[94] In fact, the British were quite willing to hold a conference on a revision of war aims since such a conference might serve to lessen Italian demands. When Italy complained that such a revision of war aims might act against her interests, sympathy at the Foreign Office was not forthcoming. In a draft reply, Cecil (acting as the Foreign Secretary in Balfour's absence) noted that Italy 'cannot expect to dictate the policy of the Alliance in every particular', while Hardinge made it clear that the Italian complaints had to be sacrificed for the greater good when he noted, 'we have to consider the Russian rather than the Italian situation.'[95]

Harold Nicolson put the entire matter in perspective in a long minute dated 9 June. As far as he was concerned, revision of the agreements signed with Russia must be looked at from a 'purely British' point of view.[96] To Nicolson, all considerations seemed to favour such discussion. First, renegotiation would strengthen the new coalition government against its critics; second, if fresh agreements were reached with it, then, even should it later fall, they would be harder for any subsequent regime to repudiate than would be the old agreements signed by the Tsarist government. Of course, there was bound to be criticism:

> The difficulty will, of course, arise in regard to our Allies, but I think that we should first approach the question from a purely national stand point and consider whether it will be worth our while to exert pressure to obtain the consent of France and Italy.

Of the five treaties which involved Russia – the Anglo-Russian convention of 1907, the Pact of London of 5 September 1914, the Straits Agreement of April 1915, the Sykes–Picot Agreement and its Russian corollary of May 1916 and the preliminary to the St Jean de Maurienne Agreement signed with Italy in April 1917 – Nicolson felt that only the last three might not be acceptable to the new Russian government, although he noted of the Pact of London: 'I feel that the present Russian Govt. might ratify it though their successors would not.' As far as these final three agreements were concerned, Nicolson did not feel that their loss would be devastating; 'we do not stand to lose by a revision, provided the Arabian and Mesopotamian questions are adequately safeguarded.'

Both Hardinge and Cecil agreed with the tenor of Nicolson's remarks, but felt that any initiative for revision should come from Russia as Britain had already expressed in late May a willingness to re-examine the agreements.[97] In Russia the British attitude was seen as an expression of the Allies' lack of belief in Russia and in her military capabilities. The belief that Russia was becoming a negligible quantity in Allied councils gave support to the calls of the coalition government for a renewed Russian military effort and won substantial support for it from the CWSD.[98] What success the Provisional government would have in readjusting war aims would rest, ultimately, on the fate of the projected July offensive.

Considerations of that offensive also had an enormous impact on British military planning during June. On 11 June the first meeting of the War Policy Committee was held and during the next two weeks British military policy was subjected to a thorough examination.[99] Russia was very much the subject of deliberations. At the first meeting, the committee discussed the French mutinies with Lieutenant-Colonel Spiers, the chief British liaison officer attached to General Foch, who informed them that the Russian collapse was one of the major reasons for the drop in French morale. In relation to this, Robertson added that both he and Foch discounted Russian aid for the rest of the year and that, as a result, 'it would be very difficult to achieve all that the Allies sought' in 1917.

Haig submitted his views to the War Policy Committee on 12 June.[100] In his paper he argued that an offensive was necessary to hearten the French as well as to prevent the Germans from being encouraged by Allied inactivity. Haig was aware of the impact which the Russian situation might have on his offensive; however he did not feel that there was any reason to cancel his attack. Instead, he argued that

In my opinion the only serious doubt as to possibilities in
France lies in the action to be expected of Russia, but even that
doubt is an argument in favour of doing our utmost in France
with as little delay as possible. Russia is still holding large
German forces and every week gained makes it more impossible
for the enemy to transfer divisions to the West in time, if we act
promptly.

Further, Haig stated that there was 'still hope' of Russian military
activity and if the Allies attacked in the west this would make the
Russian task easier. On the other hand, a 'passive attitude' on the
Anglo-French front would not ease the Russian difficulties. In a
separate letter to Derby, Haig pleaded with the Secretary of State for
War not to allow the government to adopt the French policy of
waiting for the Americans, pointing out that in 1916 the argument
had been to wait for the Russians, a policy which had proved
disastrous.[101]

Robertson was caught in a dilemma by Haig's enthusiasm for the
Flanders offensive. While the CIGS felt that Haig's plan was the best
course of action for the British, Robertson did not share Haig's belief
that total victory was possible now that Russia could no longer be
relied upon. No doubt remembering the fate which had befallen
Nivelle when his offensive had failed to come up to its extravagant
expectations, Robertson cautioned Haig not to promise too much for
his plans.[102]

Haig's optimism was not sufficient for the Committee on War
Policy. Despite a definite commitment from the Russians to begin an
offensive, the Committee summoned Haig to London to defend his
views on 19 June. On this date Haig reiterated the arguments which
he had made in his paper of 12 June, but was unable to convince the
Committee that his approach was the only one possible.[103] Lloyd
George in particular favoured giving support on the Italian front
rather than continuing the attacks in France. While Robertson was
not a complete supporter of Haig's plan, the CIGS had no time for
the Prime Minister's schemes. On 20 June Robertson gave the
Committee his views on a plan for transferring troops to Italy from
France.[104] He pointed out that at present Austria could not be
forced to make a separate peace by means of an Italian offensive
since the Dual monarchy was controlled too firmly by Germany. In
addition, the CIGS explained, Germany could match any Allied

transfer of troops to Italy with forces shifted from the Russian front.

This was not what Lloyd George wanted to hear. At the subsequent meeting of the Committee on 21 June, the Prime Minister attacked Robertson sharply, claiming that the CIGS had altered his views since the Paris conference of 4–5 May.[105] Now that French participation was uncertain, Lloyd George asked Robertson whether the latter could still be confident that an offensive was bound to succeed. The Prime Minister pointed out that, in his opinion, 'if Russia went out of the War while Austria still remained in we could not win' and concluded that the British aim should therefore be 'to get Austria out.' Haig was not impressed by Lloyd George's arguments and characterised them as of the 'lawyer type', designed to show 'black is white', but they were effective.[106] The Committee asked both Haig and the CIGS to reconsider their views in the light of the Prime Minister's arguments and to resubmit their plans to the Committee.

Haig's reply, which he made the following day, was merely an elaboration of the views he had put forward on 12 June.[107] The Commander-in-Chief emphasised the danger to France and the other Allies should the British adopt a passive stance and added that this would also allow the Germans to recuperate. Robertson's rejoinder to the Committee was much more cautious than that of Haig. The CIGS stated that his advice at Paris and his present views were identical, that is to attack

> in proportion to our resources and as justified by the amount of assistance received from the French and by the opposition we encounter, to continue pressing forward towards limited objectives in a direction which may give us a good success.[108]

Robertson emphasised that he did not guarantee that Haig's offensive would reach the Belgian coast, but was certain that 'to press on in that direction' was the best course of action. Robertson pointed out that Lloyd George's alternatives – an attack in Italy or the adoption of Pétain's policy of 'punch here and punch there' – were not new, and that the first was impossible due to logistic difficulties while the second was equivalent to Robertson's own plan.

Lloyd George was not happy with what he considered the equivocal tone of Robertson's reply. At the meeting of the War

Policy Committee on 25 June there was a sharp exchange between
the two in which the Prime Minister again accused the CIGS of
changing his advice since the Paris conference and the CIGS again
denied having done so.[109] Robertson pointed out that a definite pre-
diction on the success or failure of Haig's upcoming offensive was
impossible as it depended 'to a certain extent, on circumstances
which he cannot control, for example, the co-operation of France
and Russia.' The CIGS was adamant in his belief, however, that
Haig's plan was the best one to follow, adding that there was 'quite a
good chance of success if France and Russia would pull their
weight.' This was not a strong endorsement for Haig's plan, given
the CIGS's long-standing belief that Russia was finished for 1917,
and a more telling argument was his conviction that 'if we were to
stop taking the offensive altogether, Russia would probably go out
[of the war].'

As was the case with much of British policy, a great deal depended
on Russia and the success or failure of her proposed offensive. This
offensive was less the product of Russian military thinking than it
was of political considerations. At a conference held at *Stavka* in
mid-May, the consensus of the generals was that Russia was unable
to do anything by way of an offensive.[110] This was not agreeable to
the new coalition government. It became clear to all that only a
successful military effort could strengthen the government
sufficiently to withstand the internal political opposition. To this
end, Kerensky travelled to the various fronts in early June exhorting
the soldiers to fight on.

British views of Kerensky's efforts were ambivalent. Blair advised
the government early in June that the Provisional government must
choose between fighting and surrendering as inactivity was destroying
the Russian army, but added that he felt that Kerensky's visit to the
fronts would have influence on the troops 'no longer than the length
of his stay'.[111] Buchanan was more optimistic. His dispatch of 16
June put the matter clearly to the British government.

There is no doubt that the discipline of the army has improved.
. . . The appointment of M. Kerensky as Minister for War and
his tour round the front produced an excellent effect.
Everywhere he insisted on the necessity of discipline, and had
the most enthusiastic reception. Real measures against deserters
have been taken, and at Kieff force was successfully used for

the first time against a large body of them. . . . The army is, in fact, in a position to take the offensive provided the necessary spirit is present, but this remains exceedingly questionable. That it does not exist in most corps may be regarded as certain; the only doubtful points are whether it exists in sufficient troops to make a move, and whether it will spread to the others if the move is successful. In the opinion of most observers both questions must be answered in the negative.[112]

This was indeed, in Oliphant's words, 'depressing reading', but it reflected the views of most people in Russia.[113] While there was some optimism that an offensive might be begun, no one held out any prospects of a major victory. As one of Blair's assistants put it, 'if [the] offensive starts it can only be very short-lived, as supplies are wholly inadequate for continued action.'[114]

Thus, when the so-called 'Kerensky offensive' opened at the beginning of July, it found a wait-and-see attitude prevalent in Britain. At the meeting of the War Cabinet on 2 July it was decided that a policy of 'temporisation' should be adopted with respect to the shipment of further heavy artillery to Russia, 'pending the results of the Russian offensive'.[115] In fact the possibility of Russia 'shutting up shop' was 'constantly before' the British government at this time.[116] While Robertson's lack of confidence in the Russians was mirrored by the support he gave to delaying the shipment of artillery to Russia, his views were not shared by Haig. The British Commander-in-Chief, on the contrary, seemed quite sanguine about the Russian offensive. In his operational orders to the various commanders of the British armies, Haig laid stress on the contribution which he expected the Russian advance to have on his own attack.[117]

By the middle of July the Russian offensive had won unexpected success, and the close relationship between such success and the policies of the British government was quickly apparent. At a meeting of the CIR on 7 July, Hermonious told Wyldbore Smith that it was 'impossible' for the Russian Government Committee to draw up new priority lists for supplies unless some definite commitment could be given as to the amount of tonnage which Russia would receive.[118] Further he went on to note that 'the Russian offensive was in danger of being brought to a standstill by lack of material which was entirely due to the lack of tonnage.' Such arguments were repeated to Milner two days later. In requesting a major increase in tonnage to be allotted to Russia, Hermonius pointed out that his request represented only the 'extreme minimum' of Russia's needs and that cut-backs in it would have the 'gravest consequences' for Russia's war industries and would necessitate a 'sad modification' in the Russian campaign plans.[119]

This appeal to military necessity and the Russian successes led to action by Milner. At the War Cabinet on 16 July, Milner presented a paper arguing that Hermonius be granted his request for extra tonnage 'in view of the fact that the Russian offensive now appears to be assuming serious dimensions'. This suggestion was approved by the War Cabinet while the 'general question of sending more munitions to Russia should be taken up and reviewed with the question of general military policy of the Allies to be considered during the ensuing week.'[120] This decision underlined the fact that, while the tonnage situation was grave, earlier decisions about it were based upon a negative assessment of Russia's military capacity.

By the middle of July much was unresolved in British policy. While the opening date of Haig's offensive was only a few weeks away, the War Cabinet had not yet sanctioned it. In addition, matters of finance had again emerged. This point needs to be discussed before turning to the debates over military strategy which dominated the meetings of the War Cabinet in late July.

During May and June, while the amounts of supplies which could be sent to Russia were being constrained by considerations of tonnage, the British financial position in the United States underwent a crisis brought on by the continuing Russian demands for credit. The American government was chary of extending further credit to Russia, despite the fact that Booth had managed to settle the outstanding differences between the Russian government and American contractors during May. This meant that Russian orders in the United States were a continued drain on the British Treasury, and by the end of June there was a serious crisis in the exchange rate.[121] Despite the fears of the Governor of the Bank of England that Keynes had caused a 'disaster', the American government advanced the British enough funds to avert a crash, but the matter of the United States' taking over the financial support of Russia remained an unresolved matter at the end of the month.[122]

It was in these circumstances that the Russians, on 4 July, asked the Treasury for a further £25 million of credit.[123] In a long letter to the Foreign Office, the Treasury pointed out that Russia still had £65 million of unused credit accruing to her from previous agreements and, in any case, the Treasury 'is acting, and will continue to act, on the assumption that there is a sufficient surplus to meet all present needs.'[124] These were brave words and not at all consistent with the gravity of the situation. Actually the British financial position in the United States was perilous, and Keynes was forced by 23 July to tell the American government that 'in short our resources available for payments in America are exhausted. Unless the United States Government can meet in full our expenses in the United States, including exchange, the whole financial fabric of the Alliance will collapse.'[125] This warning had its desired effect and Allied credit, including that of Russia, remained firm, but the whole issue illustrates the wide variety of ways in which the situation in Russia played upon Anglo-Russian relations.

Obviously there were a number of matters which needed resolution. At the War Cabinet on 16 July it was decided that the next week should be devoted to establishing some lines of policy in preparation for the major conference of the Allies to be held in Paris 25–26 July.[126] Before the key matter of Haig's offensive could be dealt with, there were a number of minor issues which had to be decided. The success of the Russian offensive had encouraged General Cadorna, the Italian Commander-in-Chief, to bring forward once more his plan for an offensive against Austria, an offensive which required the British to send him 100 heavy guns. Robertson was not opposed to an Italian offensive; he noted that it was essential that the unexpected success of the Russian offensive should be exploited at once on the Italian front. On the other hand, the CIGS wished to delay sending heavy artillery to Italy as long as possible lest Haig require it in France or Cadorna delay his attack in the expectation of its arrival. Robertson also had to spend some time opposing schemes for an offensive in Palestine, pointing out that the collapse of the Russian front against Turkey made success in the Middle East quite unlikely. Robertson hammered home these points at a secret session of the War Cabinet on 20 July, emphasising as well that any Russo-Romanian offensive against Bulgaria was unlikely due to the chaotic situation on that front.[127]

Only on 21 July did the War Cabinet attack the main issue: the

question of whether or not Haig should begin his proposed
offensive. While Robertson described this meeting as a 'rough and
tumble' one, the War Cabinet decided to sanction Haig's advance,
although the CIGS felt that Lloyd George still hoped to find support
for his idea of an Italian offensive.[128] By the time that the British
representatives reached Paris for the inter-Allied conference, the
situation in Russia had changed sharply. The early promise of the
offensive had turned to defeat and defeat brought with it political
unrest.[129] The conference now had to consider the prospect of
Russian defection from the Alliance.

At a preliminary meeting of the British, French and Italian
military authorities it was agreed that the policy of an offensive in
Flanders should be adhered to and that no further aid should be
given to Italy at the moment.[130] The conference proper offered little
more by way of novelty. With respect to Russia, the Allies agreed
that 'every sacrifice' should be made to keep her in the war.[131] In
practical terms this meant that the Provisional government should be
supported against 'extremist elements', should be given economic
aid and should be assisted in restoring discipline to the Russian
armed forces. Should Russia be forced out of the war, it was
recognised that Allied war aims would have to be re-examined since
victory would be 'either more remote or less decisive' than hoped. In
military terms Russian secession would mean the adoption of a
'purely defensive attitude' in all secondary theatres, the preparation
of the transport to do both this and bring the Americans to Europe as
soon as possible and the creation of some sort of permanent
inter-Allied body to co-ordinate military plans.

While these were the official results of the conference, its real
purpose in Lloyd George's eyes was to find a wider audience for his
alternate strategies, prompting Robertson to label it 'the *worst*
conference I ever attended'.[132] To Robertson's disgust, the Prime
Minister had introduced his plans for a Balkan offensive at the
conference and 'this held the floor for 2 hours & was finally knocked
out. But fancy it!' None the less, the critical issue of Haig's offensive
had been resolved, and the Commander-in-Chief was able to make
his final plans. Haig's concentration on his own proposals was clear.
No longer able to count on any Russian support in the east, Haig was
heartened to see from intelligence reports that German forces were
being sent to the Eastern front in what he supposed to be an effort to
'knock out' Russia.[133]

While Robertson and Lloyd George were in Paris discussing Allied strategy, the War Cabinet examined the problems of supplies for Russia. At the meeting of 25 July no decisions were made, although Russia's growing dissatisfaction over the lack of supplies sent from Britain was noted. The following day, General Poole (who had just returned from Russia) advised the War Cabinet that the transportation difficulties at Archangel would soon be overcome, and it was decided to ship a further 75,000 tons of supplies to Russia.[134] Any discussion of the vital matter of heavy artillery for Russia was, in the absence of the Prime Minister and the CIGS, deferred to a later date.

When the latter two returned to Britain, the issue of Russia was considered once again by the War Cabinet. Lloyd George was not convinced that all the ramifications of the subject had been considered fully at Paris and a secret session of the War Cabinet was held 31 July to rectify this omission. The focus of discussion was a paper which Robertson had prepared on the eventuality of Russia's leaving the war.[135] Robertson's advice remained unchanged from what it had been the previous week in Paris. He opined that Russia and Romania could best be helped by the British continuing to exert the 'utmost pressure' in the west, while as many troops as possible were removed from the secondary theatres. With the Russians out, the CIGS was concerned especially with the situation in Palestine and Mesopotamia. Robertson wished to send at least one British division from Salonika to Egypt to act as a general reserve for the British forces in the Middle East. As well, he felt it was vital for the Allies to aid Russia by helping her to reorganise both her military forces and her internal transportation system, the breakdown of which had paralysed her fighting capacity. Equally important, Robertson argued, the Allies must review their war aims, since it would be 'folly' to expect to achieve the present aims without Russia's aid.

These arguments were not accepted readily by the War Cabinet. It was felt that less than total victory would not be acceptable to the public (especially when some leading politicians had promised a 'knock-out blow'!).[136] As well, a separate peace with Germany's allies was thought to be unlikely unless defeats were inflicted upon them, an occurrence which was impossible if Robertson's advice to evacuate the secondary theatres were acted upon. Since there was no agreement at the War Cabinet, no decisions about future military plans were adopted; instead it was concluded that such decisions would be taken in conjunction with the Allies at a meeting of the French, British, Italian (and, significantly, no Russian) military and political heads in London on 7–8 August.

In the mean time, Robertson wrote to Kiggell, Haig's Chief of the General Staff, for news of events in France.[137] This letter underlined the difficulties which Robertson was having in convincing the War Cabinet of the soundness of the General Staff's views on the war and the pressure which was on him from the politicians. 'It would be well worth while', the CIGS wrote, 'for you to drop me a line once or twice a week during the operations and give me such information as will enable me to show that things are going on satisfactorily.' The ministers, Robertson noted, were quite anxious, and the 'awkward blow' of Russia's collapse made it imperative that he have detailed information available to dispel their doubts.

This letter revealed several things. First, it was not addressed to Haig but to Kiggell. While Robertson and Haig still maintained good working relations, their views on the war were no longer coincident. Ever since the spring of 1917 and the Russian revolution, Robertson had been noticeably less sanguine than Haig and refused to state that victory was imminent. On the other hand, Haig was always full of optimism and found Robertson's caution 'unsound'. While in 1916 Robertson had written to Haig for information about the offensive in order to placate the politicians, in 1917 he wrote to Kiggell. Second, the fact that the CIGS had to ask specifically for information suggests that co-ordination between the army in the field and the War Office in London was not good. Finally, the phrasing of Robertson's request implied that the CIGS was not above slanting the reports from France so as to suggest that the military situation was better than it really was. The fact that the government's chief military adviser felt so uncertain of his advice being accepted that he had to stoop to such means reflected the unhealthy turn that civil-military relations were taking in the Lloyd George government. Such tensions were apparent at the London conference.

The conference of the Allies opened on 7 August in two separate sessions, one military, the other political.[138] Foch and Robertson confirmed at the opening meeting that no artillery or troops could be sent to Italy until after the end of the British offensive. The decisions of the political meeting were in complete contradiction to those of the military gathering. The politicians agreed that the General

Staffs of the three Allies should be instructed to draw up plans for operations to put Austria out of the war and for means to provide more guns for Italy. Robertson attempted to be offhand when he described the conference to Haig as being 'of the usual character and result[ing] in the usual waste of time', but this was a mask of his true feelings.[139] The CIGS was extremely unhappy with Lloyd George's continued attempts to undermine the Flanders offensive, and made his anger clear in an unrestrained letter to Kiggell. 'I have had some bad times during the last eighteen months', the CIGS wrote wrathfully, 'but this Conference was about the worst of all. . . . the Prime Minister . . . is an underbred swine.'[140]

Despite Lloyd George's efforts, the final report of the Committee on War Policy issued on 10 August supported Haig's offensive.[141] The Committee's recommendation was not unalloyed; it was felt 'strongly, however, that the offensive must on no account be allowed to drift into protracted, costly, and indecisive operations as occurred in the offensive on the Somme in 1916.' Should this appear likely, particularly as it was no longer 'prudent' to assume either a Russian military effort in 1917 or that she would not go out of the war completely, the Committee stated that the Flanders offensive should be halted and guns sent to the Italian front. This was Robertson's victory, but it had been earned at a cost. After this decision, Lloyd George retreated from his direct attempts to challenge the' military advice given by Haig and Robertson. Somewhat incapacitated by illness, the Prime Minister, except for a brief and unsuccessful attempt in early September to divert guns to Italy, spent much of his time until late September in Wales, pondering ways to get his own strategical views accepted as policy.[142]

The rancour which Russia's weakness brought to discussions of strategy was not without its repercussions in British domestic politics. The dismissal of Arthur Henderson from the War Cabinet was related to the intensity of debate over how best to deal with Russia. Henderson had been included as the Labour representative in the War Cabinet when it was formed in December 1916. In political views Henderson was (in the opinion of a recent writer) 'indistinguishable' from most non-conformist Liberals and had been criticised by the Independent Labour Party.[143] During the war he had worked with patriotic labour and had opposed the discontent with the war which was prevalent inside the Labour party. In May 1917 Henderson had convinced the Labour Party executive that

British labour should not send a delegation to the Stockholm conference and had instead supported an alternate conference in London and the sending of a British fact-finding mission of labour representatives, including himself, to Russia.[144]

Henderson's proposals not only found support in the War Cabinet, but also suggested some additional thoughts to Lloyd George. The Prime Minister had long been an opponent of the 'old diplomacy' and favoured the use of personal emissaries instead of the traditional apparatus of ambassadors and embassies. When Robert Cecil suggested that Buchanan might no longer be a man acceptable to the new regime in Russia – arguing that the ambassador was too closely identified with the Tsarist government – Lloyd George seized upon Henderson's proposed visit to Russia with the British socialist delegation as a way to kill two birds with one stone. On 23 May the War Cabinet approved Henderson's trip to Russia and gave him the authority to supersede Buchanan.[145]

Henderson's time in Russia brought about a change in his attitudes. While Henderson soon realised that Buchanan's standing with the Provisional government was excellent, the British minister became converted to a belief that the Stockholm conference should be supported. This should not be interpreted as suggesting that Henderson had any great faith in the Provisional government; instead it reflected his belief that a failure to support the Stockholm conference would play into the hands of the Bolsheviks whom he perceived as profoundly anti-war. When he returned to Britain late in July (on the same boat, incidentally, as the Russian delegates to Stockholm), Henderson arrived just as the failure of the Russian offensive became manifest. This event convinced him, as J. M. Winter has written, that 'support for Stockholm was probably the only way to keep Russia in the war and to keep a moderate government in power.'[146]

Such a view found little support in the War Cabinet. The collapse of discipline in the Russian army after the ill-fated July offensive made the British representatives in Petrograd call strongly for a firmer policy with respect to the restoration of order both in the military and civilian spheres. General Sir Charles Barter, who had replaced Hanbury Williams at *Stavka* in May, went so far in an interview with Alekseev on 31 July as to intimate that Russia's request for an Allied offensive would not receive a 'sympathetic response' unless firm discipline were reinstituted in the army. On 4

August Buchanan suggested that a joint Anglo-French note embodying Barter's ideas be presented to the Provisional government.[147] When the War Cabinet met on 7 August this proposal was felt to be too radical, but it was clear that attitudes towards the Provisional government were hardening and that Henderson's arguments, based as they were on the need to support Kerensky, would be unlikely to find much support.[148] The following day it was evident that this was so; the War Cabinet rejected Henderson's position unequivocally. When Henderson none the less called for delegates to be sent to Stockholm at the special Labour Party conference on 10 August, his political fate was sealed and he resigned the next day. Russia had had her impact on British political solidarity.

By the middle of August it was clear that British attitudes towards Russia hinged on the position which the Provisional government took towards the effective prosecution of the war. Evaluations of this attitude centred around the degree of authority which Kerensky was willing to cede to the new commander of the Russian army, General L. Kornilov. Kornilov, a man of 'magnificent personal courage' if little political judgement, had been appointed Commander-in-Chief on 31 July in the aftermath of the Russian collapse.[149] Barter and Buchanan felt that it was of the 'utmost importance' that the British government inform the Russian government that Kornilov's conditions for assuming command – the restoration of the death penalty in the army and the elimination of the Soldiers' Committees in the army – were 'cordially' approved by the British.[150] Unless this were done, Barter further suggested, Kornilov's position would be undermined and if the latter were to resign 'I see no hope of any improvement of efficiency [in the Russian army] for a considerable time.'

In an interview with Kornilov on 13 August, Barter 'hinted' that England might have to 'reconsider seriously' both continuing her offensive in the west and supplying guns to Russia unless there was an effort made to restore the fighting capacity of the Russian army.[151] While Barter attempted to force the Russian hand, the War Cabinet debated on 14 August the perennial and related issue of whether or not to ship heavy guns to Russia. General Maurice, the Director of Military Operations, read to the War Cabinet a telegram in which Kerensky complained that the British were attempting to 'bargain' with guns, by threatening to withhold them unless concessions were made on matters which were the concern of the Russian government. Maurice then noted that to stop shipment of guns 'altogether might have grave political consequences.'[152] The following day, the War Cabinet debated the matter vigorously. Robertson, Derby and the Master-General of the Ordnance, General Furse, all argued that the guns would better be used in France where they would aid Haig's offensive and lend indirect support to Russia by keeping German forces pinned in the west. This view was opposed by Milner, Balfour and Churchill. Milner and Balfour both argued that it was psychologically important to let the Provisional government know that Britain supported it fully, and Milner went so far as to state that 'in his judgement we should lose the war from a military point of view if we did not keep Russia in the war.'[153] These arguments proved decisive. The War Cabinet decided to send two batteries of 6-inch howitzers to Russia, as the 'risk of discouraging Russia by a neglect to continue the supply of guns was too great to be ignored.'

The intensity of these arguments was exceptional. Robertson and Derby were incensed by the decision and wrote to Lloyd George after the meeting to express their dissent.[154] In addition, they pointed out that Churchill was not, as Minister of Munitions, technically a member of the War Cabinet and should not have been allowed to participate in the discussions. Robertson's anger continued after the meeting, and he chided Hankey for failing to include in the minutes of the session Robertson's reminder to the War Cabinet that the decision to send guns to Russia rather than to France was to deny Haig the support formerly promised.[155] There still remained Barter's proposal to put pressure on the Russian government to accept Kornilov's demands. This was discussed on 17 August, two days after the heated debate on artillery. In line with the latter decision, the War Cabinet resolved not to recommend such a policy, lest 'it might be said that the British Government were urging the Russian Government to shoot soldiers.'[156] The instructions sent to Buchanan, however, were not so straightforward. As the matter was so 'delicate', the ambassador was given authority, 'if you think it would strengthen Korniloff's hand', to speak to the Russian government about conceding Kornilov's demands.[157] British opinion in Petrograd was divided on this matter. For his part Buchanan felt that the time was not yet ripe to push for complete acceptance of Kornilov's demands, but Barter felt otherwise and suggested that Kornilov might attempt a *coup d'état* if he were not given full authority by Kerensky.[158] Despite Barter's views, when the War Cabinet reviewed its position on 24 August, it reiterated its decision to leave matters in the ambassador's hands.[159] In line with this, and to check Barter's tendency towards supporting a more reckless policy by Kornilov, Robertson informed the latter that 'you should not fail to remember that your mission is purely military.'[160]

Events in Russia soon brought the differences between Kerensky and Kornilov into the open. On 25 August the Moscow conference of notables opened with representatives of the entire spectrum of Russian political life in attendance. Kerensky's opening speech called for all elements in Russia to work together, but he refused to sanction a return to 'iron discipline' in the army. Kornilov's speech two days later underlined the differences between his position and that of Kerensky and was met with enthusiasm by the conference. The General repeated his call for a return to order and a restoration of the authority of the officers within the army. Buchanan felt that the conference had served only to illustrate Kerensky's impotence (he has, Buchanan wrote to Hardinge, 'I think, almost played his part') and considered that the Prime Minister must soon resign.[161] Despite this, however, Buchanan did not feel that the 'moment is ripe' for a military dictatorship under Kornilov.

Relations between Kerensky and his Commander-in-Chief continued to worsen in early September, and on 5 September Buchanan was approached by a 'Russian colonel' who told the British ambassador of a plan, putatively the work of Kornilov, for a coup.[162] Buchanan refused to be drawn on the topic and informed the messenger that he 'strongly disapproved of the whole scheme which could only lead to civil war and end in a disaster.' Reaction at the Foreign Office to Buchanan's remarks illustrated just how opinion there was swinging towards support for drastic measures to improve Russia's military capacity. Hardinge minuted revealingly on Buchanan's telegram:

I do not quite understand why Sir G. Buchanan is so strongly opposed to a military coup d'etat. There will certainly be bloodshed before discipline in the Army is restored & it seems that it is only through the Army that the Soviet can be abolished & order & discipline restored.

This attitude was shared by Cecil, who was serving as Foreign

Secretary while Balfour was ill, but the latter felt that Buchanan had acted properly in avoiding compromising himself.[163]

Much of the reason for the British attitude had to do with the military situation. By the beginning of September Riga was threatened by a possible German attack and the complete collapse of Russia seemed a possibility. On 5 September the War Cabinet considered whether to hold back supplies now ready to be shipped to Russia in light of the military situation. The meeting decided to continue the shipments, but the entire issue of the situation in Russia was not so easily resolved.[164] On 7 September, with Knox present to provide expert advice, the War Cabinet met to consider Britain's policy towards Russia.[165] As far as Knox was concerned, the situation in Russia was *'almost desperate.'*[166] While he felt Kornilov to be 'a strong character, an honest patriot, and the best man in sight', the military attaché was not convinced that the situation was rescuable. Despite this, Knox 'strongly urged' that diplomatic pressure be placed on Kerensky – in whom Knox had 'no faith' – to accept Kornilov's demands. He also suggested that it should be ascertained by Barter whether or not Kornilov would appreciate a *'loyal core'* of troops, provided by either the Americans or the Japanese, around which he could rally the Russia army. While the War Cabinet came to no decision on Knox's suggestions, Milner wrote to Lloyd George that he himself was 'prepared to be guided by Knox' since he found the military attaché to be a 'man of knowledge and sound judgement'.[167] Later that same day, 7 September, Milner had a separate meeting with Knox and representatives of the Shipping Controller to discuss the matter of continuing to send supplies to Russia.[168] This meeting decided that, considering the fact that the War Cabinet had promised Kerensky in mid-August to continue shipping supplies, the present shipping programme should be taken to its completion date of 30 September.

This cautious and prudent British policy quickly found itself overtaken by events. On 9 September Kornilov began his fateful march towards Petrograd, an event which was to end in the collapse of the prestige both of the army and of the Provisional government. The instructions sent to Buchanan on 9 September, and belatedly approved by the War Cabinet the following day, reflected the uncertainty of British policy with respect to Russia.[169] Buchanan was instructed to advise the British government whether he felt that giving Kornilov support 'would be useful'. At the same time, the

War Cabinet approved Milner's recommendation to complete the shipping programme to Russia, an approval which was the economic equivalent of the instructions to Buchanan; both were motivated by a desire to increase Russia's military effectiveness and both were circumscribed by the caution which events in Russia made prudent.

The Kornilov affair remains shrouded in mystery to the present day.[170] Opinions vary on whether Kornilov attempted to overthrow Kerensky and the Provisional government or whether his march on the capital was part of a plan which he and Kerensky had concocted to end the power of the Soviets and from which the Russian Prime Minister withdrew at the last moment out of fear that Kornilov would supplant him as head of government. Such confusion existed at the time for the British representatives. On 11 September Buchanan informed the British government that

> Accounts which I receive are so contradictory that it is impossible to foretell issue of contest but even if Korniloff is completely successful I am still of opinion his action was ill advised and inopportune. . . . it would no doubt be a great advantage were [a] really strong Government established and Soviet to be suppressed; but choice of Minister which he [Kornilov] seems so far to have made is not very promising . . . [and a] week will have to be wasted before new Ministers will be in a position to take them [problems of administration] in hand.[171]

Faced with such advice, the War Cabinet decided on 12 September that an appeal to Kerensky to come to an understanding with Kornilov was the best course to pursue.[172] Events in Russia made such a course of action unworkable; by 12 September Kornilov's advance had failed and only the impact of this failure was a matter for discussion.

Opinions varied, but all were pessimistic. While Buchanan felt that it was 'too soon' to estimate the effect of Kornilov's action on Russia's military capacity, the ambassador lamented the inevitable disappearance of the general from the Russian political scene: in Kornilov the Allies had 'lost' their most capable and energetic supporter of a 'vigorous prosecution of the war by Russia.'[173] Others were not so reticent to give an opinion on the Russian army. On 15 September Blair reported that it was 'incapable of affording any further assistance to the Allies' and Robertson wrote to Haig that the most which could be expected of Russia was that, after she had concluded a separate peace, the chaos on the Eastern front would necessitate the retention of Germans troops there.[174] Haig, however, did not seem overly concerned about the Russian situation. In reply to Robertson, the Commander-in-Chief opined that Russia would be able 'to pull herself together during the winter.'[175] Haig was confident that his own advance, scheduled to begin 20 September, would be a success and saw 'no cause for anxiety' about the military situation provided that sound strategical principles – a concentration on the western front – were adhered to.

With respect to the provision of supplies for Russia, the effect of Kornilov's débâcle was quickly apparent. On 12 September Milner met with the assistant secretary of the Milner Committee and Ormsby-Gore to explain the ramifications of the War Cabinet's decision of 10 September to continue the present shipping programme to Russia.[176] Milner pointed out that no new shipments were to go forward to Russia and emphasised that this latter point was entirely for the information of the Milner Committee and 'was not to be communicated to the Russian delegates or form the subject of any discussion outside the Committee.' This decision was implemented by the Milner Committee at a meeting on 14 September where it was concluded that 'it was desirable not to sanction the placing of more new orders than was absolutely necessary until both the Economie [one of the major wharves on the White Sea where bottlenecks had occurred in the off-loading of supplies] position and the general Russian situation were clearer.'[177] A set of guidelines for the various departments was drawn up in order to make it clear what sort of goods could be ordered for Russia and these guidelines pointed up the lack of British confidence in the Russian situation. The only goods for which orders were to be sanctioned were those which either could be delivered in six months' time or were of a 'standard type and could therefore be utilised [by the Allies] in the event of diversion being necessary.' This was a return to the policy which had existed before the Kerensky offensive, a policy which contemplated a Russian withdrawal from the war.

This was a question which exercised everyone, not least Lloyd George. The Prime Minister, filled with resolve after his rest in Wales, was not so hopeful about Russia as was Haig. Any confidence

which he might have felt about possible victory in the west was
shaken by a conference with French military and political figures at
Boulogne on 25 September.[178] Here Lloyd George was apprised of
the weakened state of the French army and the following day the
Prime Minister asked Haig to prepare a paper on British strategy
should Russia withdraw from the war and Italy and France play a
largely passive role. Robertson, who had accompanied Lloyd George
to France, immediately sent Haig a paper outlining the CIGS's view
on the subject in an attempt to ensure that there was a common
General Staff position presented to the Prime Minister.[179]
Robertson's paper was little more than a reiteration of his earlier
papers of 5 May and 29 July on the same topic, but his real feelings
were revealed in a letter which accompanied the paper.

Robertson pointed out in his letter that the collapse of Russia had
raised doubts in the War Cabinet as to the possibility of defeating
Germany by means of direct attacks in the west.[180] The opinion was
gaining ground that it was best to detach some of the German allies.
To do this it was necessary to strike at these allies, an approach
which meant diverting resources from the Western front. Robertson
then showed that he was not the blind adherent of the Western front
that Lloyd George was later to allege. The CIGS wrote:

> My views are known to you. They have always been 'defensive'
> in all theatres but the West. But the difficulty is to *prove* the
> wisdom of this now that Russia is out. I confess I stick to it
> more because I see nothing better and because my instinct
> prompts me to stick to it, than to any convincing argument by
> which I can support it.

In fact, at this same time Robertson urged Lloyd George to press the
Foreign Office to make an attempt to induce Bulgaria into signing a
separate peace; as the CIGS argued, 'we *must* detach some of the
enemy countries if we possibly can.'[181] Robertson left no stone
unturned in his search for military victory.

The clash of opinion between Lloyd George and his military
advisers took place on 10 October and many of the arguments raised
there centred on Russia.[182] While both Robertson and Haig
presented papers which called for a continuance of the offensive on
the Western front, there was a marked difference in tone between
the two: Haig was optimistic; Robertson less so. The British

commander in France argued that only about one-third of the
German divisions now on the Russian front would be able to come
over to the west, thus making an offensive in France entirely
possible in 1918. Robertson's support for the Western front was
presented more negatively; he pointed out that other alternatives,
and particularly Lloyd George's proposed attack on Turkey, were
impracticable for logistic reasons and that the Western front
remained the most feasible area for British attacks. These arguments
were the sort for which Lloyd George was prepared, and he rejected
them. The following day the Prime Minister unveiled his plan to
circumvent Haig and Robertson by suggesting that the opinions of
Generals French and Wilson be obtained.[183] The struggle between
Lloyd George and Robertson which was to culminate in the latter's
dismissal in 1918 was begun in earnest.

While the debate on military strategy took on new dimensions, the
change in policy with respect to supplying munitions to Russia was
evident. A Russian request for anti-aircraft guns was rejected by the
War Cabinet on 2 October, despite, as the Milner Committee noted
three days later, the fact that for 'political and other reasons' it was
advisable to send them.[184] The matter of guns for Russia in a more
general sense was discussed on 8 October at the first meeting of the
Allocation of Guns Committee, a War Cabinet body set up to deal
with the competing Allied demands for artillery. Of the 253 guns
promised to Russia, Churchill suggested that only 50 4.5-inch
howitzers and 60 8-inch howitzers should be sent. No final decision
was taken on the final numbers for Russia, but 'it was generally
agreed that sending guns to Russia at present was a political rather
than a military operation and that while it was essential to send
batteries for political purposes, these should be kept within as
narrow a margin as possible.'[185]

The decline of Russia's military capacity was mirrored also by the
British attitude to Russian finance. By the end of August the
Treasury decided that they could no longer afford to provide the
dollars necessary for Russian purchases in the United States. The
reason for this was the attitude of the American government towards
lending money to Britain. The Americans were suspicious of the way
that Allied purchasing was centralised in British hands and preferred
to lend money to each of the Allies separately. As the Treasury
informed the Foreign Office, the money given by the Americans to
the British was based solely on British requirements, and not 'on the

needs of His Majesty's Government and the Russian Government combined'.[186] The Americans were not inclined to discuss this problem, and by the beginning of October the Treasury decided to refuse funds for the purchase of raw materials in the United States to be used for the manufacture of Russian cartridges in England. Colonel Beliaev immediately cabled to Petrograd to ask General Mikhelson to press the American government into providing funds for such purchase but the Americans were steadfast in their refusal to let funds loaned to Russia be diverted into what they saw as English hands.[187] This American attitude towards loans to the Allies persisted until after the end of the war and was one of the matters dealt with in the postwar Anglo-American settlement of debts.

Keynes made this financial problem clear at a special meeting of the Milner Committee on 23 October.[188] Milner pointed out that since the United States had entered the war, the British government had provided $160–180 million to Russia for purchases in the United States. The Russian government had requested the Americans to disburse an equal amount to the British, but, apart from agreeing to finance the Westinghouse and Remington rifle contracts, the United States had refused to do so. Keynes was adamant that the British government must push for such funds to be allotted, as the pressure on the Treasury to provide funds for Russia was insupportable. No one was willing to spend the limited dollar reserves of Britain on an uncertain ally.

By the end of October British attitudes with respect to supplies for Russia had hardened further. At the second meeting of the Allocation of Guns Committee on 22 October, it was agreed that Romania's needs for artillery rated above those of Russia; in fact, 'Russia deserved very little consideration.'[189] No further 4.5-inch or 6-inch howitzers were to be sent to Russia, although – and it was a 'waste' – 183 9.2-inch and 8-inch howitzers of a type 'which we were ourselves replacing' but which 'would be quite good enough' for Russia would be sent for political reasons.

Meanwhile, much discussion had taken place about military strategy for the winter months. While French and Wilson prepared their arguments for the War Cabinet, Haig met with Pétain at Amiens on 18 October.[190] The French Commander-in-Chief felt that, as Russia was likely to go out of the war, the French and British must remain on the defensive throughout the winter. To facilitate this, Pétain wanted the British to take over more of the French line in order to strengthen the Anglo-French defensive position. Only if Russia could be counted in did Pétain feel that an offensive could be risked. Haig did not agree. Haig was opposed to taking over any line as he felt that his Passchendaele offensive must continue for some time and that at the end of that time the British troops would need to rest, not move. This aside, Haig felt that all depended on what the British and French intended to do in 1918. 'If we are to gain a decision', Haig argued, 'we must have an offensive plan', and with Russia out, the British Commander felt that only his forces would be in a position to launch an attack. Since Haig contemplated another attack in Flanders, he did not wish to move them over the winter to take over lines from the French as this would necessitate regrouping them again in the spring. Initially the War Cabinet agreed with Haig's views, but the Italian collapse at Caporetto on 24 October meant that Allied troops were diverted to Italy from France to stem the enemy offensive, and Haig's plans for a further offensive were shelved.[191]

While Haig struggled to get his views accepted, the War Cabinet considered what to do about Russia. Schemes to revive her abounded. On 23 October a memorandum by Professor Pares, advocating support for a Volunteer Army raised by Alekseev, was discussed, but the War Cabinet decided that it would be 'quite impossible' for the British government to give active support to this body unless such help were requested by the Russian government.[192] Blair's suggestion that British propaganda in Russia be increased in order to counter the pacifistic agitation of the Bolsheviks was rejected as impracticable; it would require 'sending our very best men out to run it' and would be resented by the Russian government as an interference in internal politics.[193]

By the end of October the situation in Russia looked bleak. Official Russian military and political opinion inclined to the view that the Allies should make peace and Buchanan felt that the Russian soldiers 'could not be induced' to fight further.[194] The Bolshevik revolution served to make this view unanimous. On 22 November Major Neilson reported that the 'Russian Army no longer exists' and stated that unless 'severe' measures were taken '*immediately*' Russia would leave the war.[195] Knox was even less optimistic. He suspected that a coalition government of the socialist parties would emerge from the revolution, but noted that 'from the allied point of view, the complexion of this government is of little interest for neither socialist wing has any knowledge of affairs or desire to fight.'[196] Meanwhile, Buchanan was being bombarded at the embassy by callers asking for British assistance to set up alternate governments. To all of these the ambassador gave noncommital answers, despite his feeling that the Allies should support some group which would promise to continue the war.[197]

The revolution also had a sharp impact on supplies. While there was a dearth of reliable information about the situation in Russia, immediately after the Bolshevik coup Hermonius informed Callwell that he (Hermonius) was refusing to take orders from Petrograd: 'In view of the great sums of money, lent by HM Government' Hermonius decided to wait until the Allied governments recognised the new regime before he authorised any spending.[198] In Petrograd the Mikhelson committee was paralysed and Mikhelson himself was reported to have 'aged enormously & is getting quite thin & wasting away with worry.'[199] The British representatives in charge of supplies in Petrograd seemed particularly bitter that their hard work in organising matters in Russia had evaporated with the revolution. Byrne's replacement as the Ministry of Munition's representative in Petrograd put his feelings vividly: 'damn all these chicken hearted people who have no guts to stick out a war!!!'[200] Faced with chaos in Russia, the Milner Committee decided on 20 November that it could no longer 'usefully' discuss issues of supply until the War Cabinet laid down a general policy with regard to Russia.[201]

British policy centred on the issue of the war. With the Italian collapse, the situation in Russia was even more crucial to Allied plans, for if Russia and Italy both were to drop out the future was indeed dark. Robertson was not optimistic that Russia could be saved. In a paper prepared 19 November, he argued that it was 'hardly conceivable' that Russia could be counted on in 1918 and that Britain must press on with the offensive in the hope that it would 'galvanise' her Allies.[202] As to Russia, opinion seemed to be turning towards the idea of supporting the Cossack forces under their ataman, General Kaledin. An undated paper written at the War Office suggested that Kaledin would need to be supported by some 100,000 Allied troops 'to guard railways, and in part to exercise police duties in the agricultural districts'.[203] The fantastic nature of this proposal was underlined by its belief that a 500,000-man Polish army could be raised by declaring Poland to be independent and that this force could then be combined with the Czech legion to form a

major army in the east. In any case on 26 November Buchanan was
asked to investigate the possibility of supporting Kaledin.[204] The
matter was debated at the War Council on 29 November, but
opinion was divided and the matter was referred to Lloyd George,
Milner and Balfour all of whom were in Paris. Despite the pessimism
about Kaledin expressed by the British minister in Romania, on 3
December the War Cabinet decided to give support to Kaledin.[205]

While the War Cabinet was deciding policy with respect to Russia,
Milner attempted to arrive at some conclusions about supply. In an
interview with Hermonius on 22 November, Milner covered the
entire spectrum of munitions.[206] While Hermonius said that he felt
that to cease sending supplies to Russia would encourage the
Bolsheviks and discourage those elements loyal to the Allies, Milner
pointed out that the 'only course' open to the British was to
'postpone' all shipments. This view was supported by Poole. The
latter wrote from Russia that 'I consider you should send nothing to
and do no work for Russia which can be of the slightest use to us if
applied to our own needs. Nothing we can do for her now will make
any difference to her policy as regards the war.'[207]

Poole's opinion was shared by the War Cabinet, who were in any
case studying the matter of extending aid to Kaledin. On 30
November that body decided to suspend the manufacture of
munitions for Russia.[208] As well, ships in British ports with
munitions cargoes for Russia were to be unloaded and, if possible,
those ships now *en route* to Russia from the United States should be
diverted to Britain. This decision, and that of 3 December to offer
support to Kaledin, marked the end of British munitions assistance
to the existing Russian army. In future munitions shipped to Russia
would be for one of the numerous groups which promised to
continue the war, and the Milner Committee itself, the culmination
of three and a half years of development in the field of Anglo-Russian
co-operation, was dissolved early in February 1918; its records were
transferred to the Foreign Office.

The preliminaries to the signing of the armistice of Brest-Litovsk
hardened the resolve of the War Cabinet to give support to Kaledin,
despite the worries that this might push the Bolsheviks into the arms
of the Germans. On 14 December the War Cabinet authorised giving
'any sum of money for the purpose of maintaining alive in
South-East Russia the resistance to the Central Powers considered
necessary by the War Office, in consultation with the Foreign

Office'.[209] Despite this support for Kaledin, the British policy was by no means anti-Bolshevik in principle. As Cecil pointed out, the main concern was to ensure that the armistice would not give the Germans a chance to strengthen their forces in the west.[210] In fact, this was embodied in the agreement between the French and British governments signed on 23 December dividing Russia into zones in which the two governments would support forces willing to resist the Germans.

There are several points of interest which are revealed by an examination of Anglo-Russian relations in the period from March to December 1917. It is clear that any serious Russian offensive was discounted by Robertson as early as the days just after the first revolution, and that, despite the early success of the Kerensky offensive, the CIGS never considered that Russia could do more than hold on the Eastern front the enemy forces already committed there. Haig, on the other hand, was more optimistic about a Russian revival and included the possibility of a Russian offensive in his strategical plans as late as November.

This difference of opinion between the two principal military advisers of the British government led to Robertson's having to defend in London a strategy with which he was not in complete agreement. The CIGS was much more pessimistic than Haig about the capability of the Allies to win an absolute victory with Russia incapable of mounting an offensive, and he supported Haig's policy only because the alternatives were impracticable. Robertson's pessimism was reflected by his repeated suggestion that one or more of Germany's allies be detached by diplomatic means, and this pessimism occasionally soured relations between Haig and the CIGS. Haig's dislike of having to keep Robertson informed on events in France made the latter's position difficult as he often had to defend Haig's plans without knowing fully the circumstances which influenced them.

To Lloyd George, the collapse of Russia was a further reason to abandon the offensive in France, an offensive which he had opposed even before the revolution. Whereas Lloyd George had favoured a Balkan offensive in 1915 and 1916 as an alternative to one in France, the final extinction of Serbia and the weakened condition of Romania led him to switch his support in 1917 to an offensive against Austria via Italy. Initially unable to win support for his views, the Prime Minister obtained the necessary leverage to oppose his military advisers through Haig's continued inability to break through in the west and the increasing deterioration of the position on the Eastern front. The Italian collapse at Caporetto and the Bolshevik intention to make peace allowed the Prime Minister to go as far as to press for a unified Allied military command in December 1917.

The lack of British confidence in Russia was reflected as well with respect to supply. The creation of the Milner Committee in March 1917 meant that, for the first time, close co-ordination was effected between British policy with respect to supply and British policy towards Russia generally. The British policy, adopted in March and maintained until July, not to send guns to Russia, was evidence of the link between supply and estimations of Russia's military capacity. The illusion of success which the Kerensky offensive provided in July led to a temporary reversal of this policy, a reversal which was maintained until the failure of the Kornilov revolt signalled the final collapse of Russian military power. After the Kornilov episode, British policy reverted to its earlier form and supplies for Russia were delayed once again.

Implicit in British policy was the estimation by the War Cabinet that the Provisional government was incapable of carrying on the war. As early as the end of March, there were serious doubts about Russia's military ability, doubts which became belief by June.[211] While the July offensive raised hopes briefly of a military threat on the Eastern front, these hopes were soon dashed, and the British government began to consider the alternative which General Kornilov appeared to offer. While there is no evidence that the British government gave Kornilov any overt support, the attitude which General Barter took in his conversations with the Russian military commander must have raised the latter's hopes for such support. The failure of the Kornilov revolt meant the end of any possible military support from the Provisional government, and the British government promptly ceased to provide it with any material support.

After the Bolshevik revolution, the British government searched for a policy which would ensure a renewed military presence on the Eastern front. While the Bolsheviks were not regarded highly by the British, negotiations were pursued with them as well as with the White forces, in the hope that somehow a renewed Russian ally would emerge. British policy in Russia was not always coherent, but it never lost sight of its goal: the creation in Russia of a replacement for the now defunct Imperial army.

Notes

1 Buchanan to FO, 9 March 1917, FO 371/2995/51436.
2 Knox to DMI, 12 March 1917, FO 371/2995/53302.
3 Buchanan to FO, 12 March 1917, FO 371/2995/53569.
4 Buchanan to FO, 12 March 1917, FO 371/2995/53859.
5 Buchanan to FO, 14 March 1917, 371/2995/55576.
6 Robertson to Murray, 14 March 1917, Robertson–Murray Correspondence, Add MSS 52462.
7 Addison diary entry, 16 March 1917, Addison Papers, Box 98.
8 98th meeting of the War Cabinet, 16 March 1917, Cab 23/2; FO to Buchanan, 17 March 1917, FO 371/2995/57143.
9 G. Grahame (the Counsellor at the Paris embassy) to Drummond, 17 March 1917, Bertie Papers, FO 800/178.
10 On the Provisional government's confirmation of their participation in the war, see the note presented by Nabokov, the Russian chargé d'affaires in London, to FO, 18 March 1917, FO 371/2998/58022; C. Nabokoff, *The Ordeal of a Diplomat* (London, 1921), 82. Russian refusal is in Buchanan to FO, 18 and 19 March 1917, FO 371/2995/58053 and FO 371/2998/58781 respectively.
11 'Despatch of reinforcements from the Western to the Italian front', Robertson, 17 March 1917, Maurice Papers, WO 106/1512.
12 'A general review of the situation in all theatres of war', General Staff, WO, 20 March 1917, ibid.
13 100th meeting of the War Cabinet, 21 March 1917, Cab 23/2.
14 Untitled memorandum, Alekseev, text sent to Robertson 26 March 1917, Cab 24/9/GT 311.
15 Robertson to Haig, 28 March 1917, WO 158/23.
16 Haig to Robertson, 1 April 1917, ibid.
17 'Addendum to General Staff memorandum of 31st August 1916', General Staff, 28 March 1917, Maurice Papers, WO 106/1512 and 'Addendum to note by the Chief of the Imperial General Staff, dated 12th February 1916', Robertson, 29 March 1917, ibid.
18 Robertson to Knox and Hanbury Williams, 14 April 1917, Cab 24/10/GT 487.
19 Knox to Robertson, 16 April 1917 and Hanbury Williams to Robertson, two telegrams of 16 April 1917, all in 122nd meeting of the War Cabinet, 18 April 1917, Cab 23/2.
20 ibid.
21 Robertson to Haig, 14 April 1917, Robertson Papers I/23/18.
22 'Minutes of a meeting held to discuss the Russian munitions programme for the year 1917, at 4 Whitehall Gardens, on Wednesday March 14th', n.s., 14 March 1917, Layton Papers, Mun 4/367.
23 'Memorandum on Commission Internationale de Ravitaillement. Ministry of Munitions procedure', Wyldbore Smith, 20 January 1917, Mun 5/137/1010; Addison diary entries, 12 and 15 January 1917, Addison Papers, Box 98; correspondence among various munitions officials in Mun 4/533.
24 Hermonius to Ministry of Munitions, 8 and 10 January 1917, Black Papers, Mun 4/533.
25 Poole to CIGS, 22 March 1917, Mun 4/6395.
26 'Minutes of the 2nd interdepartmental conference on the Russian munitions programme', Captain W. Ormsby-Gore, n.d. (but late March 1917), Layton Papers, Mun 4/367.
27 113th meeting of the War Cabinet, 4 April 1917, Cab 23/2.

28   Membership listed in ibid.; see also, *History of the Ministry of Munitions*, II, pt VIII, 16.

29   'Russian Supplies Section of the ministry – suggestions for co-ordination with the Lord Milner Committee', W. J. Benson, 2 April 1917, Layton Papers, Mun 4/367.

30   Untitled memorandum, Wyldbore Smith, n.d. (but early April 1917), Cab 27/189.

31   'Note on question of policy to be determined by the Russian Cabinet Committee', n.s., 30 March 1917, Layton Papers, Mun 4/367.

32   Babichev, 'Deiatelnost Russkogo pravitelstvennogo komiteta v Londone v gody pervoi mirovoi voiny (1914–1917)', 276-92.

33   Untitled memorandum, Wyldbore Smith, n.d. (but early April 1917), Cab 27/189.

34   117th meeting of the War Cabinet, 11 April 1917, Cab 23/2; 3rd meeting of the Milner Committee, 11 April 1917, Worthington Evans Papers, Mun 4/396.

35   Keynes to Hermonius, 11 April 1917, Cab 27/189, pt I.

36   The views of Hermonius are found in Hermonius to Keynes, 14 April 1917, ibid.

37   102nd meeting of the War Cabinet, 22 March 1917, Cab 23/2.

38   'Shipping Resources Committee: interim report', Carson, 24 March 1917, Cab 24/8/GT 276.

39   Ministry of Munitions to Booth, 27 March 1917, Mun 4/5525; FO to Buchanan, 28 March 1917, FO 371/3005/66017.

40   Details in 'Notes of a conference with Mr. Keynes. Machine tools and machinery for Russia', n.s., 29 March 1917, Mun 4/3024. The implementation of this decision was discussed at 3rd meeting of the Milner Committee, 11 April 1917, Worthington Evans Papers, Mun 4/396.

41   'Note on the financial agreements between the United Kingdom and the Allies', Keynes, 9 April 1917, T 172/422 and printed in Johnson (ed.), *Keynes*, XVI, 226–38.

42   For the background of the American unwillingness to provide money for the Allies, see Burk, 'Diplomacy of finance', 360–9.

43   Treasury to FO, 17 April 1917, FO 371/3008/79435.

44   117th and 120th meetings of the War Cabinet, 11 and 18 April 1917, Cab 23/2; 4th meeting of the Milner Committee, 17 April 1917, Worthington Evans Papers, Mun 4/396.

45   123rd meeting of the War Cabinet, 20 April 1917, Cab 23/2; Keynes to Booth, 20 April 1917, Mun 4/5515.

46   Buchanan to FO, 21 April 1917, FO 371/2996/82536.

47   Undated minute by Cecil on ibid.

48   Haig to Robertson, 19 April 1917, Haig Papers, 112.

49   Robertson to Haig, 20 April 1917, Robertson Papers I/23/21; Robertson to Monro, 19 April 1917, Robertson Papers I/32/57.

50   Sir L. Woodward, *Great Britain and the War of 1914-1918* (London, 1967), 274.

51   Robertson to Haig, 28 April 1917, Robertson Papers I/23/24.

52   'Operations on West Front', Robertson, 30 April 1917, Cab 24/11/GT 599.

53   'Present situation and future plans', Haig, 1 May 1917, Haig Papers, 113.

54   128th meeting of the War Cabinet, 1 May 1917, 'A' minutes, Cab 23/13. 'A' minutes were taken in longhand by Hankey of particularly secret meetings of the War Cabinet and were not circulated.

55   Haig diary entry, 4 May 1917, Haig Papers, 113; Robert Cecil to Drummond, 7 May 1917, Balfour Papers, Add MSS 49738. See also the account of the conference in Woodward, *Great Britain and the War*, 276–7.

56 Knox to MI 3, 'Northern Front', 1 May 1917, WO 106/1092.
57 Buchanan to FO, 8 May 1917, FO 371/3011/93586 and minute by Oliphant, 9 May 1917.
58 134th meeting of the War Cabinet, 8 May 1917, Cab 23/2.
59 135th meeting of the War Cabinet, 9 May 1917, 'A' minutes, Cab 23/13.
60 'Military effect of Russia seceding from the Entente', Robertson, 9 May 1917, Cab 24/12/GT 678.
61 137th meeting of the War Cabinet, 14 May 1917, Cab 23/2.
62 'Policy in view of Russian developments', Curzon, 12 May 1917, Cab 24/13/GT 703; Jellicoe's paper, 'Naval effect of Russia seceding from the Entente', 10 May 1917, Cab 24/12/GT 688.
63 See Robertson's comments at the 139th meeting of the War Cabinet, 16 May 1917, Cab 23/2.
64 Haig to Robertson, 16 May 1917, Haig Papers, 113.
65 Henry Wilson also suggested to Robertson that the CIGS himself should speak with the French about the military situation. See Wilson to Robertson, 18 May 1917, Kiggell Papers III/3/2.
66 144th meeting of the War Cabinet, 23 May 1917, Cab 23/2.
67 Robertson to Foch, 23 May 1917, Robertson Papers I/34/28.
68 Wilson to Robertson, 2 June 1917, Kiggell Papers III/4/2.
69 Robertson to Wilson, personal and secret, 4 June 1917, Robertson Papers I/36/91; 155th meeting of the War Cabinet, 5 June 1917, Cab 23/2.
70 'Conference held at Abbeville on 7th June, 1917, between General Foch and Sir William Robertson', n.s., 8 June 1917, Maurice Papers, WO 106/1513.
71 Haig diary entries, 9 and 10 June 1917, Haig Papers, 114.
72 'Note by Lord Milner', Milner, 7 June 1917, Cab 21/88.
73 159th meeting of the War Cabinet, 8 June 1917, Cab 23/2. The members were Lloyd George, Curzon, Milner, Smuts and Hankey. Hankey's account of this committee is in *Supreme Command*, II, 670–86.
74 Poole to Milner Committee, 26 April 1917, Cab 27/189, part 2. General Mikhelson was a financial expert who had accompanied General Beliaev on the latter's mission to the west in the summer of 1916.
75 Knox to Buckley, 15 October 1917, WO 106/5128; Poole to Milner Committee, 26 April 1917, Cab 27/189, pt 2.
76 Keynes to Poole, 3 May 1917, ibid.
77 134th meeting of the War Cabinet, 8 May 1917, Cab 23/2.
78 FO to Buchanan, 9 May 1917, FO 371/3012/94450; Buchanan to FO 12 May 1917, FO 371/3012/96852.
79 Milner to Robertson, 15 May 1917, Milner Papers 144(VI); quoted in J. E. Wrench, *Alfred Lord Milner. Man of No Illusions* (London, 1958), 328.
80 Hermonius to Addison, 23 May 1917, Mun 4/3026.
81 7th meeting of the Milner Committee, 17 May 1917, Worthington Evans Papers, Mun 4/396.
82 Hermonius to Milner, 29 May 1917, Cab 17/197.
83 Milner to Hermonius, 4 June 1917, ibid.
84 8th meeting of the Milner Committee, 24 May 1917, Worthington Evans Papers, Mun 4/397. The tonnage reductions are outlined and explained in G. Thomson to Hankey, 26 May 1917, ibid.
85 My figures are derived from those given in ibid.
86 9th meeting of the Milner Committee, 31 May 1917; Milner to Hermonius, 5 June 1917, both in ibid.
87 155th meeting of the War Cabinet, 5 June 1917, Cab 23/2; Robertson to Poole and Knox, 5 June 1917, Cab 24/16/GT 1044.

88 Blair to CIGS, 9 June 1917; Poole to CIGS, 10 June 1917, both in ibid. 'Supply of guns to Russia', Derby, 16 June 1917, Cab 24/16/GT 1076.
89 173rd meeting of the War Cabinet, 2 July 1917, Cab 23/3.
90 For an excellent study of the Provisional government's attempt to modify war aims, see R. A. Wade, *The Russian Search for Peace February–October 1917* (Stanford, 1969), especially 74–92. For the general course of Russian diplomacy, see Johnson, *Tradition Versus Revolution*.
91 Buchanan to FO, 15 April 1917, FO 371/2996/77718 and minute by Ronald Graham, 16 April 1917.
92 Buchanan to FO, personal, 17 May 1917, FO 371/2998/100809.
93 Rothwell, *British War Aims*, 131–4; Lowe and Dockrill, *Mirage of Power*, II, 223–7.
94 See the British reply to a Russian note of 3 June 1917, FO 371/3010/90801.
95 R. Rodd (British ambassador to Italy) to FO, 29 May 1917, FO 371/3010/107508 and reply by Cecil; undated minute by Hardinge on Rodd to FO, 31 May 1917, FO 371/3010/111199.
96 'Revision of agreements with Russia', H. Nicolson, 9 June 1917, FO 371/2998/114164.
97 Undated minutes by Hardinge and Cecil on ibid.
98 Wade, *Russian Search*, 88–90.
99 1st meeting of the Cabinet Committee on War Policy, 11 June 1917, Cab 27/6.
100 'Present situation and future plans', Haig, 12 June 1917, Cab 27/7.
101 Haig to Derby, 12 June 1917, Haig Papers, 114.
102 Robertson to Haig, 13 June 1917, ibid.
103 7th meeting of the Cabinet Committee on War Policy, 19 June 1917, Cab 27/6.
104 9th meeting of the Cabinet Committee on War Policy, 20 June 1917, ibid.
105 10th meeting of the Cabinet Committee on War Policy, 21 June 1917, ibid.
106 Haig to Kiggell, 23 June 1917, Kiggell Papers II/11/1.
107 Untitled memorandum, Haig, 22 June 1917, Cab 27/7, WP 18.
108 'Note by CIGS on P.M.'s memo on future conduct', Robertson, 23 June 1917, Cab 27/7, WP 19.
109 11th meeting of the Cabinet Committee on War Policy, 25 June 1917, Cab 27/6.
110 A. I. Denikin, *The Russian Turmoil. Memoirs: Military, Social and Political* (London, 1922), 175–86.
111 Blair to DMI, reports of 7 and 8 June 1917, Cab 24/16/GT 985 and 1009.
112 Buchanan to FO, 16 June 1917, FO 371/2997/130560.
113 Minute by Oliphant, 2 July 1917, on ibid.
114 As reported in Blair to DMI, 18 June 1917, Cab 24/17/GT 1105.
115 173rd meeting of the War Cabinet, 2 July 1917, Cab 23/3.
116 Buckley to Blair, 3 July 1917, WO 106/5128.
117 Haig's operational orders, 5 July 1917, Haig Papers, 122.
118 Meeting of the CIR, 7 July 1917, Mun 5/137/1010.
119 Hermonius to Milner, 9 July 1917, Cab 24/19/GT 1376.
120 'British Assistance to Russia – 1917 Programme', Milner, 12 July 1917; 187th meeting of the War Cabinet, 16 July 1917, both in Cab 23/3.
121 Johnson (ed.), *Keynes*, XVI, 238–40 and 243–5. See also K. Burk, 'J. M. Keynes and the exchange rate crisis of July 1917', *Economic History Review*, 2nd series, 32, 3 (1979), 405–16.
122 Cunliffe to Lloyd George, 3 July 1917, Lloyd George Papers F/11/7/1.
123 Buchanan to FO, 4 July 1917, FO 371/3004/134853.
124 Chalmers (Treasury) to FO, 14 July 1917, FO 371/3004/139885.
125 As cited in Burk, 'J. M. Keynes', 411.
126 187th meeting of the War Cabinet, 16 July 1917, Cab 23/3.

127 Cadorna to Foch, 16 July 1917, Cab 27/7 GT 1430; 'War policy on West front', Robertson, 19 July 1917, Cab 27/7 WP 43; 'Palestine', Robertson, 19 July 1917, Cab 27/7 WP 45; 'Military policy in the Balkans', Robertson, 19 July 1917, Cab 27/7 WP 44; 191st meeting of the War Cabinet, 20 July 1917, 'A' minutes, Cab 23/13.

128 Robertson to Haig, 21 July 1917, Robertson Papers I/23/40; 192nd meeting of the War Cabinet, 21 July 1917, Cab 23/3.

129 See the reports of defeat in Buchanan to FO, 21, 22, 23 and 24 July 1917, FO 371/2997/144202, 144986, 145890 and 146814.

130 See Cab 24/21/GT 1529, 1530, 1531 and 1533.

131 'Suggestions for support to be given to Russia in order to prevent a possible defection', n.s., 26 July 1917, Cab 24/21/GT 1531.

132 Robertson to Kiggell, 27 July 1917, Kiggell Papers IV/7, original emphasis.

133 'Note on the situation, 29 July 1917', Charteris (head of British Military Intelligence in France), 29 July 1917, Haig Papers, 115; Haig diary entry, 28 July 1917, ibid.

134 195th meeting of the War Cabinet, 25 July 1917, Cab 23/2; 196th meeting of the War Cabinet, 26 July 1917, ibid.

135 'The present military situation in Russia and its effect on our future plans', Robertson, 29 July 1917, Cab 24/21/GT 1549; 200th meeting of the War Cabinet, 31 July 1917, 'A' minutes, Cab 23/13.

136 D. R. Woodward makes this point with respect to Lloyd George's attitude toward a negotiated peace and such a concern applies generally; see Woodward, 'David Lloyd George, a negotiated peace with Germany and the Kuhlmann Peace Kite of September, 1917', *Canadian Journal of History*, 6, 1 (1971), 75–93.

137 Robertson to Kiggell, secret, 2 August 1917, Kiggell Papers IV/8.

138 'Military conference – August 7th, 1917', n.s., 7 August 1917, Cab 24/22/GT 1641; 'Resolutions reached at a meeting between representatives of the British, French and Italian governments at 10 Downing Street, London, S.W. on August 8, 1917 at 3.30 p.m.' n.s., 8 August 1917, FO 371/3009/158117. The Russian representatives in London were not even informed of this meeting and discovered it only by chance; see Nabokov, *Ordeal of a Diplomat*, 126–7.

139 Robertson to Haig, 9 August 1917, Haig Papers, 116.

140 Robertson to Kiggell, 9 August 1917, Kiggell Papers IV/9.

141 'Report of Committee. G. 179', n.s., 10 August 1917, Cab 27/6.

142 See P. Rowland, *Lloyd George* (London, 1975), 412–17.

143 J. M. Winter, 'Arthur Henderson, the Russian Revolution, and the reconstruction of the Labour Party', *Historical Journal*, 15, 4 (1972), 754–5.

144 ibid., 758–9.

145 144th meeting of the War Cabinet, 23 May 1917, Cab 23/2.

146 Winter, 'Arthur Henderson', 766. On Henderson's return, see R. A. Wade, 'Argonauts of peace: the Soviet delegation to Western Europe in the summer of 1917', *Slavic Review*, 26, 3 (1967), 451–67.

147 Barter to Robertson, 31 July 1917, Cab 24/21/GT 1583; Buchanan to FO, 4 August 1917, FO 371/2997/153782.

148 205th meeting of the War Cabinet, 7 August 1917, Cab 23/3.

149 Brusilov, *A Soldier's Note-book*, 101–2. Similar views were held by the British; see Blair's report, 18, 15 September 1917, WO 106/1036, where Kornilov was described as 'strong, fearless, admittedly straightforward and a true patriot, though no politician'.

150 Barter to Robertson, 12 August 1917, Cab 24/23/GT 1705.

151 Barter to Robertson, 13 August 1917, FO 371/2997/154559.

152 214th meeting of the War Cabinet, 14 August 1917, Cab 23/3.
153 215th meeting of the War Cabinet, 15 August 1917, ibid.
154 Derby and Robertson to Lloyd George, 15 August 1917, Lloyd George Papers F/14/4/63.
155 Hankey to Robertson, 17 August 1917, Robertson Papers I/21/38/1; Robertson to Hankey, 20 August 1917, Robertson Papers I/21/39.
156 217th meeting of the War Cabinet, 17 August 1917, Cab 23/3.
157 FO to Buchanan, 17 August 1917, FO 371/3015/180414.
158 Buchanan to FO, 21 August 1917, FO 371/3015/165148; Barter to Robertson, 20 and 22 August 1917, Cab 24/24/GT 1828 and 1844.
159 223rd meeting of the War Cabinet, 24 August 1917, Cab 23/3.
160 Robertson to Barter, 25 August 1917, as cited in Kettle, *Russia and the Allies*, 69.
161 Buchanan to Hardinge, 3 September 1917, Hardinge Papers, 34.
162 Buchanan to FO, 5 September 1917, FO 371/3015/174458.
163 Minutes by Hardinge and Cecil, n.d. (but 7 September 1917), on ibid.
164 228th meeting of the War Cabinet, 5 September 1917, Cab 23/4.
165 229th meeting of the War Cabinet, 7 September 1917, ibid.
166 Milner to Lloyd George, very confidential, 8 September 1917, Cab 17/187, original emphasis.
167 ibid.
168 'Supplies for Russia', Milner, n.d. (but 8 September 1917), Cab 24/25/GT 1980.
169 FO to Buchanan, 9 September 1917, FO 371/3011/176534; 230th meeting of the War Cabinet, 10 September 1917, Cab 23/4.
170 The Kornilov affair and varying historical interpretations of it are discussed ably in G. Katov, *Russia 1917: the Kornilov Affair* (New York, 1980).
171 Buchanan to FO, 11 September 1917, FO 371/2999/178592.
172 231st meeting of the War Cabinet, 12 September 1917, Cab 23/4.
173 Buchanan to FO, 12 September 1917, FO 371/2999/178508.
174 Blair's report 18, 15 September 1917, WO 106/1036.
175 Haig to Robertson, 17 September 1917, Robertson Papers I/23/52.
176 Untitled memorandum, 12 September 1917, Mun 4/3644.
177 14th meeting of the Milner Committee, 14 September 1917, Layton Papers, Mun 4/373.
178 The conference was held to discuss German peace proposals; see Woodward, 'Lloyd George, a negotiated peace', 75–88, but turned into a general evaluation of the military position; see Edmonds, *France and Belgium, 1918*, I, 10–11.
179 'The present military situation in Russia', Robertson, 24 September 1917, Haig Papers, 117.
180 Robertson to Haig, 27 September 1917, ibid.
181 Robertson to Lloyd George, 29 September 1917, Maurice Papers WO 106/1515, original emphasis.
182 Haig's paper took the form of a letter to Robertson, dated 8 October 1917, Cab 24/28/GT 2243; 'Future military policy', Robertson, 8 October 1917, Cab 24/28/GT 2242; 247th meeting of the War Cabinet, 10 October 1917, Cab 23/13, 'A' minutes.
183 247(b)th meeting of the War Cabinet, 11 October 1917, Cab 23/13, 'A' minutes.
184 243rd meeting of the War Cabinet, 2 October 1917, Cab 23/4; 17th meeting of the Milner Committee, 5 October 1917, Layton Papers, Mun 4/373.
185 1st meeting of the Allocation of Guns Committee, 8 October 1917, Cab 27/10. Members were Curzon (chairman), Balfour, Derby, Churchill and Captain Leo

Amery (secretary). The Committee's existence was approved by the War Cabinet the day after the initial meeting; see 247th meeting of the War Cabinet, 9 October 1917, Cab 23/4.

186 Treasury to FO, 27 August 1917, FO 371/3004/167848.

187 Beliaev to Mikhelson, 16 October 1917 and Ughet (of the Russian mission in the United States) to Hermonius, n.d. (but late October 1917), Cab 27/189, part 7.

188 18th meeting of the Milner Committee, 23 October 1917, Layton Papers, Mun 4/373.

189 2nd meeting of the Allocation of Guns Committee, 22 October 1917, Cab 27/10.

190 Haig diary entry, 18 October 1917; 'Note sur le Plan du Campagne en 1918', GQG, 17 October 1917; 'Considerations bearing on the question of taking over more line from the French', Haig, 18 October 1917, all in Haig Papers, 118.

191 Robertson to Haig, 24 October 1917 and Haig to Robertson, 15 November 1917, Haig Papers, 118 and 119 respectively.

192 255th meeting of the War Cabinet, 23 October 1917, Cab 23/4; 'Memorandum on the Russian Volunteer Army', Pares, 16 August 1917, Cab 24/29/GT 2337. The formation of the Volunteer Army is discussed in G. A. Brinkley, *The Volunteer Army and Allied Intervention in South Russia, 1917–1921* (South Bend, Ind., 1966), 11–16.

193 Buckley to Blair, 18 October 1917, WO 106/5128. This did not mean, however, that interest in and schemes for improving Russia's morale by means of propaganda were not taken seriously; see my own, ' "Joy Rides"?', 895–6.

194 Buchanan to FO, 30 October 1917, FO 371/3012/209545. Barter, on the other hand, remained more optimistic; see Barter to Robertson, 28 and 29 October 1917, Cab 24/30/GT 2463 and 2469.

195 Neilson's report of 22 November 1917, WO 106/1132, original emphasis.

196 Knox to DMI, 17 November 1917, Cab 24/32/GT 2683.

197 Buchanan to FO, private and secret, 21 and 23 November 1917, FO 371/2999/223261 and FO 371/3018/224839 respectively.

198 Callwell to Hardinge, 9 November 1917, FO 371/2999/214870.

199 Banting to Byrne, n.d. (but just after the Bolshevik coup), Cab 27/189, pt 4.

200 Banting to Byrne, 13 November 1917, ibid.

201 20th meeting of the Milner Committee, 20 November 1917, Layton Papers, Mun 4/373.

202 'Future military policy', Robertson, 19 November 1917, Cab 27/8 WP 68.

203 Untitled memorandum, n.s., Maurice Papers, WO 106/1516.

204 FO to Buchanan, 26 November 1917, FO 371/3018/225396.

205 286th meeting of the War Cabinet, 29 November 1917, Cab 23/4; Cecil to Balfour, confidential, 29 November 1917, Balfour Papers, Add MSS 49738; 289th meeting of the War Cabinet, 3 December 1917, Cab 23/4; Barclay to FO, secret, 29 November 1917, FO 371/3018/228092.

206 'Lord Milner's Committee on Russian & Roumanian supplies', Byrne, 23 November 1917, Mun 4/3670.

207 Poole to Byrne, 27 November 1917, Cab 27/189, part 9.

208 288th meeting of the War Cabinet, 30 November 1917, Cab 23/4.

209 298th meeting of the War Cabinet, 14 December 1917, ibid.

210 See his comments at the 304th and 306th meetings of the War Cabinet, 21 and 26 December 1917, ibid., and his comment of 25 December 1917 on a telegram from Foch to General Berthelot (the head of the French military mission in Romania), FO 371/3019/245940.

211 This same conclusion is reached by L. P. Morris, 'The Russians, the Allies and the War, February–July, 1917', *Slavonic and East European Review*, 50, 118 (1972), 29, 45–6, but Morris feels that British confidence in Russia ended only after the failure of the July offensive, whereas I believe that it ended earlier, in March and April.

8
Conclusion

The British will to win the war is the key to understanding the Anglo-Russian alliance. The decisions taken by those who made British policy with respect to Russia were shaped by military considerations. What the British desired from Russia was a militarily capable ally who would ensure the defeat of the Central Powers; the debate in policy-making circles was over how to bring this about. The outcome of such debate determined Anglo-Russian relations.

When viewed in the Russian lens, the British strategy in the First World War takes on a new appearance. It is not that the issues discussed are different from those which have dominated discussions of civil–military relations and the controversy over the views of 'westerners' and 'easterners'; rather, it is that the reasoning behind these decisions is given a different emphasis. This emphasis is one which centres around the Anglo-Russian alliance. In schematic form, the 'alliance' view of British strategy holds that during the first year of the war the British presence on the continent was so slight, and fears of an Allied defeat in the west were so great, that Russia and the Eastern front became the determining factor in British military planning. It was these considerations which shaped the Dardanelles campaign. By the end of 1915, with the great expansion of the British army in France and the massive defeat suffered by the Russians, the military strengths of Britain and Russia within the *Entente* were more equal. None the less, Russia was still a major component of the Allied cause and her wishes needed to be respected. This was evident in the continued British participation at Salonika, where Russian and French pressure dictated that the Allies must stay. Equally the timing of the Somme offensive, its continuation throughout the autumn of 1916 and the debate over Passchendaele all were influenced markedly by considerations of Russia and the Eastern front. The end of the Russian army as a capable fighting force in 1917 brought about a search for an alternative force, one which would keep the Eastern front in being.

Was such a strategy sound? Even in retrospect it seems difficult to imagine that there was any other which could have been followed. Once Britain was committed to a continental war and once it became the long, drawn-out, bloody affair of trench warfare, she was obligated to fight alongside of and in co-operation with allies. In a war where naval power was only a long-term weapon, initially Britain was distinctly the weakest of the three major *Entente* powers. While her economic and financial resources, coupled with her reserves of manpower, gave Britain the ability to remedy this weakness, until the end of 1915 this remedy had not yet worked. As a consequence, British military policy was necessarily one which was acceptable to her allies.

Britain's relationship with Russia was different from that which she had with France. Since the two western allies shared a common front, a certain degree of co-operation was forced upon them by necessity. While many arguments arose over practical matters concerning, for example, how much line each was to hold, and how heavily, the Anglo-French alliance was cemented by common need. Not so the Anglo-Russian. The latter was held together only by the fact that Britain and Russia faced a common foe. Russia, however, had a long land front with both Germany and Austria-Hungary and was in a position where a separate peace with one or both of them was a constant possibility. The achievement of Anglo-French aims in the west was thought to depend on the existence of an Eastern front; some Russian goals could be obtained through negotiation. Therefore, even when Britain became an equal partner militarily, Russia had always to be considered.

Given the importance of Russia in British strategic planning, there are a number of conclusions which can be drawn about other aspects of the British effort during the war, conclusions which affect the reputations of several of the individuals who made up the élite which dealt with Russia. One such is Grey. The Foreign Secretary was roundly criticised by some of his contemporaries for his handling of British diplomacy in the war and particularly with respect to the lack of success which Britain had in creating a Balkan bloc against the Central Powers. The leading expert on the Foreign Office has written that Grey 'failed to recognise the integral connection between strategy and diplomacy and never understood how one could assist the other if properly coordinated.'[1] It is difficult to see the soundness of such contentions. Once war broke out, a settlement in the Balkans depended on force of arms. Britain lacked such force; Russia did not. Britain was eager to create a Balkan alliance; Russia was inclined to do so only on her own terms. Given the British dependence on Russian military strength, Grey was forced to respect Sazonov's wishes. Indeed, the need to ensure Russia's continued adherence to the *Entente* persuaded Grey in the autumn of 1914 to give Russia a promise of Constantinople. The freedom of action which had allowed the Foreign Secretary to bring a negotiated end to the Balkan Wars in 1913 was no longer available, and he had to pursue his diplomacy within the confines of a coalition. Conceivably some means could have been found to satisfy the disparate aims of the Balkan states at the same time as satisfying Russia, but Grey's inability to do so reflected only the near-impossibility of the task and not any lack of understanding of the link between diplomacy and strategy.

A defence of Grey can also be made concerning another specific matter: the British decision, following the Calais conference of December 1915, to go back on their policy to abandon Salonika. The fact that Grey decided to capitulate to Russian and French pressure over the issue of troop withdrawal has drawn heavy fire from historians. One has called the conference one of the 'travesties of international diplomacy' and argued that 'it was perhaps typical of British diplomacy at its most arrogant that this humiliating and ultimately costly collapse of policy could be represented . . . as a tactical success.'[2] Is such a charge accurate and fair? Only, it would seem, if it is forgotten that a war was on, a war in which the views of allies were important. While the War Committee had been unanimous in favour of withdrawal, the Russians and the French had been unanimous in favour of remaining. Once again, British policy was necessarily shaped by the fact that it was made within the context of a coalition. Should Grey have ignored the wishes of his allies, the *Entente* would have been subjected to strains which would have taxed its ability to function, strains which would have been as serious as any diversion of British forces to Salonika. The Russian military hierarchy in particular resented the fact that Britain deprecated the importance which *Stavka* placed on the Balkans. The price of Salonika does not seem extravagant when the alternative was increased suspicion and disharmony between Britain and Russia.

Kitchener is another central figure whose dealings with Russia should prompt a re-examination of his reputation. Was he simply, as

Margot Asquith cruelly maintained, a 'great poster', or was he the great man which his prewar reputation suggested? Since Kitchener was the architect of British strategy during the first year of the war, it is largely upon this strategy which he must be judged. I have argued elsewhere that Kitchener's strategy, the 'alliance' strategy based upon Russia, was a sound one.[3] When his dealings with Russia concerning munitions are considered, the case for rehabilitation seems even stronger. In his memoirs, Lloyd George castigated the indifference of his colleagues towards Russia: 'had we sent to Russia half the shells subsequently wasted [in the West] and one-fifth of the guns that fired them, not only would the Russian defeat have been averted, but the Germans would have sustained a [severe] repulse'.[4] Kitchener's repeated efforts to provide munitions for Russia belie such criticism. He pressed the Russians to place orders, he chivvied them to make their needs clear and he requested frequently that they set their bureaucratic house in order so that close liaison between the two countries over munitions could be established. The Russians refused to accept such urgings until the defeats of the spring of 1915 made them unavoidable; by then British manufacturing capacity and that of the United States was fully occupied. When Lloyd George dealt with the Russians about munitions, he, too, found that providing supplies for Russia was no easy matter.

Support for Grey and Kitchener carries with it an implicit criticism of Lloyd George, for the Welshman was the greatest critic of his two colleagues. In his memoirs Lloyd George made clear that he felt neither the Foreign Secretary nor the War Secretary had pursued policies designed to win the war: Grey was a man whose silences were overrated as profundity and who failed to forge a Balkan alliance; Kitchener had an 'incomprehensible fear' of sending troops away from Britain and kept his colleagues uninformed of events.[5] These charges are intimately connected with the conduct of Anglo-Russian relations. As argued above, Lloyd George's strictures lack force when Russia and Russian desires are looked at closely.

Nor was Lloyd George's attitude towards Russia quite what he portrays in his memoirs. While he was the leading 'easterner' in the political élite and supported a greater concentration on the various Mediterranean projects which Russia advocated, he did not pursue a consistent policy with respect to providing munitions for that country. When Lloyd George became Minister of Munitions he had tied his political future to his ability to provide vast amounts of supplies for the British army. As a result, when Russia requested that munitions be diverted to her, Lloyd George always deferred to the wishes of the British General Staff. In addition, when he became Secretary of War, Lloyd George tended to support the calls for arms from the General Staff, again at the expense of Russia. Like many politicians, Lloyd George's position was much more coherent and consistent in reminiscence than it was in the event.

Lloyd George's ignorance of technical matters was never more evident than in connection with Russia and her impact on British policy. The question of providing munitions for Russia was surrounded by a number of complicated logistical issues. Such issues were the sort of thing which Lloyd George loathed, suspecting that they were advanced by those trying to balk his wishes. And this was the case even more with respect to strategy. Lloyd George was the leading advocate of finding a 'way round' the German defences in the west and offered either an Italian or a Salonikan offensive as an alternative. Were such campaigns logistically possible? Even a brief look at the situation in the Mediterranean in 1917 makes it seem unlikely. By this time the increased activity of German submarines in the Mediterranean had forced a near-closure of that sea to Allied shipping.[6] This meant that an overland route to Italy and to Salonika (as far as possible in the case of the latter) had to be found to replace the supplies normally shipped from Marseilles and Egypt. The route used was based on Cherbourg and ran to Modena, Brindisi, and hence to Taranto where supplies could be taken by boat to Salonika.[7] This trip required some five days. In addition, the amount of material which could be transported by this route was limited, first by the fact that the loading facilities at Cherbourg and Taranto were not well developed and second by the fact that the maximum number of trains which could pass from France to Italy was fixed by the limitations of the Mount Cenis tunnel and the gradient along the Ventimiglia route.[8] Further, if large numbers of troops were sent on this route, then regular traffic would have to be suspended resulting in a cut in the amount of coal and wheat sent to aid the beleaguered Italian economy.[9] This effect would have been ongoing; a large-scale commitment in the Mediterranean would have required continual supply by rail. It also would have required an augmented naval presence in the Mediterranean, a difficult proposition in times of overall shortages of tonnage.[10] Even if sea transport could have been arranged, German reserves could have been transferred to the fronts faster than could the Allied troops.[11] On logistic grounds alone, then, Lloyd George's proposals were largely impractical.

In fact, it is tempting to dismiss the entire 'easterner' argument advanced by Lloyd George as an attempt to avoid the brutal realities of the war. If troops had to die to win the war, the 'easterners' seem to have felt it would be better if they were someone else's troops. Lloyd George's ongoing commitment to providing supplies to Russia and his championing of strategic alternatives in the Mediterranean were linked to his feeling that attacks in the west only cost lives. There was more than a little truth in the Russian allegation that Britain would fight to the last drop of Russian blood.

Lloyd George's policy was based on a number of quite dubious assumptions. The first was that Russia, properly equipped, was capable of winning the war on her own. Lloyd George continued to believe in the 'steamroller', since its existence would mean that British troops could be spared. The second was that the strategic alternatives in the Mediterranean would lead to the formation of a Balkan bloc and that this would prove decisive in the war. Given the performance in the field of such countries as Romania, this was fantasy. When the logistic difficulties of such a campaign are added, the whole project seems ill-advised in the extreme. Most important, Lloyd George assumed that Russia and France would be willing to carry the brunt of the fighting while Britain provided only supplies and financial support. But, as a recent commentator has remarked, 'a cash nexus was not a stable basis for a wartime alliance.'[12] Russia in particular would not have accepted a less than wholehearted British commitment to the war.

Lloyd George's technical and strategic ignorance was balanced by the fact that Robertson was a master of these very points. The CIGS produced endless papers which pointed out lucidly the flaws inherent in proposals such as those Lloyd George advanced. Robertson was a product of the reforms in the British army designed to rectify the woeful technical ignorance of the nineteenth century.[13] 'Wully', as befitted a man who had served as the Quartermaster-General of the BEF, was always fully aware of the logistic difficulties involved in a military campaign, and his careful arguments normally were decisive among the political élite. Even when Lloyd George became Prime Minister, he was unable to find arguments sufficient to persuade others that Robertson was wrong; Robertson's dismissal in 1918 centred around who was to be master, not around the soundness of his military views.

The policy which the CIGS followed with respect to Russia suggests that some modification should be made of the idea that he rarely lifted his eyes from the Western front. While Robertson was a 'westerner', that appellation covers several points of view. One was Kitchener's. When he was in charge of British strategy, Kitchener accepted the primacy of the Western front. However, the minuscule size of the BEF meant that Britain could not play a major role until the New Armies were raised, and Russia was essential if Britain were to have the time necessary to create this new force. Robertson was a different kind of 'westerner'. When he became CIGS, the situation had changed. The British army was on a scale comparable to that of the French, and Robertson intended to use this force to strike decisive blows against the Germans. This did not prevent him from appreciating the value of Russia and the Eastern front. For Robertson, Russia was not the *deus ex machina* that Lloyd George believed it to be, but the CIGS believed in close co-operation with Russia and a frank exchange of information between the two Allies. Only by means of a concerted attack by Britain and France in the west and Russia in the east could victory be achieved.

Indeed, it is evident that Robertson's awareness of the military problems in Russia during 1917 was the cause of a deepening rift between the CIGS and Haig concerning British policy.[14] Haig's views were those of the third type of 'westerner'. The commander of the BEF refused to countenance the fact that the Eastern front was in danger of collapse, or that such collapse would necessarily affect his plans for the west. Robertson was more realistic. Russia thus placed the CIGS in an awkward position: he rejected the alternatives to an attack in the west for the reasons discussed above, but doubted that a victory in the west was attainable without Russia. Thus Robertson was forced to support Haig's policy despite his own reservations. In this way, Anglo-Russian relations were intimately connected with the growing civil–military tensions within the British government, tensions which culminated in Robertson's dismissal.

Russia also had an impact on British domestic politics. Recently it has been shown that it was clear to many by the beginning of May 1915 that Britain must pursue a policy of total war in order to achieve victory.[15] The Russian collapse at Gorlice-Tarnow on 1 May must have reinforced such thinking. With the demise of the 'steamroller' came the final blow to any hopes for a short war and this created a climate of opinion wherein the policy of total war seemed the only solution. The central position which Russia occupied in British military plans and hopes made a re-evaluation of British military policy necessary when Russia proved to be less than invincible. Many Liberals found the methods necessary for total war repugnant and the formation of the coalition government was, as one writer puts it, 'a terminal point for Liberalism as a force in British politics.'[16] Fittingly, the alliance with Russia, which had long been opposed by many within the Liberal party, had led to a collapse of the Liberal ascendency.

The functioning of the Anglo-Russian alliance was impeded at a purely military level by a number of things. While the British representatives in Russia – Blair, Knox and even Hanbury Williams – did a first-rate job, the liaison between the two military establishments was amateurish in the extreme. In the beginning, the Russians were under the misapprehension that the British were merely an 'annexe' of the French and so provided little information about military plans. Both Kitchener and Robertson made strenuous efforts to overcome this situation, but even when a British intelligence mission was established in Russia and the Russians were aware of the increased size and importance of the British war effort, close co-operation between the two sides did not materialise.[17] The Russians still treated the British representatives with suspicion and were never forthcoming about information with respect to military plans or munitions needs. Anglo-Russian co-operation, unlike Franco-Russian, was co-operation at arm's length, almost as if the two countries were rivals rather than allies.

Partly this was due to geography. British and French commanders could hold meetings at short notice without removing key personnel from the various headquarters for any length of time. These meetings ensured that Anglo-French relations remained reasonably cordial and eliminated possible misunderstandings at source. Such opportunities were impossible for British and Russian commanders. Lloyd George had a valid point when he suggested that Alekseev and Robertson should meet at Petrograd, but the obvious impossibility of having the CIGS in Russia for six weeks, and Robertson's suspicions of Lloyd George's motives, prevented such a meeting. With direct high-level consultation out of the question, Anglo-Russian military liaison depended upon the representatives of each country. As pointed out, while Blair, Knox and even Hanbury Williams did commendable jobs, the Russians were chary of giving them information. This meant that the exchange of ideas between the two staffs was at best incomplete and often nonexistent. The Russian representatives abroad did not improve the situation much. General I. G. Zhilinskii, who represented *Stavka* in Paris from 1915 until late 1916, was not kept informed of events by his superiors. By June 1916 Robertson wrote to Hanbury Williams that 'you can realise that Gilinski's views are never entitled to serious consideration' and his recall at the end of the year was due to the realisation by the Russian government of his incapacity.[18] The other Russian military representative, General K. N. Dessino, was appointed to British headquarters only in June 1916. While Dessino was 'an excellent fellow' in Knox's opinion, he was also 'probably not a great worker', and his mission did not provide much in the way of improved communications between the British and Russian military hierarchies.[19] The fact that the Russian government had waited until the middle of 1916 to appoint a separate representative to the British underlined their tendency to view the British as a junior partner of the French, to the detriment of close co-ordination.

The study of Anglo-Russian relations also throws some light upon how the British governmental structure adapted to the changed circumstances of war. For the most part, no satisfactory bureaucratic arrangement was reached until 1917 to deal with the complex military, financial and supply questions between the two countries. Generally, decisions about Anglo-Russian affairs were taken by the departments concerned, with little reference to the effect which such decisions might have on other aspects of Anglo-Russian dealings. At a structural level, only the fact that most information was conveyed to and from Russia via the Foreign Office provided any kind of co-ordination within the British government. This co-ordination was augmented by the fact that several key figures enjoyed plural memberships on the various bodies which dealt with Russia. Unfortunately the priorities of the War Office, the Ministry of Munitions and the Treasury were determined by different criteria and there was no means to resolve any conflicts without recourse to the political élite. At this highest level of the British government the lack of any agreed policy with respect to Russia was evident, although everyone was keenly aware of her importance for Allied victory. Only in 1917, with the creation of the Milner Committee, was a body set up to deal with Russian matters on a concerted, regular basis, a body which had the requisite authority to resolve interdepartmental disputes.[20] While this was a noticeable improvement, it was not the complete answer. The recommendations of the Milner Committee still had to be confirmed by the politicians, and the War Cabinet was rarely unanimous in its views on Russia.

British attempts to aid Russia were also hindered by the massive incompetence of the Russian government's administrative apparatus. If the British governmental machinery for dealing with Russia was cumbersome, it was a thing of shining efficiency in comparison with that of Russia. There was virtually no co-operation between the various departments of the Russian government, and relations between the front and the rear were strained as well. Further, foreign purchasing was a political football in Russia to the detriment of efficiency. Russian internal political quarrels meant confused Anglo-Russian dealings with respect to munitions. This led to the continual frustration of the British attempts to set up any business-like arrangement between the two countries and created in London a highly critical attitude towards Russia.

What then did either side get out of the Anglo-Russian alliance during the forty months from the outbreak of war to December 1917? Britain had entered the war in the expectation that the Russian 'steamroller' would ensure a quick victory, Russia in the belief that Britain would provide the supplies and money necessary for victory. These were extravagant hopes and both were disappointed. While Russia was a rising military power prior to 1914, she suffered from certain intrinsic weaknesses which the pressures of war magnified. While Britain was the world's leading trading and financial nation prior to 1914, she was not able to provide an unlimited supply of goods for Russia. Many of the strains in the alliance resulted from the disappointment of great expectations.

None the less, the Anglo-Russian alliance did to some extent satisfy the prewar expectations of both sides. The Russian army fought valiantly against three opponents. A front against Turkey was maintained on difficult terrain and at the end of long lines of communication and supply. The Austro-Hungarian army was twice rolled back by the Russians and, by the end of 1916, largely destroyed as an effective fighting force. Against Germany the Russians had less success, but prior to 1917 Germany suffered more deaths in the east than in the west and was forced to maintain about

100 divisions on the Russian front until nearly the end of 1917.[21] Most importantly, during the first year of the war, when Britain was busy transforming her tiny prewar army into a major fighting force, Russia took the brunt of the Central Powers' attacks. Had the Germans attacked in the west during 1915, the situation for the British would have been desperate. Perhaps the British simply had the wrong metaphor for the Russians: 'steamroller' suggested a mobility which the Russians lacked; however, Russia's military contribution was extremely important for Britain.[22]

The question of what Russia received from Britain is more difficult to answer, at least in terms of how significant was the British munitions contribution to Russian military success. There is little doubt that the vast majority of Russian munitions were produced on Russian soil and that foreign supplies, with the exception of rifles, were of limited importance.[23] However, much of Russia's dramatic increase in domestic munitions production was due to the importation of machine tools, railway stock and essential raw materials.[24] In fact, any argument over just how important imported munitions were to Russia's war effort is similar to the parallel arguments made about Western contributions to the Soviet war effort in the Second World War, and like them, difficult to resolve.[25]

A much easier evaluation can be made of just what it was that Britain did provide for Russia, especially in terms of the overall contribution which Britain made to all the Allies. Some figures are illustrative.[26] Britain provided Russia with some 776 guns of all varieties, nearly 58 per cent of all guns given to the Allies. Similarly, Russia received 2,719,453 complete rounds of shell from Britain, or 59 per cent of the total produced for the Allies. The figures for incomplete shell are even more striking: nearly 98 per cent of the almost 11 million empty shell and just over 99 per cent of the approximately 25 million shell components which Britain provided for the Allies were sent to Russia. Even with respect to railway material, where Russian complaints were loudest, the British contribution was substantial. Russia received about 16 per cent by weight of the total British contribution of railway material to the Allies, despite the obvious difficulties of shipping. Only the British contribution of locomotives and wagons was slight; some 208 out of a total of 3,444 provided for the Allies went to Russia. Russia might complain that Britain did not provide as much as was requested, but the British contribution was by no means slight.

With respect to finance, the magnitude of the British contribution is even more evident. Of the £1,852 million which Britain loaned to the Allies and Dominions during the war some £568 million (or just over 30 per cent) was loaned to Russia.[27] If the comparative figures for the amounts lent to Russia and France only to the end of the period 1917–18 are examined, the special treatment accorded Russia is evident. By this time Russia had borrowed some £571.6 million whereas France had received only £373 million, less than two-thirds of the Russian total. Not only did Russia receive more in loans than did France, but also she contributed less gold to the British attempt to maintain Allied credit.[28] Keynes was quite justified in arguing that Britain had only one ally in the financial war, and that Russia was a mercenary.

Such figures do not answer the essential question: could the British have done more for Russia? After all, the Russians were never unhappy about what they received from Britain; rather their complaint was that the British did less than was needed and less than was possible. The answer to this is a qualified no. When the war broke out, Britain was forced to make several economic choices, and, as W. H. B. Court notes, 'two of the largest transfers of resources of the war were forced upon Great Britain by enemy decisions.'[29] These two, the need to manufacture resources for the New Armies and the changed food and shipping policies necessitated by unrestricted submarine warfare, meant that the resources left over for Russia were necessarily curtailed. The British had to decide between providing supplies for the British army or for the Russian army; and the deciding point was which one promised the likelihood of eventual victory. Greater help for Russia necessarily meant less for Britain. The arguments between 'westerners' and 'easterners' often boiled down to differences of opinion over just this issue.

British dependence on the United States both for credit and for supplies also had a major impact on Anglo-Russian relations. Russia had attempted to negotiate munitions contracts in the United States prior to placing foreign ordering in British hands, and this attempt had failed disastrously. Shaky Russian credit, obstructionism with respect to inspection procedures and a fundamental difference in business outlooks had all resulted in a suspicion of and hard feelings towards Russia being built up in America. Britain was the legatee of such problems. When this was combined with the general difficulties which Britain experienced in maintaining Allied credit in the United

States, Britain's failure to provide Russia's entire needs is seen less as a lack of will and more as a lack of ability. The American involvement meant that decisions about Russia's needs were formulated often on Wall Street, not in London.

The question of transportation was a particular sore point and was typical of the technical issues which often divided the two allies. The Russians did not believe that Britain, whose merchant marine accounted for just over 40 per cent of the world's total in 1914, could be short of bottoms to ship goods to Russia.[30] However, by 1917 this was the case. For a wide variety of reasons – the poor North American wheat harvest which forced diversion of ships to the longer Australian run, steel shortages, increased congestion at all ports, and, most important, the beginning of unrestricted submarine warfare – there were acute shortages throughout the year.[31] None the less, the British did manage to send a good deal to Russia. In 1916 some 2.5 million tons were sent by the Allies to the White Sea ports and in 1917 just over 2 million tons were added.[32] In all, more than 5 million tons were sent to the northern ports, almost a quarter more than in the well-publicised convoys of the Second World War.[33]

Of course, Britain was not above using technical arguments to serve her own ends. In 1917, for example, political and strategic decisions not to provide Russia with munitions were justified by appeals to shortages of shipping. Such mendacity did not mean that such technical arguments were specious; only that they could be used to serve other ends. In general, and despite the suspicions of the Russians, British arguments about transport and shipping reflected the reality of the war, where too many customers chased too few goods.

Obviously, the concrete problems of the Anglo-Russian alliance were not ones which could have been solved easily, if at all. The gap between what Britain expected of Russia and what Russia expected of Britain was just too wide to bridge. But the problems of distrust and poor co-ordination between the two were not insurmountable. Why then did they exist? Partially they stemmed from the fact that Britain and Russia did not share a common front. While the British did not always agree with the French, the latter's complaints and problems were comprehensible as they were basically the same ones that beset the BEF. Russian problems were not so easily understood. The British failed to appreciate the nature of the Eastern front, with its vast distances and poor communications. Similarly, they had difficulty in understanding the Russian economy and its needs. What appeared to the British to be a Russian inability to separate essential war needs from inessential general economic needs often reflected instead the complex problems of Russia's wartime economy. The expansion of the Russian economy led to what one writer has called 'crises of growth' wherein uneven economic expansion led to the creation of bottlenecks which choked off further increases of production.[34] The British were slow to recognise this fact and tended to begrudge Russia all supplies except those that were directly applicable to the war effort.

It is unfashionable to speak of things like 'national characteristics'. In 1914 it was not. British attitudes towards Russia coloured all aspects of the alliance. In addition to feeling that Russia could not be defeated and was a potential 'steamroller', most of the élite believed that Imperial Russia was despotic, corrupt and backward. Given this, all Russian economic and financial problems tended to be explained in a simplistic fashion instead of considered carefully. The condescension exhibited by so many Englishmen towards their Russian counterparts naturally resulted in difficult relations. The honest Russian official resented the easy assumption that he was corrupt, the highly capable Russian technician resented well-meaning British experts, and the overworked Tsarist bureaucrat resented the belief that all his problems were due to administrative bungling.[35] The fact that there was more than a kernel of truth in the British charges only made matters worse. The point is that true differences of opinion and of national interest were often overlooked or ignored due to innate prejudice. Nor was the matter entirely one-sided.

There is no doubt that Russian dislike and distrust of foreigners was a major reason for many of the problems which occurred throughout the duration of the alliance. The Russians accused the British of not pulling their weight in the actual fighting, were highly secretive about their munitions needs yet unhappy when they were not met, and were convinced that Britain failed to appreciate the magnitude of the Russian war effort. Such attitudes appear to be innately Russian. In October 1941 the British ambassador to the Soviet Union, Sir Stafford Cripps, wrote to his government that the feeling in Moscow was that Britain would fight 'to the last drop of Russian blood'.[36] In addition, like their Tsarist counterparts before them, Soviet officials refused to give the British information about war plans and munitions needs and demanded more supplies than existed transport to haul.[37] The parallels between the attitudes exhibited in the two wars is striking, and suggests that the ideological differences often cited as the root of the Anglo-Soviet distrust in the Second World War can be exaggerated.

Any British 'attempt to scrutinise Russia', Sellar and Yeatman noted amusingly, generally resulted in the conclusion that Russia was *'quite inscrutable'*.[38] This was particularly true in the First World War. The Anglo-Russian alliance was an awkward one. Neither side had confidence in the other's reliability; neither side understood the other's problems. Russia viewed Britain as a junior partner in the war on land; Britain saw Russia as a subordinate, often dependent, partner in the economic war. The alliance was between two countries with little in common but an enemy. None the less, the alliance persevered for over three years and achieved a great deal. War, as well as politics, makes strange bedfellows.

Notes

1 Steiner, 'The Foreign Office and the War', 517.
2 Dutton, 'Calais Conference', 156.
3 Neilson, 'Kitchener', 223–7.
4 Lloyd George, *War Memoirs*, I, 477. Kitchener has been defended in a general sense against Lloyd George's most inflammatory charges concerning munitions; see C. Wrigley, 'The Ministry of Munitions: an innovatory department', in Burk (ed.), *War and the State*, 34–40.
5 Lloyd George, *War Memoirs*, I, 91–2; 390–1.
6 Fayle, *Seaborne Trade*, III, 397.
7 Henniker, *Transportation*, 288–9.
8 ibid., 298.
9 The British experience at Gallipoli had shown how many ships could be tied up by inadequate harbour facilities, and those at Taranto and Salonika were primitive. On the Italian economy and its needs, see Fayle, *Seaborne Trade*, II, 317.
10 Shortages of tonnage were seasonal, based on such things as the needs of the North American grain harvest; see J. A. Salter, *Allied Shipping Control: an Experiment in International Administration* (Oxford, 1921) 141, 285–95.
11 Edmonds, *France and Belgium, 1916*, I, 550–1.
12 French, *British Planning*, 34–5.
13 On this see B. Bond, *The Victorian Army and the Staff College, 1854–1914* (London, 1972), especially 7–50, 274–95.
14 Haig's biographer, J. Terraine, *Haig the Educated Soldier* (London, 1961), 364, argues that a split between Haig and the CIGS did not occur until late September 1917. I agree with V. Bonham-Carter, *Soldier True* (London, 1963), 248–51, that the split began much earlier, in the spring of 1917.
15 French, *British Planning*, 170–2.

16   Fraser, 'British war policy', 26.
17   On the intelligence mission, see Neilson, ' "Joy Rides"?', 886–9, 896–900.
18   Robertson to Hanbury Williams, 10 June 1916, Macdonogh Papers, WO 106/1510.
19   Knox to MI 3, 20 June 1916, WO 106/1050.
20   Milner's Committee was typical of wartime attempts to co-ordinate departments through the creation of *ad hoc* bodies; see J. Turner, 'Cabinets, committees and secretariats: the higher direction of war,' in Burk (ed.) *War and the State*, 67–9.
21   Stone, *Eastern Front*, 12.
22   See Knox to MO 3, dispatch U, 7 May 1915, WO 106/1058, where Knox suggests that the French metaphor for the Russian army of a 'threshing machine' would be more apt.
23   Sidorov, *Ekonomicheskoe polozhenie*, 316–17, 332; Stone, *Eastern Front*, 209–11.
24   ibid., 159.
25   See the discussion of the debate over the importance of Western contributions to the Soviet war effort in J. Beaumont, *Comrades in Arms: British Aid to Russia 1941–1945* (London, 1980), 202–17.
26   All figures are from *History of Ministry of Munitions*, II, 88–9, appendix V.
27   The figures are from E. V. Morgan, *Studies in British Financial Policy, 1914–1925* (London, 1952), 317, table 48. A slightly different value for Russia's borrowings can be reached by including moneys provided directly to the Russian government by Barings; see A. M. Michelson *et al.*, *Russian Public Finance during the War* (New Haven, Conn., 1928), 312.
28   Morgan, *British Financial Policy*, 336–7.
29   W. H. B. Court, *Scarcity and Choice in History* (London, 1970), 92.
30   Fayle, *Seaborne Trade*, I, 6.
31   ibid., II, 339–42, 353, 386–7; III, the figures in appendix C, table 1(a) on tonnage lost to submarines. On steel shortages, see *History of Ministry of Munitions*, X, pt II, ch. 1.
32   Fayle, *Seaborne Trade*, III, 33.
33   D. W. Mitchell, *A History of Russian and Soviet Sea Power* (London, 1974), 310.
34   Stone, *Eastern Front*, 208 and 282–301.
35   See Fedotoff White, *Survival Through War and Revolution*, 57–8, for the reaction of an honest Russian bureaucrat faced with such accusations.
36   As cited in Beaumont, *Comrades in Arms*, 70.
37   See ibid., 44–5, 51–5, 61–2, 76–86, 99–111, 121–42, 166–75.
38   Sellar and Yeatman, *1066 and All That. And Now All This*, 77, original emphasis.

Select Bibliography

I Manuscript Sources

All collections are in the Public Record Office unless otherwise stated.

1 Records of the Departments of State

ADMIRALTY
Adm. 137 Historical Section: 1914–1918 War Histories

CABINET OFFICE
Cab. 1   Miscellaneous Records
Cab. 17   Correspondence and Miscellaneous Papers
Cab. 19   War Cabinet: Dardanelles and Mesopotamia Special Commissions
Cab. 21   Registered Files
Cab. 23   Minutes to 1939
Cab. 24   Memoranda to 1939.
Cab. 27. Committees; General Series to 1939
Cab. 28. Allied (War) Conferences
Cab. 42   Photographic Copies of the Papers of War Council, Dardanelles Committee and War Committee

FOREIGN OFFICE
FO 368   General Correspondence: Commercial
FO 371   General Correspondence: Political
FO 800   Private Collections: Ministers and Officials: Various

MINISTRY OF MUNITIONS
Mun. 4   Records of the Central Registry
Mun. 5   Historical Records
Mun. 7   Ministry of Munitions, Files transferred to War Office

PUBLIC RECORD OFFICE
PRO 30   Documents Acquired by Gift, Deposit or Purchase

TREASURY
T 170   Bradbury Papers
T 171   Chancellor of the Exchequer's Office: Budget and Finance Bill Papers
T 172   Chancellor of the Exchequer's Office: Miscellaneous papers

WAR OFFICE
WO 32   Registered Papers, Central Series
WO 106   Directorate of Military Operations and Intelligence

WO 157   War of 1914–1918; Intelligence Summaries
WO 158   War of 1914–1918; Correspondence and Papers of
         Military HQ
WO 159   Kitchener Papers
WO 161   War of 1914–1918; Miscellaneous Unregistered Papers

2   *Papers of Public Figures*

Addison	Bodleian Library, Oxford
Balfour	FO 800/199–217
Balfour	British Museum Add MSS 49583–49962
Bertie	FO 800/159–191
Black	Mun. 4/327, 452–575
Bradbury	T 170
Cecil	FO 800/195–198
Grey	FO 800/35–118
Haig	National Library of Scotland, Edinburgh
Hardinge	University Library, Cambridge
Kiggell	Centre for Military Archives, King's College, London
Kitchener	PRO 30/57
Kitchener	WO 159
Layton	Mun. 4/339–395
Llewellyn Smith	Mun. 4/7054
Lloyd George	House of Lords Record Office
Macdonogh	WO 106/1510–1516
McKenna	Churchill College Archives Centre, Cambridge
Milner	Bodleian Library, Oxford
Nicolson	FO 800/22, 336–381
Robertson	Centre for Military Archives, King's College, London
Robertson–Murray correspondence	British Museum Add MSS 52461–52463
Wintour	Mun. 5/7/170/25
Worthington Evans	Mun. 4/396–451

II   Printed Sources

1   *Official Histories*

Aspinall-Oglander, C. F., *History of the Great War based on official documents by Direction of the Historical Section Committee of Imperial Defence. Military Operations Gallipoli* (2 vols, London, 1929–32).

Edmonds, J. E. (chief ed.), *History of the Great War based on official documents by Direction of the Historical Section Committee of Imperial Defence. Military Operations in France and Belgium.* (14 vols, London, 1922–48).

Falls, C., *History of the Great War based on official documents by Direction of the Historical Section Committee of Imperial Defence. Military Operations Macedonia* (2 vols, London, 1933–5).

Fayle, C. E., *History of the Great War based on official documents by Direction of the Historical Section Committee of Imperial Defence. Seaborne Trade* (3 vols, London, 1920–4).

General Staff, *The Russo-Japanese War* (3 vols, London, 1908).

Great Britain, *History of the Ministry of Munitions* (12 vols, London, 1920–4).

Henniker, A. M., *History of the Great War based on official documents by Direction of the Historical Section Committee of Imperial Defence. Transportation on the Western Front* (London, 1937).

2   *Semi-official Histories*

Vinogradoff, Sir Paul and M. T. Florinsky (eds.), Carnegie Endowment for International Peace. Division of Economics and History. Economic and Social History of the World War. Russian Series. Selected Volumes.

Golovine, N. N., *The Russian Army in the World War* (New Haven, Conn., 1931).

Gronsky, P. P. and N. J. Astrov, *The War and the Russian Government* (New Haven, Conn., 1929).

Michelson, A. M. *et. al.*, *Russian Public Finance during the War* (New Haven, Conn., 1928).

Nolde, N. E., *Russia in the Economic War* (New Haven, Conn., 1928).

Zagorsky, S. O., *State Control of Industry in Russia during the War* (New Haven, Conn., 1928).

3   *Memoir Material and Biographies*

Adams, R. J. Q., *Arms and the Wizard: Lloyd George and the Ministry of Munitions* (London, 1978).

Asquith, H. H., *Memories and Reflections* (2 vols, Boston, 1928).

Bonham-Carter, V., *Soldier True* (London, 1963).

Brusilov, A. A., *A Soldier's Note-book 1914–1918* (London, 1930).

Buchanan, Sir G., *My Mission to Russia and Other Diplomatic Memories* (2 vols, London, 1923).

Buchanan, M., *Ambassador's Daughter* (London, 1958).

Buchanan, M., *The Dissolution of an Empire* (London, 1932).

Busch, B., *Hardinge of Penshurst: a Study in the Old Diplomacy* (Hamden, Conn., 1980).

Callwell, C. E., *Experiences of a Dug-Out 1914–1918* (London, 1920).

Callwell, C. E., *Field-Marshal Sir Henry Wilson: his Life and Diaries* (2 vols, London, 1927).

Cassar, G. H., *Kitchener: Architect of Victory* (London, 1977).

Churchill, R. S., *Lord Derby 'King of Lancashire'* (London, 1959).

Churchill, W. S., *The World Crisis* (6 vols, London, 1923–31).

Conwell-Evans, T. P., *Foreign Policy from a Back Bench 1904–1918: a Study Based on the Papers of Lord Noel-Buxton* (London, 1932).

Crow, D., *A Man of Push and Go: the Life of George Macauley Booth* (London, 1965).

David, E. (ed.), *Inside Asquith's Cabinet: from the Diaries of Charles Hobhouse* (London, 1977).

Denikin, A. I., *The Russian Turmoil Memoirs: Military, Social, and Political* (London, 1922).

Dugdale, B. E. C., *Arthur James Balfour* (2 vols, New York, 1934).

Egremont, M., *Balfour: a Life of Arthur James Balfour* (London, 1980).

Fedotoff White, D., *Survival Through War and Revolution in Russia* (London, 1939).

Foch, Marshal, *The Memoirs of Marshal Foch*, trans. T. Bentley Mott (New York, 1931).

Fowler, W. B., *British–American Relations, 1917–1918 The Role of Sir William Wiseman* (Princeton, NJ, 1969).

French of Ypres, Field Marshal Viscount, *1914* (London, 1919).

Fry, M. G., *Lloyd George and Foreign Policy. Vol. I The Education of a Statesman: 1890–1916* (Montreal and London, 1977).

Gerhardi, W., *Memoirs of a Polyglot* (New York, 1931).

Gilbert, M., *Winston S. Churchill. Vol. III The Challenge of War 1914–1916* (Boston, 1971).

Gilbert, M., *Winston S. Churchill. Vol. IV 1917–1922* (London, 1975).

Gollin, A. M., *Proconsul in Politics: a Study of Lord Milner in opposition and in power* (New York, 1965).

Grey of Fallodon, *Twenty-five Years* (2 vols, New York, 1925).

Gurko, V. I., *Memories & Impressions of War and Revolution in Russia 1914–1917* (London, 1918).

Hanbury-Williams, J., *The Emperor Nicholas II As I Knew Him* (New York, 1923).

Hankey, Lord, *The Supreme Command* (2 vols, London, 1961).

Hardinge of Penshurst, *Old Diplomacy: the Reminiscences of Lord Hardinge of Penshurst* (London, 1947).

Hart-Davies, R. (ed.), *The Autobiography of Arthur Ransome* (London, 1976).

Hinsley, F. H. (ed.), *British Foreign Policy Under Sir Edward Grey* (Cambridge, 1977).

Hoare, Sir S., *The Fourth Seal* (London, 1930).

Holmes, R., *The Little Field Marshal John French* (London, 1981).

Hyde, H. M., *Lord Reading* (New York, 1967).

Jenkins, R., *Asquith: Portrait of a Man and an Era* (New York, 1966).

Johnson, E. (ed.), *The Collected Writings of J. M. Keynes, XVI, Activities 1914–1918, The Treasury and Versailles* (London, 1971).

Keynes, M. (ed.), *Essays on John Maynard Keynes* (Cambridge, 1975).

Knox, A. F. W., *With the Russian Army 1914–1917. Being Chiefly Extracts From the Diary of a Military Attache* (2 vols, London, 1921).

Koss, S., *Asquith* (London, 1976).

Lennox, Lady A. G. (ed.), *The Diary of Lord Bertie of Thame 1914–1918* (2 vols, London, 1924).

Lloyd George, D., *War Memoirs of David Lloyd George* (6 vols, London, 1933–6).

Lockhart, R. H. B., *British Agent* (New York and London, 1933).

Lockhart, R. H. B., *Retreat from Glory* (London, 1934).

Magnus, Sir P., *Kitchener: Portrait of an Imperialist* (London, 1958).

Marye, G. T., *Nearing the End in Imperial Russia* (Philadelphia, 1929; reprinted New York 1970).

Morgan, K. and J., *Portrait of a Progressive* (Oxford, 1980).

Nabokoff, C., *The Ordeal of a Diplomat* (London, 1921).

Nicolson, H. G., *Sir Arthur Nicolson, Bart., First Lord Carnock: a Study in the Old Diplomacy* (London, 1930).

Oliphant, L., *An Ambassador in Bonds* (London, 1946).

Pares, B., *A Wandering Student* (Syracuse, NY, 1948).

Pares, B., *My Russian Memoirs* (London, 1931).

Petrie, Sir C., *The Life and Letters of the Right Honourable Sir Austen Chamberlain* (2 vols, London, 1939–40).

Rhodes James, R., *Memoirs of a Conservative: J. C. C. Davidson's Memoirs and Papers, 1910–1937* (London, 1969).

Ribot, A., *Lettres à un ami: souvenirs de ma vie politique* (Paris, 1924).

Robertson, W. S., *Soldiers and Statesmen 1914–1918* (2 vols, London, 1926).

Robbins, K., *Sir Edward Grey* (London, 1971).

Rodzianko, P., *Tattered Banners: an Autobiography* (London, 1938).

Roskill, S., *Hankey Man of Secrets* (3 vols, London, 1970–4).

Rowland, P., *Lloyd George* (London, 1975).

Salter, J. A., *Memoirs of a Public Servant* (London, 1961).

Tanenbaum, J. K., *General Maurice Sarrail 1856–1929 The French Army and Left-Wing Politics* (Chapel Hill, NC, 1974).

Taylor, A. J. P. (ed.), *Lloyd George: Twelve Essays* (London, 1971).

Terraine, J., *Haig, the Educated Soldier* (London, 1961).

Tyrkova-Williams, A., *Cheerful Giver: the Life of Harold Williams* (London, 1935).

Waters, W. H-H., *'Secret and Confidential': the Experiences of a Military Attache* (London, 1926).

Wilson, T. (ed.), *The Political Diaries of C. P. Scott* (London, 1970).

Wrench, J. E., *Alfred Lord Milner: Man of No Illusions* (London, 1967).

Young, K. (ed.), *The Diaries of Sir Robert Bruce Lockhart* (New York, 1973).

III Printed Secondary Works

1 Books

Alt, J. and V. Herman (eds), *Cabinet Studies* (London, 1974).

Anderson, M. S., *Britain's Discovery of Russia 1533–1815* (London, 1958).

Beaumont, J., *Comrades in Arms: British Aid to Russia 1941–1945* (London, 1980).

Bond, B., *The Victorian Army and the Staff College, 1854–1914* (London, 1972).

Brinkley, G. A., *The Volunteer Army and Allied Intervention in South Russia, 1917–1921* (South Bend, Ind., 1966).

Brown, K. D. (ed.), *Essays in Anti-Labour History: Responses to the Rise of Labour in Britain* (London, 1974).

Burk, K. (ed.), *War and the State: the Transformation of British Government 1914–1919* (London, 1982).

Cassar, G. H., *The French and the Dardanelles: a Study of Failure in the Conduct of War* (London, 1971).

Court, W. H. B., *Scarcity and Choice in History* (London, 1970).

Cross, A. (ed.), *Russia Under Western Eyes 1517–1825* (London, 1971).

Dallin, A. (ed.), *Russian Diplomacy and Eastern Europe 1914–1917* (New York, 1963).

Diakin, V. S., *Russkaia burzhuazia i tsarism v gody pervoi mirovoi voiny* (Leningrad, 1967).

Dilkes, D. (ed.), *Retreat from Power: Studies in Britain's Foreign Policy of the Twentieth Century* (2 vols, London, 1981).

D'Ombrain, N., *War Machinery and High Policy Defence Administration in Peacetime Britain 1902–1914* (Oxford, 1973).

Dreisziger, F. (ed.), *Mobilization for Total War: the Canadian, American and British Experience 1914–1918, 1939–1945* (Waterloo, Ontario, 1981).

Farrar, L. L., jun., *Divide and Conquer: German Efforts to Conclude a Separate Peace, 1914–1918* (Boulder, Col., 1978).

Farrar, L. L., jun., *The Short War Illusion* (Santa Barbara, Calif., 1974).

Ferro, M., *The Great War 1914–1918*, trans. N. Stone (London, 1973).

Flint, J. E. and G. Williams (eds), *Perspectives of Empire: Essays presented to Gerald S. Graham* (London, 1973).

Foot, M. R. D. (ed.), *War and Society* (New York, 1973).

French, D., *British Economic and Strategic Planning 1905–1915* (London, 1982).

Gleason, J. H., *The Genesis of Russophobia in Great Britain* (Cambridge, Mass., 1950).

Gooch, J., *The Plans of War: the General Staff and British Military Strategy c. 1900–1916* (London, 1974).

Gooch, J., *The Prospect of War Studies in British Defence Policy 1847–1942* (London, 1981).

Gottlieb, W. W., *Studies in Secret Diplomacy during the First World War* (London, 1957).

Guinn, P., *British Strategy and Politics 1914 to 1918* (Oxford, 1965).

Hanak, H., *Great Britain and Austria-Hungary during the First World War* (London, 1962).

Hardach, G., *The First World War 1914–1918* (London, 1977).

Hazlehurst, C., *Politicians at War* (London, 1971).

Howard, M., *The Continental Commitment: the Dilemma of British Defence Policy in the Era of Two World Wars* (Harmondsworth, 1975).

Hunt, B. and A. Preston (eds), *War Aims and Strategic Policy in the Great War* (London, 1977).

Ignatev, A. V., *Russko-angliiskie otnosheniia v 1917 g.* (Moscow, 1966).

Johnson, R. H., *Tradition versus Revolution: Russia and the Balkans in 1917* (Boulder, Col., 1977).

Joll, J., *1914 The Unspoken Assumptions* (London, 1968).

Katkov, G., *Russia 1917: the Kornilov Affair* (New York, 1980).

Kettle, M., *Russia and the Allies 1917–1920* (5 vols projected, London, 1981–).

Knightley, P., *The First Casualty* (New York and London, 1975).

Lowe, C. J. and M. L. Dockrill, *The Mirage of Power* (3 vols, London, 1972).

Lowe, C. J. and F. Marzari, *Italian Foreign Policy 1870–1945* (London, 1975).

McKay, J. P., *Pioneers for Profit: Foreign Entrepreneurs and Russian Industrialization* (Chicago and London, 1970).

Marder, A. J., *From the Dreadnought to Scapa Flow. Vol. I. 1904–1914 The Road to War* (London, 1961).

Mitchell, D. W., *A History of Russian and Soviet Sea Power* (London, 1974).

Morgan, E. V., *Studies in British Financial Policy, 1914–1925* (London, 1952).

Morris, A. J. A., *Radicalism Against War, 1906–1914* (Totowa, NJ, 1972).

Nowell-Smith, S. (ed.), *Edwardian England 1901–1914* (London, 1964).

Pearson, R., *The Russian Moderates and the Crisis of Tsarism 1914–1917* (London, 1977).

Rostunov, I. I. (ed.), *Istoriia pervoi mirovoi voiny 1914–1918* (2 vols, Moscow, 1975).

Rostunov, I. I., *Russkii front pervoi mirovoi voiny* (Moscow, 1976).

Rothwell, V. H., *British War Aims and Peace Diplomacy 1914–1918* (Oxford, 1971).

Salter, J. A., *Allied Shipping Control: an Experiment in International Administration* (Oxford, 1921).

Sellar, W. C. and R. J. Yeatman, *1066 and All That. And Now All This* (New York, 1932).

Sidorov, A. L., *Ekonomicheskoe polozhenie Rossii v gody pervoi mirovoi voiny* (Moscow, 1973).

Sidorov, A. L., *Finansovoe polozhenie Rossii v gody pervoi mirovoi voiny* (Moscow, 1960).

Smith, C. J., jun., *The Russian Struggle for Power 1914–1917* (New York, 1956).

Steiner, Z., *Britain and the Origins of the First World War* (London, 1977).

Steiner, Z., *The Foreign Office and Foreign Policy 1898–1914* (London, 1969).

Stone, N., *The Eastern Front 1914–1917* (London, 1975).

Tarle, E. V. (ed.), *Problemy istorii mezhdunarodnykh otnoshenii* (Leningrad, 1972).

Taylor, A. J. P., *English History 1914–1945* (Oxford, paper 1970).

Taylor, A. J. P., *Politics in Wartime and other Essays* (London, 1964).

Taylor, A. J. P., *The Struggle for Mastery in Europe 1848–1918* (Oxford paper, 1971).

Timberlake, C. E. (ed.), *Essays on Russian Liberalism* (Missouri, 1972).

Trask, D. F., *Captains and Cabinets: Anglo-American Naval Relations, 1917–1918* (Columbia, 1972).

Trask, D. F., *The United States in the Supreme War Council* (Middleton, Conn., 1961).

Trebilcock, C., *The Vickers Brothers, Armaments and Enterprise 1854–1914* (London, 1977).

Tsifrinovich, G. P. (ed.), *Vnutreniaia politika tsarizma* (Leningrad, 1967).

Tuchman, B., *The Proud Tower, a Portrait of Europe Before the War: 1890–1914* (New York, 1967).

Ullman, R. H., *Anglo-Soviet Relations 1917–1921* (3 vols, Princeton, NJ, 1961–73).

Van Creveld, M., *Supplying War: Logistics from Wallenstein to Patton* (Cambridge, 1977).

Wade, R. A., *The Russian Search for Peace February–October 1917* (Stanford, 1969).

Wallace, L. P. and W. C. Askew (eds), *Power, Public Opinion and Diplomacy* (New York, 1959).

Watt, D. C., *Personalities and Policies: Studies in the Formulation of British Foreign Policy in the Twentieth Century* (London, 1965).

Wildman, A. K., *The End of the Russian Imperial Army: the Old Army and the Soldiers' Revolt* (Princeton, NJ, 1980).

Williamson, S. R., *The Politics of Grand Strategy* (Cambridge, Mass., 1969).

Woodward, Sir L., *Great Britain and the War of 1914–1918* (London, 1967).

2 *Articles*

Alt, J., 'Continuity, turnover and experience in the British Cabinet 1866–1970', in Alt and Herman (eds), *Cabinet Studies*, 33–54.

Babichev, D. S., 'Deiatelnost Russkogo pravitelstvennogo komiteta v Londone v gody pervoi mirovoi voiny (1914–1917)', *Istoricheskie zapiski*, 57 (1956), 276–92.

Bark, P., 'Finansovia sovershchaniia soiuznikov vo vremia voiny', *Krasny arkhiv*, 5 (1927), 50–81.

Bridges-Adams, W., 'Theatre', in Nowell-Smith (ed.), *Edwardian England 1901–1914*, 367–410.

Brooks, D., 'Lloyd George, for and against', *Historical Journal*, 24, 1 (1981), 223–30.

Burk, K., 'The diplomacy of finance: British financial missions to the United States 1914–1918', *Historical Journal*, 22, 2 (1979), 351–72.

Burk, K., 'J. M. Keynes and the exchange crisis of July 1917', *Economic History Review*, 2nd series, 32, 3 (1979), 405–16.

Burk, K., 'The mobilization of Anglo-American finance during World War I', in Dreisziger (ed.), *Mobilization*, 23–42.

Burk, K., 'The Treasury: from impotence to power', in Burk (ed.), *War and the State*, 84–107.

Campbell, J. P., 'Refighting Britain's great patriotic war', *International Journal*, 26, 4 (1971), 686–705.

Cline, P. K., 'Eric Geddes and the "Experiment" with business in government, 1915–22', in Brown (ed.), *Essays in Anti-Labour History: Responses to the Rise of Labour in Britain*, 74–104.

Cohen, S., 'Sir Arthur Nicolson and Russia: the case of the Baghdad railway', *Historical Journal*, 18, 4 (1975), 863–72.

Collier, Sir L., 'The old Foreign Office', *Blackwood's Magazine* (September, 1972), 256–61.

Corp, E. T., 'Sir Eyre Crowe and the administration of the Foreign Office', *Historical Journal*, 22, 2 (1979), 443–54.

Debo, R. K., 'Lockhart Plot or Dzerzhinskii Plot?', *Journal of Modern History*, 42, 3 (1971), 413–39.

Dockrill, M. L., 'British policy during the Agadir crisis of 1911', in Hinsley (ed.), *British Foreign Policy*, 271–87.

Dockrill, M. L., 'David Lloyd George and foreign policy before 1914', in Taylor (ed.), *Lloyd George: Twelve Essays*, 3–31.

Dutton, D. J., 'The Calais Conference of December 1915', *Historical Journal*, 21, 1 (1978), 143–56.

Dutton, D. J., 'The union sacrée and the French Cabinet crisis of October 1915', *European Studies Review*, 8 (1978), 411–24.

Ekstein, M. G., 'Russia, Constantinople and the Straits 1914–1915', in Hinsley (ed.), *British Foreign Policy*, 423–35.

Emets, V. A., 'O roli russkoi armii v pervyi period mirovoi voiny 1914–1918 gg.', *Istoricheskie zapiski*, 77 (1965), 57–84.

Emets, V. A., 'Petrogradskaia kontferentsiia 1917 g. i Frantsiia', *Istoricheskie zapiski*, 83 (1969), 23–37.

Emets, V. A., 'Pozitsiia Rossii i ee soiuznikov v voprose o pomoshchi Serbii oseniu 1915 g.', *Istoricheskie zapiski*, 75 (1965), 122–46.

Emets, V. A., 'Protivorechiia mezhdu Rossiei i soiuznikami po voprosu o vstuplenii Rumynii v voinu (1915–1916 gg.)', *Istoricheskie zapiski*, 56 (1956), 52–90.

Farrar, M. M., 'Politics versus patriotism: Alexandre Millerand as French Minister of War', *French Historical Studies*, 11, 4 (1980), 577–609.

Fellows, T., 'Politics and the war effort in Russia: the Union of Zemstvos and the organization of food supplies', *Slavic Review*, 37, 1 (1978), 70–90.

Fraser, P., 'British war policy and the crisis of Liberalism in May 1915', *Journal of Modern History*, 54, 1 (1982), 1–26.

Fraser, P., 'The impact of the war of 1914–1918 on the British political system', in Foot (ed.), *War and Society*, 123–39.

Fraser, P., 'The Unionist debacle of 1911 and Balfour's retirement', *Journal of Modern History*, 35, 4 (1963), 354–65.

French, D., 'The military background to the "Shells Crisis" of May 1915', *Journal of Strategic Studies*, 2, 2 (1979), 192–205.

Ganelin, R. Sh., 'Storonniki separatnogo mira s Germaiei v tsarskoi Rossii', in Tarle (ed.), *Problemy istorii*, 126–55.

Gleason, W. E., 'The All-Russian Union of Towns and the politics of urban reform in Tsarist Russia', *Russian Review*, 35, 3 (1976), 290–302.

Goldstein, E. R., 'Vickers Limited and the Tsarist regime', *Slavonic and East European Review*, 58, 4 (1980), 561–9.

Gooch, J., 'Soldiers, strategy and war aims in Britain 1914–18', in Hunt and Preston (eds), *War Aims and Strategic Policy in the Great War*, 21–40.

Graf, D. W., 'Military rule behind the Russian front, 1914–1917', *Jahrbücher für Geschichte Osteuropas*, 22, 3 (1974), 390–411.

Guttsman, W. L., 'Aristocracy and the middle class in the British political élite, 1886–1916', *British Journal of Sociology*, 5 (1954), 12–32.

Hamm, M. F., 'Liberal politics in wartime Russia: an analysis of the Progressive Bloc', *Slavic Review*, 33, 3 (1974), 453–68.

Hazlehurst, C., 'Asquith as Prime Minister', *English Historical Review*, 85, 336 (1970), 516–29.

House, F., 'Music', in Nowell-Smith (ed.), *Edwardian England 1901–1914*, 411–40.

Karliner, M. M., 'Angliia i Petrogradskaia kontferentsiia Antanty 1917 g.', in *Mezhdunarodnye otnosheniia politika diplomatiia XVI–XX veka* (Moscow, 1964), 322–58.

Knox, A. F. W., 'James M. Blair', *Slavonic and East European Review*, 4 (1925/6), 482–84.

Koch, H. W., 'Das Britische Russlandbild im Spiegel Der Britischen Propaganda 1914–1918', *Zeitschrift für Politik*, 27, 1 (1980), 71–96.

Krupina, T. D., 'Politicheskii krizis 1915 g. i sozdanie osobogo sobeshchaniia po oborone', *Istoricheskie zapiski*, 83 (1969), 58–75.

Levy, P., 'The Bloomsbury Group', in Keynes (ed.), *Essays on John Maynard Keynes*, 60–72.

Lockwood, P. A., 'Milner's entry into the war cabinet, December 1916', *Historical Journal*, 7, 1 (1964), 120–34.

McDermott, J., 'The revolution in British military thinking from the Boer war to the Moroccan crisis', *Canadian Journal of History*, 9, 2 (1974), 159–77.

McEwen, J. M., 'Northcliffe and Lloyd George at War, 1914–1918', *Historical Journal*, 24, 3 (1981), 651–72.

McLean, D., 'English Radicals, Russia and the fate of Persia 1907–1913', *English Historical Review*, 93, 367 (1978), 338–52.

Morris, L. P., 'The Russians, the Allies and the war, February–July 1917', *Slavonic and East European Review*, 50, 118 (1972), 29–48.

Murray, J. A., 'Foreign policy debated: Sir Edward Grey and his critics, 1911–1912', in Wallace and Askew (eds), *Power, Public Opinion and Diplomacy*, 141–71.

Neilson, K., ' "Joy Rides"? British intelligence and propaganda in Russia, 1914–1917', *Historical Journal*, 24, 4 (1981), 885–906.

Neilson, K., 'Kitchener: a reputation refurbished?', *Canadian Journal of History*, 15, 2 (1980), 207–27.

Neilson, K., 'Russian foreign purchasing in the Great War: a test case', *Slavonic and East European Review*, 60, 4 (1982), 572–90.

Pogrebinskii, A. P., 'K istorii soiuzov zemstv i gorodov v gody imperialisticheskoi voiny', *Istoricheskie zapiski*, 12 (1941), 39–60.

Pogrebinskii, A. P., 'Voenno-promyshchlennye komitety', *Istoricheskie zapiski*, 11 (1941), 160–200.

Potts, J. M., 'The loss of Bulgaria', in Dallin (ed.), *Russian Diplomacy*, 194–234.

Pugh, M. A., 'Asquith, Bonar Law and the first coalition', *Historical Journal*, 17, 4 (1974), 813–36.

Renzi, W. A., 'The Russian Foreign Office and Italy's entrance into the Great War, 1914–1915: a study in wartime diplomacy', *Historian*, 28, 4 (1966), 648–68.

Rieber, A. J., 'Russian diplomacy and Rumania', in Dallin (ed.), *Russian Diplomacy*, 235–75.

Robbins, K., 'British diplomacy and Bulgaria, 1914–1915', *Slavonic and East European Review*, 49, 117 (1971), 560–85.

Robbins, K., 'Sir Edward Grey and the British Empire', *Journal of Imperial and Commonwealth History*, 1, 2 (1973), 213–21.

Robbins, K. G., 'The Foreign Secretary, the Cabinet, Parliament and the parties', in Hinsley (ed.), *British Foreign Policy*, 3–21.

Robbins, K. G., 'Public opinion, the press and pressure groups', in Hinsley (ed.), *British Foreign Policy*, 70–88.

Schurman, D. M., 'Historians and Britain's imperial strategic stance in 1914', in Flint and Williams (eds), *Perspectives of Empire*, 172–88.

Shatsillo, K. F., 'O disproportsii v razvitii vooruzhennykh sil Rossii nakanune pervoi mirovoi voiny (1906–1914 gg.)', *Istoricheskie zapiski*, 83 (1969), 123–46.

Sidorov, A. L., 'K voprosu o stroitelstve kazenykh voennykh zavodov v Rossii v gody pervoi mirovoi voiny', *Istoricheskie zapiski*, 54 (1955), 156–69.

Sidorov, A. L., 'Missiia v Angliiu i Frantsiiu po voprosu snabzheniia Rossii predmetami vooruzheniia', *Istoricheskii arkhiv*, 4 (1949), 351–86.

Siegelbaum, L. H., 'Moscow industrialists and the War-Industries Committees during World War I', *Russian History*, 5, 1 (1978), 64–83.

Silberstein, G. E., 'The Serbian campaign of 1915: its diplomatic background', *American Historical Review*, 73, 1 (1967), 51–69.

Smith, C. J., jun., 'Great Britain and the 1914–1915 Straits Agreement with Russia: the British promise of November 1914', *American Historical Review*, 70, 4 (1965), 1015–34.

Steiner, Z., 'The Foreign Office and the war', in Hinsley (ed.), *British Foreign Policy*, 516–31.

Steiner, Z., 'The Foreign Office under Sir Edward Grey', in Hinsley (ed.), *British Foreign Policy*, 22–69.

Steiner, Z. and M. L. Dockrill, 'The Foreign Office reforms, 1919–21', *Historical Journal*, 17, 1 (1974), 131–56.

Stoliarenko, M. A., 'Anglo-russkie soglasheniia o severnykh portakh Rossii v gody pervoi mirovoi voiny', *Vestnik Leningradskogo Universiteta*, 16, 8 (1961), 46–58.

Sweet, D. W. and R. T. B. Langborne, 'Great Britain and Russia, 1907–1914', in Hinsley (ed.), *British Foreign Policy*, 236–55.

Taylor, A. J. P., 'Politics in the First World War', in Taylor, *Politics in Wartime and other Essays*, 11–44.

Taylor, P. M., 'The Foreign Office and British propaganda during the First World War', *Historical Journal*, 23, 4 (1980), 875–98.

Torrey, G. E., 'The Rumanian–Italian Agreement of 23 September 1914', *Slavonic and East European Review*, 44, 103 (1966), 403–20.

Towle, P., 'The European balance of power in 1914', *Army Quarterly and Defence Journal*, 104, 3 (1974), 333–42.

Towle, P., 'The Russo-Japanese War and the defence of India', *Military Affairs*, 44, 3 (1980), 111–17.

Turner, J., 'Cabinets, committees and secretariats: the higher direction of war', in Burk (ed.), *War and the State*, 57–83.

Turner, J., 'The formation of Lloyd George's "Garden Suburb": "Fabian-like Milnerite penetration"?', *Historical Journal*, 20, 1 (1977), 165–84.

Verkhovskii, D. V. and F. S. Krinitsyn, 'Plany voiny', in Rostunov (ed.), *Istoriia pervoi mirovoi voiny 1914–1918*, I, 185–206.

Wade, R. A., 'Argonauts of Peace: the Soviet delegation to Western Europe in the summer of 1917', *Slavic Review*, 27, 3 (1967), 451–67.

Warman, R. M., 'The erosion of Foreign Office influence in the making of foreign policy, 1916–1918', *Historical Journal*, 15, 1 (1972), 133–59.

Watt, D. C., 'The nature of the foreign-policy-making élite in Britain', in Watt, *Personalities and Policies*, 1–15.

Weinroth, H. S., 'The British Radicals and the balance of power, 1902–1914', *Historical Journal*, 13, 4 (1970), 653–82.

Wilkinson, R., 'Political leadership and the late Victorian public school', *British Journal of Sociology*, 13 (1952), 320–30.

Wilson, K., 'British power in the European balance, 1906–14', in Dilkes, *Retreat from Power*, I, 21–41.

Wilson, K., 'The opposition and the crisis in the Liberal Party over foreign policy in November 1911', *International History Review*, 3, 3 (1981), 399–413.

Wilson, T., 'Britain's "Moral Commitment" to France in August 1914', *History*, 64 (1979), 380–90.

Winter, J. M., 'Arthur Henderson, the Russian revolution, and the reconstruction of the Labour Party', *Historical Journal*, 15, 4 (1972), 753–73.

Wrigley, C., 'The Ministry of Munitions: an innovatory department', in Burk (ed.), *War and the State*, 32–56.

Woodward, D. R., 'Britain in a continental war: the civil-military debate over the strategical direction of the Great War of 1914–1918', *Albion*, 12 (1980), 37–65.

Woodward, D. R., 'David Lloyd George, a negotiated peace with Germany and the Kuhlmann Peace Kite of September, 1917', *Canadian Journal of History*, 6, 1 (1979), 75–93.

Index

Abbeville,
  military conference at (7 June 1917) 264
Addison, Dr. Christopher 5, 102, 126–8, 133, 195, 198, 214, 216, 239–40, 251–2, 267
Alekseev, Gen. M. V. xii, 120–2, 124, 125, 144, 146–7, 148–50, 152, 154, 155–7, 160, 164, 228, 232–3, 253–4, 266, 292, 312
Allison, 'Col.' J. Wesley 66–7, 73–4, 173
American Locomotive Company 76, 88
Anglo-Russian Convention (1907) 2, 6, 16
Anglo-Russian Sub-Committee 199, 204–5, 207–9, 217, 256
Archangel 176, 180–1, 196–7, 233, 241
Asquith, Herbert Henry x, 11, 14–15, 24, 33, 46, 58, 60, 78, 89, 116, 119, 122, 124, 162–3, 172, 196, 203, 225

Balfour, Arthur J. 13–14, 33, 59, 72–3, 93, 119, 122, 124, 142, 144, 145, 147, 148, 153, 175, 177–80, 192, 209, 226–7, 259, 270, 284, 294
'Balkan bloc' 44–8, 72–3, 77–8, 306–8, 310
Bark, P. L. 55–6, 65–6, 68, 104–5, 111–14, 173, 182–4, 192, 198–200, 202–4, 212, 226, 232, 237
Barter, Gen. Sir Charles 282–5, 286, 296
Beliaev, Col. N. 100–1
Beliaev, Gen. M. A. 101, 192, 195, 197, 199–201, 208, 210, 214, 233–4, 236, 241, 242, 291, 299 n74
Benckendorff, Count A. 48, 52, 54, 117, 121, 202
Benson, W. J. 256
Bertie, Sir Francis 7, 43, 49, 57, 72–3, 226
Bethlehem Steel Co. 74–5, 88, 187–8, 213–15
Black, Adm. Sir Frederick W. 130
Blackett, Sir Basil P. 23, 55–6, 65–6, 67
Blair, Capt. James 32–3, 34, 53, 75, 95, 104, 111, 116, 117, 118–19, 223 n148, 240, 274–5, 287, 292, 301 n149, 312–13
Booth, George M. 22–3, 101, 125–8, 189, 197, 212, 214–15, 216, 255–6, 258
Boulogne
  financial conference at (20–22 Aug. 1915) 106–7, 112
  military conference at (19–20 June 1915) 93
  military conference at (20 Oct. 1916) 159
Bradbury, Sir John 54, 106

Brest-Litovsk, armistice of 250, 294
Bratianu, I. 45–7, 146
Briand, A. 118, 122, 150, 151–2, 158, 162
British intelligence and propaganda mission in Russia 28, 31, 32, 42 n182, 232, 292
British Military Equipment Section (BMES) 239–40
Brusilov, Gen. A. A. 152, 195, 265
Buchanan, Sir George 18, 19, 20, 21, 24–7, 28, 30, 31, 32, 33, 48, 49, 52, 56, 58, 59, 60, 74, 88, 95, 104, 105, 110, 116, 202–3, 205, 212, 229, 231–2, 243, 250–2, 259, 261, 266, 267, 269, 274, 282–3, 284–7, 292–4
Bulgaria 45, 62, 65, 72–3, 78, 110, 114–16, 120, 143, 149, 151–5, 157–8, 162, 277
Buxton, Charles R. 33–4, 47
Buxton, Noel E. 33–4, 42 n176, 47
Byrne, Col. Frederick 240, 257, 293

Cadorna, Gen. L. 152, 164–5, 277
Calais
  financial conference at (24 Aug. 1916) 203
  military conference at (5–6 July 1915) 92–5, 102
  military conference at (11 Sept. 1915) 108–9
  military conference at (5 Oct. 1915) 115
  military conference at (4 Dec. 1915) 121–2, 307
Callwell, Gen. Sir Charles 6, 10, 31, 69, 73, 144, 205, 209, 256, 293
Cambon, P. 51, 70–1, 152
Canada 66, 113, 173–4, 186
Canadian Car and Foundry Co. (CCFC) 173, 186–8, 207–8
Cecil, Lord Robert 259, 270–1, 282, 285
Chamberlain, J. Austen 33, 226
Chantilly
  military conference at (27 Dec. 1914) 60–1
  military conference at (March 1915) 71
  military conference at (24 June 1915) 93
  military conference at (7 July 1915) 95
  military conference at (14 Sept. 1915) 109
  military conference at (8 Oct. 1915) 115
  military conference at (6–8 Dec. 1915) 122–4, 130, 142–3
  military conference at (14 Feb. 1916) 146
  military conference at (12 Mar. 1916) 148